MAJOR-GENERAL ROBERT ROSS.

Drawn by Walter Tomlinson, from an oil painting, which was presented to the officers of the 1st Battalion by the late General Falls.

MAJOR-GENERAL JAMES WOLFE.

Drawn by Walter Tomlinson, from a mezzotint (1782) presented to the officers of the 1st Battalion by Lieutenant R. Woodforde Deane.

HISTORY

OF THE

XX REGIMENT.

1688—1888.

COMPILED BY

B. SMYTH, Lieutenant;
Quartermaster, 1st Lancashire Fusiliers.

The Naval & Military Press Ltd

Published by

The Naval & Military Press Ltd
Unit 10 Ridgewood Industrial Park,
Uckfield, East Sussex,
TN22 5QE England

Tel: +44 (0) 1825 749494
Fax: +44 (0) 1825 765701

www.naval-military-press.com
www.military-genealogy.com
www.militarymaproom.com

In reprinting in facsimile from the original, any imperfections are inevitably reproduced and the quality may fall short of modern type and cartographic standards.

PREFACE.

THE object of this work has been to supply in some measure a want long felt by the XX Regiment: a fuller and more complete account of the history of their corps. With this object steadfastly in view, no effort has been spared to render it, in so far as completeness is concerned, worthy of the exploits it chronicles; but the absence of manuscript and other regimental records of the first hundred years, and the meagreness of the details extant concerning the subsequent half century, have made this portion of the narrative less full than that of the later periods. To add to the intrinsic value of the work, authorities have been quoted, and the sources of information acknowledged. Should there be any instances of the names and services of individual officers being omitted, it is only because they could not be traced or could not be introduced with any degree of relevancy into the narrative.

As Englishmen are proud of the history of their country, and look upon it as their common heritage; as the descendants of great soldiers cherish and venerate the glory of their forefathers; so also do the XX Regiment prize that long roll of fame to which they are successors.

CONTENTS.

                                                                                                        PAGE

CHAPTER I. 1688–1702   1

    Landing of the Prince of Orange—Raising of the XX by Sir R. Peyton—Gustavus Hamilton—In Garrison at Carrickfergus—Battle of the Boyne—First Siege of Limerick—Ballymore—Siege of Athlone—Battle of Aghrim—Second Siege of Limerick—The Regiment moved to the Isle of Wight.

CHAPTER II. 1702–1704   8

    The Grand Alliance—Accession of Queen Anne—War declared against France and Spain—Regiments for Sea Service—Embarkation for Spain—Disembarkation—Surrender of Rota and Fort Catalina—XX selected for Service in the West Indies—Attack on Guadalope—Landing at Jamaica—Return to Ireland.

CHAPTER III. 1704–1713   12

    Arrival from the West Indies—Embarkation for Portugal—Winter Quarters—Restricted to Defensive Operations during 1708—Battle of La Gudiña—Winter Quarters—Advance across the Guadiana, 1710—Attack on Cabaleros—Campaign of 1711—Capture of Small Towns—The Clandestine Treaty—Suspension of Hostilities—XX sail for Gibraltar.

CHAPTER IV. 1713–1741   17

    Gibraltar threatened—Critical Situation—Arrival of Reinforcements—Second Demonstration against the Rock—The Thirteenth Siege—The Garrison open Fire on the Spaniards—The Enemy constructing a Mine—Sixty Guns playing on the Garrison—Arrival of Colonel Fitzgerald—Cessation of the Siege—Casualties—Embark for Ireland, 1728—To England, 1741.

CHAPTER V. 1741–1745   24

    War of the Austrian Succession—Embarkation for Flanders—Winter Quarters in Ghent—Campaign of 1743—Battle of Dettingen—Field-Marshal Wade's abortive Campaign—Siege of Tournay Battle of Fontenoy.

CONTENTS.

CHAPTER VI. 1745-1748 ... 29
Insurrection in Scotland—XX land in England—March to Lancashire—Siege of Carlisle—Battle of Culloden—Re-embarkation for the Netherlands—Return to Scotland.

CHAPTER VII. 1749-1758 ... 31
Wolfe joins the XX—Fire at Glasgow—Change of Stations—Unpleasant Duties—Special Thanks of His Majesty King George II—March to Dover—Inspection by H.R.H. the Duke of Cumberland—Social duties—Cantonment on the Coast of Kent—Wolfe's Orders—Colonel Kingsley joins—The Second Battalion—Sir John Mordaunt's Expedition—Wolfe's Letters—The Second Battalion constituted the 67th Regiment—Wolfe leaves the Corps—His Letter to Captain Parr.

CHAPTER VIII. 1758-1759 ... 46
Expedition to St. Malo—Return to England—Embarkation for Germany—Winter Quarters in Munster.

CHAPTER IX. 1759-1760 ... 48
The Seven Years' War—Grenadier Battalion—Battle of Minden—Glory of the XX—Casualties—Prince Ferdinand's General Order—The Virginians—Colonel Beckwith—Attack on the Headquarter Camp—Campaign of 1760—Battle of Warburg—The XX Grenadier Company—Colonel Beckwith—Surprise of Zieremberg—March to the Lower Rhine—Battle of Kloster-Kampen—Winter Quarters.

CHAPTER X. 1761 ... 68
Cautious Advance—Battle of Kirch-Denkern—Maxwell's Brigade—Camp at Ol-Weilmar—Skirmishes.

CHAPTER XI. 1762-1763 ... 73
Sortie from Gottingen—Combat at Wilhelmsthal—Attack on the Fulda—A General Engagement—Skirmishes—Battle of Brucker-Muhl, the Last in the Seven Years' War—Cessation of Hostilities—Winter Quarters—Prince Ferdinand's Letter to the Army—Lord Granby—The Total Casualties of the XX—Embarkation for England.

CHAPTER XII. 1763-1776 ... 79
Service in Gibraltar—Death of General Kingsley—Removal to Ireland.

CHAPTER XIII. 1776-1781 ... 80
Embarkation for Quebec—Lieutenant Norman—Operations on Lake Champlain—Isle Aux Noix—Advance against the Enemy—Major Acland at Hubbardton—Difficulties of the March—Battles of Freeman's Farm and Bemus Heights—Surrender of the Army—Colours of the XX Burnt—Affecting Scenes—Prisoners of War—Return of the Regiment to England.

CONTENTS.

CHAPTER XIV. 1782–1796 94
    Service in Ireland and British North America—The West Indies—State of Affairs in St. Domingo—Arrival of the XX—Attack on Tiburon—Storming of L'Acul—Casualties—Reverse at Bompard—Death of Lieutenant-Colonel Markham—His Character—Return of the XX to England—March to Exeter.

CHAPTER XV. 1796–1799 100
    Change of Stations—Recruiting—Volunteers from the Militia—Distinguished Officers join the XX—Formation of Two Battalions—Embarkation for Holland—Arrival at the Helder—Battle of Krabbendam—The XX would not be beaten—Remember "Minden"—Thanked by Sir R. Abercromby—Casualties—Advance against Hoorn—A Night March—The First Battle of Egmont op Zee—The Second Battle—Return to England.

CHAPTER XVI. 1800–1801 108
    Stationed at Cork—Expedition to Belle Isle—Minorca—The Flank Battalion—Service in Egypt—Capture of the Batteries—A Night Attack—General Coote's Despatch—Constructing Batteries—Forts des Bains and Triangular—Ophthalmia—Gold Medals awarded to the Officers.

CHAPTER XVII. 1801–1808 113
    Arrival at Malta—Bounties Offered—Reduction of the Establishment by One Battalion—Presentation to Colonel George Smyth—New Colours—Efficiency of the Corps—Departure from Malta—The Flank Companies—Disembarkation at Castelamare—Night-March—Severe Winter—Sail for Messina—Detention on Board Ship—Causing a Diversion—Battle of Maida—Death of Captain McLean—Arrival of the XX—Colonel Ross—Captain Colborne—March to Maida—French Prisoners—Scylla Castle—Messina—Unhealthy Quarters—Wreck of the "Windermere"—Gibraltar—Disembarkation at Portsmouth.

CHAPTER XVIII. 1808–1809 125
    Embarkation at Harwich—Portugal—Battle of Vimiera—March to the Frontier of Portugal—Fort Lalippe—March into Spain—The Regiment joins Sir John Moore's Army—The Retreat on Coruña—The Battle—Arrival in England—Mortality among the Survivors.

CHAPTER XIX. 1809–1812 137
    Recruiting—March to Dover—Embarkation at Deal—Landing at South Beveland—Malarial Fever—Return to England—A Skeleton Battalion—Deaths—Presentation to Colonel Ross—Sail for Ireland—Kinsale—Mallow—Training for Active Service—Fermoy—March to Middleton—Suppression of Illegal Assemblies—Inspection by Lord Forbes.

CONTENTS.

	PAGE
CHAPTER XX. 1812-1813	141

Embarkation for Coruña—Landed at Lisbon—*En route* to join the Army—Forced Marches—Battle of Vittoria—Pursuit of the Enemy—Colonel Ross promoted Major-General—Combat at Roncesvalles—Captain Tovey's Company—Casualties—Soult's Despatch—The Retreat—Battle of Sauroren—Lord Wellington's Despatch—Pursuit—Skirmishes—Colonel Wauchope mortally Wounded—The Light Troops—Colonel Steevens succeeds to the Command—First Distribution of Colour Badges—Casualties in the Battles of the Pyrenees.

CHAPTER XXI. 1813 ... 152

The Storming of St. Sebastian—Death of Major Rose.

CHAPTER XXII. 1813-1814 ... 154

Spanish Attack—The Fall of St. Sebastian—Battle of Nivelle—Impassable Roads—Surrender of Two German Regiments—Advance on Orthes—The Battle—The Fight at St. Boës—General Ross wounded—Pursuit to Bordeaux and Toulouse—Battle of Toulouse—Reviewed by Lord Wellington—Embarkation for Ireland.

CHAPTER XXIII. 1814-1818 ... 162

Arrived at Cork—March to Mallow—Death of General Ross—New Colours—Change of Station—Suppression of Unlawful Meetings—Move to Dublin—Colonel Charles Steevens retires from the Army—His Services.

CHAPTER XXIV. 1818-1821 ... 166

Departure from Dublin—Embarkation for St. Helena—Arrival—Lieutenant-Colonel South retires—His Services—On Duty over the Emperor Napoleon—Surgeon Arnott consulted by the Emperor—Panegyric on Marlborough—Presentation by the Emperor to the XX—Napoleonic Relics—Change of Stations.

CHAPTER XXV. 1822-1837 ... 170

Sail for Bombay—Service in India—Koolapoor Field Force—Cholera—Colonel Thomas joins—Inspection by Sir John Keane—His Address and General Order to the Corps—Volunteers—Embarkation.

CHAPTER XXVI. 1837 ... 175

Arrival in England—Quartered at Canterbury—Joined by the Depôt.

CHAPTER XXVII. 1838 ... 176

March to London—Guards of Honour—The Coronation of Queen Victoria—Presentation of Colours by the Duke of Wellington—His Speech.

CONTENTS.   xi

PAGE

CHAPTER XXVIII. 1838-1841 181
 March to Weedon and Manchester—Changes among the Officers—Inspections—Change of Stations—The First Railway Journey—Arrival at Dublin—Death of Captain Barlow—Retirement of Colonel Thomas, C.B.—Embarkation for Bermuda.

CHAPTER XXIX. 1841-1853 185
 Arrival at Bermuda—Formation of a 2nd Battalion—Epidemic of Yellow Fever—Change of Stations—Arrival at Halifax, Nova Scotia—Embark for Quebec—Change of Commanding Officers— Amalgamation of the Two Battalions—Fire at Montreal—Complimentary General Order—Sail for England—Winchester and Plymouth—Active Service—Sail for Turkey.

CHAPTER XXX. 1854 194
 Voyage to the East—Varna—Crimea—The Disembarkation—March to the Alma—The Battle—Bivouac on the Field—March into the Interior—Cholera—Sebastopol—Commencement of the Siege—Heavy Fire on the Trenches—Battle of Balaklava—Attack on the 2nd Division—Casualties to 1st November.

CHAPTER XXXI. 1854 199
 The Battle of Inkerman.

CHAPTER XXXII. 1854-1855... 222
 Day after Inkerman—Burial of Sir George Cathcart—The Siege of Sebastopol—The Great Storm—Hardships and Sufferings endured—The Regimental arrangements—Working Parties Commended—Armed with the Enfield—Attack of the 23rd March—Lord Raglan's Despatch—Assault of the 18th June—Operations during July and August—Assault of the 8th September—Death of Major Chapman.

CHAPTER XXXIII. 1855-1856 233
 The Kinburn Expedition—Deaths from Sickness during the Campaign—Honours bestowed on the Corps—Peace Proclaimed—The XX Quartered in Sebastopol—Embarkation for England—Arrival at Spithead.

CHAPTER XXXIV. 1856-1858 239
 Reviewed by Queen Victoria—Sergeant James Campbell—Banquet at Portsmouth—Colonel F. C. Evelegh, C.B.—Orders for Immediate Embarkation for India—Departure from Aldershot—Embarkation at Spithead—List of Officers—Landing at Calcutta—March to Benares—XX Posted to the 4th Division—Colonel Evelegh appointed Brigadier—Battles of Chanda—Ameerapore—Sultanpore—Arrival at Lucknow—The Siege—Storming of the Engine House—Capture of the Residency—Captain Warren—Lieutenant W. F. F. Gordon—Capture of Gao Ghat and Moosa Bagh—Officers mentioned in Lord Clyde's despatches—Raising of the 2nd Battalion—Field Operations—Sickness.

xii   CONTENTS.

PAGE

CHAPTER XXXV. 1858–1859 251
    March from Lucknow—Camp at Nawabgunge—Duties of the Field Force—Expedition to Mohan—Actions at Hussengunge, Meangunge, and Poorwah—Attack and Destruction of Fort Simree—Engagement at Berah—Instructions to Brigadier Evelegh—Defeat of the Rebels at Buxer-Ghat—Colour captured by Private Bray—Casualties—Anecdote of Colonel Evelegh—Return to Nawabgunge—Evelegh selected to Command a Special Field Force—Major Butler commands the XX—March to Churda—Attack on Fort Musjeidia—Night-March to Bankee—Surprise and Defeat of the Rebels—Two Companies with Colonel Christie's Column—Deaths since Landing—Evelegh leaves the Regiment—Lieutenant-Colonel Cormick succeeds to the Command—Lieutenant-Colonel Butler—Gondah.

CHAPTER XXXVI. 1859–1867 264
    Death of Major-General Thomas, Colonel of the Regiment—Cantonments at Gondah—Building of Barracks—Convoys Plundered—Field Operations by Lieutenant-Colonel Cormick—Actions at Muchlee Goan and Khyber Jungle—Colonel Cormick's Despatch—Captain Vaughan's special Service Column—Defeat of the Rebels—Occupation of the Barracks at Gondah—Final Operations under Colonel A. Holdich, C.B.—Death of Lieutenants Holmes and Horn—Inspection by General Sir Hugh Rose—Change of Stations—Formation of a Field Service Column—Sir William Mansfield inspects the Regiment—Quartered at Calcutta—Preparations for the Return to England—Volunteering—Arrival at Plymouth.

CHAPTER XXXVII. 1867–1881 271
    Quartered at Plymouth—Detachment to Exeter Riots—Detachments at Bristol and Trowbridge—Removal to Aldershot—Death of Colonel Cormick—Change of Stations—Sent to Ireland—Inspection—Presentation of Colours by Lord Strathnairn—Change of Stations—Embark for Bermuda—Sir F. Horn, Colonel of the XX—Quartered at Halifax, N.S.—Embark for Cyprus—Change of Camps—Headquarters to Malta—XX Return Home.

CHAPTER XXXVIII. 1881–1888 282
    The XX at Cork—Change of Title—Transfers from the Battalion—Stations in Ireland—Guards of Honour—Fermoy—Liverpool—Manchester—Inspection by H.R.H. the Duke of Cambridge at Manchester and Fleetwood.

THE SECOND BATTALION.

CHAPTER XXXIX. 1588–1863 289
    A National Emergency—Raising of the 2nd Battalion—Lieutenant-Colonel Radcliffe—Clonmel—Waterford—Tralee—Inspections—Presentation of Colours—Speech of General Lord Seaton—Curragh Camp and Dublin—Move to England—Aldershot—Portsmouth—Retirement of Colonel Radcliffe—Embarkation for India—Arrival at Calcutta.

CONTENTS.   xiii

                                                  PAGE
CHAPTER XL. 1863–1868 299
   Ordered to China—Outline of the History of Japan—The Daïmios—Attack on the Legation—Landed at Hong-Kong—Detachment to Yokohama—The 67th Regiment—Headquarters to Japan—Cholera—Death of Captain Honourable A. E. P. Vereker—Review at Yokohama—Assassination of Major G. W. Baldwin and Lieutenant R. N. Bird—Their Characters and Services—Execution of the Murderers—Sir Rutherford Alcock—Letter to Colonel Browne—Approbation of Major-General Guy—The Field Battery—Inspection by General Guy—The Taku Forts—The Legation Guard—Embarkation for Hong-Kong—Letter of thanks from Sir H. S. Parkes—Presentation of a Farewell Cup—Embarkation for South Africa—Stations.

CHAPTER XLI. 1869–1888 313
   G Company struck by Lightning—Change of Stations—The Mauritius—Complimentary Order by Major-General G. S. Smyth—Wing to South Africa—The Return Home—Service in Ireland—Colonel H. R. Browne exchanges to the 37th Regiment—State of the Battalion during his Command—Service in England—Ordered to Ireland—Mullingar—Colonel John Davis retires upon Half Pay—Under Orders for India—Numerous Detachments—Volunteers—The Embarkation—Arrival in India—Stationed at Mhow—Inspections by Generals Stewart and Hardinge—Retirement of Lieutenant-Colonel O'Neill—Change of Stations—Guard of Honour at Ajmere—Inspection by Sir R. Phayre—Death of Major Randolph and Captain Furlonger—Inspection by H.R.H. the Duke of Connaught—Move to Ahmednagar—Colonel Webster retires—Lieutenant-Colonel G. D. Wahab succeeds to the command.

APPENDIX.

(IN CHRONOLOGICAL ORDER.)

GUSTAVUS HAMILTON, VISCOUNT BOYNE 325
LIEUTENANT-GENERAL WILLIAM KINGSLEY 326
MAJOR-GENERAL JAMES WOLFE 327
GENERAL THOMAS CARLETON 333
LADY HARRIET ACLAND 335
MAJOR-GENERAL ROBERT ROSS 340
FIELD-MARSHAL LORD SEATON, G.C.B., G.C.M.G., G.C.H. 350
SURGEON ARCHIBALD ARNOTT 355
MAJOR-GENERAL HENRY THOMAS, C.B. 357

CONTENTS.

	PAGE
CAPTAIN HENRY HOLLINSWORTH, MILITARY KNIGHT OF WINDSOR	359
GENERAL SIR FREDERICK HORN, K.C.B.	361
COLONEL FREDERICK C. EVELEGH, C.B.	363
GENERAL SIR W. P. RADCLIFFE, K.C.B.	366
COLONEL JOHN CORMICK	369
COLONEL SIR OWEN TUDOR BURNE, K.C.S.I., C.I.E.	371
THE ORIGIN OF THE XX.—COUNTY TITLES	375
THE ORDERS OF WOLFE	377
EXTRACT FROM A MINDEN LETTER	383
LETTER FROM FIELD-MARSHAL LORD SEATON, G.C.B., TO MAJOR-GENERAL P. BAINBRIGGE	385
GENERAL BAINBRIGGE'S NARRATIVE OF RONCESVALLES AND SAUROREN	387
LETTERS OF CAPTAIN J. KINCAID, RIFLE BRIGADE, AND LIEUTENANT-COLONEL G. TOVEY	406
CANADIAN AFFAIRS	409

MAPS.

	PAGE
BATTLE OF MINDEN	58
OF SPAIN, PORTUGAL, AND THE SOUTH OF FRANCE, SHOWING THE ROUTE TAKEN BY THE REGIMENT DURING THE RETREAT ON CORUNA, AND IN THE OPERATIONS IN THE PENINSULAR WAR	160
THE FIGHT ON MOUNT INKERMAN	208
THE FIGHT AT THE SANDBAG BATTERY	216
OF THE COUNTRY ROUND LUCKNOW	266

ILLUSTRATIONS.

PORTRAITS OF GENERALS WOLFE AND ROSS	*Frontispiece*
PRIVATE SOLDIER, 1750	*after xv*
PRIVATE SOLDIER, 1777	,,
SERGEANT, 1800	,,
PRIVATE SOLDIER, 1812	,,
OFFICER OF THE GRENADIER COMPANY, 1838 ...	,,
OFFICER OF THE LIGHT COMPANY, 1838...	,,
OFFICER OF THE GRENADIER COMPANY, 1853 ...	,,
OFFICER OF THE LIGHT COMPANY, 1853...	,,
PRIVATE SOLDIER, 1867	,,
PRIVATE SOLDIER, 1880	,,
PRIVATE SOLDIER, 1888	,,

Private.
1750

Private,
1777

Sergeant
1800

Private,
1812.

Officer, Grenadier Company, 1838.

Officer, Light Company.
1838.

Officer,
1853.

Officer Light Company
1853

Private.
1862

CHAPTER I.

1688–1702.

Landing of the Prince of Orange—Raising of the XX by Sir R. Peyton—Gustavus Hamilton—In Garrison at Carrickfergus—Battle of the Boyne—First Siege of Limerick—Ballymore—Siege of Athlone—Battle of Aghrim—Second Siege of Limerick—The Regiment moved to the Isle of Wight.

THE Prince of Orange was the chief of a foreign State, but was also an exalted member of our own Royal Family; and it was in that last character that, at a time of emergency, he found himself entreated to come to England, and even to come in strength. He landed with a Dutch army at Torbay, on the 5th November, 1688, to enable the country to assert the rights of the constitution in Parliament against the illegal proceedings of King James II. The Prince reached Exeter on the 8th of November, when a large number of persons, from all ranks of society, joined his standard. His Highness issued commissions to Lord Mordaunt, Sir R. Peyton, and Sir J. Guise to raise regiments of foot for his service.

Sir Robert Peyton (whose commission as Colonel was dated 20th November, 1688) raised in the city of Exeter and its vicinity a regiment which has served in the army, without intermission, to the present time, and which now bears the title of "The Lancashire Fusiliers," but still retains its numerical order of succession (XX).

In February, 1689, after the flight of King James to France and the elevation of the Prince and Princess of Orange to the throne of England, the regiment was

B

reduced to six companies; but, when it was found necessary to send an army to Ireland to deliver that country from the power of King James, the corps was augmented to thirteen companies.

Sir Robert Peyton withdrew from active service in June, 1689, and was succeeded in the command of the regiment by Colonel Gustavus Hamilton, a distinguished soldier, who had quitted the service of King James in Ireland.[1] The regiment was recruited to its establishment in time to accompany the second division of the army, commanded by the Duke of Schomberg, to Ireland, where it arrived during the siege of Carrickfergus. The XX was placed in garrison at Carrickfergus. After passing the winter in garrison, the regiment took the field in the spring of 1690, and joined the army commanded by King William III, who advanced to the banks of the Boyne, where the French and Irish troops, under King James, had taken up a position to oppose the passage of the river.

The battle of the Boyne was fought on the 1st July, 1690, and was the first engagement in which the XX Regiment took part. The loss in this battle was slight.

After the victory of the Boyne the regiment advanced with the army to Dublin, whence it was detached under General Douglas against Athlone. This place, however, was found too strongly garrisoned, and King James's adherents too numerous in the neighbourhood, to admit of its being captured by so small a force. The regiment, therefore, re-joined the army commanded by King William III, which appeared before the walls of Limerick, and commenced what is known in history as the first siege of Limerick.

---

[1] See Appendix.

King William's army was accompanied by small cannon only; several large pieces of ordnance, with ammunition, &c., had been left at Cashel, and were now slowly following the army; but when about seven miles from William's camp, they were surprised and captured by Sarsfield. The loss of the artillery and the heavy autumnal rains began to tell upon the besiegers, and it was determined to make one great effort.

The assault was made on the 27th August, at three in the afternoon. The English, overwhelmed by numbers, were driven back with great loss. The siege was raised, and the army went into winter quarters.

During the period that active operations were suspended, detachments of the regiment had frequent encounters with bands of armed peasantry, called Rapparees.

In June, 1691, the XX joined the army commanded by General de Ginkell (a Dutch officer of great experience). The Irish were in considerable force at Ballymore, an ill-built town on the road between Athlone and Mullingar. They were devoid of discipline, whereas the army to oppose them was in splendid order. General de Ginkell had, as his seconds, Talmash and Mackay, two of the best officers (except Marlborough) in the British Isles. The XX formed part of the force, commanded by Major-General Sir John Lanier, which advanced on Ballymore. Here, upon a peninsula surrounded by a swamp, stood an ancient fortification, towards which the Irish retired before the advancing troops, but soon continued their retreat to a hill, where the main body of their force was drawn up. They subsequently retreated precipitately into the town, at the entrance to which they had thrown up a trench, but, not finding it defensible, they abandoned the place on the 8th of June. The whole army then moved westward, and, on the 19th June, appeared before the walls of Athlone, as the ramparts of earth around it were named.

The town lay partly in Leinster and partly in Connaught. The English quarter was in the former and the Celtic in the latter. The Shannon, which is the boundary of the two provinces, poured through Athlone in a deep and rapid stream, and turned two large mills which rose on the arches of a stone bridge. Sixty yards below the bridge was a ford, and above it rose a Norman castle, with a tower seventy feet high, and a curtain wall having a frontage to the river of about sixty yards. Encamped within a short distance of the town was a French army of 25,000 men under General St. Ruth. During the night of the 19th the English placed their cannon in position; on the morning of the 20th the firing began, and at five in the afternoon the assault was made. In a few hours de Ginkell was master of the English quarter of Athlone; and this success had cost him only twenty men killed and forty wounded. Between him and the Celtic quarter there yet flowed the Shannon. Several days were spent in the erection of batteries, to cover the passage of the troops, and in the attempts to repair the bridge. On the 30th of June, de Ginkell called a council of war. It was proposed to try the ford, which proposition was agreed upon; and it was determined that the attempt should be made that very afternoon.

The XX led the way on the daring, if not desperate, enterprise of crossing, in the face of the enemy, a rapid river, passable only in the heat of summer when the water was low, and then only at a place barely wide enough to admit of twenty men abreast.

Lord Macaulay thus describes this forlorn hope:—
"It was six o'clock. A peal from the steeple of the church gave the signal. Prince George of Hesse-Darmstadt, and a brave soldier named Hamilton, whose services were afterwards rewarded with the title of Viscount Boyne, descended first into the Shannon. Then the Grenadiers lifted the Duke of Würtemberg on their shoulders, and with a great shout plunged twenty abreast up to their cravats in the water. The stream ran deep and strong, but in a few moments the head of the column reached dry land."[1]

Fifty pieces of cannon and mortars were at that moment firing upon them.[2] The stout fellows of the Scots Brigade and of Hamilton's (XX) regiment now placed planks on the broken arches of the bridge and laid pontoons on the river; the whole army commenced to cross, and with the loss of only forty-two men killed and wounded—so rapidly was the movement made—the troops of King William forced their way into Connaught.[3]

Of the Irish, a thousand men were slain. General St. Ruth retired in the direction of Ballinasloe, and pitched his camp about thirty miles from Athlone, on the road to Galway, near the ruined castle of Aghrim, where he decided to make a last stand.

On the 11th of July, General de Ginkell, having repaired the fortifications of Athlone and left a garrison there, fixed his headquarters at Ballinasloe, about four miles from Aghrim.

In firm and orderly array the troops of King William, "their ranks ablaze with scarlet," after some delay occasioned by a thick fog, and a further delay caused

---

[1] Macaulay's *History of England*, vol. iii, page 273.
[2] General Kane's *Memoirs*. [3] *British Battles*.

by the necessity of dislodging the Irish outposts, came in sight of the battalions of St. Ruth, occupying a position which had been chosen with great judgment. At five o'clock in the evening this memorable battle commenced. Major-General Mackay advanced with the regiments of Kirk (2nd) and Hamilton (XX), and drove the enemy from the lines of hedges in front, also from the right and left of the castle of Aghrim. To drive them, however, was not such easy work, as the troops had to advance over slippery and uneven ground, sinking at every foot of the way in the mud or bog, and meeting with a determined resistance from the defenders posted behind the walls and hedges. The Irish were never known to fight with more resolute bravery.[1]

"We still pursued them," records General Kane, "until we drove them out of four or five rows of hedges, into an open plain."

General Saint Ruth was killed by a cannon ball, there was no one to take his place, and the crisis had arrived. At this moment Mackay made a flank movement, and Talmash led a vigorous attack in front, and the whole of the Irish gave way.

"Only four hundred prisoners were taken. The number slain was, in proportion to the number engaged, greater than in any other battle of the age. But for the coming on of a moonless night, made darker by a misty rain, scarcely a man would have escaped. Of the conquerors, six hundred were killed and about a thousand wounded."[2]

From Aghrim the regiment marched to Galway, which place capitulated after a short resistance. What

---

[1] *London Gazette.*
[2] Macaulay's *History of England*, vol. iii, page 276.

remained of King James's army took refuge in the city of Limerick. The army under General de Ginkell marched against Limerick, and the "second" siege began on the 14th August.

The regiment was engaged in this service until the surrender of the city by treaty and the cessation of hostilities in Ireland, on the 3rd of October, 1691.

The XX remained in Ireland until June, 1702, when it was moved to the Isle of Wight.

Chapter II.

1702–1704.

The Grand Alliance—Accession of Queen Anne—War declared against France and Spain—Regiments for Sea Service—Embarkation for Spain—Disembarkation—Surrender of Rota and Fort Catalina—XX selected for Service in the West Indies—Attack on Guadalope—Landing at Jamaica—Return to Ireland.

ON concluding the "Grand Alliance" against France and Spain, in the latter part of 1701, King William immediately adopted measures for augmenting the army and navy. Eleven battalions were added to the army (from the 29th to the 39th). These and other warlike preparations were in progress when King William III died at Hampton Court Palace on the 8th of March, 1702. He was succeeded on the throne by Queen Anne, who resolved to carry out the policy and views of the late King.

War was declared against France and Spain on the 4th May; additional forces were sent to Flanders, the Earl of Marlborough being appointed to command the British, Dutch, and auxiliary troops.

By a Special Royal Warrant, dated St. James's, 1st June, 1702, the six following regiments were detailed for sea service:—Colonel Ventris Columbine's, 6th; Colonel Thomas Earle's, 19th; Colonel Gustavus Hamilton's, XX; Colonel Lord Lucas's, 34th; Colonel Earl of Donegal's, 35th; Colonel Viscount Charlemont's, 36th.

Thirteen battalions were sent to Holland to assist the Dutch in opposing the advance of the French army towards their frontier.

The XX was not destined to share in the victories of Marlborough, triumphs then unequalled since the days of Crecy and Agincourt. But an expedition against Spain, with the specific object of reducing Cadiz, having been decided upon, the regiment[1] formed part of the expeditionary force commanded by the Duke of Ormond, General of Horse; and embarked on board four transports of the fleet, under Sir George Rooke, Vice-Admiral of England, which sailed from St. Helens on the 1st July, 1702, and, on the 23rd August, came to anchor in the Bay of Bulls, two leagues distant from Cadiz.

Officers and men were impatient to engage the enemy, and every hour was of consequence in giving time to the Spaniards to add further to their preparations for defence; yet, in spite of these considerations, three days were lost by the chiefs in debate upon the best place for landing. At length a decision was arrived at, and, at early dawn on the morning of the 26th, the troops commenced to disembark between the

---

[1] Embarkation return of Brigadier-General Gustavus Hamilton's regiment, 1st July, 1702.

The Colonel's Company	52 men	On board the "Berwick."
The Lieut.-Colonel's Company	52 ,,	
The Major's Company	51 ,,	On board the "James and Sarah."
Captain Ward's Company	51 ,,	
,, Weighton's Company	51 ,,	
,, John Hamilton's Company	51 ,,	On board the "Friend's Adventure."
,, Asle's Company	51 ,,	
,, Fredk. Hamilton's Company	49 ,,	
,, Parker's Company	52 ,,	On board the "Nicolas."
,, St. Clair's Company	49 ,,	
,, Wightman's Company	51 ,,	
,, Lord Lambert's Company	49 ,,	
Total	609	

GEORGE WHITEHEAD, Lieut.-Colonel.

N.B.—One of the soldiers of Captain St. Clair's Company proved to be a female.

promontory of Rota and Fort Santa Catalina. Two days' rations of bread, cheese, and beer were issued to every man. In rear of each regiment was an officer of artillery with twenty *chevaux-de-Frise*. No drum was to be beaten, no colour uncased, save in the boat of the General commanding. When a drum beat, then the lines of boats were to row; when it ceased, the men were to lie upon their oars.

No soldier to fire under pain of death while in the boat, or to unshoulder his musket when landed. At four o'clock precisely, one thousand two hundred British Grenadiers sprang ashore, and the rest followed in quick succession, though a high wind was rolling the sea upon the beach with such fury that more than thirty boats were upset; many soldiers were drowned, and many had to swim ashore, or wade out of water that flowed over their cravats.

Four pieces of cannon, which were firing on the disembarking troops, were carried at the point of the bayonet, and spiked, under cover of the fire of H.M. ship "Lennox."

The coast being now open, in the afternoon the English and Dutch began their march towards Rota, a small town in the north side of Cadiz Bay, near the mouth of the Guadalquiver, making a halt during the night. Next day Rota was surrendered by the Alcade, and taken possession of by one hundred Grenadiers.

Fort Catalina was surrendered, and capitulated on the 22nd August, though the French had recently strengthened it by a new battery mounted with forty pieces of cannon.

Early in September an unsuccessful attack was made on Fort Matagorda; but the batteries of the allied forces sank so deep in the soft sand and marshy ground as they recoiled in firing, that, after a loss of sixty-five men killed and wounded, further attempts were relinquished. Intelligence having reached the Duke of Ormond that a Spanish army, said to be 40,000 strong, commanded by the Marquis de Villadarius, was advancing, he retired with the army to Rota, and embarked on board the fleet.

The XX, together with the 19th, 35th, and 36th Regiments, were selected for service in the West Indies, and sailed for the Leeward Islands on the 24th September, 1702, with a division (six ships) of the Royal Navy under Commodore Walker. The commodore called at Antigua, where the military forces were increased by some troops under Colonel Codrington. A descent was made on the island of Guadalope, where the troops raised the fort, burnt the town, ravaged the country, and re-embarked. They then retired to Nevis, where they suffered great privations, and must have perished by famine had they not been relieved by Vice-Admiral Graydon, who was on his way to Jamaica.[1]

Extensive arrangements were made for further raids on the French and Spanish settlements in the West Indies. The Earl of Peterborough was nominated to the command of the armament to be employed in this service, but the design was abandoned.

The regiment suffered considerable loss from the unhealthy climate of Jamaica, where it remained until June, 1704, when it was removed to Europe and quartered in Ireland.

---

[1] Smollett's *History of England*, page 933.

CHAPTER III.

1704-1713.

Arrival from the West Indies—Embarkation for Portugal—Winter Quarters—Restricted to Defensive Operations during 1708—Battle of La Gudiña—Winter Quarters—Advance across the Guadiana, 1710—Attack on Cabaleros—Campaign of 1711—Capture of Small Towns—The Clandestine Treaty—Suspension of Hostilities—XX sail for Gibraltar.

THE regiment was stationed in the south of Ireland on arrival from the West Indies in the summer of 1704. On the 25th April, 1707, the allied forces under the Earl of Galway were defeated by the French and Spaniards, commanded by the Duke of Berwick (son of James II), at Almanza. This defeat materially changed the aspect of affairs in Spain.

Additional troops were shortly afterwards selected for embarkation for Portugal, and the XX, together with the 5th, 39th, and a newly-raised regiment (since disbanded), commanded by Colonel Stanwix, embarked at Cork on the 22nd May, 1707, and landed at Lisbon on the 8th of June. This seasonable reinforcement, arriving soon after the defeat of the allies at Almanza, in the south-east of Spain, and at the moment when the enemy, having captured Serpa and Moura in the Alemtejo, had seized on the bridge of Olivenza, in Portuguese Estremadura, and menaced that important place, revived by its presence the drooping spirits of the Portuguese. These four regiments, being the only British troops in that part of the country, were disembarked in great haste, and reached the frontier under the command of the Marquis de Montandre. The enemy, having resolved to besiege Olivenza, or to oblige the Portuguese to give battle, had all their heavy cannon and fascines in readiness before the town; but, upon the approach of the four regiments, they retired in great precipitation, and sent away their cannon to Badajoz.

The British halted at Estremoz, a strongly-fortified town of the Alemtejo, situated in an agreeable tract of country on the Tarra, and remained in this pleasant quarter during the summer, afterwards encamping in the fruitful valley of the Caya, near Elvas, having detached parties on the flanks to prevent the enemy making incursions into Portugal.

The regiment was engaged in this service until November, when they went into quarters in the frontier towns of Portugal. In the spring of 1708, the XX again took the field, and was encamped at Fuente de Supatores, between Elvas and Campo Mayor. The British division was soon afterwards increased to six regiments, by the arrival from England of the 13th and a newly-raised regiment (Paston's).

The little army in the Alemtejo was commanded by the Marquis de Fronteira, but the characteristic inactivity of the Portuguese caused the services of the British to be restricted to defensive operations. The XX was encamped in the autumn at Campo Mayor, and afterwards went into cantonments.

The regiment moved from its quarters in the spring of 1709, and was soon actively engaged. It was encamped near Estremoz, and proceeded thence to Elvas on the 23rd April, 1709. The regiment was subsequently encamped with the army on the banks of the Caya, where the Earl of Galway, who had been removed from the army in Catalonia, appeared at the head of the British division. On the 7th May, 1709, the Spaniards, commanded by the Marquis de Bay, made a movement to forage the adjacent country, when the Portuguese General (Marquis de Fronteira), contrary to the Earl of Galway's advice, passed the Caya with most of the forces, and drew them out on the plain of La Gudiña, which has given its name to the battle. The onset was begun by the Spaniards, who were three times bravely repulsed by the English and Portuguese infantry in the centre.[1] But the Marquis of Bay, leading the attack in person, then made a charge upon the right of the allies, which consisted entirely of some raw Portuguese cavalry, which, after a slight resistance, was routed. The Portuguese cannon fell into the hands of the enemy; their cavalry on the left also gave way: and Lord Galway advanced at this juncture, to recover the cannon, with the 13th, Stanwix's, and Galway's regiments. His brigade was intercepted and, for the greater part, obliged to surrender, with Lord Barrymore, Generals Sankey and Pearce, and his other principal officers; as to himself, his horse was shot under him, and he had great difficulty in effecting his escape.

At the same time the 5th, XX, 39th, and Lord Paston's regiments, though deserted by the whole of the cavalry, made a determined stand against the enemy's repeated attacks with admirable firmness until the Portuguese infantry retired, and then withdrew fighting from the field.

In the *Monthly Mercury* of May, 1709, this scene is thus described:—"The enemy advanced in full career, threatening the destruction of this little band, yet, with

---

[1] *London Gazette*, May 16th—19th, 1709.

ranks unbroken and steady tread, these undaunted English calmly retraced their steps, exhibiting one of the noblest spectacles of war, and occasionally punishing the temerity of their pursuers with a cool and deliberate resolution, which laid a thousand Spaniards dead upon the field."

The heroic conduct of this brigade impressed the enemy, and likewise the Portuguese, with a sense of British courage.

The brigade effected its retreat with the loss of only one hundred and fifty men killed and wounded, and passed the night at Arronches. The XX, in common with the three other regiments of the brigade, acquired great honour by its gallant behaviour on this occasion. The regiment afterwards encamped at Elvas, was subsequently in position on the banks of the Guadiana, and again passed the winter in cantonments in the Alemtejo.

The casualties of the preceding campaign having been replaced by recruits from England, the regiment was again in the field in the spring of 1710, and was employed in the Alemtejo; but the army was weak and unequal to any important undertaking, and the French, having obtained some success in the province of Tras os Montes, occasioned a detachment to be sent thither.

In the autumn the army advanced across the Guadiana, and on the 4th of October arrived on the rich plains of Xeres de los Cabaleros, on the river Ardilla, in Spanish Estremadura.

It was determined to attack this place by storm on the following day, and the 5th, XX, and 39th Regiments, having been selected for this service under the command of Brigadier-General Stanwix, advanced at four in the afternoon to attack the works near St.

Catherine's Gate by escalade.[1] A few minutes after the regiments had commenced the assault the governor sent proposals to surrender, which were agreed to, and the garrison, consisting of seven hundred men, became prisoners of war. The army afterwards retired to Portugal by the mountains of Orlor, and went into quarters. During the campaign of 1711, the XX formed part of the army which assembled at Olivenza in May, and, having passed the Guadiana by the pontoon bridge at Jereumenla, advanced against the enemy, who took refuge under the guns of Badajoz.

The regiment was engaged in the capture of several small towns in Spanish Estremadura; but the summer passed without any achievement of importance. About this time a discovery was made by the Earl of Portmore, who commanded the British troops in Portugal, of a Clandestine Treaty[2] in progress between the Crown of Portugal and the enemy, in which the former had agreed to separate from the allies; to give an excuse for this, a mock battle was to have been fought, in which the British troops were to have been sacrificed. This treaty was broken off, but the British Government soon afterwards entered into negotiations with France.

The XX remained in Portugal, and during the summer of 1712 was encamped on the plains of the Tarra. In the autumn a suspension of hostilities was proclaimed at the camp by Major-General Pearce, and the regiment went into cantonments. On the 11th of April, 1713, the Treaty of Utrecht was signed. By its provisions the fortress of Gibraltar and the island of Minorca, which had been taken by the English during the war, were ceded to Great Britain. The XX proceeded to Gibraltar from Portugal in July, 1713.

---

[1] *London Gazette.*   [2] *Annals of Queen Anne.*

Chapter IV.

1713-1741.

Gibraltar threatened—Critical Situation—Arrival of Reinforcements—Second Demonstration against the Rock—The Thirteenth Siege—The Garrison open Fire on the Spaniards—The Enemy constructing a Mine—Sixty Guns playing on the Garrison—Arrival of Colonel Fitzgerald—Cessation of the Siege—Casualties—Embark for Ireland, 1728—To England, 1741.

THERE is no record forthcoming of the first seven years of the regiment's sojourn in Gibraltar.

In 1720 the fortress was threatened by the Spaniards. Ceuta, a Spanish fortress in Morocco, had been besieged many years by the Moors, and a formidable force, commanded by the Marquis de Leda, was assembled in Gibraltar Bay under pretence of relieving it, but with a secret intention of first surprising Gibraltar, for which purpose they had procured scaling ladders, &c. This armament was not fitted out so secretly, but that the British Ministry had timely notice, and suspecting some finesse, despatched orders to Colonel Kane, Governor of Minorca, to immediately embark a part of his garrison and repair to Gibraltar under convoy of the fleet in the Mediterranean. On his arrival, he found Gibraltar in a very critical state of unpreparedness. The garrison consisted of the 5th, 13th, and XX Regiments. These battalions were weak in numbers; they were commanded by Major Hetherington, who, with the exception of Major Batteroux, was the only field officer in the place. Many officers were absent; only provisions for fourteen days were in the stores; a large number of Spaniards were in the town; and a fleet was before its walls.

Such was the feeble state of affairs when Colonel Kane opportunely arrived with five hundred men, provisions, and ammunition.

The British Commodore acted forthwith in so spirited a manner, that the Marquis de Leda was obliged to sail for Ceuta, though he was still of opinion that the fortress might have been taken by general assault.

This scheme proving abortive, Gibraltar remained unmolested until the latter end of the year 1726, when the Spaniards, who had kept a watchful eye on the garrison, assembled an army in the neighbourhood of Algeciras. On the 20th of January, 1727, they encamped on the plain below St. Roque, and began to erect a battery on the beach to protect their camp. The formidable fleet of Admiral Hobson was then at anchor in the bay, but, as he had not received any intelligence of hostilities having commenced between England and Spain, he was with reluctance compelled to overlook the transporting of provisions, artillery, and ammunition from Algeciras (where the Spaniards had formed their depôts) to the camp. Bragadier-General Kane, who had been a second time ordered from Minorca to Gibraltar, lay under similar embarrassments. The operations of the enemy, however, tending towards a direct attack upon the garrison, he thought it prudent to order the Spaniards out of the town, and forbid their galleys anchoring under his guns. Gibraltar had undergone considerable alterations since the siege of 1705. Several works had been erected on the heights above the lines, which were distinguished by the name of Willis's batteries; the Prince's lines were also extended to the extremity of the Rock, and an inundation with a causeway was formed out of the morass that was in front of the grand battery.

The Count de Las Torres commanded the Spanish forces, amounting to near 20,000 men; and soon after his camp was formed he advanced within reach of the garrison. The Brigadier therefore despatched a parley, to desire "That he would withdraw from the range of his guns, or otherwise he would do his utmost to force him." The Count answered, "That as the garrison could command no more than they had power to maintain, he should obey his Catholic Majesty's orders, and encroach as far as he was able." Notwithstanding this insult, as war had not been formally declared, the Brigadier would not commence hostilities, until the Spaniards, by their proceedings, should oblige him to take such a course in defence of his command. The British Government decided to reinforce the garrison. The 26th, 29th, and 39th Regiments embarked on board six men-of-war at Portsmouth, and, in addition, the 25th and 34th Regiments embarked at Cork.[1] The fleet sailed under Admiral Sir Charles Wager, early in January, and, after a stormy passage, arrived in the bay of Gibraltar on the 2nd of February.

Brigadier Clayton, the Lieutenant-Governor, arrived with these reinforcements, and a council of war was immediately summoned; but the result was a determination not to fire upon the Spaniards.

On the 10th February, the enemy brought materials for batteries to the old windmill on the neutral ground. In consequence of this move a second council was held, and it was agreed that the Spanish General had made open war by encroaching so far on the liberties of the garrison. In the evening the out-guard was withdrawn, and on the following afternoon the old

---

[1] The regiments from Cork did not reach Gibraltar until the 27th of March.

mole and Willis's batteries opened fire on the Spanish workmen. They persisted, nevertheless, in carrying on the operations, and at night a large party marched down to the Devil's Tower, where they immediately broke ground and began a communication with their other work. This party was greatly annoyed in marching to their post, but were soon at a point, under cover of the rock, where the guns could not be depressed to bear upon them. Numbers of the enemy deserted to the garrison, by whom, on the 17th, the Lieutenant-Governor was informed that the Spaniards were constructing a mine in a cave under Willis's, with the intention, if possible, of blowing up that battery. On receipt of this intelligence the Engineers were sent to reconnoitre the cave, which, after some difficulty, they discovered, with a sentry at its entrance; a party was immediately stationed to annoy the communication with musketry. On the morning of the 22nd, the Count opened fire on the garrison with seventeen pieces of cannon besides mortars.

In the meantime, Sir Charles Wager and Admiral Hobson, with the fleet under their command, were constantly harassing the enemy by intercepting their homeward-bound ships; any that were captured being brought into the bay proving of great benefit to the besieged. On the 3rd March, the enemy opened a new battery of twenty-two guns and directed its fire on the old mole and town; on the 8th, another of fifteen guns, bearing upon the old mole, which, it appears, proved a troublesome battery to the western flank of their approaches. On the 10th April, Colonel Cosby arrived in the "Solebay," with five hundred men from Minorca. Two days afterwards the Admirals sailed westward, leaving Commodore Davis behind with six men-of-war and the sloops. Lord Portmore, the Governor, arrived on the 21st, with a battalion of Guards, and another of the line; also Colonel Watson, of the Artillery, with several noblemen as volunteers. On the 26th, the Spaniards opened a new battery against Willis's and the extremity of Prince's lines.

Their batteries now mounted sixty cannon, besides mortars. In the beginning of May, the garrison had intelligence that the enemy designed an assault; precautions were accordingly taken, the guns on the lower defences being loaded with grape.

The Spaniards added still to their approaches, raising various communications to and from their advanced batteries. Towards the 16th and 20th their firing abated, but their engineers continued to advance their trenches. The firing continued until the 12th of June, on which date, about ten p.m., Colonel Fitzgerald,[1] of the Irish Brigade, in the Spanish service, appeared carrying a flag of truce; on being admitted into the garrison, he delivered letters to Lord Portmore from the Dutch Minister at the Court of Madrid, with a copy of the preliminaries of a general peace; whereupon a suspension of arms took place, and all hostilities ceased on both sides.

A Spanish journal of the siege is given in the *Historical Register* for 1727, and in fuller detail in Dodd's *History of Gibraltar*.

From that journal it appears that of the one hundred and fifteen days from the 23rd February to the 17th of June inclusive, the Spaniards had some casualties on every day but six, and that their losses amounted to three hundred and ninety-two killed and one thousand

---

[1] *History of Gibraltar*, J. H. Mann, page 246.

and nineteen wounded. From other sources it has been ascertained that eight hundred and ninety-five deserted, and that more than five thousand died of sickness or were invalided. Their total loss, then, was seven thousand two hundred and eighty-six.

In the journal of an English officer, published in 1727, it was stated that the number of rounds fired by the guns of the different forts in Gibraltar was 52,292; during the first week in May the defenders seemed to "live in flames," so incessant was the enemy's cannonade.

The loss of the garrison was comparatively slight. The following is a return of the killed and wounded during the siege, from the 11th February to 12th June, 1727. This information is taken from *The Political State of Great Britain*, vol. xxxiv, p. 413.

Regiments.	Officers Killed.	Men Killed.	Men Wounded.	Died of Wounds.	Total.
Foot Guards	...	2	19	2	23
Royal Artillery	1	11	16	2	29
Pearce's 5th Regiment	...	4	9	...	13
Lord Mark Kerr's 13th Regiment	...	7	26	3	36
Clayton's 14th Regiment ...	...	7	13	5	25
Egerton's XX Regiment ...	1	8	12	8	28
Middleton's 25th Regiment ...	1	3	14	...	17
Anstruther's 26th Regiment ...	...	6	29	3	38
Disney's 29th Regiment ...	...	2	12	...	14
Bissett's 30th Regiment ...	...	8	15	4	27
Hayes's 34th Regiment	...	2	16	2	20
Newton's 39th Regiment ...	...	6	4	4	14
Detachments from the Regiments at Minorca, under Colonel Cuby, 18th Foot.	...	6	17	1	24
Total	3	72	202	34	308

In addition to the foregoing, twenty-eight men died of disease and fourteen deserted, making a total of three hundred and fifty casualties. The actual loss, however, is found in most cases to be more than the numbers returned. Dodd makes a significant note:—
"The Guards lost upwards of a hundred and six men, and the other regiments in proportion, but 'twas chiefly by sickness, and, as it appears, after the 12th June; so that by the lists above, which are most exact and true, above eight times as many died from distemper, occasioned, as it was thought, by want of fresh provisions, as fell by all the accidents attending the siege."

During this, the thirteenth siege of Gibraltar, no regiment seems to have rendered itself conspicuous above the others by any particular act of service; but, as will be perceived, the XX had more men killed, including those who died from their wounds, than any other corps engaged in this memorable defence, at the commencement of which its strength was only four hundred and fifteen all ranks. In April, 1728, the XX embarked from Gibraltar and proceeded to Ireland, where it arrived in May. In 1741, the regiment was withdrawn from Ireland and stationed in the south of England.

CHAPTER V.

1741–1745.

War of the Austrian Succession—Embarkation for Flanders—Winter Quarters in Ghent—Campaign of 1743—Battle of Dettingen—Field-Marshal Wade's abortive Campaign—Siege of Tournay—Battle of Fontenoy.

ENGLAND being one of the signatory powers to the settlement known as the "Pragmatic Sanction," the country became involved in the "War of the Austrian Succession," and despatched an army under the command of Field-Marshal the Earl of Stair to Flanders. The XX formed part of this force, and embarked in the month of May, 1742.

The regiment was not actively engaged during this year, but was somewhat suddenly ordered into quarters in the town of Ghent, where it remained until the early part of May, 1743, when the whole of the allies or the "Pragmatic," as it was called, encamped on the river Mayn. Many futile attempts were made to bring the French army under Marshal de Noailles to battle, but, although the English crossed to the French side of the river, de Noailles contented himself with the minor operations of cutting off our supplies.

On Sunday, the 16th of June, the army under the Earl of Stair re-crossed the river and took possession of Aschaffenburg. This position was badly chosen, and the French Marshal made the occupation of it impossible by seizing two villages, which enabled him to cut off the British from their base and source of supplies. After many abortive councils of war, it was decided on the 26th June that the army should retire on Hanau, and about one o'clock on the 27th the allies commenced their retreat. The British rear-guard had hardly left Aschaffenburg when the French pushed across the river and seized that post.

The village of Dettingen is about eight miles from Aschaffenburg and close to the river Mayn. At eight o'clock, as our advanced parties approached the village, they found it occupied by a considerable French force under the Duke de Grammont, who had drawn up 24,000 men, horse and foot, on a moor in front of the village.

During the morning the march of the English had been harassed by the fire of five batteries which the enemy had established on the opposite side of the river. As the troops neared Dettingen, their position became still more disadvantageous. On their right flank they had an impassable bog, and in consequence they were crushed and jammed together from want of space. Some six hours were spent in deployment and in other intricate movements before a satisfactory order of battle was fixed upon. The infantry were ranged in six lines, with the cavalry on the flanks and in rear. At two p.m. the battle was commenced by a furious charge of the French cavalry; two of their regiments, the Maison du Roi and Black Mousquitaires, pierced our first three lines, but were utterly destroyed and broken by the fire of the fourth. After four hours' fighting the French gave way, and were totally defeated. Their infantry behaved badly. At the last final attack by our men absolute terror seemed to have seized them; they threw away their arms and plunged into the river, many being drowned. *"Sauve qui peut"* was the cry on all sides.[1]

---

[1] *Age of Louis XII*, Voltaire.

Many English officers of distinction were killed and wounded. The loss of the XX is not accurately recorded, but it was slight. Dettingen is the first honour borne on the colours of the corps, but it was not until the year 1883 that it was placed thereon by the gracious permission of Her Majesty Queen Victoria.

The XX remained on the field of battle until ten o'clock, when it commenced a weary night march of twenty-five miles under a drenching rain. The regiment remained for some time at Hanau, and subsequently went into winter quarters.

During the year 1744 no action of any importance took place; it was a year void of results to either side. The allies left their winter quarters on the 3rd May, and assembled at Ascke and Affligen; the English were encamped near Oudenard, on the 25th of June. On the 20th August, the allied army passed the Scheldt, and advanced into French territory, but, owing to the

---

NOTE.—Although the results of the battle of Dettingen, fought on the 27th of June, 1743, were not equal to those attending the victories gained over the French by Edward III and Henry V, yet there are circumstances which render the conflict of Dettingen similar to those of Crecy and Agincourt. At Crecy, on the 26th of August, 1346, King Edward III and his son, Edward the Black Prince, were present; at Dettingen, King George II was accompanied by his son, the Duke of Cumberland.

It was the *début* of both the royal princes on the tented plain, and the chivalrous bearing of the Black Prince, particularly his behaviour to the prisoners, finds a parallel in the conduct of the Duke of Cumberland, who refused to have his wound attended to until the surgeons had examined that of a French officer (Giradau).

The disadvantage, under which the British fought at Dettingen, was equal to that under which they laboured at Agincourt; and the impetuosity of the enemy, in both instances, prevented the English army perishing from want of provisions.

All these battles are likewise noted for the number of the French royal family and nobility who were present.

The battle of Dettingen is further remarkable as being the last action in which a British monarch commanded the army.

The want of provisions and tents, unfortunately, compelled the victors to abandon the field of battle, otherwise Dettingen might have rivalled many of the achievements recorded in British history.

scarcity of provisions, forage, &c., they were obliged to retreat, and returned to winter quarters at Ghent and Bruges on the 17th September. So ended the abortive campaign of 1744 under Field-Marshal Wade.

The French opened their trenches before Tournay on the night of the 30th of April, 1745. This fortress was besieged by an army of 80,000 men, under Marshal Saxe. The allies, under His Royal Highness the Duke of Cumberland, marched to the relief of the beleaguered fortress on the 9th of May. They found the French encamped on some gentle heights, with the village of Antoin and the river Scheldt on the right, the village of Fontenoy and a narrow valley in their front, and a small wood named Barré on their left.

Abatis were constructed in the wood of Barré; redoubts between Antoin and Fontenoy; and the villages were carefully fortified. The French outposts and pickets were attacked and driven in on the 10th May. The night was passed by both armies under arms. The attack commenced at two a.m.

A trustworthy English account of the battle of Fontenoy has yet to be written. Its brilliant narrator, Voltaire (though now proved to have been wildly misled[1]), was not only copied throughout his own century, but even in this later age has been echoed by historians no less able than Lord Stanhope and Thomas Carlyle.

A corrective history, based upon the authentic materials now given to the world, or rather to Germany, may hereafter appear; but for the present it must suffice to say that Marshal de Saxe in the end (having with him the King of France) retained his entrenched

---

[1] Karl von Weber, Leipzig, 1863; *Edinburgh Review*, October, 1864.

position against the allies, thus successfully covering the siege of Tournay (which fell soon after the action), and that the famous column of British and Hanoverian troops (with which the XX was acting) then won a renown which never has ceased to be great in the eyes of military men.

In this battle the XX suffered severely. Lieutenant-Colonel Gee (commanding), one sergeant, and twenty-seven rank and file were killed; Captains Meyrac and Maxwell, Lieutenants Boutchiere, Vickers, and Ensign Hartley, one sergeant, thirty-four rank and file were wounded. Major Hon. E. Cornwallis succeeded to the command on the death of Lieutenant-Colonel Gee.

After failing to carry the entrenched position of Fontenoy, the allies could only act on the defensive, and cover Brussels and Antwerp.

CHAPTER VI.

1745–1748.

Insurrection in Scotland—XX land in England—March to Lancashire—Siege of Carlisle—Battle of Culloden—Re-embarkation for the Netherlands—Return to Scotland.

WHILE the army was in Flanders, Charles Edward, eldest son of the Pretender, raised his father's standard in the Highlands of Scotland, and, being joined by several clans, made a desperate effort to overturn the existing Government, and to establish his father's pretensions. The XX was ordered to return to England, and arrived in the Thames on the 4th of November, 1745, and marched to the borders of Lancashire, under General Ligonier. The regiment was subsequently employed in pursuit of the Highlanders, on their retreat from Derby; it was also engaged in the siege of Carlisle, when the garrison agreed to surrender, and Brigadier-General Bligh, Colonel of the XX, with a body of infantry, took possession of the place on the 30th December, 1745. On the 17th January, 1746, the Royal army in Scotland sustained a serious defeat at Falkirk. The XX was ordered to proceed to North Britain; it arrived in Edinburgh in February, and embarked from Leith for passage to Aberdeen, where it arrived on the 25th of March.

Having joined the army under the Duke of Cumberland, the regiment took part in the battle of Culloden on the 16th of April, being stationed in the second line under Major-General Huske. So resistless was the onslaught of the Highlanders, that they broke through Monro's and Burrel's regiments, in the first line, and captured two pieces of cannon.[1] The second line was drawn up three deep, the front rank kneeling, the second bending forward, the third standing upright. These, reserving their fire till the Highlanders were close upon them, poured in such a deadly volley as to completely disorder them. Before they could recover, these gallant soldiers of the second line improved the advantage, and driving the clans together until they became one mingled mass turned them from assailants into fugitives.

This victory proved decisive, and the attempts of the Pretender were frustrated.

Four men only of the XX were killed; Lieutenant Trapaud and seventeen men wounded.

Brigadier-General Thomas Bligh was removed to the 12th Dragoons, and the Colonelcy of the XX was conferred on Lieutenant-Colonel Lord George Sackville, dated 9th April, 1746.

After the victory at Culloden the regiment was stationed for some time at Perth, and was employed in searching for arms and in executing measures of necessary severity against the clans, which had taken part in the rebellion. Meanwhile, hostilities had been continued on the continent, and, in 1748, the XX re-embarked for the Netherlands.

The war, however, was soon after terminated by the treaty of Aix-la-Chapelle, which was signed on the 7th October. The British troops returned to Great Britain, the XX being stationed at Stirling.

---

[1] Lord Mahon's *History of England*, vol. iii, page 455; and *Forty Five*, by Lord Mahon.

CHAPTER VII.

1749–1758.

Wolfe joins the XX—Fire at Glasgow—Change of Stations—Unpleasant Duties—Special Thanks of His Majesty King George II—March to Dover—Inspection by H.R.H. the Duke of Cumberland—Social duties—Cantonment on the Coast of Kent—Wolfe's Orders—Colonel Kingsley joins—The Second Battalion—Sir John Mordaunt's Expedition—Wolfe's Letters—The Second Battalion constituted the 67th Regiment—Wolfe leaves the Corps—His Letter to Captain Parr.

ON the 5th January, 1749, Brevet Major James Wolfe was gazetted Major of the XX, and joined the regiment at Stirling early in February. The corps moved to Glasgow in the following month. On the 25th April, a detachment[1] of the regiment was ordered to work on the road from the Pass of Leny to the head of Loch Earn. While the regiment was stationed in Glasgow a tremendous fire devastated the Gorbals on the south side of the Clyde, by which one hundred and fifty families were rendered homeless. The following notice appeared in the local paper:—
"Major Wolfe and the officers of Lord George Sackville's regiment were present all the time, and were of singular service, by placing guards upon the bridge and all the avenues, to keep off the crowd to prevent their stealing the effects belonging to the poor sufferers. Many of the soldiers exerted themselves in quenching the flames, and saving people's lives."[2] The officers of the regiment subscribed liberally towards a fund for

---

[1] All paviors, carpenters, smiths, miners, and bricklayers to be sent. Extra pay to military road makers was—lieutenants 2s. 6d., sergeants 1s., corporals 8d., privates 6d. a day.
[2] *Glasgow Courant.*

the relief of the sufferers, Lord George Sackville heading the list with fifty pounds. The regiment marched from Glasgow to Perth on the 16th October, 1749. George, Viscount Bury, was gazetted Colonel of the XX on the 1st November, 1749, vice Sackville. On the 20th March, 1750, Major James Wolfe was promoted Lieutenant-Colonel, vice Lieutenant-Colonel Hon. Edward Cornwallis, appointed[1] Governor of Nova Scotia.

In July, 1750, Lord Bury visited the corps for the first time. The last division of the regiment arrived at Dundee on the 1st October, 1750. Early in 1751, the regiment moved to Banff, and thence to Inverness about the end of September of the same year, where it remained until the 18th May, 1752, when it was ordered to Fort Augustus. The duties of military officers in command of out-stations were as unpleasant as the execution of them was vexatious, owing to the severity

---

[1] A very popular officer: Wolfe, writing to a friend in America, says:—"Tell Cornwallis that I thank him for making me a Lieutenant-Colonel; he promised to write to some of us, but has not; they are not the less ardent for his prosperity, and the whole corps unites in one common wish for his welfare and success." The Honourable Edward Cornwallis was the sixth son of Charles Lord Cornwallis. He was the eldest of twin children born on the 22nd February, 1713; the other twin being Frederick Charles, who became Archbishop of Canterbury in the reign of George III. Edward Cornwallis entered the XX at an early age, and rose to the rank of Lieutenant-Colonel. He served with the corps through the campaigns in Flanders and Scotland, in 1744-1745. On the death of Lieutenant-Colonel Gee at the battle of Fontenoy, Major Cornwallis succeeded to the command of the corps. In 1743 he was nominated member of Parliament for Eye, and in 1745 he obtained a position at Court as Groom of His Majesty's Bedchamber. He commanded the XX at Stirling, and, on being appointed Governor of Nova Scotia, was succeeded by Major Wolfe. In May, 1749, Lieutenant-Colonel Cornwallis sailed for Nova Scotia in charge of one thousand one hundred and forty-nine settlers, and he was the first Governor and founder of the province of Nova Scotia. In 1752 he resigned the Governorship, but continued to serve in the army, and was promoted Major-General in February, 1757, and Governor of Gibraltar in 1759. General Cornwallis died in the year 1776, aged 63.—*Collections of the Nova Scotia Historical Society*, for the years 1879-80.

of the rebellion statutes. Captain Trapaud reports:—
"The sergeant stationed at Knockfin apprehended, on Sunday, the 15th instant, one John Farquharson, a popish priest, dressed in his sacerdotal vestments, as he was preaching to above three hundred persons. The sergeant ran great hazard of his life in taking the above priest, as he was disguised, by a small sword and two soldiers with their bayonets, the people making an attempt to rescue the priest." Another officer reports "that a sergeant took a fellow for wearing a blanket in the form of a philibeg." Captain Walter Johnson states, "In this country we have great scarcity of provisions. A great many cattle have died, and what are alive are scarcely able to crawl, so that the men get very little to buy, except milk and eggs." The XX was again quartered in Glasgow early in 1753. His Majesty King George II sent his thanks, in particular to Lord Bury's regiment, for their behaviour in the Highlands.

In May, 1753, detachments of the regiment left Glasgow for the Highlands, to be employed in road-making. One detachment was so employed upon the side of Loch Lomond, in Argyleshire, and five companies, under Wolfe, were encamped for the same purpose at Inverdouglas, situated on the west side of the Loch in Dumbartonshire. It was the custom for regiments, on completing their allotted task, to erect a tablet by the roadside, recording the date and name of the regiment. One of these tablets, put up by the men under Wolfe in 1753, was pulled down some years ago by a farmer at Ardvoirlich, and turned into a hearthstone. Another, on the road near Tynaclach, Arrochar, bore the mark of the XX, but without the date and name of the commanding officer.

The various detachments returned to Glasgow on the 24th August, and the corps proceeded by march route on the 8th September for England. Carlisle was reached on the 8th September, Warrington (in Lancashire) on the 30th, Warwick on the 16th October, and Reading on the 22nd of the same month. The old tradition, "that good sportsmen are invariably good soldiers," is verified by the life of Wolfe, who appears to have been what would now be termed a good all-round sportsman. During his command, the XX kept a pack of hounds. In one of his letters he mentions that the officers hunted when passing through Lancashire. He was an excellent horseman,[1] and from the subjoined extract from a letter to his mother, it will be seen that he did not despise the gun and rod :—" My cousin Goldsmith has sent me the finest young pointer that ever was seen; he eclipses Workie, and outdoes all. He sent me a fishing rod and wheel at the same time, of his own workmanship, that are inestimable. This, with a salmon rod from my uncle Wat, your flies and my own guns, puts me in condition to undertake Highland sport, and to adventure myself amongst mountains, lakes, and wildest wastes."

During the period the XX remained at Reading, the corps was inspected by His Royal Highness the Duke of Cumberland. On the arrival of the headquarters and six companies at Dover, the following regimental order was published by Lieutenant-Colonel Wolfe :—"Dover, 23rd December, 1753. His Royal Highness the Duke, when he reviewed the regiment at Reading, was pleased to express his approbation of several parts of the discipline of it, such as the manner

---

[1] *Glasgow, Past and Present,* vol. iii, page 759.

of carrying the arms, of levelling, of marching, and of wheeling, and in particular of the silence and obedience that he observed, and ready compliance with orders without the confusion sometimes perceived in the execution of things that seem new." At this time some companies were stationed at Maidstone.

The only incident of any importance that occurred while the regiment was quartered at Dover was a complaint made against the officers for neglecting their social duties, particularly in the matter of not giving or attending balls, &c. In reply, Lieutenant-Colonel Wolfe wrote: "Some of our finest performers are at present disabled and the rest disheartened. Notwithstanding this, I always encourage our young people to frequent balls and assemblies. It softens their manners and makes them civil; and commonly I go along with them to see how they conduct themselves. I am only afraid they shall fall in love and marry. Whenever I perceive the symptoms, or anybody else makes the discovery, we fall upon the delinquent without mercy until he grows out of conceit with his new passion. By this method we have broke through many an amorous alliance, and dissolved many ties of eternal love and affection."

In the middle of January, 1754, the regiment was ordered to prepare for cantonment on the Kentish coast, to prevent suspicious vessels from approaching the shore. After a considerable suspense, the XX left Dover and marched to Sittingbourne, where it remained until the end of March, when five companies left for Guildford, to be reviewed by Lord Bury, and the remaining companies for Bristol, to aid the civil authorities. In the autumn of 1754 the regiment moved to Exeter. The XX had to send a draft of one hundred men to Colonel

Dunbar's regiment, for the Virginian expedition; and it was found no easy matter to replace so many men where industry was well paid.

In February, 1755, the XX was held in readiness to go on board the fleet for special service. The regiment moved to Winchester, where it arrived about the 20th March, 1755. The Earl of Albemarle (Lord Bury had succeeded to the earldom on the death of his father) was transferred to the 3rd Dragoon Guards, and was succeeded in the Colonelcy of the XX by Colonel Philip Honeywood on the 8th April, 1755. Colonel Honeywood's promotion was a very great disappointment to Lieutenant-Colonel Wolfe, who justly considered that, having efficiently commanded the regiment for six years, he had a right to the promotion, or, at least, that none but a general officer should be placed over him.

The XX moved from Winchester to Canterbury early in November. It was at the latter place that Wolfe issued his celebrated "Instructions for the XX Regiment in case the French should land." They were published in several periodicals after his death.[1]

The following regimental order was published at Winchester. "The Lieutenant-Colonel takes this opportunity to thank the officers and soldiers of the companies here for their extreme handsome behaviour under arms; the knowledge and the diligence of the officers, and the obedience and attention of the soldiers was very conspicuous; and Sir John Mordaunt, who inspected (on the 6th October, 1755) the regiment, expressed his satisfaction in the strongest terms, and will

---

[1] *Gentlemen's Magazine*, vol. xxx, pages 528—530.

make a proper report to His Majesty and the Duke of what he saw." At Canterbury the regiment was again inspected by the Duke of Cumberland. Wolfe conveyed the praise of the Commander-in-chief in a regimental order of which this is an extract: "The Lieutenant-Colonel desires that the captains will acquaint their men that H.R.H. the Duke has expressed his approbation of their appearance and behaviour under arms in very strong terms.; and he has been pleased to say that he has conceived a good opinion of the corps, and does not doubt but they will take the first opportunity to distinguish themselves. As the regiment has been particularly distinguished in the late promotions, and a number of officers of great merit taken out of the corps, it is hoped it will be the constant endeavours of their successors to promote the discipline, and consequently the honour, of the regiment."

Early in 1756, the regiment moved to Dover, thence to Portsmouth, and almost immediately returned to Canterbury. Colonel William Kingsley was gazetted to the Colonelcy of the XX, vice Honeywood, on the 22nd May, 1756.

On the 20th May, 1756, the regiment left Canterbury, arrived at Basingstoke on the 1st June, and marched to Devizes on the 7th. Colonel Kingsley joined the regiment at Devizes on the 27th June, 1756.[1] The XX left Devizes on the 27th July, 1756, and encamped (with five other battalions) at Shroton, near Blandford, in Dorsetshire. By a Royal Warrant, dated 25th August, 1756, second battalions of seven hundred and eighty men each were added to fifteen infantry regi-

---

[1] Of Colonel Kingsley, Wolfe wrote, "Our new colonel is a sensible man, very sociable and polite."

ments. The XX was one of the corps selected. This was the first introduction of "second battalions" into the British army. On the 20th October, 1756, three companies of the XX, accompanied by three companies of the Buffs, under the command of Lieutenant-Colonel Wolfe, marched into Gloucestershire, to assist the civil power in suppressing riots.

Both battalions were encamped at Budford Heath, near Dorchester, where a large body of troops had been assembled during the month of May. Towards the middle of July, Lieutenant-Colonel Wolfe was summoned to London, to advise the authorities on the formation of an expedition that had been decided upon for the destruction of Rochefort, on the coast of France. By the 10th August, ten infantry regiments (both battalions of the XX), with fifty light-horse and a large train of artillery, were assembled at Newport, Isle of Wight. The expeditionary force was commanded by Lieutenant-General Sir John Mordaunt, Major-Generals Conway and Cornwallis. Lieutenant-Colonel Wolfe was appointed Quartermaster-General. As the enterprise failed through want of capacity on the part of the leaders, and as the third in command (Major-General Hon. Cornwallis) and the Quartermaster-General were both XX officers, it will not be inappropriate to record their characters as sketched by Walpole. After describing the two seniors, he says: "Cornwallis was a man of very different complexion, as cool as Conway, and as brave; he was indifferent to everything but to being in the right. He held fame cheap, and smiled at reproach." Walpole continues: "Under these was Wolfe, a young officer who had contracted reputation from his intelligence of discipline and from the perfection to which he brought his own regiment. The world could not expect more from him than he thought himself capable of performing. He looked upon danger as the favourable moment that would call forth his talents." The transports arrived on the 6th September and the troops embarked immediately, and sailed from St. Helens on the 8th. The fleet arrived off the Isles of Rhé and Oleron on the morning of the 20th. From the 20th to the 29th nothing was done but to assemble and re-assemble councils of war; in this way valuable time and opportunities were lost. Lieutenant-Colonel Wolfe made a reconnaissance and strongly recommended that Fouras should be attacked. This met with the approval of one council of war, but was rejected by a second council. Of the operations, Wolfe wrote: "We lost the lucky moment in war, and are not able to recover it. We shall return to England with reproach and dishonour; though, in my mind, there never was in any troops, sea and land, a better disposition to serve." Great national disappointment was caused by the failure of the expedition against Rochefort, as the people counted upon success. A Board of General Officers was appointed to inquire into the causes of the failure, and delivered their report upon the 21st November. They attributed the frustration of the design, in the first instance, to not attacking Fouras agreeably to Lieutenant-Colonel Wolfe's plan; "which certainly," says the Report, "must have been of the greatest utility towards carrying your Majesty's instructions into execution." General Mordaunt was tried by court-martial, but acquitted.

Lieutenant-Colonel J. Wolfe was promoted Brevet-Colonel on the 21st October, 1757, for his services on this expedition.

The following is an extract from a letter dated Bath,

29th December, 1757, written by Wolfe to Captain Parr,[1] of the regiment who was recruiting at Wigan in Lancashire :—

"Dear Parr,—Your success gives me double satisfaction, for the regiment and yourself, and I know full well that you will omit nothing that may tend to improve or continue it. I thank God our officers, and those who have left us, profess a sense of duty and spirit that needs no quickening, no urging. I explained the nature of our discipline some days ago to the Prince of Wales, who is extremely desirous of being informed of these sort of things.[2] I told him there was in the corps a necessary degree of obedience, joined with high spirit of service and love of duty, with which he appeared to be greatly pleased, knowing well that from good inclinations, joined with order and discipline, great military performances usually spring. As I profess to introduce as many young gentlemen as I possibly can into the army, and to exclude *canaille* as much as in me lies, I am ready to give all possible assistance to the young man you speak of."

Brevet-Colonel Wolfe was appointed by Mr. Pitt to the command of a brigade in the expeditionary force under Major-General Amherst, for the reduction of Louisbourg, the key to the River St. Lawrence. Wolfe left the regiment at Exeter on the 7th January, 1758, and never rejoined the XX again; but his official connection with the corps did not cease until he was promoted Colonel.

---

[1] Captain Parr had been, for two years, Wolfe's Adjutant.
[2] Of Wolfe's contemporaries, King George III was perhaps one of the last survivors.

1749—1758. 41

The second battalions of the regiments (fifteen[1]) having been formed into distinct corps, that of the XX was numbered the 67th.

The following are the names of the officers who were transferred with the 2nd Battalion of the regiment on its being constituted the 67th Regiment, on the 21st April, 1758:—Colonel, James Wolfe; Lieutenant-Colonel, Robert Robinson; Captains, Charles Veaitch, Edward Goodenough, William Delaune, James Dunne, Thomas Osborne, George Sherwin; Lieutenants, James Nesbitt, William Dughe, William Edwards, Francis Raper, Frecheride Dykes, Marmaduke Green, John Gardener, John Cane, Richard Faulkner, George Smith, William Yorke, Phillip Hales, Henry Nesbitt, Thomas Wilkinson, Alexander Rose, John Matson, Despard Crosdale; Ensigns, William Massey, Thomas Barker, Joseph Collings, Royston Barton; Surgeon, Joseph Harris; Adjutant, James England.

That the 67th Regiment are proud of their parentage will be seen by the following extract from the concluding chapter of the historical records of that distinguished corps:—"The details contained in the foregoing pages show that the reputation acquired by the XX Regiment in the wars during the reigns of King William III and of Queen Anne—in the defence

[1] 2nd Battalion.	Constituted.	2nd Battalion.	Constituted.
3rd Foot	the 61st Foot.	24th Foot	the 69th Foot.
4th ,,	,, 62nd ,,	31st ,,	,, 70th ,,
8th ,,	,, 63rd ,,	32nd ,,	,, 71st ,,
11th ,,	,, 64th ,,	33rd ,,	,, 72nd ,,
12th ,,	,, 65th ,,	34th ,,	,, 73rd ,,
19th ,,	,, 66th ,,	36th ,,	,, 74th ,,
XX ,,	,, 67th ,,	37th ,,	,, 75th ,,
23rd ,,	,, 68th ,,		

The 71st, 72nd, 73rd, 74th, and 75th were disbanded after the peace of Fontainbleau in 1763.

of Gibraltar, 1727, and at the battles of Dettingen and Fontenoy—has been preserved unsullied by the 2nd Battalion of that corps since the year 1758, at which period it was constituted the 67th Regiment."

Wolfe's promotion terminated his official connection with the XX, and his biographer thus describes the feeling of the corps towards their late commander:— "On Wolfe's promotion to the Colonelcy of the 67th Regiment, he was succeeded in the Lieutenant-Colonelcy of the XX by Major Beckwith, Captain Maxwell obtaining the Majority. By none of his numerous friends was he more highly esteemed than by the officers whom he had formerly commanded, and by none of his countrymen was he more respected and beloved than by the men whom he had trained to a state of discipline until then unknown in the British army."

The following letter from Wolfe (after his return from the Louisbourg expedition) to Captain Parr[1] is

---

[1] Captain Parr remained in the regiment until January, 1776; he had then completed twenty-six years' service, and for the last six had been in command. He was wounded at Minden, and took part in most of the actions of the Seven Years' War. He was promoted Major, 31st January, 1763, and Lieutenant-Colonel 23rd January, 1770. Lieutenant-Colonel Parr was appointed Governor of the Tower of London on the 14th April, 1778, and Lieutenant-Governor of the province of Nova Scotia on the 8th October, 1782; this position he held until his death, which occurred on the 21st November, 1791. In Murdoch's *History of Nova Scotia*, vol. iii, page 97, Lieutenant-Colonel Parr's character (official and private) is described in these words: "During his administration, which was upwards of nine years, the welfare and happiness of His Majesty's subjects in this province was his invariable study and pursuit. From all I can gather of authentic evidence, he seems to have been a candid man of business, disposed to act honestly, and to listen to good advice. He had been a captain in the battle of Minden, and had risen gradually in his profession to the command of his regiment. His habits are said to have been frugal and parsimonious. He has left us no indications of extraordinary ability, but seems to have been the very man to suit the time in which he acted, being plain, simple, and diligent." Colonel Parr was buried in the aisle of St. Paul's Church, Halifax. The XX was at that time stationed in Halifax, and formed the firing party.

peculiarly regimental and of the greatest possible interest:—

"Salisbury, 6th December, 1758.

"Dear Parr,—Your remembrance and congratulations upon my return to Europe are most acceptable, and I shall always set a high value upon your friendship and good opinion. It gives me the utmost satisfaction to hear of the good behaviour of your regiment, and I don't at all doubt but that they will be still more distinguished when they are more tried.

"They are led by the same captains who have assisted in establishing the sound discipline that prevails amongst you; and there is no reason to suppose other than the natural effects whenever it comes to the proof.[1] My people, I find, are much out of humour with your chief. I hope there is no such temper amongst you. It is my fortune to be cursed with American service, yours to serve in an army commanded by a great and able prince, where I would have been if my choice and inclinations had been consulted. Our old comrade, Howe, is at the head of one of the best trained battalions in all America, and his conduct in the course of the last campaign corresponded entirely with the opinion we had all entertained of him.[2] His Majesty has not a better soldier in those parts—modest, diligent, and valiant. His brother was a great man; this country has not produced his like in my time; his death cannot be enough lamented. You must continue to be upon good terms with the Hano-

---

[1] The proof came on the 1st of August of the following year, at Minden, when Wolfe was lying before Quebec.

[2] The Honourable William Howe, who had been a captain in the XX, was now Lieutenant-Colonel commanding 58th Regiment. His brother, Lord Howe, was killed in America. Lieutenant-Colonel Howe commanded Wolfe's advanced guard up the Heights of Abraham.—Smollett's *History of England*, page 1294.

verian Guards, they deserve your esteem. Your quarters are not, I fear, amongst the best, nor, I fear, amongst the cheapest. The first news I heard at Portsmouth was the death of McDowall. What a loss was there! I have hardly ever known a better foot officer, or a better man—clear, firm, resolute, and cool.[1] My health is mightily impaired by the long confinement at sea. I am going directly to the Bath, to refit for another campaign. We shall look, I imagine, at the famous post of Ticonderoga, where Mr. Abercromby, by a little soldiership and a little patience, might, I think, have put an end to the war in America. You will always have my best wishes. I asked immediately—'Did Kingsley's come into action?' 'How did they behave?' The answer was: 'There is no doubt they would have done well, but there was no enemy to try them.' My compliments to the corps. I hope Grey has his health, and Carleton.[2] Fare ye well.—I am, dear Parr, your faithful and obedient servant.

"J. W.

"To Captain Parr, of the XX Regiment,
 "At Munster, Westphalia."

It may be considered that in the preceding chapters the life of the Commander has been too much merged into the history of the corps; this may to a certain extent be true, but it is a matter of sincere congratulation that for eight years the XX was commanded by the "Immortal Wolfe." He brought the corps to the highest possible state of efficiency: officers were specially selected from it to command other corps:

---

[1] Alexander McDowall, Captain of the Grenadier Company of the XX. Captain McDowall was Adjutant of the corps when Wolfe joined, and held the appointment until the 20th August, 1754.

[2] See Appendix.

men of high character and members of great families joined it: and commissions in it were eagerly sought for. And lastly, Wolfe established and fostered that *esprit de corps* which is the true foundation of all regimental efficiency.[1]

---

[1] The whole of the letters, and almost all the particulars and details contained in this chapter, have been taken from *The Life of Wolfe*, by R. Wright, published in 1864.

CHAPTER VIII.

1758–1759.

Expedition to St. Malo—Return to England—Embarkation for Germany—Winter Quarters in Munster.

ON Friday, the 26th of May, 1758, a force of about 13,000 fighting men in all, under the command of the Duke of Marlborough, embarked at the Isle of Wight. The XX formed part of the 2nd Brigade[1] of the expedition, which was commanded by Major-General Waldegrave. The transports sailed to Spithead, and thence to St. Helens, where they were detained by contrary winds until the 31st May. On the 4th June, St. Malo was sighted, but the fleet proceeded to Cancalle Bay. The Grenadiers of the army were landed, and Lord Down, with twenty men of Kingsley's,[2] marched through a narrow pass into the village, where they were met by the Marquis of Landal (Intendant of the coast and Colonel of the Militia), with his servant. Lord Down called to him, and told him if he would surrender he had nothing to fear; but he foolishly refused to do so, and consequently, together with his servant and two horses, was shot dead upon the spot. The party then took possession of the village. The whole force disembarked on the 6th June, and encamped at Cancalle. At daybreak on the 7th, the army marched in two divisions towards St. Malo (distant about seven miles), where they arrived in the evening. The route lay across country, the difficulties of marching

---

[1] The regiments of the 2nd Brigade were Kingsley's (XX), Wolfe's (67th), and Loudon's (30th).—*London Gazette*, June 6th—10th, 1758.

[2] *Gentleman's Magazine*, vol. xviii, 1758, page 298.

were great. A party of two hundred pioneers preceded the army to remove obstacles, &c. Pickets supported by the 2nd Brigade advanced under the walls of St. Malo, and set fire to all the shipping in the harbour.[1]

The 2nd Brigade returned to camp on the night of the 8th. A terrible storm raged during the night, not a tent was left standing. About noon on the 9th, the army struck their tents and marched in one column to Cancalle. On the 12th, the whole force re-embarked on board the transports, sailed on the 21st, arrived off the Isle of Wight on the 25th, returned to the French coast on the 27th, sailed for England on the 29th, and disembarked at St. Helens on the 30th June, 1758.

The XX was selected to proceed to Germany, to join the allied army in that country, under H.S.H. Prince Ferdinand of Brunswick. It embarked from Gravesend in July, landed at Embden[2] on the 3rd August, and, advancing up the country, joined the army before the end of the month.

The XX, 25th, and 51st Regiments formed a brigade under Major-General Kingsley at Soest on the 20th of August, 1758, at which place and date Prince Ferdinand joined the English. ("Grand looking fellows," said the Germans.)[3] During the first campaign the army was employed in changes of encampments and positions only, from the last of which, on the 18th November, 1758, the corps was ordered to winter quarters in Munster, on the River Aa, where it remained until the spring of 1759.

---

[1] *Gentleman's Magazine*, vol. xviii, 1758.

[2] The Duke of Marlborough, Commander-in-Chief of the British division, in a letter to Mr. Pitt, dated Kossfeld, 15th August, 1758, says: "Nothing but rains and uncertainties; marching latterly up to our middles in water; have come from Embden straight towards Wesel country, almost one hundred and fifty miles (Soest still a good sixty miles to south-east of us)."

[3] *Frederick the Great*, vol. viii, page 123.

Chapter IX.

1759-1760.

The Seven Years' War—Grenadier Battalion—Battle of Minden—Glory of the XX—Casualties—Prince Ferdinand's General Order—The Virginians—Colonel Beckwith—Attack on the Headquarter Camp—Campaign of 1760—Battle of Warburg—The XX Grenadier Company—Colonel Beckwith—Surprise of Zieremberg—March to the Lower Rhine—Battle of Kloster-Kampen—Winter Quarters.

THE "Seven Years' War" commenced in the year 1756, but it was not until 1758 that England declared war against France, and landed troops in Germany, the particulars of which are mentioned in the preceding chapter. The chief battles in which the English were engaged in this long struggle were "Minden," "Warburg," "Surprise of Zieremberg," "Kloster-Kampen," "Kirch-Denkern," and "Vellinghausen," in all of which, with the exception of the last-named engagement, Kingsley's (XX) bore a most conspicuous and distinguished part. "Skirmishes" and "affairs of outposts" were innumerable. Divisions of the army were engaged for days, and suffered considerable loss; but it has been found impossible to trace the particulars or details of these small engagements or of the casualties incurred by the corps engaged. "Beckwith's Brigade" (Lieutenant-Colonel XX) and "Maxwell's Battalion of Grenadiers" (Major XX) have found a place in the history of England and Germany. Two companies of the XX served in the battalion of Grenadiers.

On the 3rd June, 1759, the British infantry quitted their cantonments, and encamped near Lynen. The allied army was assembled by the 11th June in the neighbourhood of Werle and Soest. The Grenadier companies of the six British regiments were formed into a battalion (2nd Grenadier Battalion), the command of which was given to Major Maxwell,[1] of Kingsley's. On the 13th June, the army marched to Anrachte; and on the 14th to Buren, where it encamped. The allies advanced to Lipstadt on the 19th; they passed the river Lippe, both above and below the town, and then retired towards Rhittberg, pitching their camp near to that town, and in an advantageous position. The army moved in three columns from Stoltyenau to Petershagen Heath; but the position of the enemy was found to be too strong to admit of its being attacked with any prospect of success. On the 17th, the whole of the allied forces advanced in nine columns to the plain of Minden, and was formed in line of battle in rear of the village of Todtenhausen. They remained in this position until four o'clock in the afternoon, when they retired, and occupied the camp of the previous day. The army marched in three columns, by the right of Petershagen camp to that of Hille, on the 29th. The headquarters of Prince Ferdinand were at the village of Hille, and were covered by Napier's (12th) and Kingsley's (XX) regiments. This was the last disposition of any importance previous to the 1st of August.

The following graphic and lucid description of Minden is taken from Carlyle's *Frederick the Great*, vol. viii, pages 189-198:—"For the last ten days of July, about Minden, the manœuvring, especially on Prince Ferdinand's part, had been intense; a great idea in the

---

[1] *Operations of the Allied Army*, by an Officer, 1764, page 93.

head of Ferdinand, more or less unintelligible to Contades. Contades, with some 30,000, which is the better half of his force, has taken one of the unassailablest positions. He lies looking northward, his right wing on the Weser with posts to 'Minden' (Minden perhaps a mile north-eastward there), on his left impassable peatbogs and quagmires; in front a quaggy river or impassable black brook, called the Bastau, coming from the westward, which disembogues at Minden;—there lies *Contades*, as if in a rabbit-hole, say military men; for defence, if that were the sole object, no post can be stronger. Contades has in person say 30,000; and round him, on both sides of the Weser, are *Broglio* with 20,000; besides other divisions, I know not how many, besieging Münster, capturing Osnabrück (our hay magazine), attempting Lippstadt by surprise (to no purpose), and diligently working forward, day by day, to *Ferdinand's* ruin in those Minden regions.

"Three or four divisions busy in that manner;—and above all, we say, he has Broglio with a 20,000 on the right or east bank of the Weser,—who, if Ferdinand quit him even for a day, seems to have Hanover at discretion, and can march any day upon Hanover city, where his light troops have already been more than once.

"Why doesn't Ferdinand cross Weser, re-cross Weser; coerce Broglio back; and save Hanover? cry the Gazetteers and a public of weak judgment.

"Pitt's public is inclined to murmur about Ferdinand; Pitt himself never. Ferdinand persists in sticking by 'Minden' neighbourhood; and, in a scarcely accountable way, manœuvring there, shooting out therefrom what mischief he can upon the various Contades people in their sieges and the like. The attempt on Gohfeld was a serious mischief to Contades, if it succeeded. But the detaching of the Prince of Brunswick on it, and weakening one's too weak army, 'What a rashness, what an oversight!' thinks Contades (as Ferdinand wished him to do): 'Is our skilful enemy, in this extreme embarrassment, losing head, then? Look at his left wing yonder'—(General Wangenheim, sitting behind batteries, in his village of Todtenhausen, looking into Minden from the north):—'Wangenheim's left leans on the Weser, yes; but his right, observe, has no support within three miles of it: tear Wangenheim out, Ferdinand's flank is bare!' These things seemed to Contades the very chance he has been waiting for; and brought him triumphantly out of his rabbit-hole, into the Heath of Minden, as Ferdinand hoped they would do.

"And so, Tuesday evening, July 31st, things being now all ripe, upwards of 50,000 French are industriously in motion. Contades has nineteen bridges ready on the Bastau brook, in front of him. *Tattoo* this night, in Contades's camp, is to mean general march, 'March, all of you, across these nineteen bridges, to your stations on the Plain or Heath of "Minden" yonder,—and be punctual.' Broglio crosses Weser by the Town Bridge, ranks himself opposite Todtenhausen; and through the livelong night there is, on the part of the 50,000 French, a very great marching and deploying. Contades and Broglio together are 51,400 foot and horse. Ferdinand's entire force will be near 46,000; but on the day of battle he is only 36,000,—having detached the Hereditary Prince on Gohfeld, in what view we know.—

"*The battle of 'Minden,'* called also of *Tonhausen* (meaning *Todtenhausen*), which hereupon fell out, has still its fame in the world. Ferdinand's posts extend from the Weser river and Todtenhausen round by

Stemmern, Holzhausen, to Hartum and the Bog of Bastau (the chief part of him towards Bastau),—in various villages, and woody patches and favourable spots; all looking in upon 'Minden,' from a distance of five or seven miles; forming a kind of arc, with Minden for centre. He will march up in eight columns; of course, with wide intervals between them,—wide, but continually narrowing as he advances; which will indeed be ruinous gaps, if Ferdinand wait to be attacked; but which will coalesce close enough, if he be speedy upon Contades. For Contades's line is also of arc-like or almost semicircular form, behind it Minden as centre; 'Minden,' which is at the intersection of Weser and the Brook; his right flank is on Weser, Broglio *versus* Wangenheim the extreme right; his left, with infantry and artillery, rests on that black brook of Bastau with its nineteen bridges. As the ground on both wings is rough, not so fit for cavalry, Contades puts his cavalry wholly in the centre: they are the flower of the French army, about 10,000 horse in all; firm open ground ahead of them there, with strong batteries, masses of infantry to support on each flank; batteries to ply with cross-fire any assailant that may come on. What becomes of Ferdinand's left flank, with a gap of three miles between Wangenheim and him, and 10,000 chosen horse to take advantage of it! Had the French been of Prussian dexterity and nimbleness in marching, it is very possible something might have come of this latter circumstance: but Ferdinand knows they are not; and intends to take good care of his flank. 'Contades and his people were of willing mind; but had no skill in marching up:' and, once got across the Bastau by their nineteen bridges, they wasted many hours:—Broglio was in his place, silently looking into Wangenheim, by five o'clock; but unfortunately did nothing (except cannonade a little);—and indeed all through did nothing. The morning was very misty; but Ferdinand has himself been out examining since the earliest daybreak: his orders last night were, 'Cavalry be saddled at one in the morning,'—having a guess there would be work, as he now finds there will. From five a.m. Ferdinand is issuing from his camp, flowing down eastward, beautifully concentric, closing on Contades; horse not in centre, but English infantry in centre (six battalions, or six regiments by English reckoning); right opposite those 10,000 horse of Contades's, the sight of whom seems to be very animating to them.

"Soon after eight the fight begins: attack, by certain Hessians, on Hahlen and its batteries; attempt to drive the French out of Hahlen, as the first thing,—which does not succeed at once (indeed took three attacks in all); and perhaps looks rather tedious to those English battalions.

"Ferdinand's order to them was, 'You shall march up to attack, you six, on sound of drum;' but, it seems, they read it, 'by sound of drum:' 'Beating our own drums; yes, of course!'—and being weary of this Hahlen work, or fancying they had no concern with it, strode on, double quick, without waiting for Hahlen at all! To the horror of their Hanoverian comrades, who nevertheless determined to follow as a second line. The Contades cross-fire of artillery, battery of thirty guns on one flank, of thirty-six on the other, does its best upon this forward-minded infantry, but they seem to heed it little; walk right forward; and, to the astonishment of those French Horse and of all the world, entirely break and ruin the charge made on them, and tramp forward in chase of the same. The 10,000 Horse feel astonished, insulted; and rush out again, furiously charging; the English halt and serry themselves: 'No fire till they are within forty paces;' and then such pouring torrents of it as no horse or man can endure. Rally after rally there is, on the part of those 10,000; mass after mass of them indignantly plunges on,—again, ever again, about six charges in all;—but do not break the English lines: one of them (regiment Mestre-de-Camp, raised to paroxysm) does once get through, across the first line, but is blown back in dreadful circumstances by the second. After which they give it up, as a thing that cannot be done. And rush rearward, hither, thither, the whole seventy-five squadrons of them; and 'between their two wings of infantry are seen boiling in complete disorder.'

"This lasted about an hour: *this is essentially the soul of the fight*,—though there wanted not other activities, to right of it and to left, on both sides; artilleries going on at mighty rate on both wings; and counter-artilleries. Broglio cannonading Wangenheim very loudly, but with little harm done or suffered, on their right wing.

"Wangenheim is watchful of that gap between Ferdinand and him, till it close itself sufficiently. Their right-wing infantry did once make some attempt there; but the Prussian horse shot out, and in a brilliant manner swept them home again. Artillery and that pretty charge of Prussian horse are all one remembers, except this of the English and Hanoverian foot in the centre: '*an unsurpassable thing*,' says Tempelhof (though it so easily might have been a fatal!)—which has set Contades's centre boiling, and reduced Contades altogether to water, as it were. Contades said bitterly: 'I have seen what I never thought to be possible,—a single line of infantry break through three lines of cavalry ranked in order of battle, and tumble them to ruin.'

"This was the feat, this hour's work in the centre, the essential soul of the fight:—and had Lord George Sackville, General of the horse, come on when galloped for and bidden, here had been such a ruin, say all judges, as seldom came upon an army. By about ten in the morning all was over.

"Contades retired into his rabbit-hole by those nineteen bridges: a defeated army, thanks to Lord George, not an annihilated one. The allies' loss amounted to two thousand eight hundred and twenty-two men, full half of it falling on those six battalions. The loss of the French being seven thousand and eighty-six men, with heavy guns, colours, cavalry flags, and the like.

"Of the English infantry, historians say, what is not now much heard of in this country, '*That these unsurpassable six*' (*in industrious valour* unsurpassable, though they mistook orders, and might have fared badly!) 'are ever since called the "Minden Regiments;" that they are the 12th, XX, 23rd, 25th, 37th, and 51st of the British line; and carry "Minden" on their colours'—with silent profit, I hope!"

The XX was on the right of the line, in the 2nd[1] Brigade, commanded by the Colonel of the regiment, Major-General William Kingsley. From its position on the flank, the regiment suffered severely from the fire of a French battery, to which it was exposed during the march to the attack on the French cavalry.

The loss of the six English regiments was one thousand three hundred and ninety-four officers and men

---

[1] The regiments of the 1st Brigade, under Major-General Waldegrave, were the 12th, 23rd, and 37th; those of the 2nd were the XX, 25th, and 51st.

killed and wounded; of this number the XX had the largest proportion, which was as follows:—Captains J. Frearson, W. Stewart, and W. Cowley, Lieutenants E. Brown, G. Norbury, Ensign J. Crawford, one sergeant, and seventy-nine rank and file were killed; Captains Charles Grey, John Parr, Alexander Tennant, Captain-Lieutenant David Parry, Lieutenants Luke Nugent, John Thompson,[1] George Denshire, and William Bosswell, Ensigns N. Irwin, William Dent, and William Renton, twelve sergeants, and two hundred and twelve rank and file were wounded.

Lieutenant-Colonel Beckwith, the officer commanding the XX, was appointed aide-de-camp to H.S.H. Prince Ferdinand on the field of Minden, in recognition of his own and the regiment's distinguished services at this ever memorable victory.[2]

The severe loss sustained by the regiment at Minden caused the following general order to be issued by Prince Ferdinand:—

"Minden, 2nd August, 1759.
"Kingsley's regiment of the British line, from its severe loss, will cease to do duty."

But the zeal and *esprit de corps* which animated the survivors of the XX is shown in the general order dated—

"Minden, 4th August, 1759.
"Kingsley's regiment, at its own request, will resume its portion of duty in the line."

---

[1] In Appendix, see extract from a letter from this officer, dated Hospital at Minden, 18th August, 1759.

[2] "Colonel Lawrence, who carried the colours of the XX Regiment at the battle of Minden, was ever fond of repeating that his regimental comrades bore the brunt on that celebrated day."—*Fifty Years' Recollections*, by Cyrus Ridding, page 27, vol. i.

The following are extracts from the general order issued by H.S.H. Prince Ferdinand of Brunswick to the army after the battle:—

"His Serene Highness orders his greatest thanks to be given to the whole army, for their bravery and good behaviour yesterday, particularly to the English infantry and the two battalions of Hanoverian guards; to all the cavalry of the left wing: His Serene Highness states publicly, that next to God, he attributes the glory of the day to the intrepidity and extraordinary good behaviour of these troops, which he assures them he shall retain the strongest sense of as long as he lives; and if ever, upon any occasion, he shall be able to serve these brave troops, or any of them in particular, it will give him the utmost pleasure.

"His Serene Highness thinks himself infinitely obliged to Major-Generals Kingsley and Waldegrave for their great courage, and the good order in which they conducted their brigades."

We will now quote from another authority to show that His Serene Highness did not forget the British infantry and their services in this brilliant victory.

On the 28th June, 1827, General Sir George Don, in presenting colours to the 12th Regiment, said:—"In 1797, I attended the renowned Duke of Brunswick on the spot where this battle ('Minden') was fought; after His Serene Highness had shown me the position occupied by the British, he said, *It was here the conflict was most obstinate, and it was here that the British infantry gained immortal glory.*"

In Smollett's *History of England*,[1] the victory is ascribed to the "extraordinary prowess of the gallant

---

[1] Page 1303.

brigades under Major-Generals Kingsley and Waldegrave." The victory afforded the greatest satisfaction to the people of England. Horace Walpole writes: "Every house in London is illuminated, every street has two bonfires, every bonfire has two hundred squibs."

Minden and Kingsley's have found a place in works of fiction. In the *Virginians*,[1] after describing General Wolfe as he lived, Thackeray thus introduces the XX:— "Why are you gone back to rugged rocks, bleak shores, burning summers, nipping winters, at home, when you might have been cropping ever so many laurels in Germany? Kingsley's are coming back as covered with them as Jack a-Green on May-day." The anniversary of Minden has always been celebrated in the corps. The late Lieutenant-General P. Bainbrigge mentions being present at a Minden dinner at Malta in 1802, when the Minden toast was given. When in India, the 1st Battalion's festivities extended over three days, and included horse-racing, &c. In recent years, the celebrations have been worthily carried out. Trooping of the colours at noon (every officer and man wears a rose[2]), athletic sports, Minden dinners, &c.

For its services at Minden the regiment was honoured by the "laurel wreath" being placed on its colours and appointments, as a never-failing memorial of its conduct in this glorious victory.[3] On the night of the

---

[1] Vol. ii, p. 163.

[2] A tradition, believed to be well founded, is handed down that at Minden, the XX at one time was marching through flower gardens, and that many of the men put roses in their button-holes. This circumstance has united the rose with the memory of the battle. See also Colonel Thomas's speech at the presentation of colours by the Duke of Wellington.

[3] By the victory of Minden, the dominions of Hanover and Brunswick were preserved, and the enemy obliged to evacuate the greater part of Westphalia.

Sketch Map of the Field of Minden.

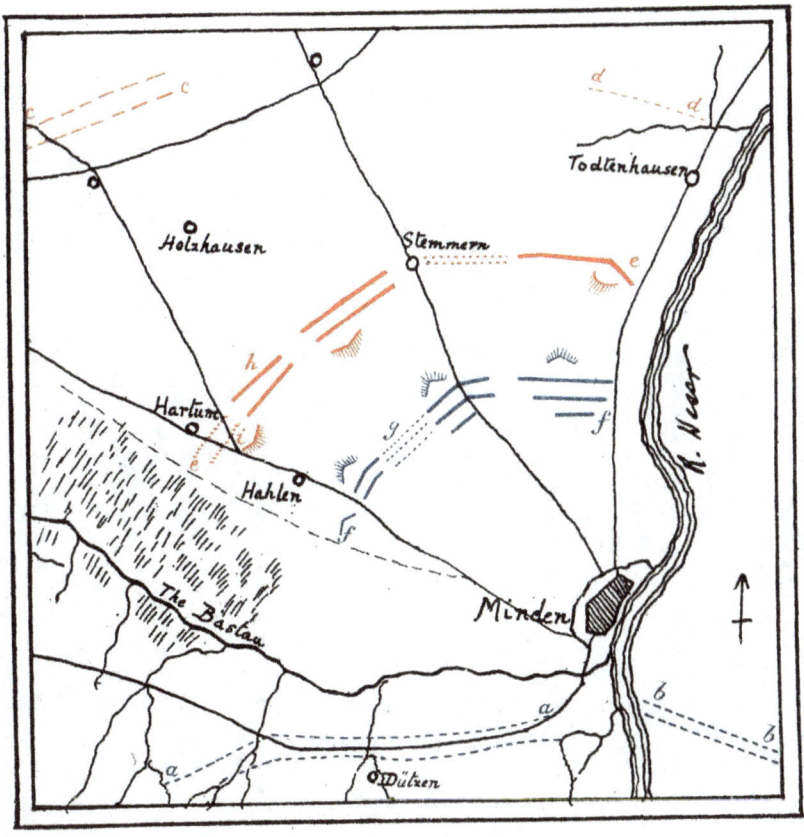

a a Contades Camp   b b Broglio's Camp
c c Ferdinand's position, night of July 31st
d d Wangenheim's position, night of July 31st
e e Ferdinand's Line of Battle
f f French Line of Battle
  g French Cavalry   h English Infantry
  i English & Hanoverian Cavalry under Sackville.

1st, the enemy passed the Weser, and burned the bridges over that river.

The garrison of Minden surrendered themselves prisoners of war on the morning of the 2nd: at noon the same day, Prince Ferdinand entered the town of Minden. Prince Ferdinand followed up the victory at Minden with great energy: on the 4th, the army marched to Gosfeld; to Hervorden on the 5th; to Bielefeld on the 6th; to Stakenbroeck on the 8th; and to Paderborn on the 9th.

On the 10th, the rear-guard of the enemy was attacked, and fifty waggons laden with provisions were captured. The allied army marched to Delem on the 11th, and on the 12th encamped at Stalberg; it entered the country of Waldeck on the 13th, then directing its march so as to gain the flank of the enemy, who was in position near Cassel. This position, however, was abandoned on the 18th.

On the night of the 26th of August, the Hereditary Prince of Brunswick marched towards Wetzler, and, early in the morning of the 27th, surprised Colonel Filcher's corps, consisting of two thousand men, whom they attacked and entirely defeated with a loss of sixty men. Numbers were wounded and four hundred made prisoners; the camp equipage and a great number of horses were also captured.

Colonel Beckwith, at the head of the British Grenadiers, particularly distinguished himself on this occasion.[1] The allies captured the town of Marpurg on the 5th September, encamped at Elermhausen on the 6th, and, on the 10th, marched to Neider-Weimar.

On the 12th of October, the allies occupied Crossdoff,

---

[1] *Operations of the Allied Army*, page 121.

where they remained until the 5th December, when they were cantoned in the villages surrounding that place. For the greater convenience of the troops the position was changed to Marpurg on the 4th January, 1760. On the 19th January, the different corps of the allied army began their march to their respective winter quarters, the British were assigned the town of Osnaburg, where they arrived on the 29th January.

Major-General Kingsley, Colonel of the regiment, was appointed Governor of Fort William on the 22nd March, 1760.

On the 5th May, the army again took the field. The last division reached Paderborn on the 12th, and marched on the 14th towards Fritzlar, where they encamped on the 20th. The Marquis of Granby joined the army on the latter date and assumed command of the British forces. The allies quitted their camp on the 24th June, and encamped at Frillingdorff; on the 25th they advanced to Neustadt.

On the 17th of July, a large body of the French appeared upon the right of our line, where the Marquis of Granby had his headquarters. Their irregulars advanced and fired upon our pickets, which were posted in a wood. The regiments of Kingsley (XX) and Home (25th), who were posted at the headquarters, immediately joined the pickets, and the enemy were repulsed. The Marquis removed his camp to Saltsbach, and the two regiments rejoined the line.[1] The army encamped at Wolfshagen on the 25th; at Zieremberg on the 26th; and at Kalle on the 27th. On the 30th, the troops were under arms all day. About eleven o'clock at night, they marched in six columns to

---

[1] *Operations of the Allied Army*, page 157.

Liebenau. At five o'clock on the morning of the 31st, the whole were assembled, and formed on the heights, near Corbeke, on the other side of the Diemel. On the morning of the following day, August the 1st, 1760, was fought the battle of Warburg, which ended victoriously for the allies. The following account is taken from Carlyle's *Frederick the Great*:[1]—" Warburg is a pleasant little Hessian Town, some twenty-five miles west of Cassel, standing on the north or left bank of the Diemel, among fruitful knolls and hollows. The famous 'Battle of Warburg' went thus: Chevalier du Muy, who is Broglio's rear-guard or reserve, 30,000 foot and horse, with his back to the Diemel, and eight bridges across it in case of accident, has his right flank leaning on Warburg, and his left on the village of Ossendorf, some two miles to north of that. Two days ago (July 29th), Erbprinz, Hereditary Duke of Brunswick, crossed over into these neighbourhoods, with a strong vanguard, nearly equal to Du Muy; and, after studious reconnoitring and survey, means, this morning (July 31st), to knock him over the Diemel again, if he can. No time to be lost; Broglio near and in such force. Duke Ferdinand too, quitting Broglio for a moment, is on march this way; crossed about midnight, some ten miles farther down, or eastward; at his best speed, to support the Erbprinz, if necessary, and beset the Diemel when got;—Erbprinz not, however, in any wise, to wait for him; such the pressure from Broglio and others. A most busy swift-going scene that morning. The plan of attack, which is still dark to Du Muy, commences about eight a.m., by launching the British Legion upon Warburg Town, there to take charge of

---

[1] Vol. ix, pages 44-46.

Du Muy's right, who cannot get it attended to. The attack was well aided by a mist which now fell, and which hung on the higher ground, and covered the march of Erbprinz and Ferdinand for an hour or more.

"They burst simultaneously upon Du Muy's right and left wing, coercing his front the while; squelches both these wings furiously together; forces the coerced centre, most horse, to plunge back into the Diemel, and swim. Horse could swim; but many of the Foot, who tried, got drowned. And, on the whole, Du Muy is a good deal wrecked—fifteen hundred killed, two thousand prisoners, not to speak of cannon and flags,—and, but for his eight bridges, would have been totally ruined. The fight was uncommonly furious, especially on Du Muy's left; Maxwell's Battalion[1] going at it, with the finest bayonet practice, musketry practice; obstinate as bears. The fight generally was of the hot and stubborn kind, for hours, perhaps two or more;—and some say, would not have ended so triumphantly, had it not been for Duke Ferdinand's vanguard, Lord Granby and the British Horse. Mauvillon[2] says, 'the English greatly distinguished themselves this day, and accordingly they suffered by far the most; their loss amounting to five hundred and ninety men:' or, as others count,—out of twelve hundred killed and wounded, eight hundred were English."

The battle commenced before the British infantry could reach the scene of action; but, to quote from Lord Granby's despatch,[3] "they pressed their march as much as possible, many of the men, from the heat of

---

[1] See page 49.

[2] Colonel Mauvillon, German Engineer Officer, serving on the staff of Prince Ferdinand: author of the *History of Prince Ferdinand of Brunswick's Wars.*

[3] *Gentleman's Magazine*, vol. xxx, pages 386, 387.

the weather and over-straining themselves to get on, through morassy and difficult ground, suddenly dropped down on their march."

The chief loss fell on the British Grenadiers and Highlanders, who had four hundred and fifteen men killed and wounded.

The Grenadier company of the XX, being the first to get into action, was sharply engaged. The loss in killed and wounded was immense: two sergeants and thirteen rank and file were killed; Captain Tennant, three sergeants, and thirty-five rank and file wounded.[1] In this action Colonel Beckwith commanded a brigade. Prince Ferdinand, in a letter to His Majesty King George II, dated Warburg, August 1st, says: "Colonel Beckwith, who commanded the English brigade, formed of English Grenadiers and Scotch Highlanders, distinguished himself greatly, and has been wounded in the head."

On the evening of the battle, the English division of the army was ordered to pursue the enemy: the division crossed the Diemel, and encamped upon the heights of Wilda, about four miles from Warburg.

By Warburg, Ferdinand had got the Diemel, on the left bank of which he spread his army, rendering the river impassable to Broglio, who lay on the opposite bank. A detachment, consisting of Maxwell's battalion of Grenadiers, one hundred and fifty Highlanders, and the XX, the whole being under the command of the Hereditary Prince of Brunswick, was selected to form the head of the column for the surprise of the town of Zieremberg.[2] This force marched from camp at eight p.m., on the 5th September.

---

[1] "Our loss is moderate, and falls chiefly upon Maxwell's battalion of Grenadiers, which did wonders."—*London Gazette*, Saturday, August 9th, 1760.

[2] *Operations of the Allied Army*, page 169.

At a mill about two English miles from the town, and within sight of the enemy's guards, Maxwell's Grenadiers took one road, the XX and the Highlanders another; when they came within half a mile of the town the videttes of the grand guard challenged them, but did not push forward to reconnoitre. The men marched in the most profound silence, and in a few moments they saw the fires of the enemy's pickets. The noise of their trampling over the gardens gave the alarm, and the enemy began to fire; upon which the attacking force ran towards the town with unloaded firelocks, and, having killed the guard at the gate, rushed into the town and drove everything before them. Never was there a more complete surprise. The attack was so sudden that the enemy had not time to get together in any numbers, but fired from the windows upon the assailants, who rushed into the houses and made a severe use of their bayonets. The number of killed and wounded was considerable, from an ill-judged resistance on the part of those in the houses; but in justice to our men it must be said that they gave quarter to all who asked it; there were also several instances of their refusing to take money from the prisoners, who offered them their purses. The troops were withdrawn from the town about three o'clock in the morning, and arrived in camp about eight. The bravery of the troops upon this occasion received the highest commendation. The loss of the English was less than ten men, which was considered wonderful in a night attack. General Griffen, who went into the town with the Prince at the head of Kingsley's, received a bayonet thrust from one of his own men, who heard him speaking in French to a soldier whom he had seized.[1]

---

[1] *Operations of the Allied Army*, page 170.

Brigadier-General de Norman, thirty-five officers, and four hundred and twenty-eight men were taken prisoners, and two guns captured. On the 1st of October, General Waldegrave marched towards the lower Rhine with a detachment of the army, consisting of two battalions of British Grenadiers, Highlanders, the XX and 25th Regiments.[1] General Waldegrave's corps passed the Rhine by a bridge about two miles below the town of Wesel, and joined the Hereditary Prince of Brunswick at eleven o'clock. At ten o'clock, on the night of the 15th, the troops, under the direction of the Prince, began their march towards Kampen. In order to reach the enemy's camp, it was necessary to dislodge Filcher's corps, which occupied a convent half a league from their advanced posts. This gave the alarm to Marshal de Castrides, and enabled him to put his troops under arms. He was, however, attacked, and twice driven from his position; and now began a battle, which was, after an hour's cessation, recommenced at five in the morning—16th October—with a terrible and well-sustained musketry fire, which lasted until about nine at night without ceasing.

This was a complex, determined fight; both sides fought with uncommon obstinacy, and it ended by the withdrawal of the allies. The retreat was conducted in good order; the enemy did not pursue, which was fortunate, as our men had expended all their ammunition. The Hereditary Prince of Brunswick halted upon a moor, not far distant from the scene of action, where his exhausted troops lay upon their arms all night.[2] Of the allies, ten officers, sixteen non-commissioned officers, two hundred and twenty-one rank and file were killed;

---

[1] *Operations of the Allied Army*, page 176.
[2] *Gentleman's Magazine*, vol. xxx, page 484.

sixty-eight officers, forty-three non-commissioned officers, and eight hundred and twelve rank and file wounded; and four hundred and twenty-nine rank and file were taken prisoners. The casualties of the XX were one sergeant and twenty-two rank and file killed. Captain Grey, Lieutenants Nugent, Pringle, Power, five sergeants, and one hundred and twenty-six rank and file wounded; Lieutenants Boswell and Bailey wounded and taken prisoners; forty-nine rank and file, nearly all of whom were wounded, were taken prisoners. During the action of the 16th, the regiment was opposed to very superior numbers of the French, who also had the advantage of occupying a naturally strong position in a wood. Of this battle Carlyle writes: " And there ensued, not the surprisal as it turned out, but the battle of Kloster-Kampen; which again proved unsuccessful, or only half successful, to the Hereditary Prince. A many-winged, intricate Night-Battle; to be read of in books. Many English fallen in it, too: the English showed here again a *ganz ausnehmende Tapferkeit*,[1] says Mauvillon; and probably their loss was proportionate."[2] In the French account of the battle, they acknowledge a loss of eight hundred and forty-one men killed, and one thousand seven hundred and ninety-five men wounded. Lieutenant-General de Segur and several other French officers, together with four hundred men, were taken prisoners: one pair of colours and several guns were captured.

The Hereditary Prince marched by Genderick on the morning of the 17th; an attack was made on the advanced column, but no authentic details are forthcoming. It was a desultory sort of engagement, which

---

[1] Quite exceptional bravery.
[2] Carlyle's *Frederick the Great*, vol. ix, pages 139-140.

lasted all day. The Rhine was much swollen by the heavy rains, and the troops had to repair the bridges before they could pass over. This work was accomplished early in the morning of the 18th in the presence of the enemy, who, however, did not attempt to molest them.[1] On the night of the 18th, the troops marched to Brunnen: on the 26th to Scheremberg: to Limbeck on the 27th: thence to Klein-Reckeim, where they encamped. The XX went into winter quarters in the Bishopric of Munster, on the 11th of December, and remained there until the early part of the following February.

---

[1] *Operations of the Allied Army*, page 179.

CHAPTER X.
1761.

Cautious Advance—Battle of Kirch-Denkern—Maxwell's Brigade—Camp at Ol-Weilmar—Skirmishes.

DURING the month of January, 1761, and early part of February, the army remained in winter quarters; but on the 9th of the latter month they assembled at their respective rendezvous. On the 13th February, the army was cantoned in the neighbourhood of Neidenstein. After several unimportant movements, a general advance was made on the 17th, covering a wide tract of country to the extent of seventy miles. During these operations, the allies drove all before them. The English division occupied the centre, moving with great caution, and was accompanied by Prince Ferdinand and Lord Granby. The French army, under Marshal de Broglio, having been reinforced by 12,000 men, the allies retired into Westphalia, where they arrived about the 28th March. The army crossed the Diemel on the 1st April, and on the 19th June were in position on the heights above Neuhass. On the 24th, an advance was made on Soest. The march was resumed on the 28th, and an advantageous position, within sight of the enemy's camp, was seized and occupied on the 29th. About one o'clock in the morning of the 4th July, the allies made a general attack on the enemy's position. The attack was delivered against the rear of the position, as the front was too strongly fortified. The French at once evacuated their camp and earthworks, and retired behind Werle. The allies encamped on the heights of Hemmeren. On the 14th July, the English division occupied the heights above Kirch-Denkern. For an account of the battle of Vellinghausen or Kirch-Denkern, which was fought on the 15th and 16th July, we again turn to the pages of Carlyle[1]:—

"Vellinghausen is a poor little moory hamlet in Paderborn country, near the south or left bank of the Lippe River; lies to the north of Soest,—some fifteen miles to your left hand, as you go by rail from Aachen to Paderborn.

"Prince Ferdinand's first business was to guard Lippstadt, with 95,000 men against the two armies under Broglio and Soubise numbering together 160,000 men. Ferdinand took up a position at Vellinghausen, when the French formed a junction at Soest on the 6th July.

"Ferdinand threw up earthworks at the villages of *Kirch-Denkern*, Scheidingen, Wambeln, and others; bogs, rough places, and woods are all turned to advantage; his right is covered by a quaggy brook; and his left rests on Vellinghausen.

"On Tuesday, the 15th July, 1761, at about six in the evening, Broglio suddenly burst into onslaught on Ferdinand's position. Granby and the English are in camp near Vellinghausen; and are quite taken on the sudden: but they drew out rapidly, in a state of bottled indignation, and fought, all of them, *Maxwell's Brigade* and the others, in a highly satisfactory way.

"Broglio burst out into enormous cannonade, musketade, and cavalry work, in this part, and struggles at it, almost four hours,—but finds he can make nothing of it; and about ten at night, leaves off till a new morning.

---

[1] *Frederick the Great*, vol. ix, pages 200-203.

"Next morning, about four, Broglio recommenced; again very fiercely, and with loud cannonading; but with result worse than before. About ten in the morning he gives up the bad job; and sets about retiring.

"If retiring be now permissible; which it is not altogether. Ferdinand orders a general charge of the left wing upon Broglio; which considerably quickened his retreat, and broke it into flight, and distressful wreck and capture, in some parts,—Regiment Rouge,[1] for one item, falling wholly, men, cannon, flags, and furniture, to that Maxwell and his brigade.

"Ferdinand lost, by the indistinct accounts, from fifteen hundred men to two thousand: Broglio's loss was above five thousand; two thousand of them prisoners."

In this engagement the XX served in the army corps commanded by Lieutenant-General Conway; and in the brigade[2] of Major-General Townshend. Prior to the action of the 15th, General Conway's corps was ordered to occupy and defend a position between Illigen and Hohenover; at this particular point the enemy made a very feeble attack, and were easily repulsed.[3] On this occasion the regiment lost only three men, exclusive of those serving in Maxwell's battalion. On the 27th, the allied forces marched in the direction of Paderborn, and encamped near Evitte on the 28th. There were frequent skirmishes with the enemy on the 29th, between Paderborn and Dribourg.[4]

The march was continued in four columns until the

---

[1] Four battalions.—*Gentleman's Magazine*, vol. xxxi, page 317.

[2] The 8th, XX, 25th, and 50th were the regiments of the brigade.

[3] *Operations of the Allied Army*, pages 213—215; *Gentleman's Magazine*, vol. xxxi, page 316.

[4] *Operations of the Allied Army*, page 223.

13th August, on which date they encamped near Blomberg, on the heights of Reilen-Kirchen. As the Quartermasters were marking out the camp, the enemy appeared in force, and some smart skirmishes ensued.[1] Marshal de Broglio intended to occupy the same ground for his camp, but the allies were first in possession, which in this instance gave them considerable advantage. On the 19th, the French resumed their march, and crossed the Weser; they were pursued by the allies, and their rear-guard was much harassed by the English under Lord Granby. On the 24th August, Prince Ferdinand, at the head of all the British troops (except the Guards), proceeded by forced marches towards the Diemel, capturing the enemy's posts, *en route;* at Deinglebourg, they made over three hundred prisoners.[2] They crossed the river, and, on the 26th August, encamped at Hoff-Giesmar, within six leagues of Cassel, pushing forward an advanced party to Winter-Kasten. On the 30th August, the English division recrossed the river, and encamped at Corbeke.

The French army retired to its strong entrenchments, near Cassel, on the 17th September, being closely followed by the allies, who established their camp at Ol-Weilmar.

During the month of October, no important movement or action took place; both armies remained inactive.

Prince Ferdinand's army was in position at Obr, on the left bank of the Weser, on the 1st November; the Prince moved towards Eimbeck to prevent, if possible, the junction of the French forces.

The 5th and 6th November were passed in a long

---

[1] *Operations of the Allied Army*, page 226.
[2] *Ibid.*, page 230.

series of skirmishes on all sides,[1] in all of which the French were repulsed.

At three o'clock, on the morning of the 9th, the army marched to and occupied the heights between Mackensen and Lithorst. As this movement turned the enemy's flank, Marshal de Broglio retreated from Eimbeck during the night of the 10th, and evacuated the adjacent country.

The army moved into cantonments and winter quarters, in the Bishopric of Osnaburg, on the 4th December. Thus ended the campaign of 1761.

---

[1] *Operations of the Allied Army*, pages 237-238; *Gentleman's Magazine*, vol. xxxi, page 530.

CHAPTER XI.

1762-1763.

Sortie from Gottingen—Combat at Wilhelmsthal—Attack on the Fulda—A General Engagement—Skirmishes—Battle of Brucker-Muhl, the Last in the Seven Years' War—Cessation of Hostilities—Winter Quarters—Prince Ferdinand's Letter to the Army—Lord Granby—The Total Casualties of the XX—Embarkation for England.

IN the campaign of 1762, the XX served in Lieutenant-General Waldegrave's army corps, and in the brigade commanded by Major-General C. Mompleson. Active operations commenced on the night of the 10th March, when the French, sallying forth from Gottingen, fell upon the lines of the allies at daybreak; the attack was unexpected; the enemy was, however, repulsed in every direction, but with considerable loss to both sides.[1] The XX was at Blomberg on the 4th June. The allies surrounded the French army in their camp at Grevenstein and Carldoff on the 23rd June, and attacked the enemy on the following morning; the French retired with great precipitation, and endeavoured to gain the heights of Wilhelmsthal.[2] The retreat was covered by the Grenadiers of France, the Royal Grenadiers, the Regiment of Aquitain, and some other corps, being the flower of the French infantry. These troops, finding that they were cut off from the main body of the army, gained the wood of Mejenbrecken, where they were attacked by the English under Lord

---

[1] *Operations of the Allied Army*, page 243.
[2] *Operations of the Allied Army*, page 250; *Gentleman's Magazine*, vol. xxxii, page 335.

Granby, and, with the exception of two regiments, were utterly destroyed, the whole being either killed or taken prisoners.[1] The despatches announcing this action say: "All the troops in general behaved with uncommon spirit, but particularly the 1st Battalion of Grenadiers, belonging to Colonel Beckwith's brigade, who distinguished themselves greatly."[2] Lieutenants Power and Irwin, of the XX, were taken prisoners in this battle; they were serving in Major Maxwell's battalion of Grenadiers.[3]

There were eighteen hundred men of the French army killed; and two thousand seven hundred and thirty-two taken prisoners, the Grenadiers of France alone had six hundred and thirty-five made prisoners, The trophies captured were one standard, six pairs of colours, and two pieces of cannon.

On the 6th July, both armies were in position in the vicinity of Cassel. A general attack was made on all the enemy's posts on the Fulda, on the 15th July; but, as they were strongly reinforced, the attack was suspended and the allies retired to their camp.

Both armies were in close proximity to each other on the 1st August, and both had a chain of sentries on the banks of the Fulda. During this day many skirmishes occurred, with varying success, but without important results to either side. There was a general engagement on the 8th August. The army bivouacked on the nights of the 8th and 9th, and returned to camp on the morning of the 10th. Prince Ferdinand advanced the army on the 3rd September, with the object of attacking the enemy, but halted at Staten. During

---

[1] *Operations of the Allied Army*, page 250.
[2] *Gentleman's Magazine*, vol. xxxii, page 335.
[3] *Ibid.*, page 336.

the night of the 10th and morning of the 11th, several smart skirmishes took place between the English and French, in all of which the latter were repulsed with loss.

On the 15th September, the French were driven out of the town of Wetzler by General Conway's division. The enemy retired in great haste and confusion, and crossed the river Lahn.[1] About six a.m. (a foggy morning) on the 21st, the French attacked a redoubt, which was garrisoned by some Hanoverians. On the fog clearing, it was discovered that the enemy was advancing in force. They were held in check for a time by our guns, but were immediately reinforced by large bodies of fresh troops, and a severe engagement ensued, which lasted fourteen hours without a moment's intermission and without advantage to either side.[2] The allies lost about eight hundred men. The French acknowledge casualties to the number of three hundred killed and eight hundred wounded. All the British regiments were engaged, but the particulars of their casualties cannot be traced. This action was fought near the Castle of Amöneburg —in the *London Gazette* it is called the Battle of Brucker-Muhl—on a narrow confined piece of ground; forty pieces of cannon had a clear frontage of four hundred paces only during the fourteen hours the battle raged. This was the last battle of the "Seven Years' War;" subsequent operations were confined to a few minor skirmishes.

During the month of October, both armies were employed making redoubts and batteries in front of their respective camps on the banks of the rivers Ohm and Lahn.

---

[1] *Operations of the Allied Army*, page 272.
[2] *Ibid.*, page 273.

His Serene Highness Prince Ferdinand of Brunswick issued orders to the army on the 15th November that hostilities were to cease from that date.

On the 19th, both armies marched to their winter quarters; the English had theirs in the bishopric of Munster.

On the 30th December, General Conway published to the army the following letter from His Serene Highness Prince Ferdinand:—

"His Serene Highness declares to the army, that he shall always preserve the most flattering remembrance of having fought successfully at the head of those brave troops, who, composed of different nations, exerted themselves so vigorously for the public liberty, and for the honour of their own and his country; that this remembrance will not cease but with his life, and will never fail to recall to him the obligations which he has to the Generals and other officers, who, by their valour and experience, have assisted and enabled him, at the same time, to serve his country, and to make a suitable return for the confidence which His Britannic Majesty has been pleased to honour him with; he therefore returns them his thanks for the same, and to the army in general for their obedience which they have constantly shewn during the time he has commanded them."

On the 13th January, 1763, General Conway communicated to the army the thanks of the House of Commons, "for the meritorious and eminent services which they had done for their King and country during the course of the war;" and at the same time published the following letter from His Excellency the Marquis of Granby:—

"Lord Granby had hoped to have it in his power to

have seen and taken his leave of the troops before their embarkation for England, but a severe illness having detained him at Warburg, and his present state of health obliging him to take another route, he could not leave this country without this public testimony of his entire approbation of their conduct since he has had the honour to command them.

"These sentiments naturally call for his utmost acknowledgments; he, therefore, returns his warmest thanks to the generals, officers, and private men, composing the whole British corps, for the bravery, zeal, discipline, and good conduct, he has constantly experienced from every individual, and his most particular and personal thanks are due to them upon their ready obedience upon all occasions to such orders as his station obliged him to give. His best endeavours have always been directed to their good by every means in his power, and he has some satisfaction to think he has some reason to flatter himself of their being convinced, if not of the efficacy, at least of the sincerity of his intentions, if he may judge by the noble return their behaviour has made him; a behaviour, that while it fills him with gratitude, has endeared them to their King and country, and has covered them with glory and honour.

"Highly sensible of their merit, he shall continue, while he lives, to look upon it as much his duty, as it will for ever be his inclination to give them every possible proof of his affection and esteem, which he should be happy to make as apparent as their valour has been, and will be, conspicuous and exemplary to after ages."

The German historian Mauvillon, in his history of the war, thus describes the English: "The first in rank of Ferdinand's force were the English; about a fourth part of the whole army. Braver troops, when on the field of battle and under arms against the enemy, you will not find in the world: that is a truth."[1]

The total casualties—killed, wounded, and taken prisoners—of the XX, during the three years the regiment served in Germany, was twenty-eight officers, twenty-five sergeants, and five hundred and thirty-eight men.

On the 25th January, 1763, the XX commenced its march to Williamstadt, where it embarked for England in February. On returning to England, the strength of the regiment was twenty-seven officers, and seven hundred and six non-commissioned officers and privates.

---

[1] Carlyle's *Frederick the Great*, vol. ix, page 205.

Chapter XII.
1763–1776.

Service in Gibraltar—Death of General Kingsley—Removal to Ireland.

THE history of the corps for the next thirteen years is uneventful, so far as warlike services are concerned. In March, 1763, the XX proceeded to Gibraltar, and remained there until the summer of 1769, when it returned to England. The Colonel of the regiment, Lieutenant-General William Kingsley, under whose name it fought in the campaigns in Germany, died on the 17th November, 1769.

In 1774, the regiment proceeded to Ireland, where it was stationed until April, 1776.

CHAPTER XIII.

1776–1781.

Embarkation for Quebec—Lieutenant Norman—Operations on Lake Champlain—Isle Aux Noix—Advance against the Enemy—Major Acland at Hubbardton—Difficulties of the March—Battles of Freeman's Farm and Bemus Heights—Surrender of the Army—Colours of the XX Burnt—Affecting Scenes—Prisoners of War—Return of the Regiment to England.

THE XX—with six other regiments[1]—embarked at Cork on the 5th of April, 1776, sailed on the 8th, arrived at Quebec on the 29th of May, and proceeded thence to Montreal. The regiment was at once employed on outpost duty, which was a most difficult and arduous service, the whole country being infested with spies and deserters. Lieutenant-General Sir Guy Carleton was at this time preparing a force for service against the insurgents. On reaching Vercherres on the 17th June, Major Carleton was appointed to the command of the advanced guard, which consisted of two companies of the XX, three of the 24th, and two guns.[2]

At Longuiel—a village on the banks of the St. Lawrence, opposite Montreal—on the 18th June, Major Carleton was joined by a large number of Canadians, whom he employed night and day in making roads for the army.[3] On the 20th June, the regiment was cantoned at Bellouiel, and at Chamblée on the 26th, where it remained until the early part of October. The nature

---

[1] The 9th, 24th, 31st, 34th, 53rd, and 62nd Regiments.
[2] General order dated Vercherres, 17th June, 1776.
[3] General order, dated Longuiel, 18th June, 1776.

of the duties which the regiment was called upon to perform at this period is shown by the following general order, which was published by Lieutenant-General Sir John Burgoyne:—

"Chamblée, 9th August, 1776.

"It cannot but give satisfaction to the army to know that the whole gang of deserters from Colonel Maclean's regiment, who sought to redeem their perfidy to the rebels, in whose cause they were before engaged, by becoming a second time traitors to their King and lawful State, have been taken by the outposts and are in safe custody, except one, who received too honourable a death from the firelock of one of his guards, whom he attempted to murder after he was a prisoner. It appears by Brigadier-General Frazer's Report, that the conduct of the detachment employed in this pursuit has been truly exemplary. Lieutenant-General Burgoyne takes this occasion to express his fullest approbation and thanks to Lieutenant Norman of the XX Regiment, who commanded it, and General Frazer will please to direct a dollar to be given to each man of the party, in consideration of the activity, perseverance, and spirit with which they seconded those principles in their officer."

The regiment moved to the Isle Aux Noix on the 29th September.

General Sir Guy Carleton concentrated the army at Point au Fer, and the XX arrived at this place on the 11th of October. The object was a combined attack by the naval and military forces against the western shore of Lake Champlain. Early on the morning of the same day, the fleet, consisting of twenty-seven gun-boats, and carrying eighty-seven pieces of ordnance, proceeded under General Carleton and Captain Pringle,

Royal Navy, in search of the enemy. The fleet was preceded by a large body of Indians in birch bark canoes, led by Captain and Brevet-Major Thomas Carleton, XX Regiment, who commanded the advance guard of the expedition.[1]

The enemy's fleet of sixteen gunboats, carrying ninety pieces of ordnance, was discovered at Valcour Island; an engagement ensued in which the Americans were totally defeated, with the loss of thirteen gunboats. The original plan of the campaign included an attack on Ticonderoga; but this was abandoned owing to the lateness of the season, and the army returned to Canada for winter quarters. The XX was placed in garrison at the Isle Aux Noix (the advanced post of the army) about the 15th of November.[2] This island is at the entrance of Lake Champlain, fifteen miles from St. John; it is about one mile long and five hundred yards wide, and capable of being stubbornly defended; the ground rises in the centre, and is marshy near the water on both sides. The XX erected several block houses and earthworks for the defence of the island.[3]

The island was extremely barren, but during the open season the scarcity of provisions was not felt, owing to the large quantities of fish of all kinds, which were caught round the island. During the winter months, when the lake was frozen, the men were afflicted with scurvy; many were in hospital, some died, but the

---

[1] Lieutenant Hadden's *Journal*, pages 18 and 19. J. M. Hadden, Lieutenant Royal Artillery, served throughout the campaigns under General Carleton and Burgoyne. His MS. Journal and six order books were sold in London in 1874, and have since been published by Brigadier-General Rogers, U.S. army, with no less than three hundred and eighty-eight references.

[2] Anburey's *Travels*, vol. i, page 122.

[3] Hadden's *Journal*, page 54.

majority recovered.[1] The advance of the army into the revolted provinces having commenced under Lieutenant-General Burgoyne, the XX left the Isle Aux Noix about the middle of June, and joined Brigadier-General Frazer's brigade; but, by a general order dated Cumberland Head, 18th June, 1777, it was placed in the right wing, 2nd Brigade, commanded by Brigadier-General Powell.[2] On Tuesday, the 1st July, the army marched to Crown Point, whence it embarked and crossed Lake Champlain, and encamped within four miles of Ticonderoga; the German troops occupying the opposite shore. The total strength of the XX on this day (sick included) was five hundred and twenty-eight rank and file.[3]

During the night of the 5th July, the Americans abandoned their works at Ticonderoga and Mount Independence, leaving all their guns, stores, and provisions; a large detachment proceeded towards Hubbardton; the remainder, embarking on board their vessels, sailed in the direction of Skeensborough. The retreat of the enemy was discovered at daybreak, on the 6th of July; they were pursued by a portion of Brigadier Frazer's corps towards Hubbardton. The remainder of the army embarked on board the fleet at eight a.m., forced the enemy's boom, and made for Skeensborough. About two p.m., Brigadier-General Frazer came up with the enemy, who considerably outnumbered his force; owing to this superiority, the enemy nearly succeeded in out-flanking the British force, and, for a time, the result of the action seemed doubtful, when a detachment under Major-General

---

[1] Lieutenant Hadden's *Journal*, page 54.
[2] *Ibid.*, page 68.
[3] Adjutant-General's state.

Reideseil, which had been sent as a support, fortunately arrived, and the enemy were repulsed on all sides. In the battle of Hubbardton, as this engagement was called, the Americans lost their commander—Colonel Francis—and two hundred men killed, and the same number wounded and taken prisoners. The British loss was seventeen officers and one hundred and nine men killed and wounded. The action was commenced by the Grenadiers of the army, who were commanded by Major Acland of the XX, who was wounded in the thigh.[1] Two companies only of the XX were engaged, and there is no record of their casualties.

About three o'clock in the afternoon of the 6th July, the 9th, XX—commanded by Lieutenant-Colonel John Lind—and 21st Regiments landed near Skeensborough, and ascended the mountains to get behind a fort occupied by the Americans at that place; but as the three regiments gained the summit, the enemy set fire to their fort and fled with such haste that only thirty of their number were made prisoners. Another party of the enemy were pursued towards Castleton, and, being overtaken, a sharp fight ensued, in which the Americans sustained severe loss. On the 8th July, the XX was detached with two field pieces towards Fort Anne, to support the 9th Regiment. On the 12th July, the whole British force (excepting one English and one German regiment) was concentrated at Skeensborough.[2]

The roads having been repaired, obstructions removed, bridges constructed, &c., the army advanced on the 25th July to Fort Anne, fourteen miles from Skeensborough. On the afternoon of the 29th July,

---

[1] Hadden's *Journal;* and Anburey's *Travels*, vol. i, page 295.
[2] Hadden's *Journal*, page 98.

the XX advanced with the right wing of the army to Fort Edward, fourteen miles from Fort Anne.[1]

An idea of the enormous physical difficulties of this campaign can be gleaned from General Burgoyne's despatches. Writing to Lord George Germain from Fort Edward, near the Hudson river, on the 22nd July, he says:—"In the several skirmishes, the loss of the enemy, including killed and wounded, amounted to about three hundred. The enemy cut large timber trees on both sides of the road, so as to fall across and lengthways, with branches interwoven. The troops had not only layers of these to remove in places where it was impossible to take any other direction, but also they had about forty bridges to construct, and others to repair, one of which was of log-wood over a morass two miles in extent."

On Saturday, the 13th September, at two p.m., the advanced corps and right wing, consisting of the 9th, XX, 21st, and 62nd Regiments, under Brigadier Hamilton, with all the artillery, crossed the Hudson river on a bridge of boats, near Batten Kill, and encamped at Saratoga.[2] The XX were ordered to advance four companies to cover the headquarters, which were at Schuyler's house.[3] At twelve noon, on the 15th September, the army moved forward in three columns, and halted at a farm, called Dovogat,[4] three miles from the former position. On the 17th, the army advanced three and a half miles to Sword's Farm. At ten a.m., on Friday, the 19th, the army moved forward in three columns. About two p.m., the British regi-

---

[1] *Political and Military Episodes*, page 254.
[2] Hadden's *Journal*, page 144.
[3] *Ibid.*, page 145.
[4] *Campaign of General John Burgoyne*, by W. L. Stone, page 41. (The house is still standing in good preservation.)

ments arrived opposite Freeman's house, which they passed, and took post on the skirt of a wood, a little beyond it. They were almost immediately attacked by the enemy, who were in possession of the wood, which was eventually cleared, after a stubborn resistance, by the 24th Regiment, with a loss of fifty men. The enemy continued the attack, chiefly on the flank and rear of the 62nd Regiment, which corps suffered very much, losing one hundred and eighty-seven men killed and wounded, and twenty-five men taken prisoners. The regiment was forced to abandon its position, and with it two guns of the artillery.[1] The British line then retreated under Major-General Phillips, closely followed by the Americans.

During this attack the XX was thrown into a wood on the left of a cornfield, and they repulsed the enemy, thus saving the rear of the 62nd Regiment from being galled by the hostile fire.[2] The whole British line advanced a second time under Major-General Phillips, and regained the captured guns and the position from which the 62nd had retired; the Grenadiers, led by General Frazer, moved forward on the right at the same moment, and the enemy being thus pressed retreated to their works.[3] It was now nearly dark, and further pursuit was not attempted. In his despatch, dated Still Water, 19th September, 1777, General

---

[1] Lieutenant Hadden's *Journal*, page 166. Lieutenant Hadden was in charge of the guns; nineteen out of twenty-two men had either been killed or wounded.

[2] Hadden's *Journal*, page 166.

[3] Of this action, the American historian (Stone) says: "The Continentals (nine regiments under Arnold) had, for the sixth time, hurled fresh troops against the three British Regiments, the XX, 21st, and 62nd. The guns on this wing were already silenced. These three regiments had lost half their men, and now formed a small band surrounded by heaps of the dead and dying."—*Campaign of Burgoyne* page 47.

Burgoyne says: "About three o'clock the action began by a very vigorous attack on the British line, and continued with great obstinacy until after sunset, the enemy being constantly supplied with fresh troops. The stress lay upon the XX, 21st, and 62nd Regiments, most parts of which were engaged near four hours without intermission." In bringing the services of Major-General Phillips to the notice of the King, General Burgoyne wrote: "I am indebted to him, particularly for restoring the action in a point which was critically pressed by a great superiority of fire, and to which he led up the XX at the utmost personal hazard."

Of the XX, Lieutenants Cook, Lucas, and Obins,[1] and many men were killed. Lieutenant-Colonel Lind was wounded in two different actions; Captain Farquhar, Lieutenants Wemys, Stanley, and Ensign Connell were wounded, also a large number of men. Burgoyne's army lay upon their arms that night, and early on the following morning took up a position within cannon shot of the enemy. The long and tedious marches, absence of all opportunities of plundering, and the strict discipline in which they were held, made the Indians discontented, and they deserted in large numbers; and as soon as the result of the campaign became doubtful, the provincial volunteers either returned to their homes or went over to the enemy.[2]

In the meanwhile the army was employed throwing up earthworks, and, by all means which the ground

---

[1] Lamb, in his *Memoirs*, says: "Three subalterns of the XX, on this occasion, the oldest of whom did not exceed seventeen years, were buried together."—Quoted at page xcviii, Explanatory Chapter, Hadden's *Journal;* also Anburey's *Travels*, page 373, vol. i.

[2] *Political and Military Episodes*, page 286.

afforded, strengthening the position, which was now extended to the meadows bordering upon the Hudson.[1]

On the 3rd October, it was found necessary to place the army upon reduced rations, a measure to which it submitted without murmuring.[2] On the 7th October, the regular troops (one thousand five hundred men with ten guns) deployed into line, within three quarters of a mile of the left of the American position, while a body of Provincials and Indians were sent through the woods to gain the rear of the enemy's camp. The attack was anticipated by the Americans, who advanced rapidly and in great force upon our left, where Major Acland, XX Regiment, at the head of the Grenadiers, received and checked them.[3] The Grenadiers were posted on a gentle eminence. The American troops marched steadily forward until our men had delivered their fire, when the Americans poured in a destructive volley, and charged on both our flanks. For thirty minutes, a bloody and hand-to-hand struggle ensued on this hill; but on Major Acland being dangerously wounded, and being pressed by enormous

---

[1] The following story is told of a XX man by Ensign Thomas Anburey, 24th Regiment, who served in General Burgoyne's army as a volunteer, and was attached to Major Acland's Grenadiers. Ensign Anburey's work is entitled "*Travels through the Interior Parts of America*, in a Series of Letters, by an Officer." It was published in 1791, ran through several editions, and appeared both in France and Germany. "The gallant behaviour of an old soldier of the XX deserves to be remembered. He had been wounded at the battle of Minden, and as he lay on the ground a French Dragoon rode over him, and the horse's feet rested on his breast. After having recovered from this accident, he thought himself invulnerable, and held the Americans in great contempt. When they attacked the foraging party, the hardy old veteran, sitting upon the forage which he had got on the horse, kept loading and firing his piece at the enemy, and in this manner brought his forage into camp."

[2] Major-General Riedesel, quoted in *Campaign of General Burgoyne*, page 48; Lamb's *Journal*, page 163.

[3] *Political and Military Episodes*, page 292.

odds, the Grenadiers fell back, leaving the ground thickly strewn with their dead and wounded. In the square space of twelve or fifteen yards lay eighteen Grenadiers in the agonies of death, and three officers were propped up against stumps of trees, two of them mortally wounded, bleeding, and almost speechless.[1] In a few minutes the action was extended along the whole line, and is thus described by General Burgoyne's biographer: "Meanwhile, the American forces were pouring, in ever-increasing masses, upon the British, and the contest became a hand-to-hand struggle; bayonets were crossed again and again; guns were taken and retaken; but our men were falling fast under the withering fire of the riflemen, and there were no reserves to fill up the big gaps in their ranks. General Benedict Arnold, at the head of a column of fresh troops, charged upon the British centre, carrying all before him; thrown into irretrievable disorder, Burgoyne's broken columns regained their camp, leaving ten guns and hundreds of dead upon the field."[2] The Americans attacked the British in their camp, but the darkness of an autumn evening interposed its shadows between them. In this action, called by different authorities the battle of Bemus Heights, Stillwater, and Saratoga, the British were defeated, with great loss. It was fought about half a mile from the scene of the action of Freeman's Farm, and ended on the same ground. Bemus Heights is fully a mile and a quarter south of the battle ground. The exact site of the battle is nearly midway between the villages of Schuylerville and Stillwater, and nine miles east of Saratoga

---

[1] *Campaign of General Burgoyne*, page 59.
[2] *Political and Military Episodes*, page 294.

Springs.[1] Of the XX, Major Acland[2] was shot through both legs. He was taken prisoner as a Grenadier was carrying him into camp.[3] Lieutenant Dowling, of the 29th Regiment, who was attached to the XX for duty, was also wounded. Of the other casualties there is no record, but they must have been immense.[4]

General Burgoyne's position being untenable, it was changed during the night. On the evening of the following day (8th October), the enemy showed a disposition to turn the right of the British by the advance of a strong column. General Burgoyne defeated this movement by falling back on Saratoga. The march, though the distance was a little over eight miles, occupied the army twenty-four hours, such were the difficulties of the ground, and the labour of transporting material. The hospital with the sick and wounded were left in camp. On reaching Saratoga, the heights were found to be occupied by the enemy, whose numbers now amounted to fourteen thousand. The British were surrounded, and all means of retreat cut off. The troops took up the best position they could, fortified it, and waited till the 13th October, in the hope of reinforcements from Sir H. Clinton. During this time the men lay continually upon their arms, and were

---

[1] *Campaign of Burgoyne*, page 71.

[2] For the adventures of Lady Harriet Acland, wife of Major Acland, see Appendix.

[3] Letters from Cambridge, Anburey, page 396; *Campaign of Burgoyne*, page 60; Lamb's *Journal*, page 180.

[4] I have to add, my lord, a general report of the killed and wounded. I do not give it as correct, the hurry of the time and the separation of the corps having rendered it impossible to make it so.—Extract from General Burgoyne's despatch, dated Albany, 20th October, 1777.

NOTE.—In 1875, Major-General Meares (then Lieutenant-Colonel commanding the 1st Battalion) found at the scene of this fight a brass plate for the cross belt, with the XX deeply engraved. This interesting relic is now in the officers' mess of the battalion.

exposed to an incessant cannonade.[1] To add to the distress of the situation, the weather was unusually severe; and the men, worn out and exhausted by toil and privation, by hard fighting and constant watching, were without shelter, insufficiently clothed,[2] and short of food.[3] On the 12th October, General Burgoyne called a council of war; the unanimous decision of the council was that "the present position justifies a capitulation upon honourable terms." On the 17th October, 1777, the Convention of Saratoga was completed and signed. The army surrendered by marching from their encampment to the bank of the Hudson River, where they piled arms at the word of command of their own officers. Previous to the surrender the colours of the XX were burnt. The scenes that were now witnessed are described as most affecting. "Young soldiers, who had borne privation and suffering without a murmur, stood abashed and overcome with sorrow and shame; bearded veterans, for whom danger and death had no terrors, sobbed like children, as for the last time they grasped the weapons they had borne with honour on many a battlefield."[4] From the 6th July to the 12th October, the losses of the army amounted to one thousand one hundred and sixty men killed and wounded, seventy-three of whom were officers. The consequence of the surrender of General Burgoyne, at Saratoga, was the loss to England of the American colonies.

Lord Mahon says: "The surrender of three thousand five hundred fighting men, under Burgoyne, was more fruitful in results than those conflicts in which hundreds

---

[1] General Burgoyne's despatch, dated 20th October, 1777.
[2] Anburey. [3] *Political and Military Episodes*, page 304.
[4] *Political and Military Episodes*, pages 309-10.

of thousands of men have been engaged and tens of thousands fallen."[1]

According to Burgoyne's biographer, the causes of the failure were three, viz.: "The inherent strategical vices of the project; the alternate interference and negligence of the Cabinet in its executive details; and the want of administrative arrangement and preparedness in the essentials of army supply."[2]

In the House of Lords, the Earl of Shelburne[3] directly charged Lord George Germain with having brought about the disaster: the operations were intended to be carried out by two Generals in concert with one another; but the Minister sent positive orders to one General and discretionary orders to the other. Mr. Burgoyne is directed to march to New York or effect a junction with Mr. Howe; the latter goes on board his ship and gets to the other side of Philadelphia. The Earl of Chatham and Mr. Fox both censured the American Minister. After the surrender at Saratoga, the XX marched to Cambridge, near Boston, a distance of two hundred miles, where it arrived about the 15th November. The men were quartered at Prospect Hill, and the officers in the town of Cambridge.[4] The regiment was detained prisoners of war, the officers signed the "Cambridge Parole."

By article ii. of the Convention, dated Camp at Saratoga, October 16th, 1777, it was agreed that "a free passage to be granted to the army under Lieutenant-General Burgoyne to Great Britain, on condition of not serving again in North America during the

---

[1] *History of England*, vol. vi, page 288.
[2] *Political and Military Episodes*, page 333.
[3] Served in the XX under Wolfe.
[4] *Letters from Cambridge*, Anburey, vol. ii, page 55.

present contest, and that the port of Boston is assigned for the entry of transports to receive the troops whenever General Howe should so order." Congress refused to ratify this article of the Convention, and not only were the troops retained in captivity, but they were treated in the most unkind and harassing manner. A non-commissioned officer thus recounts his experiences at this time:—"It was not unfrequent for thirty or forty persons, men, women, and children, to be indiscriminately crowded together in one small open hut, their provisions and firewood on short allowance, a scanty portion of straw their bed, their own blankets their only covering. In the night time those that could lie down, and the many who sat up from the cold, were obliged frequently to rise and shake from them the snow which the wind drifted in at the openings."[1] The treatment meted out to the officers was equally offensive. They were often confined as prisoners in the guard rooms.[2]

During the year 1780, the following officers of the XX were exchanged:—Captains Rollinson, Winchester, Lieutenants Wheat, Gilbert, Gaskill, Crofts, Charlton, Ensign Cooper, and Surgeon Cahill. On the 3rd September, 1781, Lieutenant-Colonel Lind and the regiment were liberated and sent to England.

---

[1] Page 196 of *An Original and Authentic Journal of Occurrences during the late American War*, from its commencement to the year 1783, by R. Lamb, late Sergeant in the 9th and 23rd Regiments. Published 1809.

[2] Letters from Cambridge, Anburey: Lamb's *Journal*, page 196.

CHAPTER XIV.

1782—1796.

Service in Ireland and British North America—The West Indies—State of Affairs in St. Domingo—Arrival of the XX—Attack on Tiburon—Storming of L'Acul—Casualties—Reverse at Bompard—Death of Lieutenant-Colonel Markham—His Character—Return of the XX to England—March to Exeter.

IN 1783 the XX proceeded to Ireland, and was stationed in that country until the 15th June, 1789; on this date the corps embarked for Halifax, Nova Scotia, and served in this and other stations in British North America until the year 1792, when it was ordered to the West Indies and quartered in Kingston, Jamaica. The island of St. Domingo was at this time a French possession. Owing to the unwise and vexatious laws enacted by the Government at Paris, the relationship between the white population—chiefly planters—and the negroes and mulattoes, was strained and embittered. As soon as the Republic was established in France, the National Assembly entered into the dispute, and showed practical sympathy with the natives by supplying them with leaders, men, and money. On the 21st August, 1791, there was a general rising and massacre[1] of the white population, the result of a preconcerted plan. During this year the planters of St. Domingo petitioned the English Cabinet to take the island under British protection, asserting that it was the general wish and desire of the white population that the Government should do so.

---

[1] *History of the West Indies*, page 124.

These overtures were renewed in 1793; and, as the National Assembly had declared war against England, the Government favourably entertained the request of the colonists.[1] Instructions were accordingly despatched to Major-General Williamson, commanding at Jamaica, to send a sufficient force from that island to St. Domingo, to occupy and retain all places that might be surrendered, until reinforcements should arrive from England. From a miscalculation of the difficulties and strength of the enemy, General Williamson sent from Jamaica eight hundred and seventy men—fit for duty—only; this small contingent was composed of the 13th Regiment, seven companies of the 49th Regiment, and a detachment of artillery. An attack was made on Tiburon on the 4th of October, but it failed; the English were compelled to retreat, with the loss of forty men.[2] Subsequent to the reverse at Tiburon an epidemic of yellow fever, of peculiar virulence, raged in St. Domingo, and carried off half the effective force. These unfortunate events left General Williamson no alternative but to withdraw the troops, or send reinforcements from Jamaica. He decided on the latter course, and at once sent the Royals, XX, and remaining companies of the 49th Regiment, amounting, in all, to about eight hundred men. These regiments reached St. Domingo about the end of October, 1793.[3]

The garrison in Jamaica was now reduced to less than four hundred men. The British force in St. Domingo was far out-numbered by the enemy.

---

[1] *History of the West Indies*, in three volumes, by Bryan Edwards. Published 1801. Vol. iii, page 155.
[2] *Ibid.*, page 159.
[3] *Ibid.*, page 159.

The French Republican Commissioners had brought with them from France six thousand chosen French troops. There were, previous to the arrival of the Commissioners, nine thousand men enrolled in the French and Colonial Militia: this militia included the free people of colour. In addition to these there were six thousand negroes, raised by the Commissioners, making a total of 21,000 effective men opposed to 1,200 British soldiers and a force of colonists, whose strength cannot be traced, but not numbering more than a few hundred.[1] It was decided to make a second attack on Tiburon, and the XX, together with the 13th Regiment, Marines, and British Legion, embarked at Jeremie—N.W. of the island—on the 31st January, 1794, under the command of Lieutenant-Colonel Whitelocke, and anchored off Tiburon on the evening of the 2nd February. The whole disembarked at daybreak on the 3rd.

The enemy opposed the landing and fought bravely, but were repulsed and forced to retire.[2]

The following is an extract from the despatch of Major-General Williamson, dated 9th February, 1794: "At the capture of Cape Tiburon, the business was spirited and well done; it secures the passage and, with Cape Nichola Mole, commands that fine extensive bay. It has also drove the brigands as far back as Aux Cayes —sixty miles. Of the enemy, fifty were killed and one hundred and fifty were taken prisoners. The XX had one sergeant and four privates wounded."[3]

Lieutenant-Colonel Whitelocke determined to attack the post of L'Acul, about six miles from Leogane, at

---

[1] *History of the West Indies*, vol. iii, pages 151-155.
[2] *London Gazette*, 15th March, 1794.
[3] *Ibid.*, 15th March, 1794.

the extremity of the plain of the same name. The troops marched about four o'clock in the morning of the 19th February. The attack commenced at four p.m. on the 20th February. The place was carried at the point of the bayonet, under a sharp destructive fire from the hill on which the fort stood. Had the detachment (two hundred) of Colonial troops, which had been sent on the 18th by sea, been landed, the retreat of the enemy would have been cut off, and not a man would have escaped. In this brilliant little affair the flank companies of the XX were engaged; Lieutenant Tinlin, of the Grenadier company, and ten men were wounded.[1] Lieutenant Tinlin was wounded by an explosion as he entered the gates of the fort; Lieutenant Caulfield, 62nd Regiment, who was with him, was also wounded, and, after lingering for some time, died of the injuries received. The French officer, finding that he could no longer hold the place, attempted to blow it up.[2]

The next enterprise of this gallant little army had a less favourable termination; it was directed against a strong post and settlement at a place called Bompard, about eight miles from Cape Saint Nicolas, inhabited by a hardy race of German colonists.[3] A detachment of two hundred men was selected for this service— one division was commanded by Major and Brevet Lieutenant-Colonel Markham, XX, and the other by Major Spencer. The particulars of the attack and subsequent retreat of this small force are not forthcoming. All that we know is that they were repulsed, with a loss of forty men, by the enemy, who had the

---

[1] *London Gazette*, 17th April, 1794.
[2] *History of the West Indies*, vol. iii, pages 163-4.
[3] *Ibid.*, vol. iii, pages 164-5.

advantage of defending a naturally strong position with superior numbers. The enemy bore testimony to the great gallantry of our men.

The mortality among the British troops in St. Domingo in this year was appalling. They fell like autumn leaves. In two months, forty officers and six hundred men died from yellow fever.[1] On the 19th May, 1794, the 22nd, 23rd, and 41st Regiments arrived at St. Domingo from England. This was the first reinforcement since the arrival of the XX. On the 26th March, 1795, Lieutenant-Colonel David Markham, the officer in command of the regiment, was shot through the heart whilst leading an attack on an outpost of the position held by the enemy, who was at this time laying siege to Fort Bizotton.[2] This fort stood on a hill, and commanded the town and harbour of Port au Prince. The Colonel fell as the party was rapidly advancing to the charge. The detachment under the direction of Captain Honourable Colville, 13th Regiment, still pushed on, captured the outpost, colours, five pieces of cannon, destroyed the stores, and killed some hundreds of the enemy on the spot.

Of this engagement, Bryan Edwards says, page 181, vol. iii:—"But the victory was dearly obtained by the loss of so enterprising and accomplished a leader." At page 239 he states, "I cannot deny myself the melancholy satisfaction of preserving in this work the following honourable tribute to the memory of this

---

[1] *History of the West Indies*, vol. iii, page 174.
[2] *Ibid.*, vol. iii, pages 180-181.

NOTE.—Lieutenant-Colonel Markham had only succeeded to the command of the corps, by purchase, on the 29th March, 1794, on the retirement of Lieutenant-Colonel Lind. The latter officer was soon after promoted Major-General, and died 1st May, 1795. He had commanded the XX for many years.

amiable officer, which was given out in general orders after his death by the Commander-in-Chief:—

"'Headquarters, 28th March, 1795.

"'Brigadier-General Horneck begs the officers, non-commissioned officers, and privates of the detachment which on the 26th instant proceeded under the command of Lieutenant-Colonel Markham on a party of observation, to receive his very sincere thanks for their gallant behaviour at the attack on the enemy's advanced post, taking their colours and cannon, and destroying their stores. At the same time, he cannot sufficiently express his feelings on the late afflicting loss that has been sustained in Lieutenant-Colonel Markham, who, equally excellent and meritorious as an officer and a man, lived universally respected and beloved, and died leaving a bright example of military, social, and private virtue.'"

There does not appear to have been any fighting of importance after this engagement.

All that remained of the XX after four years of war and disease in St. Domingo was six officers and seventy non-commissioned officers and men. These few representatives of the corps left St. Domingo for England in March, 1796; arrived at Plymouth, where they were disembarked, and proceeded by march route to Exeter, under the command of Lieutenant-Colonel Forbes Champagné.

The following are the names of the officers who fell victims to the climate of St. Domingo:—Major Charles Boyd; Captains W. Farquhar, T. Story, R. Dobson, and J. Fenton; Captain-Lieutenants J. Eccles and R. Bateman; Lieutenants P. B. Ravencroft, E. Blennerhasset, Stewart, and Dalton; Ensigns G. Bloomer and E. W. Thorpe; Adjutants A. L. Wynyard and W. Smyth.

CHAPTER XV.

1796-1799.

Change of Stations—Recruiting—Volunteers from the Militia—Distinguished Officers join the XX—Formation of Two Battalions—Embarkation for Holland—Arrival at the Helder—Battle of Krabbendam—The XX would not be beaten—Remember "Minden"—Thanked by Sir R. Abercromby—Casualties—Advance against Hoorn—A Night March—The First Battle of Egmont op Zee—The Second Battle—Return to England.

THE XX marched from Exeter to Lichfield in November, 1796. During the month of March, 1797, the regiment moved to Liverpool, where it was stationed until the 2nd June, 1798, thence it proceeded to Manchester, and, after a short stay in that city, proceeded by march route to Preston. Recruiting was more successful at Preston than at any of the towns in which the corps had previously been quartered: three hundred recruits joined the colours. An expedition was at this time being prepared for service in Holland, and the XX was selected to form part of it, and accordingly left Preston on the 3rd July, 1799, and arrived at Barnham Downs early in the following month. The XX was here joined by one thousand eight hundred volunteers from the militia battalions of the counties of York, Lancaster, Stafford, Derby, Chester, Devon, Cornwall, and Cambridge. These were the men who composed the old fighting XX—splendid soldiers, who won honours and distinction for their corps in the campaigns in Holland, Egypt, Calabria, Spain, Portugal, and the south of France. At this period there also came to the XX distinguished officers, whose names will ever have a high and honoured place in the annals of the regiment: foremost among them stand the names of Lieutenant-Colonels G. Smyth, P. Bainbrigge, and R. Ross. On the 4th August, 1799, the regiment was formed into two battalions; Lieutenant-Colonel George Smyth was appointed to command the first, and Lieutenant-Colonel David Clephane to the second. Nothing more clearly shows the superiority of the discipline of the corps, or the ability and zeal of its officers, than the ease with which the organisation of the masses of the recruits—about two thousand—into two battalions was accomplished. Officers and men were of different corps—were strangers to each other; their uniforms were different, the only outward mark showing that they belonged to the XX was the breastplate. The facings, the militia badges on the cap and on the pack, remained; but this tended more to confusion than otherwise.[1]

After a brief stay at Barnham Downs camp, they marched on the morning of the 25th August to Deal, where they embarked. The regiment was all on board by eleven in the morning, and sailed by three

---

[1] Speaking of the regiments swollen by volunteers from militia battalions, General Bunbury says: "If only three months had been gained for them to know something of their officers and sergeants, and the ways of the regiments into which they had entered, the men would probably have done their duty well; but such was not the case, and one cannot be surprised that, with the exception of the XX and 40th Regiments, these suddenly-created battalions proved unfit to meet a brave and skilful enemy."—Page 39, *Narrative of the Great War with France from* 1799 *to* 1810, by Lieutenant-General Sir H. Bunbury, K.C.B.

NOTE.—Sir H. Bunbury was aide-de-camp to H.R.H. the Duke of York in the North Holland campaign, was at the head of the Quartermaster General's department in the Mediterranean under three successive commanders, and was Under Secretary of State for War from 1810 to 1816. During the Peninsular War, Sir Henry was sent on several occasions to advise the Duke of Wellington as to the wishes and intentions of the British Government.

in the afternoon—no drunkenness, no absentees, and no confusion.[1]

The two battalions of the XX and the 63rd Regiment formed one brigade, which was commanded by Major-General Don. Major-General Lord Charles Fitzroy was appointed Colonel-Commandant of the second battalion on the 10th August, 1799.[2] Of the embarkation at Deal, Lieutenant-Colonel Steevens, in his *Reminiscences of My Military Life*, says: "The division consisted of about four thousand men, and everything was so well arranged, the boats being all ready for us on our arrival on the beach, that from the time the division stepped into the boats, it took only twenty minutes before all was on board." At about four o'clock in the afternoon of the 28th August, both battalions of the XX disembarked under the guns of the Helder, and had to wade through the water, carrying the ammunition on the top of their knapsacks; in this way some of it was destroyed and a few stand of arms lost. One company—one hundred men—under the command of Captain George Paddon, Lieutenants Steevens and Robinson, was sent to garrison Texel Island, near the mouth of the Scheldt. As soon as the disembarkation was completed, the XX bivouacked on the sandhills about four miles to the south of Helder town. By the 4th September, Sir Ralph Abercromby had placed his army in order of battle; the most important point of his line of defence was from Krabbendam to Petten. "At the salient angle of the British position stood the village of Krabbendam, and in this village were posted both battalions of the

---

[1] Lieutenant-General P. Bainbrigge—Quartermaster General's department—and Captain Hollinsworth.

[2] *London Gazette*, 13th August, 1799.

XX."[1] At daybreak on the 10th of September, the enemy (French and Dutch), with their whole force massed in three columns, attacked the British position; they were repulsed at the Einigenbrug suburb by the 2nd Battalion. The enemy then assailed the entrenchments at Krabbendam; they rushed to the attack in swarms, and at one time it was feared they would force their way into the intrenchments; but Lieutenant-Colonel Smyth, seeing the danger, stood upon the parapet (supported by some of his men, as the blood was flowing copiously from a wound in his leg), and, brandishing his sword, shouted, in tones that could be heard above the din of battle, "Twentieth, remember Minden."[2] The battalion answered to the call by driving the French from the intrenchments with great slaughter. Of this fight, Sir Henry Bunbury says:[3] "Nor was the attack on Krabbendam less marked by valour; the Republicans, led by Dumonceau, assailed the village of Krabbendam with headlong fury; they penetrated into the village, and, in spite of the destructive fire from the houses, they fought hand to hand with our troops. But the XX was a regiment that never would be beaten; and their commander, Colonel George Smyth,[4] was an officer of first-rate ability. To him Sir Ralph Abercromby had specially assigned the defence of this important post, and worthily he discharged his trust. Although three-fourths of the two battalions of the XX were volunteers recently received from the militia, they had been already imbued with the

---

[1] *Narratives of the Great War*, pages 6 and 7.
[2] *Western Antiquary*.
[3] *Narratives of the Great War*, page 8.
[4] *Ibid.* The following footnote appears at page 8:—"This excellent officer died, unfortunately for our service, just at the beginning of the Spanish War, before he had attained the rank of a general officer."

spirit of the old regiment, and so gallantly did they maintain their post that there was no need of moving up the brigades in reserve to their support."

Sir Ralph Abercromby complimented and thanked the corps on the field for their services, and published the following army order, which he also embodied in his despatch, dated Schager Brug, 11th September, 1799:—"The two battalions of the XX Regiment, posted at Krabbendam and the Zuype Sluys, did credit to the high reputation which the regiment has always borne. Lieutenant-Colonel Smyth, of that corps, who had particular charge of the post, received a severe wound in his leg, which will deprive us for a time of his services."[1]

The casualties of the regiment were as follows:—1st Battalion: Lieutenant-Colonel George Smyth, Major Robert Ross, Captain Henry Powlett, and Lieutenant John Colborne,[2] wounded; Lieutenants Charles Des Vaux[3] and Christopher Hamilton,[4] lost a leg; Lieutenant and Adjutant Samuel South, wounded; of the rank and file fourteen were killed, twenty-five wounded, and fourteen missing; total, fifty-three. 2nd Battalion: Captain-Lieutenant L. Ferdinand Adams, one sergeant, and thirty-four rank and file, wounded; four rank and file killed, and four missing; total, forty-three.

The command of the 1st Battalion devolved upon Brevet Lieutenant-Colonel Phillip Bainbrigge, the senior Major.

Additional troops having arrived from England, and H.R.H. the Duke of York having assumed the command of the army, Sir Ralph Abercromby, with his

---

[1] *London Gazette*, 16th September, 1799.
[2] See Appendix.   [3] Afterwards Sir Charles Des Vaux, Bart.
[4] Commanded the 97th Regiment for many years, and died Major-General.

division, advanced on the town of Hoorn. The XX formed a brigade in this division.

At six o'clock in the evening of the 18th September, they began their march under a heavy rain, which continued all night. The darkness was intense, and the route lay over a narrow paved causeway, flanked on both sides by low stripes of deep mud, which were confined by broad ditches filled to the brim. After a fourteen-mile march, under these conditions, they arrived at the gates of Hoorn between three and four in the morning, and entered without opposition.

Our men had been under arms twelve hours, were dead tired, and unable to resume their march before mid-day, when, owing to the reverses suffered by the Russians at Bergen on the previous day, the division was recalled to its former position on the Zuype.[1]

On the 2nd October, the army moved forward in three bodies; Sir Ralph Abercromby's division formed the right column, and, as it was to march along the beach, was unable to start until after six a.m., the hour of departure being dependent on the state of the tide. This march was a series of skirmishes: every yard of the advance was contested, and on two occasions there were serious conflicts. At length the soldiers, wearied from fighting and marching over soft sea sand, arrived in front of a ridge of sandhills and within two miles of Egmont op Zee. Of the part taken by the corps in this, the first battle of Egmont op Zee, there is no record as distinguished from the other regiments of the brigade in which it served, which was commanded by Major-General Lord Cavan. Captain Powlett and Ensign Milnes were wounded, and fifty

---

[1] *Narratives of the Great War*, page 22.

men were killed or wounded. The enemy retired, and on the following day (3rd October) the XX advanced beyond Egmont. On Sunday, the 6th of October, the advanced posts of the allies were pushed forward to secure some villages in front and to force the detachments of the enemy to fall back on their main body. The French opposed our advance at all points, but particularly at Baacum, where the Russians received a serious check. Sir R. Abercromby advanced to their assistance, and a general action along the whole line ensued, and was maintained with great obstinacy until night, when the enemy retired. This was the second battle of Egmont op Zee. Of the 1st Battalion, Brevet Lieutenant-Colonel Bainbrigge, commanding, Brevet Major Campbell, Ensigns Favell and McCurry (colours), were killed; Captain Newman, Lieutenants Maxwell, Close, and Ensign Humphreys wounded. The 2nd Battalion had Captains Maister, Wallace,[1] and Torrens, Lieutenant Steevens,[2] and Ensign Drewry wounded. The loss in non-commissioned officers and soldiers amounted to one hundred and seventy-one killed, wounded, and missing. Captain Manley Power[3] succeeded to the command of the 1st Battalion on the death of Lieutenant-Colonel Bainbrigge, his promotion as Major being dated 7th of October, 1799. In this short campaign of five weeks' duration, the casualties of the XX were twenty-two officers, inclusive of two commanding officers and two field officers, and three hundred and seventeen non-commissioned officers and

---

[1] Captain Wallace died of wounds received in the Pyrenees, 25th July, 1813.

[2] Lieutenant C. Steevens was severely wounded and taken prisoner.

[3] Afterwards Lieutenant-General Sir Manley Power, K.C.B., died in 1826. His father, Bolton Power, served in the XX from 1757 to 1785. Was present at Minden, and in all the actions of the "Seven Years' War," also the campaign in America under Sir John Burgoyne.

men.[1] The campaign in North Holland was brought to a close by the embarkation of the British army at the Helder on the 31st October, 1799; the two battalions of the XX were disembarked at different ports in the south of England, and were subsequently concentrated at Ashford in Kent.

---

[1] See Lord Seaton's letter, Appendix.

NOTE.—The regiment received its share of £21,830. 15s. 9d., the value of four frigates and two hulks captured by the army in Holland. It was issued as bounty to the troops, each soldier receiving six shillings and eight pence (6s. 8d.).—*London Gazette.*

CHAPTER XVI.

1800–1801.

Stationed at Cork—Expedition to Belle Isle—Minorca—The Flank Battalion—Service in Egypt—Capture of the Batteries—A Night Attack—General Coote's Despatch—Constructing Batteries—Forts des Bains and Triangular—Ophthalmia—Gold Medals awarded to the Officers.

IN the months of January and February, 1800, the regiment (both battalions) proceeded to Ireland, and was stationed at Cork. On the 7th June, the XX embarked with a small expedition against Belle Isle; the ships reached the island on the 18th June; the two battalions were immediately transferred from the transports to two seventy-four-gun ships, the first battalion to the "Canada" and the second battalion to the "Captain." The attack was abandoned at the last moment; the second battalion was landed, and encamped on the Isle of Houat for a few days.

The second battalion having re-embarked, the transports sailed on the 24th June for Minorca, where they arrived early in July. The first battalion was quartered in George Town and the second at Fort George. This fort commanded the entrance of the harbour which led to Fort Mahon. The light companies of the regiment formed part of a Flank Battalion, which was commanded by Brevet Lieutenant-Colonel R. Ross,[1] and occupied quarters at Alayor. At this time (1801) the regiment was chiefly composed of men who had volunteered from the militia for the limited period of five years, and for service in Europe only; but, being anxious to join the

---

[1] Promoted Brevet Lieutenant-Colonel, 1st January, 1801, for service in Holland.

army in Egypt, the officers, particularly Lieutenant-Colonels Smyth and Ross, exerted themselves to induce the men to offer their services, which they cheerfully and willingly did, notwithstanding the great mortality among the troops then serving in Egypt. The battalions embarked on the 24th June, and arrived in Aboukir Bay on the 23rd July; they disembarked the following morning, encamped on the east side of Alexandria, and were formed in brigade with the "Ancient Irish Fencibles." On the 17th August, the 30th and 50th Regiments attacked and captured several batteries; the XX and 92nd Regiments being held in support.

The regiment embarked on the 22nd August in boats, on the inundations, and joined the division, under the command of Major-General Sir Eyre Coote, on the west side of Alexandria. On the night of the 25th of August, the 1st battalion captured an outpost occupied by the enemy. Sir Henry Bunbury thus describes this affair: "Near as Coote's position was to Fort des Bains, there was still an outpost held by the enemy which was likely to embarrass our operations against that work. Early in the night of the 25th of August the 1st battalion of the XX, under that admirable officer, Colonel George Smyth, marched silently forth with unloaded muskets; they turned the left of the French redoubt, and rushing in with the bayonet they captured or killed the whole of its defenders (about one hundred men). Irritated by the success of this exploit, a strong column of the enemy, issuing from the city under cover of a cannonade, attempted to drive the XX from the post they had so gallantly mastered, but the attack was repelled with ease."[1]

---

[1] *Narratives of the Great War*, page 152.

The following is a copy of the General's despatch:—
"Camp, West of Alexandria,
"August 26th, 1801.

"Sir,—Being anxious to push my pickets upon the left, as far as possible towards the enemy's advanced work, the redoubt des Bains, I directed Lieutenant-Colonel Smyth, with the first battalion of the XX, assisted with a small detachment of the 26th Light Dragoons, commanded by Lieutenant Kelly, to attack and drive in the French outposts, upon the right of their position. He was to be supported by a battalion of infantry disposed for that purpose upon the sandhills.

"Soon after dark last night, Lieutenant-Colonel Smyth commenced the attack by turning the left of the enemy's pickets and scouring the hills as he advanced. The cool and spirited conduct of that officer, and the corps under his command, as also the detachment 26th Light Dragoons, is well deserving of praise. *Not a man attempted to load, and the whole was executed by the bayonet.* The loss of the enemy in this affair amounted to upwards of one hundred men killed, wounded, and taken; of the latter I enclose the return. This service was performed, on our side, with the loss of only three men slightly wounded, and has placed me in a situation to erect a battery within about six hundred yards of the redoubt des Bains.

"The enemy, however, extremely exasperated at our success, made several attempts to regain the ground he had lost. With this view he kept up a very heavy fire of cannon and musketry for about an hour, when, finding all his endeavours ineffectual, he retired, leaving us in peaceful possession of the advantage we had gained in the early part of the night.—I have, &c.,

"(Signed) EYRE COOTE, Major-General."

During the night of the 27th and morning of the 28th August, both battalions were employed on the arduous and fatiguing duty of constructing gun and mortar batteries. By the most persevering exertions on the part of the officers and men, the batteries were completed and ready to open fire on Forts des Bains and Triangular by daybreak on the 28th, but at the solicitation of the French General (Menou), hostilities were suspended by an armistice of three days, agreed to by General Hutchinson.

Articles of capitulation were signed on the 30th of August, by which the French surrendered the town and forts of Alexandria, and the army, as prisoners of war, laid down their arms and returned to France. Egypt was thus delivered from the power of Napoleon. To the XX was awarded the distinguished honour of taking possession of the two principal Forts—des Bains and Triangular—in recognition of its gallant conduct in the last and final attack, which resulted in the French General's appeal for the armistice, and subsequent capitulation.

The flank companies of both battalions entered into formal occupation of the forts on the 2nd September, and on the following day rejoined the regiment in camp at Pompey's Pillar. Whilst serving in Egpyt the regiment suffered from fever, dysentery, and ophthalmia. Lieutenant H. W. Walker and many men died from fever; the majority of the officers and men were afflicted with ophthalmia : Captain Arthur Lloyd subsequently lost his sight from the effects of this disease.[1]

For its services in Egypt the regiment received the thanks of Parliament and the Royal authority to bear

---

[1] *Reminiscences of My Military Life*, page 27.

on its colours the word "Egypt" with the Sphinx, as memorials of its gallant conduct in this campaign. The officers of the regiment were permitted to accept gold medals from the Grand Vizier.[1]

---

[1] *Cannon's Historical Records*, page 32.

Chapter XVII.

1801–1808.

Arrival at Malta—Bounties Offered—Reduction of the Establishment by One Battalion—Presentation to Colonel George Smyth—New Colours—Efficiency of the Corps—Departure from Malta—The Flank Companies—Disembarkation at Castelamare — Night-March — Severe Winter—Sail for Messina—Detention on Board Ship—Causing a Diversion—Battle of Maida—Death of Captain McLean—Arrival of the XX—Colonel Ross—Captain Colborne—March to Maida—French Prisoners—Scylla Castle—Messina—Unhealthy Quarters—Wreck of the "Windermere"—Gibraltar—Disembarkation at Portsmouth.

THE regiment embarked at Alexandria, arrived at Malta on the 6th December, and disembarked on the 9th; the 1st Battalion was quartered at Vittoriosa and the 2nd at Isola. A bounty of five pounds (£5) was offered by the Government to induce the men to extend their period of service in the army; the majority of the men of the XX continued their connection with the corps, an inconsiderable number re-enlisted for other regiments, and, on the other hand, the XX was joined by volunteers from regiments then serving in Malta.

On the declaration of the Peace of Amiens, 27th March, 1802, the establishment of the regiment was reduced to one battalion; the men of the 2nd Battalion joined the 1st at Vittoriosa; the officers who were in excess of the new establishment were placed on half pay, but were reinstated as vacancies occurred. In consequence of this reduction, Lieutenant-Colonel George Smyth was transferred to the 82nd Regiment on the 14th November, 1802. Previous to his departure from Malta he was presented with a sword, by

Lieutenant-Colonel Ross and officers of the corps, accompanied by an address expressing the high estimation in which he was held, and regret that his service with the XX was terminated.

On the 3rd of May, 1803, the regiment marched to Valetta, the capital of the island. Lieutenant-Colonel Ross presented the regiment with a set of new colours on his assuming the command in September of this year. The XX remained in Malta until October, 1805. During this period there is nothing of importance to chronicle beyond the ordinary routine duties of a regiment in garrison; and the high state of military efficiency to which the corps was brought by the exertions of the commanding officer (Lieutenant-Colonel Ross), of which (says Colonel Steevens in 1839) even at this distance of time there is ample testimony.[1] Whilst at Malta, a detachment of the regiment, under the command of Captain James Bent,[2] was stationed on the island of Gozo. The regiment embarked at Valetta on the 25th October, 1805, and sailed on the 3rd November for Naples with the expeditionary force, commanded by Lieutenant-General Sir James Craig. Previous to the embarkation, the flank com-

---

[1] Colonel Steevens, in his *Reminiscences*, pages 38 and 39, tells us very plainly how the efficiency was maintained. He says: "We had plenty of occupation, as far as drilling went, during our stay in Malta; for our Colonel (Ross) used frequently to take the XX out into the country at five in the morning, and not bring us home till one p.m. I can vouch for the truth of it, and so can many others. We were repeatedly out for *eight hours* during the hot weather; frequently crossing the country, scouring the fields over the stone walls, the whole regiment acting as light infantry; and *the best* of the *joke* was, that *no other corps in the island was similarly indulged.*"

Wolfe, in his time, appears to have held and acted upon the same idea as guided Ross.

The former, when in command of the XX, in writing to a friend, expresses "regret that the men get tired after drilling for five hours," and he "considered that they had not the stamina of their forefathers."

[2] Killed at the head of the regiment at the battle of Orthes, 27th February, 1814.

panies of all the regiments detailed for service with the expedition were formed into two battalions: the Grenadier battalion, under Lieutenant-Colonel Hon. W. O'Callaghan, 39th Regiment, and the light companies into a light infantry battalion, the command of which was assigned to Lieutenant-Colonel Kempt, 81st Regiment. The corps composing Brigadier-General Ackland's brigade were the XX, 35th, and 61st. Captain W. Wallace, with fifty volunteers from the Norfolk Militia, arrived at Malta on the 27th October, and joined the battalion on board the transports: this reinforcement brought the strength of the corps to seven hundred and fourteen all ranks.[1] The transports, with General Craig's force, fell in with the Russian armament off Sicily, and the armies of both countries landed without opposition in the neighbourhood of Naples. The XX disembarked at Castelamare, in the Bay of Naples, on the 22nd November, 1805, and at night marched to Nocera. The roads were wet and heavy, and in consequence the march was unpleasant and fatiguing. To add to the general discomfort, on reaching Nocera, quarters for the men were found with difficulty and after a tiresome delay. The King of Naples reviewed the regiment on the sands at Torre-del-Nunciate. His Majesty expressed his admiration at the appearance and discipline of the corps. About the middle of December, the regiment vacated its quarters at Nocera, and marched along the coast, at the foot of Mount Vesuvius, and on the high road through Capua, in the direction of Gaeta, finally going into cantonments in the small village of Carano, near Sessa, where the British headquarters had been estab-

---

[1] On the 1st of August, 1806, the strength was six hundred and sixteen, showing a loss in nine months of ninety-eight men.

lished. The winter was remarkably severe, and our men suffered much privation. It is a curious fact that more than one Russian was frozen to death in the Kingdom of Naples.[1]

The Russian troops were withdrawn from Naples about the 10th January, 1806, and the British returned to Castelamare about the same date. The XX embarked on the 16th, sailed on the 19th, and arrived in the harbour of Messina on the 22nd. Owing to political differences with the Court of Naples, Sir James Craig's division was not allowed to land until the 17th of February, when the XX was quartered in the vicinity of Messina; subsequently it was stationed along the coast as far as the lighthouse, which was opposite the Scylla rock. Sir James Craig, the commander of the English division, was obliged, from ill-health, to resign his command, and was succeeded by Major-General Stuart, who decided, towards the latter end of June, to strike a sudden blow at the French division under General Reynier, then occupying Calabria. The troops embarked without delay, and the transports anchored in the bay of St. Euphemia on the evening of the 30th June. The troops disembarked the following morning. With the two-fold object of creating a diversion in favour of the main body of the army during the disembarkation at St. Euphemia, and of deceiving the French commander as to the strength of the British division, the XX was employed in cruising off the coast of Calabria, between Reggio and Cape Spartivento, in large open boats.[2]

---

[1] Bunbury.

[2] These boats were called feluccas, and could, on an emergency, hold one hundred men, but on this occasion there were not more than one officer and twenty men in each boat.

On the 3rd July the feluccas returned to Messina harbour, the regiment was transferred to the transports. "Britannia" and "Symmetry," and sailed the same day for St. Euphemia. The ships anchored in the bay early on the morning of the 4th, and were at once hailed by Admiral Sir Sydney Smith, who informed Colonel Ross that it was the General's intention to attack the French that morning.

With commendable and characteristic promptitude Colonel Ross ordered the disembarkation of the regiment.[1] In his *Reminiscences*, Colonel Steevens says: "Without waiting for orders, our gallant chief, Colonel Ross, gave directions for the regiment to disembark soon after daylight. We cheerfully obeyed the order and landed forthwith, after filling our haversacks and canteens, for officers as well as men carried three days' provisions, their blankets, and a change of linen. In landing, the boats had to go through a great deal of surf, and the men spoilt all their cartridges; but having some casks of ammunition in the boats, we soon replenished their pouches, and immediately hurried across the country, through woods and marshes, and reached our little army in the very nick of time."

The division had moved forward to the attack in an échelon of brigades, the Light Battalion, under Colonel Kempt, taking the lead, and on the right of this battalion was posted the light company of the XX, commanded by Captain Murdoch McLean—a force which had been separated from the main body of the regiment. As soon as they reached the left bank of the Lamato, which was steep and woody, Colonel Kempt sent the Corsician Rangers across the stream to search the

---

[1] Exclusive of the Light and Grenadier companies; these companies formed part of the battalions so called, and had disembarked with the army.

thickets and to secure his flank from ambuscades, at the same time sending out McLean's company as a support. The instant the Corsicians entered the wood they were met by a sharp fire, and a desperate charge on the part of about two hundred French; this caused them to be driven in much confusion and disorder upon McLean's light company, which with great difficulty maintained its ground. Captain McLean was at this moment shot through the heart; and, "if the men had not been of sterling stuff, the company must have been broken."[1]

For some moments the fighting was very sharp, until the French retreated, when the light company resumed its position on the right of the line, under the command of Lieutenant W. H. Russell, the subaltern of the company. While the skirmishing was going on, both armies, in much the same formation, were approaching each other. The advance of the French infantry was covered by their cavalry, who made repeated charges upon our columns, but they soon cleared away to allow their infantry to close with ours. The leading French brigade (1st Légère, three battalions, supported by a regiment of Poles), led by General Compère, advanced in line upon Kempt's battalion. Both sides opened fire at a short distance, but that of the English was so deadly that General Compère ordered his brigade to charge.

---

[1] *Narratives of the Great War with France* (page 243), by Lieutenant-General Sir Henry Bunbury, K.C.B.

NOTE.—Captain Murdoch McLean was the son of G. McLean, Esquire, of Scalle Castle, in the Isle of Mull, and was a brother of Matorga McLean. Captain McLean was a popular officer. There is a small memorial of his name and manner of death in the mess of the 1st Battalion, in the form of a silver snuff-box; it bears the following inscription, which is surmounted by a laurel wreath and the XX:—

MURDOCH MCLEAN
QUI IN PROELIO CECIDIT
4 JULII, 1806.

As they drew near, with disordered ranks, Kempt gave the word, and the light battalion sprang forward to meet them. General Bunbury thus describes this portion of the fight: "But the two lines were not parallel; the light companies of the XX and 35th encountered the extreme left of the French, but the rest of the brigade broke before their bayonets crossed. They had, however, come too close to escape; it was a headlong route; General Compère fell badly wounded within our ranks, and his brigade was utterly dispersed with fearful slaughter, which was continued over a long extent of plain, and the lower falls of the hill of Maida."[1] In the meanwhile, in other portions of the field, both sides fought without gaining any material advantage; the English position at this juncture and the advent of the XX is thus told by Sir Henry Bunbury[2] (page 246): "The heat was tremendous; and the result of the day seemed far from certain, when as I was riding along the rear of Cole's brigade, anxiously watching the French sharpshooters, who were stealing farther and farther round his left, and were backed by their horsemen, one of my assistants came galloping to me from the beach, with the welcome tidings that the XX had landed, and was coming through the brushwood at double quick time.[3] I rode instantly to meet them, and explained to Ross how matters stood. He caught the spirit of the affair in an instant, pressed onward, drove the swarm of sharpshooters before him; gave the French cavalry such a volley, as sent them off in confusion to the rear; and passing beyond the left of Cole's brigade, wheeled

---

[1] *Narratives of the Great War*, page 245.
[2] At Maida, Sir H. Bunbury was Adjutant-General in the absence of Brigadier Campbell.
[3] The main body of regiment, its light company being already in action.

the XX to their right, and opened a shattering fire on the enemy's battalions. The effect was decisive; Reynier was completely taken by surprise at the apparition of the fresh assailant; he made but a short and feeble effort to maintain his ground." By mid-day, the battle was ended, and, except by the light battalion, no attempt was made to follow the enemy; the XX returned to the beach for food and repose. In his despatch, General Stuart bore testimony to the important part played by Colonel Ross and the XX at Maida; but Sir H. Bunbury is more precise in the bestowal of praise. He says: "The most brilliant parts on this little stage were acted by Colonels Kempt and Ross: to them the glory of the fight at Maida is chiefly due." The loss of the XX in this decisive victory was slight; this satisfactory and unfrequent feature is attributable to the skilful manner in which the corps was handled by Colonel Ross, and also perhaps to the fact that it came upon the enemy unexpectedly. The casualties of the Grenadier and light companies were not separately recorded, beyond the statement that they were severe. In the remaining companies of the regiment one man was killed and six wounded.[1] Maida[2] was added to the list of honours borne on the colours of the corps; Lieutenant-Colonel Ross was awarded a gold medal, and appointed aide-de-camp to the King with the rank of colonel in the army.

At daybreak on the 5th, the XX marched from the beach to the little town of Maida, situate on a high hill

---

[1] The numbers killed, wounded, and taken prisoners of the French were enormous. More than five hundred of their bodies were buried by the English on the field of Maida.

[2] The plain of Maida was covered with myrtle bushes, and for many years the anniversary of the battle was celebrated in the regiment, all ranks wearing a sprig of myrtle in their caps.

above the plain. Colonel Kempt, with his light battalion, had advanced some distance along the hills and detached the light company of the XX (now led by Captain Colborne[1]) to follow the enemy and ascertain their intentions. Colborne pressed forward, naturally thinking that our army was following him. He overtook the rear of the French column, which was marching in very great disorder, but, discovering at the end of the second day that he was entirely without support, he was obliged to fall back on his battalion.[2] On the morning of the 8th July, the XX marched to Pizzo, *en route* for Sicily. At Pizzo the regiment was employed in searching French prisoners who had plundered the military treasury chest. A considerable sum was recovered.

The march was resumed during the night of the 9th; a halt was made at Monteleone, and thence the march was continued through Sumnara and Palma to Scylla Castle. This rock fortress was at this time besieged by the British. The XX was brought here to take part in the storming of the Castle. Unfortunately the details connected therewith are few.[3] The regiment

---

[1] Captain Colborne succeeded to the command of the light company after the battle of Maida.

[2] Many of the advantages won at Maida were thus thrown away. No attempt was made to follow up the victory. On the evening of the 4th July, the Admiral entertained the General (Sir J. Stuart) on board the flag-ship. Sir H. Bunbury, who was present, states, "that they had no discussion of ulterior objects, nor concerted any plans, but talked of Turkish ladies and Greek girls, and the Admiral closed the evening by instructing the General in the art of wreathing shawls and putting on the turban after the fashion of the most refined Turkish ladies."

NOTE.—In Allison's *History of Europe*, vol. ix, for the XX is printed 26th Regiment.

[3] We have not been able to find any official account of the siege and surrender of Scylla. In 1806 it was no doubt an event of small importance. The subjoined extracts from the *Adventures of an Aide-de-Camp*, by James Grant, refer to this operation, but we cannot vouch for their authenticity; it should, however, be stated that the author's father served with his regiment in this campaign; and further, that Grant's description of Maida and other incidents of the war agree in almost every

bivouacked on a range of low hills which commanded the fort, and it took part in the assault by which the place was carried.

Leaving a detachment under Major Walker to form part of the garrison of Scylla, the regiment commenced, on the afternoon of the 12th, a tiresome, down-hill march, mule tracks alone marking the way over very rough ground, to the town of Bagnara, where they arrived about midnight and remained until the 15th. On this day the regiment embarked on board the transport "Malabar" and some feluccas for passage to Reggio, where they were landed. On the 20th July the regiment crossed the Straits of Messina, and occupied its former cantonments along the coast from the town of Messina to the Faro light. In November a company of Sicilians was organised and added to the regiment. The XX marched from Messina to Melazzo, in relief of the 35th Regiment, during the month of November, and was joined on the line of march by the flank companies; they had been detached on the first formation of the expedition, at Malta, in October, 1805.

Melazzo proved an unhealthy station; at one time, during the summer of 1807, half the officers and about three hundred men were ill from fever. To explain the subsequent movements of the corps, it is necessary to

---

particular with the historical records, even to the names of the officers, with the exception that there was no officer of the name of Dundas serving under Sir John Stuart. "The casemates are vaulted with solid masonry, they are in the flanks of bastions, and are capable of containing a company each. They have six thirty-twos to sweep the exterior slopes of the advanced fort, in endeavouring to cross which Colonel Ross has lost some of the bravest fellows in the ranks of the XX" (page 247). In describing the forlorn hope, he says: "A glow of courage that would make one face the devil took possession of my breast when the stormers, two hundred in number, selected from the volunteers of the XX, threw off their knapsacks, blankets, and canteens, and were handed over to me by their Adjutant" (page 255).

give a brief account of one incident of the foreign policy pursued by the English Government at this time. The Government was anxious to further the emigration to the Brazils of the royal family of Portugal; for this purpose they kept a naval force, under Sir Sydney Smith, off Lisbon. Suddenly a Russian squadron, under Admiral Siniavin, took refuge in the Tagus. It was supposed, as Russia and England were in a state of hostility, that the presence of the Russian ships would intimidate the Prince Regent, and prevent his leaving Portugal. Sir Charles Cotton was, therefore, sent with instructions to force the Tagus and to attack Admiral Siniavin. To ensure success, General Spencer with five thousand, and Sir John Moore with ten thousand men (the latter being withdrawn from Sicily), were ordered to Lisbon to aid the enterprise; but, before the instructions were written, the Prince was on his voyage to the Brazils, and Marshal Junot ruled in Lisbon.

The XX proceeded from Melazzo to Messina in October, 1807, and there joined the expeditionary force under the command of Lieutenant-General Sir John Moore.[1] On the 28th of October, the transports with the division on board sailed from Messina. In clearing the harbour, the ship "Windermere," with the headquarters of the XX on board, ran aground. Three companies were immediately sent ashore to lighten the ship, and at high tide (twelve midnight) she was got off and passed safely out of the harbour, but only to strike on the rocks near the Faro Lighthouse at three o'clock on the following morning and become a total wreck. The regiment landed without loss of life or accident, and encamped until the afternoon of the 30th.

---

[1] The following regiments composed the force: 1st and 3rd battalion of Guards, XX, 35th, 52nd, 61st, 78th Regiments, and De Watteville's corps.

The companies that had been sent ashore in Messina harbour were taken on board the transport ship "Ajax." This vessel called at the Faro Light and embarked the headquarters, sailed again at nine p.m, and came up with the convoy the following evening (31st October). The transport fleet reached Gibraltar on the 2nd of December. The XX was transferred from the "Ajax" to the "Atlas" transport on the 13th December, and, together with the rest of Sir John Moore's force, sailed for England on the 18th, arriving at Spithead on the 31st of December, 1807.

In compliance with the quarantine regulations, the regiment was detained on board ship for three days. On the 3rd January, 1808, the disembarkation took place at Portsmouth, and the corps proceeded by march route to Brabourne Lees, in Kent, where it arrived on the 13th January, after an absence from England of eight years, having during this period taken part in two campaigns. The regiment being considerably below its establishment, recruiting parties were sent to Cambridge, Exeter, and Ipswich. The Sicilian company, which had been raised and added to the regiment whilst serving in Sicily, was ordered to the Isle of Wight, *en route* to join the Sicilian regiment at Malta. Some of the Sicilians were, at their own request, allowed to continue their service in the XX. On the 26th and 27th days of May, the regiment marched in two divisions to Colchester, where it arrived on the 2nd and 3rd June, and on the 23rd marched from Colchester to Ipswich, preparatory to embarkation for Portugal.

Chapter XVIII.

1808-1809.

Embarkation at Harwich—Portugal—Battle of Vimiera—March to the Frontier of Portugal—Fort Lalippe—March into Spain—The Regiment joins Sir John Moore's Army—The Retreat on Coruña—The Battle—Arrival in England—Mortality among the Survivors.

THE regiment embarked at Harwich on the 18th July, 1808, and arrived at the mouth of the Tagus on the 18th of August. Seven companies, under Lieutenant-Colonel Campbell, landed in the Bay of Maceira, near Peniché, and lay on the sands till daybreak, when they marched to Vimiera, and formed part of the 8th Brigade, commanded by Brigadier-General Ackland, in the army under Sir Arthur Wellesley. Owing to a scarcity of boats, the headquarters were not disembarked.

Already, on the 17th day of August, Sir Arthur Wellesley had defeated the French in the combat of Roriça; and at eight o'clock on the morning of the 21st August, the French cavalry were seen on the heights to the south of the village of Vimiera. The 2nd, 3rd, 4th, and 8th Brigades were immediately directed to cross the valley behind the village, and take position on the heights, which were occupied by our piquets.

As these brigades reached the ground, the second and third were disposed into two lines facing to the left; the 4th and 8th Brigades were to have furnished a third line, but before the latter had reached the summit, observing a French brigade advancing against the centre, they attacked it in the flank and forced it back on the main body.

The enemy was repulsed at all points, and the battle won by noon. The 8th Brigade suffered very little, the casualties of the XX being as follows:—Lieutenant Brook killed, Lieutenant Hogg and five men wounded, and one man missing.

In this action the light company, under Captain C. Steevens, was detached, and, together with two companies of the 95th (Rifle Brigade), was employed to clear some of the enemy's riflemen out of a wood in front of our centre.

The headquarters of the regiment, under Colonel Ross, landed on the afternoon of the 21st. The regiment marched from Vimiera[1] on the 23rd of August, and bivouacked near the village of Amilla; thence it marched to Torres Vedras on the 31st August, and on the following days to Mafra and Cintra, and encamped at Becarinha, near to the latter place. When wood could be obtained, the troops were hutted, but otherwise they were exposed to all weathers. On the conclusion of the Convention of Cintra, the XX was ordered to Elvas; it crossed the Tagus to Aldea Gallega, and thence marched through the towns of Conya, Montemor, Nuevo, Vende de Duc, Aryolas, Estremos, Alberoca, and Villa Viciosa. In all these towns the regiment was received by the people with acclamations of gratitude and joy. At Estremos the inhabitants presented it with two fine bullocks, and to both officers and men offered refreshments of bread, wine, and fruit. The bullocks, their horns decorated with ribbons, were driven out of the town at the head of the regiment. The XX remained a few days at

---

[1] In Napier's *History of the War*, the place where this battle was fought is called Vimiero, but in Sir A. Wellesley's despatch it is as above. This applies to other towns and villages in Spain and Portugal which are mentioned.

Villa Viciosa, and during its stay the Lady Abbess and nuns of the convent extended their hospitality to the officers. Colonel Ross, with the regiment, having been appointed by Sir Hew Dalrymple to receive Fort Lalippe from the French, and to escort the garrison to Lisbon under the terms of the convention, sent a flag of truce to the commandant, Colonel Girod.

Major Colborne, who carried the flag of truce, was furnished with an autograph letter from General Kellerman: he was received by Girod with civility, but the latter refused to surrender his post without more complete proof of the authenticity of the treaty, and, with this in view, proposed that a French officer should proceed to Lisbon to verify the information; not that he affected to doubt the truth of Colborne's information, but that he would not surrender his charge while the slightest doubt, capable of being removed, attached to the transaction.[1] On the 25th September, the regiment moved from Villa Viciosa to Elvas,[2] and occupied the town barracks, sending two companies to Fort St. Lucia, and a detachment to take possession of the outer works of Fort Lalippe the same evening. The French evacuated the fortress at daybreak on the 26th, and were escorted by a detachment of the XX as far as Estremos, where they were handed over to the 2nd Queen's. The regiment occupied Fort Lalippe, and remained there until the 9th October, when it returned to Elvas, and was quartered in the convent of Saint Paulo.

---

[1] Napier's *History of the Peninsular War*, vol. i, page 100.

[2] Steevens writes, "Here, as at Villa Viciosa, we used to chat with the nuns through the iron grating, and one of our officers (Lieutenant W——), a handsome young fellow, fell in love with one of them, a very pretty girl; the affection seemed reciprocal, and, I believe, they were both equally sorry when the regiment marched away."

On the 28th of October, the regiment marched from Elvas, and passing through Campo Mayor, Albuquerque, Alcede, Brosas, Alcantara, Morilezza, *en route* to Ciudad Rodrigo, arrived at the latter place on the 10th November, having covered one hundred and sixty miles in the march.

The regiment left Ciudad Rodrigo on the 15th November, and reached Salamanca on the 18th, and was quartered in the convent of Saint Thomas, with five companies of the 95th and 1st Battalion 52nd Regiments. Sir John Moore's army (of which the regiment now formed a part) was concentrated at Salamanca on the 23rd November, but want of supplies and transport obliged the Commander to order the march of his army in small and successive divisions.[1]

On the 2nd December, the XX was employed in placing the village of Castilianos da Morisco in a state of defence, so that it would be in a position to repel the enemy's cavalry, who were in the vicinity in numerous bodies, making raids on surrounding villages.

The XX marched from Salamanca on the 11th, and arrived at Toro on the 12th of December: advanced from Toro on the 16th, and on succeeding days halted at Tedra, Villapando, Valderas, Santierbo, and Graghal, the latter place being the advanced post of the army. From Salamanca to Graghal the distance was one hundred and thirty miles. The regiment halted at Graghal on the 22nd and 23rd. On the evening of the latter day they were kept under arms, and left their quarters about nine o'clock on a bitterly cold night. It was Sir John Moore's intention to make a night-march and fall on Marshal Soult's division of the French

---

[1] *History of the Peninsular War*, vol. i, page 177.

army at Saldaña at daybreak the 24th. The XX had not proceeded far when it was ordered back to its quarters. The Commander-in-Chief had gained his object; he had drawn Napoleon from Madrid, and the Emperor had now put 50,000 men in motion from the capital to compass the ruin of the British. This intelligence reached Sir John as his army was moving on Saldaña.[1]

The retreat on Coruña commenced on the following day (24th); but the XX with the reserve,[2] under the personal direction of the Commander-in-Chief, marched on the 25th (Christmas Day).[3] A heavy storm, followed by torrents of rain, with a piercing wind, was the beginning of a retreat, unparalleled for sufferings and hardships in the annals of the British army. The reserve fell back by the road of Mayorga, and crossed the Esla by the bridge of Castro Gonzalo on the morning of the 26th.[4] During this period of the retreat, the XX formed the rear-guard of the reserve. Being preceded by the other divisions of the army, the reserve fared very badly for provisions, etc. On the 27th, the XX reached the town of Benevente. At daybreak on the 29th, the town was surprised by the enemy's cavalry: the regiment turned out to support our cavalry under Lord Paget, who defeated the enemy and took their leader, General Lefebre Desnouettes, prisoner.[5] A blanket was supplied to

---

[1] *History of the Peninsular War*, vol. i, pages 190, 191.

[2] The regiments forming the reserve were the XX, 28th, 52nd, 91st, and 95th.

[3] "On this same day we lost one of our men in a melancholy way, and a fine young man he was; he was in the Grenadier company; he was eating a piece of roll or new bread, while walking along and talking to his comrades on the march, when part of it stuck in his throat and choked him."—*Reminiscences of My Military Life*, page 62.

[4] *History of the Peninsular War*, vol. i, page 191.

[5] A favourite officer of Napoleon's, to whom he bequeathed a legacy of 100,000 francs.

J

each officer and soldier at Benevente. The regiment marched from this place on the night of the 29th, arrived at Astorga on the 31st of December, and was quartered in a convent outside the town. Some Spanish fugitive troops had entered the town previous to the arrival of the British, and caused a tumult and confusion that increased the difficulties of maintaining discipline and of obtaining supplies during the remainder of the retreat. On the 31st December, the regiment marched to Cambarros, a village six miles from Astorga.

Previous to marching, Colonel Ross addressed each company, and explained to the men that upon their own perseverance, patience, and keeping their ranks depended their own safety, and perhaps that of the army. During the remainder of the retreat the officers, by the Colonel's orders, had to remain at all times with their companies, whether in billets, quarters, or in the bivouac. During the night of the 31st, the cavalry fell back upon Cambarros, and the reserve had in consequence to march to Bambibre. This was distressing— a night-march of eight miles, carried out in a heavy snowstorm and severe frost. At Bembibre our men witnessed the most disgusting scenes of drunkenness among the stragglers of the preceding divisions.

The horrors of the line of march were now appalling and touched the hearts of the most callous. One officer relates:[1] "It was dreadful to see the numbers of dead lying by the roadside, consisting of men, and sometimes women and children; once or twice I saw a little infant lying close to its mother, both dead; also horses, asses, mules, and oxen, some frozen to death,

---

[1] *Reminiscences of My Military Life*, pages 68—73.

having been overcome by fatigue; others were shot. During the retreat a little boy was found whose parents were supposed to have perished. I think he was picked up by Colonel Ross, for I recollect perfectly well seeing him with a child in front of his saddle, but whether or not this little boy was the same I cannot exactly say."[1]

Sir John Moore, with the reserve (except part of the XX) and cavalry, marched to Calcabellos. A portion of the regiment, under Colonel Ross, was left at Bembibre to cover the town and protect the stragglers, about a thousand of whom were in the town when the reserve left on the morning of the 2nd January. The French cavalry were kept in check for some time by Colonel Ross's rear-guard; but neither threats, nor the near approach of the enemy's cavalry, would induce the majority of the stragglers to leave the town. As the French cavalry was now appearing in great force, Colonel Ross ordered the destruction of the surplus arms, ammunition, stores, and baggage, and left the stragglers to their fate. The XX had hardly quitted the town when the cavalry entered it, charging through the long line of stragglers, who were so insensible from liquor, as neither to make any resistance, nor get out of the way of the horsemen as they cut to the right and left. The pursuit was continued until checked by the XX and 15th Hussars, directed by Major-General Paget. The regiment remained the night at Calcabellos, and was here joined by the Grenadier company of the Buffs, which had been sent from Portugal in charge of specie for Sir John Moore's army. This company returned to England with the XX. The regiment was present at the repulse of the

---

[1] The boy was adopted by the armourer of the regiment, but only lived for a few years.

French cavalry at Calcabellos on the 3rd January, when General Colbert, the French commander, was killed. The regiment took no part in this affair, but Colonel Ross, and all those who witnessed the death of Colbert, expressed their sorrow at the fall of such a gallant soldier.

A man, belonging to one of the regiments, who had left the ranks, and had been taken prisoner by the French, managed to escape and joined the reserve at Calcabellos. Although severely wounded, he was able to walk, his wounds being chiefly in the face and arms.

The French cavalry had cut him about terribly; he was, indeed, a ghastly object to look upon. Colonel Ross showed him to his men as a warning to them of what they might expect if they left the ranks and lagged behind. The Commander-in-Chief withdrew the reserve to Villa Franca, on the evening of the 3rd: the XX remained in rear whilst stores and magazines were being destroyed. When this work was completed, the march was continued to Villa Franca, where its progress was much impeded by the number of stragglers, and by the excesses of which the other divisions had been guilty. Passing through Villa Franca, the regiment halted at Herrerias about midnight, having marched forty miles during the preceding twelve hours. After a few hours' rest at Herrerias, the march was resumed: Noagles was reached in the afternoon of the 4th, after a long and weary tramp, through snow and rain, over almost impassable roads, and with an enterprising enemy in their rear. During this march, the enemy's light cavalry attempted to advance upon the flanks of the reserve, but were attacked and driven back by the light company of the XX, under Captain C. Steevens.

On the morning of the 5th January, £25,000 was thrown away, as the oxen could no longer draw the wagons. The money was rolled down the side of a hill. Towards the evening (5th), the reserve approached Constantino, closely followed by the French. There is a hill close to the bridge which is admirably situated for covering the passage of the river Minho. Sir John Moore ordered the 95th and artillery to occupy the top of this hill. Acting with great caution, the French remained behind another hill. In the meantime, the remainder of the reserve pushed over the bridge without loss, followed by the 95th and artillery. General Paget was then ordered to defend the bridge and banks of the river with the 28th and 95th Regiments, while Sir John Moore placed the XX, 52nd, and 91st Regiments in position on some heights near the river. The positions were hardly taken when the enemy poured down the opposite side of the valley in great force, but, although they renewed their attacks with ever increasing numbers, they were always repulsed with loss.

At ten p.m. the reserve retired to Lugo, where they arrived on the morning of the 6th, after a harassing march of eighteen miles. The XX was quartered in the convent. Between the 3rd and 6th, the regiment had been three times engaged with the enemy. At daybreak on the 7th, the XX took up its position in front of Lugo. The army was drawn up in order of battle, as the Commander-in-Chief wished to engage the French in a decisive action.

The French attacked the British centre and left, but were repulsed with a loss of between three and four hundred men. The army was in line of battle all day on the 8th, but retired during the night. A terrible storm of wind and rain, mixed with sleet, commenced as the regiments broke up from their positions; the road marks were destroyed, and the guides of the different divisions lost the true direction. One division only gained the main road, the other two were still in the vicinity of Lugo at daybreak on the 9th.[1] The XX, together with the other regiments of the reserve, covered the retreat of the army, and held a position near Betanzos during the night of the 9th. The sufferings endured by the regiment up to this date were terrible. Both officers and men were in a state of starvation; many were without shoes, and all were in rags.

On the 11th they arrived at El Burgo, and were quartered in the villages on the St. Jago road. Of the regiments forming the reserve, Napier says: "For twelve days these hardy soldiers had covered the retreat, during which time they had traversed eighty miles of road in two marches, passed several nights under arms in the snow of the mountains, were seven times engaged with the enemy, and they now assembled at the outposts, having fewer men missing from the ranks (including those who had fallen in battle) than any other division in the army."[2]

Sir John Moore accompanied the reserve during the retreat; his cheerful and courteous manner sustained the drooping spirits of the suffering soldiers; he praised and held up their superior discipline during the retreat, as an example to the rest of the army, and warmly applauded their gallant conduct in action. To its honour it must be recorded that the XX lost fewer men during the retreat than any other regiment serving

---

[1] *History of the Peninsular War*, vol. i, page 201.
[2] *Ibid.*, vol. i, page 202.

in the expedition. From the confidence the Commander-in-Chief had in its experienced and distinguished commander,[1] and from the tried character of the corps, it was selected for some of the most dangerous and arduous services during the whole retreat.

At El Burgo the regiment was relieved from all duty, on account of the arduous duties it had performed. Captain Steevens relates that he was in command of an outpost, which was visited by Sir John Moore, who, finding that the regiment was still on duty, ordered it to be at once relieved, as he wished it to get as much rest as possible. A few miles from the town, four thousand barrels of gunpowder were stored in a magazine; to prevent their falling into the hands of the enemy they were exploded on the 13th. There was a terrific crash, the ground trembled, the houses were shaken, and the vibration was felt by the vessels in the harbour. The next act of destruction was of a very painful character. It was found impossible to embark the horses; they were all shot or stabbed, and then thrown from the edge of an overhanging rock into the sea.

At two p.m. on the 16th January, a general movement was observed in the French lines. At three o'clock, Marshal Soult commenced the battle with a heavy cannonade, and at the same time three strong columns, led by a cloud of skirmishers, poured down upon the British: they carried the village of Evina, and drove in our piquets. The Commander-in-Chief ordered General Paget with the reserve, with exception of one regiment which was stationed at Airis, to turn the enemy's left and threaten their great

---

[1] In addition to his great professional ability, Colonel Ross was one of the few officers who could speak French and Spanish.

battery. The XX, with the other regiments of the reserve, descended into the valley, attacked and quickly forced the enemy to retire. They continued the pursuit to a great distance, dispersing everything that came before them, until the enemy, perceiving that their left flank was exposed, drew it entirely back. As the evening closed (six p.m.) the British were in advance of their original positions, and the French were retiring in confusion at all points. Not long after giving the order which led to this brilliant attack, Sir John Moore, the Commander of our army, was killed. After the battle the XX bivouacked, without fires, and at midnight marched through Coruña, and embarked on board the transports. On the voyage home a storm scattered the fleet, and the ships put into the nearest ports. The regiment disembarked at Falmouth, Plymouth, and Portsmouth, between the 21st and 31st of January, 1809, and marched to Colchester, where the different parties were assembled by the 20th of February. There is no record of the loss suffered by the XX in the retreat and battle of Coruña; the casualties of Sir John Moore's army were never officially reported.[1]

On landing in England the men of the regiment were in a deplorable condition. Worn and haggard in appearance; clothing in rags; many without shoes;[2] few had their arms and accoutrements complete; and all were in a state of filth, which they neither had the power nor means of avoiding. Of the survivors a large number reached England, only to become the victims of a deadly fever with which this ill-fated army was stricken, and to find an early grave in their native land.

---

[1] Not in the *London Gazette*.
[2] "During the retreat some of the officers were without shoes."—*Steevens*.

CHAPTER XIX.

1809-1812.

Recruiting—March to Dover—Embarkation at Deal—Landing at South Beveland—Malarial Fever—Return to England—A Skeleton Battalion—Deaths—Presentation to Colonel Ross—Sail for Ireland—Kinsale—Mallow—Training for Active Service—Fermoy—March to Middleton—Suppression of Illegal Assemblies—Inspection by Lord Forbes.

THE last campaign had reduced the regiment to a mere skeleton, and it was found necessary in consequence, in order to place it in a state fit to take the field, to call for volunteers from various regiments of militia. In the month of April, 1809, eleven officers and five hundred and thirteen non-commissioned officers and men joined the regiment. Many men were also drawn to the colours of the corps by recruiting parties, which were sent to Norwich, Aldborough, and Rochester.

On the 4th and 5th days of July, 1809, the XX marched from Colchester, *en route* to Dover, where the two divisions arrived on the 10th and 11th, and were quartered in Dover Castle.

The regiment was selected for service with the expedition, which was about to proceed to the Scheldt, and it was attached to the brigade of Major-General Graham, which formed part of the reserve commanded by Lieutenant-General Sir John Hope.

At daybreak, on the 26th of July, the regiment marched from Dover to Deal, and embarked on board H.M.S. "Monmouth" at nine a.m: sailed on the morning of the 28th, and arrived off the Scheldt the same evening. With the first tide the "Monmouth" moved up the eastern branch of the Scheldt, and anchored near the Katten Dyke.

The XX landed, on the 1st August, on the South Beveland, and marched to the village of Heinrichskindren. Two companies, commanded by Major C. Steevens, were sent to the village of Boesselle; they took possession of two batteries, which the French had evacuated a few days previous to the arrival of the regiment. The XX continued its march in this pestilential swamp; passed through the towns of Goes and Heytkensant, and, on the 9th of August, went into cantonments at the villages of Schore and Walke, the headquarters occupying the former. About the 1st of September, an epidemic of malarial fever (afterwards known as Walcheren fever) raged among the troops; one-third of the XX was sick and unfit for duty. On the 3rd of September, the regiment retired through Ter Goes; the invalids were sent to Katten Dyke, and were put on board ship for passage to England. On the following day, the regiment crossed to Wolversdyke, an island lying between north and south Beveland. During this expedition the XX was not engaged; on one occasion Colonel Ross pursued some of the enemy with the light company, but did not come up with them, and was not under fire.

The regiment marched to Kningspladana, on the 6th September, and embarked on board the "Spectro" and "Ganges," seventy-four-gun ships, but were transferred on the afternoon of the same day to the "Bucephalus" and "St. Fiorenzo" frigates, headquarters being on board the first-named ship. The frigates sailed on the following day, reached Harwich on the 15th, and the regiment landed on the 16th, with orders to proceed to Colchester.

The appearance of the regiment on its return to Colchester was lamentable: about three hundred men, and those weak and sickly, with barely sufficient strength to walk, was all it could muster. At this date, six hundred men were in hospital at different places.

Within the short space of nine months, the XX was twice reduced to a skeleton battalion; on the first occasion by war, pestilence, and famine, and on the second by sickness alone. Captain Robinson, Ensign Mills, and a large number of men died after the return of the corps to Colchester. Towards the end of this year (1809), Major John Murray, on behalf of the officers, presented a valuable sword to Colonel Ross, as a recognition of their appreciation of his high qualities as officer in command of the corps. On the 28th of June, 1810, the regiment marched to Harwich, and embarked on board transports, which sailed on the 5th July, and arrived at the Cove of Cork on the 25th, when it disembarked and marched to Kinsale. The headquarters and four companies were accommodated in Fort Charles, and six companies in the new barracks. On the 1st of November, the XX was relieved at Kinsale by the 6th Regiment, and proceeded to Mallow, *viâ* Cork.

The change to Mallow proved very beneficial to the men who were suffering from the Walcheren fever. The regiment remained here for eighteen months, and through the indefatigable exertions of its commanding officer, Colonel Ross, it attained the highest standard of efficiency. The whole corps passed through a course of instruction in drill, and in the duties of a regiment in the field; every conceivable contingency of actual warfare being carefully and frequently rehearsed. On the 8th of May, 1812, the regiment marched to Fermoy.

The right wing, under Colonel Ross, proceeded from Fermoy to Middleton by a circuitous route on the 29th June. The line of march lay through disaffected districts, and many illegal assemblies were suppressed *en route*. The right wing remained at Middleton, and was there joined by the left wing, on the 18th September, when the regiment was inspected by Major-General Lord Forbes.

CHAPTER XX.

1812–1813.

Embarkation for Coruña—Landed at Lisbon—*En route* to join the Army—Forced Marches—Battle of Vittoria—Pursuit of the Enemy—Colonel Ross promoted Major-General—Combat at Roncesvalles—Captain Tovey's Company—Casualties—Soult's Despatch—The Retreat—Battle of Sauroren—Lord Wellington's Despatch—Pursuit—Skirmishes—Colonel Wauchope mortally Wounded—The Light Troops—Colonel Steevens succeeds to the Command—First Distribution of Colour Badges—Casualties in the Battles of the Pyrenees.

ON the 12th of October, 1812, the regiment marched from Middleton to the Cove of Cork, and embarked; the headquarters on the "Alfred," seventy-four-gun ship, the remainder of the corps on the troop-ships "Dover" and "Roebuck." The convoy sailed on the following day, and anchored in the harbour of Coruña on the 27th October. The troops landed on the 28th, but re-embarked on the 29th and sailed for Lisbon, where they disembarked at the arsenal on the 15th November, and were quartered in some of the convents in that city. The regiment marched from Lisbon on the 15th of December, under Colonel Ross, *en route* to join the army commanded by Lord Wellington, halted at Leira on the 24th and 25th of December, and at Coimbra from the 29th to the 31st December. On the 12th of January, 1813, the XX reached St. John de Pesquira, and went into cantonments, forming, together with the 7th and 23rd Fusiliers, Major-General Skerret's brigade in the 4th Division, commanded by

Lieutenant-General Sir Lowry Cole, G.C.B.[1] On the 27th of February, the regiment was in quarters at Villacova; on the 3rd March, it crossed the Coa, and was billeted in the town of Almendra. The regiment re-crossed the Coa on the 18th of May, and encamped at Villacova. At daybreak on the 20th, it crossed the Douro, and advanced towards Miranda, which was occupied on the 23rd. The regiment was inspected at this place by Lieutenant-General Sir T. Graham, on the 26th May. On the 31st, the corps crossed the Esla by a pontoon bridge, and during this day had its first skirmish with the enemy. The regiment continued to advance by forced marches, passing through the cities of Zamora, Toro, and on the 7th of June encamped in the town of Palencia, which the French had only left that morning. The river Ebro was crossed on the 15th of June, and on the 18th the town of Osma was occupied.

In addition to long and forced marches, through a rough and mountainous country, the men had often to drag the guns of the artillery, at places where the roads were rendered impassable for horses by the heavy rains.

The XX was in position before Vittoria on the 20th June. At daybreak on the 21st, under a heavy drenching rain, it advanced on Vittoria, and formed up on the left of the main road leading to that town. It subsequently crossed the Zadora river by the bridge of Nanclares, in support of the guns of the division. In this action the regiment was only slightly engaged and its loss was trifling, viz., three men killed and two wounded. The retiring foe was closely followed by

---

[1] The regiment was posted to the 4th Division at the request of General Sir Lowry Cole.

the XX until about nine p.m., when the darkness precluded further pursuit.

The regiment had been under arms since five a.m., and during the interval of sixteen hours had had no rations[1] of any kind. While on the march, and towards the close of the day, they came to a field of beans. The pangs of hunger were so acute, that the men rushed into the field, tore up the beans by the roots, and devoured them voraciously. The officers thought it excusable, but the General expressed his displeasure.[2] On the following day the pursuit was resumed, and the regiment bivouacked at Salvateirra.

The French retreated towards Pampeluna—the XX encamped within sight of that town on the 26th of June. Since the battle of Vittoria the regiment formed part of a force with which, by a series of forced marches, Lord Wellington endeavoured to cut off the French General (Clausel) before he could enter Tudela. On the 1st of July, the XX went into quarters in the town of Aybar, after a continuous march of six weeks; during this period it had traversed six hundred miles over rugged and zigzag flinty roads, along winding valleys, over difficult mountains, and through dense forests. Colonel Robert Ross[3] was promoted Major-General on the staff of the army (dated 1st of June, 1813), and appointed to command the brigade in which the XX was serving in the Peninsular. Lieutenant-Colonel Andrew Wauchope succeeded to the command of the corps, consequent on the promotion of General Ross.

---

[1] The ration consisted of 1lb. beef, 1lb. biscuit, and a small allowance of rum or wine. The biscuit, rum, and reserve ammunition were carried by the mules, and the muleteers had also to drive the bullocks. They always followed in rear of the division, and often did not arrive in camp for some hours after the regiment, and occasionally did not reach it before the troops had commenced another march.

[2] Steevens.   [3] For services of General Ross, see Appendix.

From the 6th to the 17th July the regiment was cantoned at Villalba, and formed part of the blockading force before Pampeluna. On the 18th of July, it was relieved by a Spanish regiment, and moved to an encampment near Zubiri; on the next day, it marched to Espinal, two miles in advance of Viscayret, in the valley of Urroz.

About midnight, on the 24th of July, the regiment was called to arms, and, at daybreak on the 25th, moved up the Mendichuri Pass. On reaching a point about half way up the Lindouz ridge, Major-General Ross halted the right wing, and led the left wing and a company of Oels Brunswickers up the heights. When they gained the summit, they suddenly came upon the enemy's skirmishers, whose fire proved troublesome to the wing. General Ross called for a company to drive them away, and without waiting for further orders, Captain George Tovey doubled his (number 6 now F.) company out, and soon cleared the skirmishers from the wooded hollow in front of the wing, but when they came to the opposite side of the wood, they unexpectedly came face to face with a strong column (6th Light Infantry) of the enemy, which was in the act of mounting the ridge from the opposite side to that by which the wing had ascended. The French commander called upon the men of the company to lay down their arms; but Captain Tovey answered by ordering his company to charge with the bayonet. They rushed headlong into the French column, killing the commander and two other officers and many men with the bayonet. The French were almost paralysed with astonishment at finding themselves, a regiment in column, attacked by such a handful of men; but they soon recovered from their consternation, and Captain Tovey called aloud to his men to retire. One sergeant, one corporal, and twenty-two men of the company were killed or wounded in this affair.[1] The left wing retired to the base of the ridge (followed by Tovey's men), where the right, under Brevet-Major Bent, had taken up a strong position, and was ready to receive the enemy, who now made a series of desperate attacks, the officers leading and urging their men with great vehemence. But this furious bravery was of no avail, the XX stood firm and unshaken; the French were met with withering volleys, and any of them who happened to reach our ranks were bayoneted. No prisoners were taken during this day's fight. The post was held until the remainder of the brigade came up, and thus it was that Marshal Soult received his first repulse in the Pyrenees. In this combat (called Roncesvalles) the XX suffered severely; the adjutant (Lieutenant F. Buist), two sergeants, two corporals, and ten privates were killed; twelve privates were missing, and two sergeants, two corporals, and ninety-eight privates were wounded. The following officers were wounded: Lieutenant-Colonel W. Wallace (died of his wounds on the 15th August), Brevet-Major Bent, Lieutenants Champagné, Crokat, Walker, Smith, Ensigns Thompson and Oakley.[2]

---

[1] An interesting correspondence with regard to the action of this company took place in 1839, between Captain Tovey and an officer of the Rifle Brigade.—See Appendix.

[2] Ensign R. C. Oakley was gazetted to the XX on the 7th March, 1811. He was promoted Lieutenant on the 21st October, 1813, and Captain on the 27th December, 1827. He was present at the battle of Vittoria, the combat at Roncesvalles, where he was wounded. He served with the regiment in St. Helena and in India. Captain Oakley died at Belgaum on the 2nd June, 1835. He was an officer of great piety, whose good influence was felt throughout the regiment. He taught in the day and Sunday schools, and worked for the spiritual benefit of the men. To show the respect in which he was held by all ranks, a monument was erected to his memory in Bodmin Church by the officers, non-commissioned officers, and men of the regiment.

K

Of the earlier or first period of the fight at Roncesvalles, Napier writes:[1] "The head of Ross's column, composed of a wing of the XX regiment and a company of Brunswickers, was on the summit of the Lindouz, where most unexpectedly it encountered Reille's advance guard. The moment was critical, but Ross, an eager, hardy soldier, called aloud to charge, and Captain Tovey, of the XX, running forward with his company, crossed a slight wooded hollow and full against the front of the 6th French Light Infantry dashed with the bayonet. Brave men fell by that weapon on both sides, but, numbers prevailing, these daring soldiers were pushed back again by the French. Ross, however, gained his object; the remainder of his brigade had come up, and the pass of Atalosti was secured, yet with a loss of one hundred and forty men of the XX regiment and forty-one of the Brunswickers."

In his despatch, dated Linzoain, 26th July, 1813, Marshal Soult represents the French regiment as having made the bayonet charge, and the XX being nearly destroyed in consequence.

The Adjutant (Lieutenant Buist) was buried at night, with all the honour and ceremony that the time and circumstances would permit. At midnight the regiment was ordered to retire. From want of transport, and the difficulties of a night-march in a mountainous district, it was impossible to move the wounded with the regiment; they were, therefore, placed near the camp fires, a card being attached to each, with a few words written thereon committing him to the mercy and aid of the French, who to their honour treated

---

[1] *History of the Peninsular*, vol. iii, page 251.

ours as they did their own wounded. The fog, which had added intenseness to the darkness of the previous night, had not cleared until some hours after sunrise on the 26th; it shrouded the movements of the regiment, and enabled it to retire without molestation from the enemy. At two p.m. on the 26th, the battalion was on the heights of Linzoain, and halted there until midnight, when the retreat was resumed through the Zubiri valley, and at noon on the 27th a position was taken up on a rocky ridge above the town of Huarte, within sight of Pampeluna.

During the afternoon of the 27th, the regiment moved about a mile in advance of the position of the morning, piled arms, and bivouacked for the night. About midnight, a terrific thunderstorm raged, accompanied by wind and rain; the men were wet through as they lay without covering. On the morning of the 28th, the XX was in line of battle, on the left of the British position, which was on a rugged height overlooking the Lanz river and the road to Villalba: immediately in their front was a small chapel held by the 7th Cacadores (Portuguese). The battle of Sauroren was an affair of some importance, and the part taken in it by the XX was as follows: About noon, a column of the enemy forced its way up to the chapel; the Portuguese at once fell back, but were rallied by Major-General Ross, and, together with the XX, charged the French with a shout that rang through the hills above the rattle of the musketry, and sent them tumbling down through the woods in indescribable confusion. But the enemy quickly reformed, and again attacked, but were a second time repulsed and broken. Additional columns now appearing on the right of the XX, it was forced to retire by the strength of the assailing masses on their front and right flank. The enemy gained the crest which had been so gallantly defended; but here the struggle was renewed with the whole brigade, and both sides were mixed together in the desperate confusion of a hand-to-hand conflict. At this moment Lord Wellington brought the 27th and 48th Regiments on to the scene, and sent them against the French, who were driven down the heights, and were totally routed and defeated. We cannot refrain from giving one quotation from Sir William Napier's history, in which he deals with the struggle on the crest of the ridge before the 27th and 48th joined in the fray. He says: "The 10th Portuguese regiment fighting on the right of Ross's brigade yielded to their fury; a heavy body crowned the heights and wheeling against the exposed flank of Ross forced that gallant officer also to go back. His ground was instantly occupied by the enemies with whom he had been engaged in front, and the fight raged close and desperate on the crest of the position; charge succeeded charge, and each side yielded and recovered by turns."[1] The loss of the XX on this occasion was Captain Murdoch McKenzie and eighteen men killed; Captains John Murray, Edward Jackson (severely), Lieutenants R. L. Lewis (severely), J. H. Bainbrigge[2] (lost right arm), C. Connor, and T. Falls[3] (severely), two sergeants and eighty-one wounded.

The following extracts from the despatch of Lord Wellington, dated San Estevan, 1st August, 1813,

---

[1] *History of the Peninsular War*, vol. iii, page 261. From the same work we learn that Lord Wellington called it bludgeon work.

[2] For a narrative of these and other actions, by General J. H. Bainbrigge, see Appendix.

[3] Lieutenant Thomas Falls was aide-de-camp to General Ross, and continued to serve on the General's staff until his death at Baltimore. Lieutenant Falls reached the rank of a General Officer.

refer to these combats: "In the actions which took place this day (25th July), the XX regiment distinguished themselves." . . . "In the course of this contest (28th July) the gallant 4th Division, which had been so frequently distinguished in this army, surpassed their former good conduct. Every regiment charged with the bayonet, and the 7th, XX, 23rd, and 40th Regiments, four different times. Their officers set them the example, and Major-General Ross had two horses shot under him." The despatch concludes with this paragraph: "It is impossible to describe the enthusiastic bravery of the 4th Division; and I am much indebted to Lieutenant-General Sir Lowry Cole for the manner in which he directed their operations. Major-General Ross and all the officers commanding, and officers of the regiments, were remarkable for their gallantry."

On the 29th of July, the XX pushed through the Pass of Vilate in pursuit of the enemy. The regiment was engaged in an unimportant skirmish on the 30th. On the 1st of August, the regiment ascended the heights above San Estevan, and attacked the French rear-guard. During the day the regiment was frequently engaged in detached positions. They made several charges with the bayonet, capturing much baggage and making a large number of prisoners. Lieutenant Fitzgerald was slightly wounded. On the 2nd of August, the XX marched from Yanzi, and in the afternoon took part in an attack on the front of the enemy's position at Echallar which resulted in the defenders being driven out with considerable loss. The particulars of this engagement are very meagre, but it is recorded that the XX rendered very timely aid to the 6th Regiment. Lieutenant-Colonel Wauchope (the officer commanding the regiment) was mortally wounded whilst in the act of assisting some wounded men of the corps. He died at Passages on the 15th of September.[1] Ensign Wrixon and one man were killed, Lieutenants Rotton (severely), Lutyens, six sergeants, and twenty-five rank and file wounded.

In all the actions fought on the Pyrenees, the light companies of Major-General Ross's brigade were commanded by Major A. Rose, who proved a very enterprising leader of light troops.

Brevet Lieutenant-Colonel C. Steevens assumed the command of the regiment on Lieutenant-Colonel Wauchope being wounded.

On the 4th of August, the regiment went into camp at Lesaca: this town is about twenty miles from St. Sebastian, and one mile from Passages, where the wounded and invalids of the army were sent. The regiment remained encamped at Lesaca until the end of August: at this place Lieutenant-Colonel Steevens conferred colour badges on ten of the most meritorious sergeants of the regiment. This was the first introduction into the army of the rank of colour-sergeant. The casualties (killed and wounded) of the XX in the campaign on the Pyrenees were twenty-one officers, thirteen sergeants, and two hundred and seventy-three rank and file.

The word "Pyrenees" to commemorate the various

---

[1] "Poor Wauchope was buried at Passages, where he died. A few days before his death I sat by his bed side and wrote a letter to his father in Scotland, which he dictated, asking his father to meet him at Portsmouth, as he was daily expecting to embark at Passages for that place; but alas! it was not to be. At the time of his death, Lieutenant W. Chafin Grove, of the XX, was with him. There was always somebody of his regiment in attendance; many of us went to stay with him, but Grove was always in his quarters, and was very kind and attentive. He had the best medical advice."—*Reminiscences of My Military Life*, page 107.

actions[1] was inscribed on the colours. Under authority dated Horse Guards, 1st June, 1814, special badges were presented to Major-General Robert Ross, Lieutenant-Colonel Andrew Wauchope, Major Alexander Rose.

---

[1] Roncesvalles, which occurred on the 25th July, excepted. "Pyrenees" was granted for the actions fought between the 28th of July and 2nd of August.

CHAPTER XXI.

The Storming of St. Sebastian—Death of Major Rose.

ST. Sebastian had undergone a siege of sixty days, and still showed no signs of capitulating. Lord Wellington, irritated by the long delay, and considering that the besiegers (5th Division) had been discouraged, called for volunteers from the regiments composing the 1st, 4th, and Light Divisions: "*Men,*" he said, "*who could show other troops how to mount a breach.*"[1] The numbers demanded from and furnished by the XX were two captains, two sergeants, one drummer, and eighteen privates. This party, together with the other volunteers (two hundred in all) from the 4th Division, marched from camp at Lesaca to St. Sebastian on the 30th of August, 1813, under Brevet-Major Alexander Rose, who had been selected to command the volunteers of the division on this perilous enterprise. St. Sebastian was stormed and captured on the following day, August 31st. Every officer and man of the detachment furnished by the XX was either killed or wounded. The following are the particulars: Major Rose, Sergeant John Fletcher, Privates Samuel Wright and James Taylor, killed in the breach; Captain John Murray, Sergeant Seth Gambling, Drummer John Keays, and sixteen men wounded.

Alexander Rose joined the XX as Ensign in the year 1796, and gained his Captain's commission on the 16th June, 1800, and was promoted Brevet-Major on the 1st January, 1812. He served with the regiment

---

[1] *History of the Peninsular War,* vol. iii, page 282.

in Holland, and was present at Krabbendam and the battles of Egmont-op-Zee. He accompanied the regiment to Minorca, and thence to Egypt, and took part in the attack on the forts at Alexandria. His next service was at the battle of Maida, and the operations in Naples and Sicily. He was with the XX throughout the retreat on Coruña, and in the expedition to Walcheren; he led the light troops of the Fusilier Brigade at the battle of Vittoria, and in all the actions fought on the Pyrenees, and terminated his career in the breach at St. Sebastian. The services of Major Rose passed unrecognised; but a posthumous reward, in the form of a grant of a medal for the Pyrenees, was published in the *London Gazette* of the 1st of June, 1814, nine months after his death.

The following sketch is from the pen of his friend and brother officer, Colonel Steevens: "At the siege of St. Sebastian I lost my most intimate friend in the regiment, Major Rose; we had been together nearly eighteen years, and I felt his loss most deeply. He was a fine, high-spirited, brave young Scotchman, the handsomest officer in the XX, of an excellent temper; he was a great favourite among all ranks in the regiment, and much regretted by everybody, and by no one more than myself. When he marched his detachment from the 4th Division a day or two before the place was stormed, I went part of the way with him; he was talking to me a good deal about the duty on which he was going, well knowing what a dangerous one it was, and he seemed to have a presentiment that he should never return; for when I took leave of him, and wished him every success, and said, 'God speed you, my dear fellow,' he replied, 'God bless you, I shall never see you again.'"

CHAPTER XXII.

1813-1814.

Spanish Attack—The Fall of St. Sebastian—Battle of Nivelle—Impassable Roads—Surrender of Two German Regiments—Advance on Orthes—The Battle—The Fight at St. Boës—General Ross wounded—Pursuit to Bordeaux and Toulouse—Battle of Toulouse—Reviewed by Lord Wellington—Embarkation for Ireland.

ON the 30th of August, 1813, the XX occupied a position in support of the Spaniards, close under the foundry of San Antonio, on the Pena de Haya mountain. On the 31st the regiment was still held in reserve on the Crown mountain, near the river Bidassoa; during the forenoon the enemy crossed the river and attacked the Spaniards. Lord Wellington remained with the regiment during the whole of this day, as the position afforded an extensive and commanding view of the scene of operations. News of the fall of St. Sebastian, and the death of Major Rose, reached the regiment at three p.m.; about the same hour a storm broke over the mountains and, continuing to rage during the remainder of the day, put an end to the combat between the French and Spaniards, of which the regiment had been quiet observers.

The XX returned to the camp at Lesaca on the 3rd of September, and on the 12th encamped near the Yanzi bridge on the Bidassoa. It marched to Passages on the 22nd to receive new clothing. The XX held an advanced post on the heights of Santa Barbara on the 6th and 7th of October, and on the 8th encamped on one of the lower slopes of the great Rhune. The regiment was frequently engaged in small skirmishes.

During October and the early part of November, the regiment was encamped on the side of a bleak mountain range, exposed to the full blast of piercing winds, and the drenching autumn rains, which had now set in, and from which their tents afforded but little protection.

The battle of Nivelle was fought on the 10th of November. Before daylight on that day, the regiment moved down the passes of the Pyrenees, in the most profound silence, and lay down at the appointed place. At dawn of day the signal gun was fired, and the XX with the 4th Division assaulted the redoubt of San Barbe. Our skirmishers were not long in working their way into the rear of the work, when the French, without making a single effort to expel them, fled from it.[1] Leaving the redoubt, our men pushed on to the village of Sarre, which was soon carried, and an advance made against a position held by the enemy on the heights in rear. This was also soon disposed of, and the enemy under General Conroux was eagerly pursued. General Clausel, who endeavoured to cover the retreat of Conroux's defeated troops, was now attacked by the 4th Division; the storming of the redoubt Louis XIV being assigned to the XX. This redoubt was captured after a stubborn resistance, and the 58th French Regiment taken prisoners.[2] The regiment was still following the enemy, who had now taken to the bridges across the Nivelle, when it was halted by Lord Wellington. We have been unable to trace the losses of the XX on the day of this battle (Nivelle), during which it had marched and fought for twelve hours: they do not

---

[1] *History of the Peninsular War*, vol. iii, page 335.
[2] MSS. Records.

appear to have been published in the *London Gazette*. After the battle, the regiment went into cantonments opposite the French camp at Serres.

The XX advanced with the division on the 11th of November, but the roads were of deep clay and the men sank up to their ankles in mud, and it was found impossible to continue the march. Quarters were found for the regiment in the village of Ascain, one wing making use of the chapel, and the other the houses in the village. The regiment remained at Ascain until the night of the 8th of December, when it marched towards Bayonne.

The XX was in the reserve with the 4th Division during the passage of the Nive on the 9th. On the following day, Marshal Soult attacked the British position at Barrouilhet, which was held by the 5th Division. The XX moved up in support and occupied a ridge one mile in rear of the church of Arcangues. From this point the regiment, with the brigade under Major-General Ross, was sent to cover the village of Arbonne, and this movement had the effect of checking the enemy. At the close of this day's (10th) action, two regiments of Nassau and Frankfort, commanded by Colonel Krause, deserted from the French army and surrendered themselves to General Ross, in the camp of the XX. They were sent to the nearest port and embarked for Germany.

At this time the regiment was for eight days without baggage or tents, and for several nights all ranks were exposed to incessant rains or frosts. On the 14th of December, the regiment went into cantonments near the chateau of Arcangues at Arauntz, and erected redoubts on the banks of the Nive.

At eight o'clock on the night of the 3rd January, 1814,

the XX marched from Arauntz, and, after a journey of a few hours, went into temporary quarters in a village *en route*. The march was continued the whole day from early morning on the 5th; the Nive was passed at Ustaritz, and an encampment was formed at night. On the following day the corps again moved forward, and was placed in the centre of the allied position at Bastide de Clerence. A general action was here expected: the allies came in touch about three p.m. with the enemy, who at once retired, the affair ending in a slight skirmish.

On the 7th, the XX was in bivouac; the cold was intense, and all suffered in consequence. On the following day they marched to Ustaritz, about a league from Bayonne, and went into cantonments. The roads had now become impassable quagmires, and both armies were fastened in their respective positions.

From Ustaritz, Lieutenant-Colonel Steevens proceeded to England on leave of absence, and the command of the regiment devolved upon Major James Bent.

On the 15th of February, the regiment advanced in the direction of Bayonne, and on the 21st was in cantonments at Bidache on the Bidouze; on the 24th, it was at Sorde, and at Peyrehorade on the 25th. The army was now moving on Orthes. On the 26th, the regiment forded two tributary streams of the river Pau. On the evening of this day the march was resumed, and, at daybreak on the 27th, the XX was at the church of Baights, with the village of St. Boës in its front. This village was strongly occupied by the enemy; the heights in its rear could only be reached by a narrow tongue of ground commanded by the French reserve of sixteen guns, so placed on the Dax road, in a position covered from counter-fire, as to be able to destroy any column which should attempt to debouch from the village in this direction.

The XX, in brigade under Major-General Ross, attacked St. Boës about nine a.m., and tried to force its way from the village. Napier says,[1] "General Cole assailed St. Boës with Ross's British brigade; his object was to get to the open beyond it, but fierce and slaughtering was the struggle. Five times breaking through the scattered houses did Ross carry his battle into the wider space beyond: yet ever as the troops issued forth the French guns from the open hill smote them in front, and the reserve battery on the Dax road swept through them from flank to flank." General Ross fell dangerously wounded. The combat at the village was continued with great obstinacy for about three hours. A Portuguese regiment was sent to protect our right flank from the French riflemen, but they could not withstand the French, and soon fled from the fight. The enemy's troops now crowded in on the exposed flank, and our men with difficulty fell back through St. Boës. The French were now taken in flank by two of our divisions, and at the same time, Ross and Anson's Brigades, strongly supported, forced their way across the narrow neck and gained the ground beyond it. Here the XX charged with the bayonet a strong column of the enemy, which they forced back upon its own guns; but, as soon as their front was clear, the gunners poured a deadly fire into the ranks of the corps. The XX then charged for the guns and captured two of them.

In the battle of Orthes the regiment suffered enormously, considering the numbers engaged. Major

---

[1] *History of the Peninsular War*, vol. iii, page 413.

James Bent[1] (who commanded the regiment), Captain J. D. St. Aurien, Ensign J. Murray, and six men were killed. Captains John Murray (severely), R. Telford, A. Smith, Lieutenants C. Connor and E. L. Godfrey were wounded. Captain George Tovey was taken prisoner. Sergeant-Major H. Hollinsworth, three sergeants, two corporals, and ninety-three men were severely wounded. One man was taken prisoner. After the action fought at Orthes, the probable effective strength of the regiment did not exceed two hundred men. According to Colonel Steevens, there were nearly four hundred survivors from the fight at Roncesvalles. Between the 26th of July, 1813, and 26th of February, 1814, the casualties of the corps in battles alone were one hundred and fifty-three men; this number, added to the one hundred and five placed *hors de combat* at Orthes, would reduce the fighting line by two hundred and fifty-eight men. Some of the wounded did no doubt rejoin the ranks, but this addition would be counterbalanced by losses from other causes: there was a fair percentage of sickness in the army at this period. There is no mention made in the manuscript records, nor in any other document, so far as we have been able to ascertain, of men joining the regiment from England or elsewhere. Captain Wm. Russell[2]

---

[1] James Bent came to the XX as Ensign in 1796. He was promoted Captain on the 31st March, 1803, and Brevet-Major on the 27th August, 1812. He was present at the battles of Krabbendam and Egmont-op-Zee; attack on the forts at Alexandria; the battles of Maida and Vimiera; retreat and battle of Coruña; and the Walcheren expedition. He took part in fight at Vittoria, all the actions fought on the Pyrenees and in the South of France.

[2] This was the second occasion on which this officer succeeded to a command in action. At Maida, during the battle, the command of the light company fell to him on the death of Captain Mc. Lean. In the March number of the *U.S. Journal* for 1839, Lieutenant-Colonel George Tovey (veteran), writing of the exploits of the light company at Maida, said that he (Russell) "was as gallant an officer as ever drew a sword." Major Russell settled in New South Wales.

succeeded to the command of the regiment on the death of Major Bent.

The regiment followed in pursuit of the French on the day following Orthes; the Ardour was crossed at St. Sever, and the march was continued daily until the 10th of March, when a halt was made at Langon until the 14th. In the meanwhile the objective point was changed, and the XX was ordered to proceed by forced marches to the town of Toulouse. On the 4th of April it crossed the Garonne, by a pontoon bridge, at the town of Grenade, fifteen miles from Toulouse, and on the following day was at Croix d'Orade.

About six a.m. on the 10th of April, the XX left the bivouac of the previous night, to take part in the attack on Toulouse; it crossed the Ers at the bridge of Croix d'Orade, passed through the suburb of Mont Blanc, and for two miles struggled through the deep marshy ground which lay between the river Llers and the heights of St. Sypiere. The fighting of the regiment in this battle (Toulouse) was slight; the 4th Division, of which the regiment formed part, stormed two redoubts, from which the enemy took flight, after a very feeble resistance: from this cause the loss was trifling. Two rank and file were killed and seven wounded. Captain H. Obins XX, brigade Major of the Fusilier brigade, was wounded.

Captains G. Tovey and H. Obins were promoted Brevet-Majors for their distinguished services in this campaign (*London Gazette*, 12th April, 1814).

The Emperor Napoleon having abdicated, a convention was agreed to by Lord Wellington and Marshal Soult; and hostilities ceased on the 17th of April, 1814.

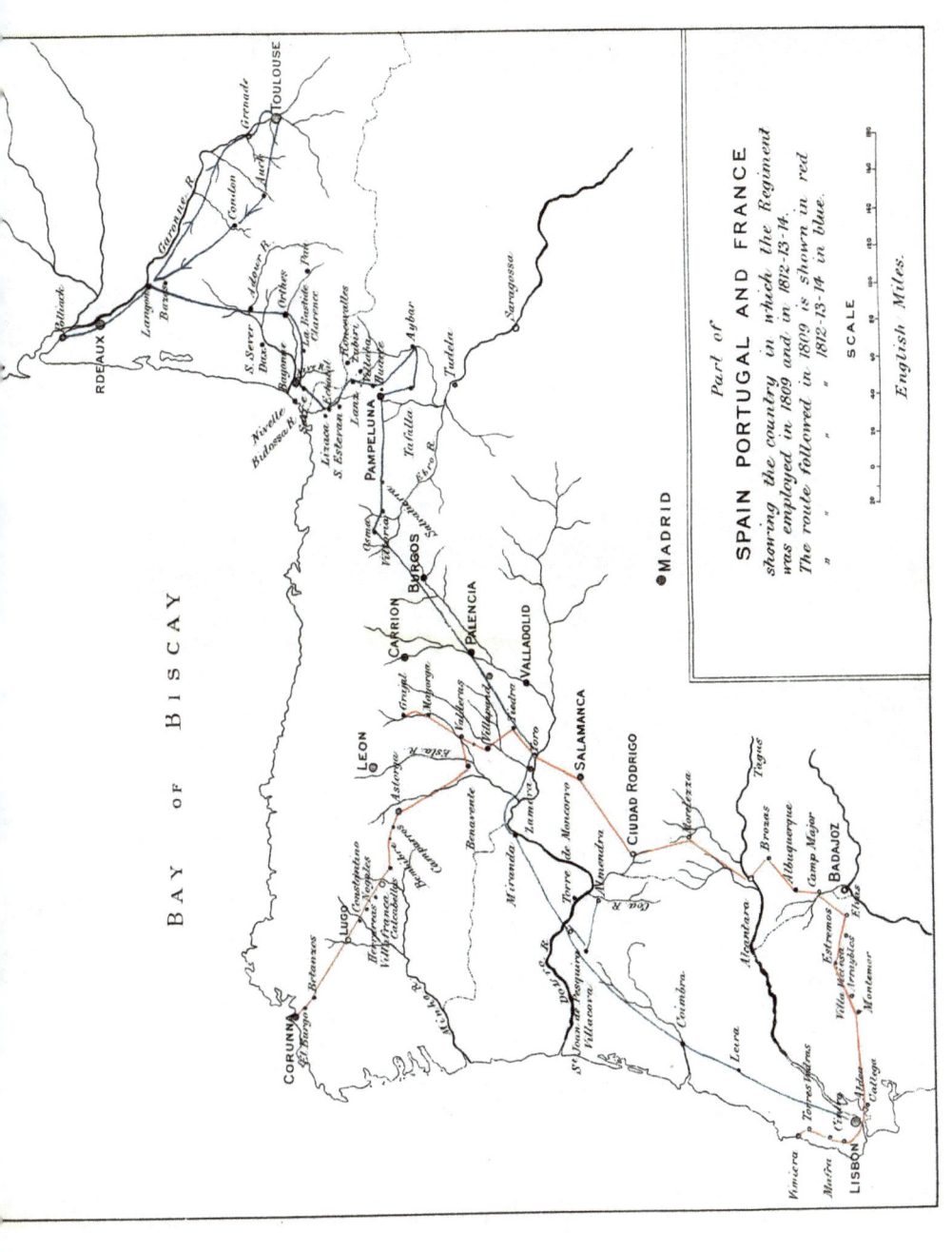

The XX marched through the town of Toulouse on the 21st of April, was at Auch on the 24th, and at Condom on the 25th, where it went into quarters and remained until the 30th May. The regiment proceeded to Bordeaux under the command of Captain and Brevet-Major Russell, on the 31st: the line of march was *viâ* Nerac and Bezas. The army was concentrated in the neighbourhood of Bordeaux on the 6th of June, and was reviewed by Field-Marshal Lord Wellington, on the 14th, when these gallant soldiers took leave of their General with three hearty cheers. The XX embarked on board two transports at Poliack on the Garonne on the 16th, and sailed for Ireland on the 22nd of June, 1814

NOTE.—The Spanish ladies, who were residing in Toulouse during the brief period the XX was quartered in the vicinity of that town, presented each officer with a silk rosette. One of these rosettes is now in the mess of the 1st Battalion.

Chapter XXIII.

1814-1818.

Arrived at Cork—March to Mallow—Death of General Ross—New Colours—Change of Station—Suppression of Unlawful Meetings—Move to Dublin—Colonel Charles Steevens retires from the Army—His Services.

THE transports with the regiment on board arrived in the Cove of Cork on the 7th July, 1814; the disembarkation took place the same day at Monkstown. The regiment marched to Cork and was billeted there for the night, and on the following day marched to Mallow, where it remained until the 21st of July. The battalion proceeded in three divisions *viâ* Mitchellstown, Cahir, Clonmel, Carrick-on-Suir, and reached Waterford on the 1st of August. While stationed at Waterford, the regiment was reduced in strength by the discharge from the service of veteran soldiers wounded and worn out in many campaigns. Lieutenant-Colonel Steevens resumed the command of the regiment on its arrival at Waterford.

The regiment heard with universal sorrow of the death of Major-General Robert Ross,[1] commander-in-chief of the forces in the United States, who was shot on the 12th of September, 1814, whilst making a reconnoissance before Baltimore. General Ross was identified with and commanded the XX during one of the most glorious periods in the history of the corps. The regiment erected a monumental tablet to his memory in the Parish Church, Rosstrevor, the family

---

[1] See Appendix.

seat in the County Down, as a testimony of how much in his life he was beloved, and in his fall regretted by the corps, for whose character and fame he had so zealously and successfully exerted himself, and to the comfort and welfare of which he was ever unceasingly devoted. It is the strongest proof of the affection in which he was held by the corps, that they thus perpetuated his fame, and handed down to succeeding generations his name and example. The regiment attended church in mourning on successive Sundays for a month.

On the death of the Colonel of the regiment, Lieutenant-General Sir John Stuart, Count of Maida, the Colonelcy was conferred upon Lieutenant-General Sir William Houstoun, K.C.B., by commission, dated 5th April, 1815. Sir William Houstoun presented the regiment with new colours, bearing the additional honours that had been gained in the Peninsular campaigns. On the 21st May, 1815, the regiment marched *via* Carrick-on-Suir, Clonmel, and Cashel to Templemore, arriving at the latter station on the 24th. From Templemore the regiment furnished no detachments and the whole regiment was quartered in barracks.

The county of Tipperary was at this time under the operation of the " Insurrection Act," and the duties the regiment was called upon to perform were disagreeable, and such as are usually carried out by police or officers of the law courts. Parties were constantly sent to seize stills to prevent illicit distillation of whiskey; preventing unlawful meetings at night; searching for arms; and assisting to seize cattle in default of payment of rent.[1] The regiment marched from Templemore on the 22nd March, 1816, the headquarters, commanded

---

[1] *Reminiscences of My Military Life*, page 121.

by Lieutenant-Colonel Steevens, for Boyle, and a wing, under Major South, for Sligo; they arrived at their several destinations on the 28th. From the two stations mentioned, the regiment sent out nineteen detachments in the counties of Roscommon, Leitrim, Mayo, and Longford. On the 18th June, 1818, the headquarters, followed by the various detached parties, marched for Dublin; the headquarters halted *en route* at Mullingar on the 11th of June, and met with a very cordial and hospitable reception from the 78th Highlanders, who thus renewed a friendship which began on the plain of Maida.

The regiment reached Dublin on the 15th of June, and was quartered in the castle barracks, six companies being detached to Naas and Wicklow. The establishment of the regiment was here fixed at six hundred and fifty rank and file. The Commander of the Forces at this time was General Sir George Beckwith, son of Colonel Beckwith, who served for many years in the XX, and commanded it at "Minden." Sir George expressed his pleasure at meeting the corps, and evinced a great interest in all that concerned it.[1] Lieutenant-Colonel Charles Steevens retired from the service by the sale of his commission on the 18th of December, 1818, and was succeeded by Lieutenant-Colonel Samuel South, an officer who had risen from the ranks. The subjoined is a *résumé* of Colonel Steeven's services in the XX:—Lieutenant-Colonel Steevens was gazetted an Ensign on the 30th of December, 1795, and joined the XX at Exeter in the spring of the following year. Lieutenant-Colonel Steevens was present with the battalion in all the

---

[1] *Reminiscences of My Military Life*, page 124.

stirring scenes and hard-fought victories in which the corps participated, from 1799 to the end of the war in 1814. He took part in the battles of Krabbendam and Egmont-op-Zee, (was severely wounded and taken prisoner,) in the attack on the forts at Alexandria, battles of Maida and Vimiera. Succeeded Lord Seaton in the command of the light company, and led it during the Coruña retreat and the Walcheren expedition. Was present at the battles of Vittoria, Roncesvalles, and all the actions on the Pyrenees. He commanded the XX at the battles of Nivelle and Nive. Lieutenant-Colonel Steevens received a gold medal for the actions on the Pyrenees, and a silver medal with clasps for Egypt, Maida, Vimiera, Coruña, Vittoria, Nivelle, and Nive. He commanded the regiment for five years, and two of his sons, Lieutenant-Colonel George Steevens and Captain Nathaniel Steevens, served in the corps. Lieutenant-Colonel N. Steevens published, in 1878, *Reminiscences of My Military Life,*[1] a work which his father had written some years after he had left the regiment, and contains his recollections of the events through which he passed, and of the men with whom he served in the XX. Colonel Steevens died at Cheltenham, on the 9th March, 1861.

---

[1] In compiling the Records, this book was of invaluable assistance.

CHAPTER XXIV.

1818–1821.

Departure from Dublin—Embarkation for St. Helena—Arrival—Lieutenant-Colonel South Retires—His Services—On Duty over the Emperor Napoleon—Surgeon Arnott consulted by the Emperor—Panegyric on Marlborough—Presentation by the Emperor to the XX—Napoleonic Relics—Change of Stations.

SOMETIME during the month of December, 1818, the regiment left Dublin for Cork, being then under orders to embark for St. Helena. The route lay through the towns of Naas, Cashel, Clogheen, to Fermoy, where the corps was concentrated and quartered in barracks. The XX marched from Fermoy in four divisions during the months of January, February, and March, 1819, and embarked at the Cove of Cork on board the chartered ships "Windermere," "Albion," and "Lloyds." The ship "Lloyds," with the headquarters of the corps on board, reached St. Helena in the month of June, 1819. On disembarkation, the headquarters were stationed at James Town, and detachments at Francis Plain, High Knoll, Lemon Valley, Ladder Hill, and other small outposts. Early in 1820, the XX moved to Deadwood, relieving the 66th Regiment in the immediate charge of and as guard over the residence of the Emperor Napoleon. The duties of all ranks were now particularly severe; the men had but one night in bed, and the fatigue and working duties were equally frequent and proportionally arduous. The regiment was at this time commanded by Major Jackson, Lieutenant-Colonel Samuel South having proceeded to England preparatory to retiring upon half pay. This officer's career in the XX was a long, successful, and eventful one. Of the date of his joining, or the particulars of the early period of his service in the corps, there are no data. He was promoted Quartermaster from Sergeant-Major, on the 29th March, 1794, and subsequently became Adjutant with the rank of Lieutenant; was promoted Captain on the 14th March, 1805, Major in 1813, and Lieutenant-Colonel in December, 1818. Colonel South's war services commenced in St. Domingo, in 1794; during this campaign he passed through the trying ordeal of several epidemics of yellow fever, which decimated the regiment, and he was one of the seventy-six survivors who returned to England. He was Adjutant of the corps in Holland, and was wounded at the battle of Krabbendam; served in Egypt; was present at the battles of Maida and Vimiera, and throughout the Coruña retreat; accompanied the regiment on the Walcheren expedition. He served with the corps at the battles of Vittoria and Roncesvalles, in all the actions on the Pyrenees, and the battles of Orthes, Nive, Nivelle, and Toulouse, and ended a remarkable career as commander of the corps, when guarding the "Great Napoleon."

His son, Charles South, joined the XX as Ensign in 1814, was promoted Lieutenant 17th December, 1818, and appointed Paymaster of the corps on the 23rd August, 1827. For Captain South's services, see chapter xxix.

The XX was singularly connected with the last days of the "Great Napoleon." On the 19th March, 1821, Doctor Arnott was first consulted by the Emperor's physician, Professor Antommarchi, and he paid his first visit to the Emperor on the evening of the 1st of April. From this date, the doctor's visits were of daily occurrence. On the 14th April, the Emperor received the doctor in the most affable manner, and after questioning him as to his case, he suddenly turned the subject from medicine to war, and began to talk about the English armies, the Generals by whom they had been commanded, and passed a most magnificent encomium upon Marlborough.[1] "Marlborough was not a man whose mind was narrowly confined to the field of battle; he fought and negotiated; he was at once a captain and a diplomatist. Has the Twentieth his campaigns?" "I think not," said Arnott. "Well," added the Emperor, "I have a copy of them, which I am glad to offer to that brave regiment; take it, doctor, and place it in their library as coming from me."

The three volumes had been given to Napoleon by Lord Robert Spencer; on the title-page are the words "L'Empereur Napoleon," but not, it is believed, in Napoleon's handwriting. Sir Hudson Lowe objected to the volumes being received by the regiment, unless the Imperial title was torn out.[2] The officers would not consent to such a mutilation; and on the books being sent to England for the opinion of His Royal Highness, the Commander-in-Chief, they were returned in their original condition, with the remark, that "such a gift from Napoleon to a British regiment was most gratifying to him, and that the safe detention of Napoleon was sufficient testimony that the regiment had done its duty, and the presentation of the books was a satisfactory and flattering acknowledgment that a delicate and difficult duty had been performed in a generous and gentlemanly spirit."

---

[1] Abbott's *History of Napoleon*, vol. ii; and *The Last Days of Napoleon*, by F. Antommarchi, vol. ii, page 96.

[2] *Times*, 12th September, 1853.

On the death of the Emperor, on the 5th of May, 1821, the body was placed in Surgeon Arnott's[1] charge, and he watched over it night and day until the funeral. The officer on duty when the Emperor died was Captain W. Crokat,[2] and he regulated and controlled the order of admittance of persons wishing to view the body of the deceased. Twelve Grenadiers of the XX carried the remains to the grave. The *London Gazette* of the 4th July, 1821, announced the arrival in London of Captain Crokat, XX Regiment, with a despatch from Sir H. Lowe, informing the Government of Napoleon's death.

In 1821, the regiment changed quarters to Francis plain. Lieutenant-Colonel James Ogilvie, C.B., having exchanged from half pay, arrived at St. Helena in the month of September, 1821, and assumed command of the corps.

---

[1] See Appendix.

[2] General William Crokat joined the XX in Sicily on the 9th April, 1807, as Ensign. He was promoted Lieutenant on the 30th June, 1808, and was present at the battle of Vimiera, and the retreat on and battle of Coruña. Lieutenant Crokat took part in the battle of Vittoria, and was severely wounded in the combat at Roncesvalles on the Pyrenees. He received the war medal and clasps for Vimiera, Coruña, Vittoria, and Pyrenees. He was promoted Captain on the 31st March, 1814. Captain Crokat was promoted Brevet-Major (5th July, 1821) for bringing home the despatches announcing the death of Napoleon. In April, 1822, he accompanied the regiment to India, and retired upon half pay on the 7th November, 1826. His subsequent promotions were: Lieutenant-Colonel, 10th January, 1837; Colonel, 11th November, 1851; Major-General, 31st August, 1855; Lieutenant-General, 21st December, 1862; and General, 25th October, 1871. General Crokat died in 1879, aged 88 years.

NOTE.—In addition to three volumes of Cox's *Life of Marlborough*, the following Napoleonic relics are in the Officers' Mess of the 1st Battalion. They were presented by Sir Owen T. Burne, K.C.S.I. :—Miniature imitation in bog-oak and gold of Napoleon's sarcophagus in the Palace of the Invalides, Paris. Lock of Napoleon's hair. Feather from his hat. A piece of the coffin which contained his remains, when first interred at St. Helena. There is also a letter bearing the signature of Marshall Soult, Duc de Dalmatia, addressed to the officers of the regiment, and dated Weedon, July, 1838.

CHAPTER XXV.

1822-1837.

Sail for Bombay—Service in India—Koolapoor Field Force—Cholera—Colonel Thomas joins—Inspection by Sir John Keane—His Address and General Order to the Corps—Volunteers—Embarkation.

THE headquarters and right wing embarked on board the East India Company's ship "Macqueen" and the left wing on board the "Orwell" on the 13th April, 1822, and sailed for Bombay on the following day. The "Macqueen" arrived in Bombay harbour on the 4th and the "Orwell" on the 14th June; on landing, the regiment was quartered in the town barracks. Lieutenant-Colonel Ogilvie assumed command of the Bombay garrison and Major Hogg that of the XX. On the 17th April, 1824, the corps embarked at Colabah on board the ships "Stewart Forbes" and "Cornwallis," and landed at Cannanore on the 29th April. Lieutenant-Colonel Ogilvie was granted leave of absence on medical certificate; the command devolved upon Colonel J. Foster Fitzgerald, C.B.[1] The XX embarked on the 1st March, 1825, for Bombay, landed there on the 17th, and proceeded, by

---

[1] J. Foster Fitzgerald received his first commission on the 29th October, 1793, when he was eight years of age. He reached the rank of Captain on the 9th May, 1794, and joined the 46th Regiment in 1801. On the 25th September, 1803, he was promoted Major, and Lieutenant-Colonel on the 10th July, 1810. Colonel Fitzgerald commanded a light battalion and a brigade in the Peninsular. He was awarded the gold cross for Badajoz, Salamanca, Vittoria, and the Pyrenees. He joined the XX as second Lieutenant-Colonel on the 5th February, 1824, succeeded to the command in this year, and served with the corps until he was promoted Major-General on the 22nd July, 1830. He was promoted Lieutenant-General on the 23rd November, 1841, General on the 20th June, 1854, and Field Marshal on the 29th May, 1875. He was Colonel of the 18th Regiment, and a Knight Grand Cross of the Bath. Field Marshal J. Foster Fitzgerald died in 1877, aged ninety-two years.

march route, in two divisions to Poonah, where the 1st Division arrived on the 29th, under Major Jackson, and the 2nd, under Brevet-Major Lutyens, on the 30th. The left wing (four hundred rank and file), under Brevet-Major G. Tovey,[1] proceeded to Koolapoor to join the field force at that place. Whilst encamped near the fort at Koolapoor, cholera broke out among the men, and two sergeants and fifteen rank and file died from this disease. The wing rejoined headquarters on the 27th February, 1826, under Brevet-Major Lutyens. Lieutenant Clinton, two sergeants, and forty rank and file joined the headquarters from the depôt in England, on the 10th of March, 1826. This party formed the guard on board a convict ship bound to New South Wales; whilst on the return passage from this colony to Madras, they were shipwrecked on the coast of New Holland, and lost all their baggage. Lieutenant-Colonel Ogilvie exchanged with Lieutenant-Colonel Henry Thomas; the latter officer joined the XX from half pay in February, 1827. The regiment marched in two divisions from Poonah on the 19th February, 1829, and arrived at Colabah on the 27th and 28th of that month. On the 5th January, 1831, the XX again changed stations, and was quartered at Belgaum, relieving the 40th Regiment. Lieutenant Donald Campbell died at Malwan, on the 26th of February, 1835.[2]

---

[1] Major George Tovey joined the XX as Ensign in 1804. He was promoted Lieutenant on the 21st November, 1805; Captain, 9th November, 1809; and Brevet-Major on the 12th April, 1814, for his distinguished conduct in the Pyrenees and in the campaign in the South of France. He was the hero of the fight at Roncesvalles. He fought in every action from Maida to Orthes, where he was taken prisoner. Major Tovey served with the corps in St. Helena and in India until 1837, when he retired upon a pension.

[2] A tablet was erected to his memory in the Cathedral, at Glasgow. It bears this inscription: "This tablet is erected by the officers, non-commissioned officers, and privates of the XX Regiment to commemorate their esteem and regard for Lieutenant Donald Campbell, who died at Malwan, East Indies, on the 26th of February, 1835; aged 34 years."

His Excellency Lieutenant-General Sir John Keane,[1] K.C.B., G.C.H., Commander-in-Chief of the Bombay army, inspected the regiment, at Belgaum, on the 11th December, 1835. He dined with the officers in their mess, on the evening of the 12th, and, in responding to the toast of his health, said: "Colonel Green,—The commander of a British regiment is at all times in an enviable position, but that of the XX, sir, most particularly so. Whatever is great! whatever is grand! whatever is glorious! has always been associated with this corps. I have known it from my earliest youth, and it is one that has upon all occasions distinguished itself. I can tell you that it has been in a great measure owing to the example of some of its officers, who were my earliest companions in military life, that I now know how to conduct myself in my present rank of Lieutenant-General, and to acquit myself, sir, as a gentleman. The names of Smyth, Power, Colborne, and Ross, will be ever dear to my memory. Those names, those names, I repeat, sir, are sufficient of themselves to make everyone composing the XX spur on to do his utmost; and it is a pleasure to me to convey to you, Colonel Green, that I am not disappointed. What I witnessed yesterday fully satisfied my expectations. Do you, then, Colonel Green, accept my warmest thanks for the manner in which the regiment went through its several duties at the inspection and review; and I have great pleasure in thanking the officers and men for their exertions; I except no one, for general attention was observable in all. I am delighted to see the XX again looking so well. My own services have almost ever been identified with those of the XX, whose colours I now behold before me can testify.

---

[1] Created Lord Keane of Guznee, in 1840.

When I come to reflect on Europe, sir, and consider what may be going on at this very moment: it may happen that ten thousand men may yet be placed under my command there: and should I be so fortunate as to have the XX among them, the result, sir, of any conflict, I know would be again, as it has been formerly, most brilliant to the British arms. Although I find myself becoming a veteran, still there is yet another campaign in me. You are about to leave India, and I wish everyone of you a most prosperous and happy voyage to old England, and trust the regiment will soon be completed in men and fit for active service."

The following is an extract from the general orders by Sir John Keane, the Commander-in-Chief of the Bombay army, after his inspection of the regiment, in December, 1835:—

"Headquarters, Camp,
"Poonah, 16th January, 1836.

" Sir John Keane has long known and served with the XX Regiment, and he has ever found it, as he did at this inspection, under the command of Lieutenant-Colonel Green, a credit to itself and the British army. Its conduct in the field has always been a proud example of steady discipline and valour; and, now that its period of service is nearly completed in India, and that it is about to leave this command on its return to England, the Lieutenant-General feels it to be due to the regiment, and it is to him a pleasing duty, to state that its fair fame has been well supported by its uniform and soldierlike conduct during the time it has served in the Bombay Presidency.

"(Signed) R. MacDonald,
" Major, Military Secretary."

During the month of September, 1836, upwards of four hundred men volunteered to remain in India, and were transferred to different corps. On the 30th of December, 1836, the left wing, under the command of Captain Deshon, embarked on board the ship "Lady Faversham," and sailed for England on the 31st. The headquarters of the corps, under the command of Lieutenant-Colonel Green, embarked on board the ship "Malabar," and sailed on the following day. Previous to embarkation, Brigadier-General Salter inspected and complimented the regiment on its behaviour, and wished all ranks a pleasant voyage to England.

Chapter XXVI.
1837.

Arrival in England—Quartered at Canterbury—Joined by the Depôt.

THE left wing, under Captain Deshon, landed at Deal on the 28th April, 1837, and marched to Canterbury on the following day. Colonel Green and the headquarters landed at Deal and proceeded to Canterbury on the 8th May; thus the XX returned to England, after a continuous absence, on foreign service, of over eighteen years. The depôt, under Captain Croad, joined headquarters at Canterbury. On arrival from India, the strength of the corps was as follows:— Lieutenant-Colonels, two; Majors, two; Captains, ten; Lieutenants, nineteen; Ensigns, eight; Paymaster, one; Adjutant, one; Quartermaster, one; Surgeon, one; Assistant-Surgeon, one; Sergeants, thirty-six; Corporals, twenty-five; Drummers, seven; Privates, three hundred and sixty; Women, twenty-seven; Children, forty-eight.

Chapter XXVII.
1838.

March to London—Guards of Honour—The Coronation of Queen Victoria—Presentation of Colours by the Duke of Wellington—His Speech.

ON the 26th March, 1838, the regiment marched, *viâ* Sittingbourne, Rochester, and Dartford, to the Tower of London, where it was stationed. The XX furnished all the "Guards of Honour," for the reception of the Ambassadors who came to London to represent their respective Governments at the coronation of Her Majesty "Queen Victoria." Marshal Soult, the French Ambassador, was received by the corps at the stairs of the Tower, on landing.

At five a.m. on the 28th of June, the corps[1] marched from the Tower, and took up its position, which extended from the gates of Buckingham Palace to Constitution Hill, and returned to the Tower at eight p.m.

On Saturday, the 7th July, 1838, Field Marshal His Grace the Duke of Wellington, High Constable of the Tower of London, presented new colours to the XX, in the presence of a large assemblage of the nobility, ladies and gentlemen. His Grace was attended by the General Commanding-in-Chief, Lord Hill, Generals Lord Fitzroy Somerset, Sir Lowry Cole, Sir Thomas Bradford, Sir Hussey Vivian, Sir William Anson, and many other distinguished officers.

---

[1] In addition to the Guards, the regiments which took part in the coronation ceremonies were the XX, 1st and 2nd Battalions of the Rifle Brigade, Detachment Royal Marines, and Hon. Artillery Company.—General order, Horse Guards, 23rd June, 1838.

Unfortunately, this ceremony, intrinsically so interesting, was marred by the weather, a furious storm having burst over the Tower at one o'clock, precisely as His Grace was about to present himself in front of the corps, which, before it could be put under cover for the moment in the armoury, was thoroughly drenched, as well as the unsheltered spectators. When the weather permitted, the regiment was re-formed on the Broad Walk of the Tower, and, having been inspected in line by the Duke, marched past in slow time, and then formed square. The new colours were held by the two Majors, and after the consecration service was performed by the Chaplain General, Doctor Daken, His Grace presented them to Majors W. N. Hutchinson and Gaspard Le Marchant and a Grenadier, who had advanced into the centre of the square to receive them.

The Noble Duke then addressed the regiment "in terms of the highest eulogy, recapitulating its services from so distant a period as the battle of 'Minden,' to its latest victory on French ground at Toulouse. He had, personally, he said, witnessed part of its career, and had seen no regiment in a higher state of conduct and discipline. With all the wisdom and kindness of a parent, he impressed on the young men who surrounded him the necessity of military subordination. Three or four hundred well-disciplined soldiers, he said, would achieve almost anything; while ten times that number, if irregular and undisciplined, were feeble in comparison; a mere tumultuous mob, easily dispersed and subdued. Order was as essential in barracks as in families; without it there could be neither comfort nor well-doing; it was even more essential, by reason of their greater numbers and more important duties. Complimenting in the highest terms the commander of the regiment, Colonel Thomas, His Grace expressed his full confidence that the colours now presented to the XX Regiment would never receive from those young soldiers the slightest stain; but that under their new flag they would emulate and, should occasion call, equal the glory of their predecessors."

To this impressive and almost parental address, Colonel Thomas replied in earnest and appropriate terms. At the close of the parade ceremonies, and after a short visit to the Ordnance Map Office, His Grace, the general officers, ladies, and gentlemen present, were entertained at luncheon, in a marquee adjoining the mess room. In proposing the health of the illustrious Duke, Colonel Thomas said: "That the most brilliant, perhaps, of the services of the XX had been performed under the immediate observation of the Duke, whose illustrious hand had now placed in their charge those honourable symbols of royal favour and national confidence;—symbols," said the gallant veteran, "while stimulating us to increased zeal and devotion, bring back to our memories that electrical cheer, 'Here he is himself!' when, in the most awful and trying moments, the presence of their great leader had given every heart assurance of victory. No man," continued the gallant Colonel, "can understand as well as does your Grace the moral effect of that *esprit de corps*, which would seem to adhere to some regiments in particular; that it has long been the characteristic of the XX is shown by the *Minden Rose*, transmitted fresh and unsullied through all its banners, and now, by your own hand, entwined with the laurel." Assuring

---

NOTE.—According to the *Times* of the 9th July, 1838, the Duke's address to the regiment took twenty minutes in delivery, but, owing to the howling of the wind, only occasional sentences could be heard outside the square.

His Grace that the officers and men of the XX would ever consider this auspicious ceremony a pledge of their constancy to defend the colours now confided to them by their Sovereign, through his illustrious hands, Colonel Thomas, in the name of the regiment, proffered to the Duke his grateful and respectful acknowledgments, amidst enthusiatic cheering.

The Duke was pleased to make the following reply: " Colonel Thomas,—I feel obliged by the flattering mention you have made of my name on the present occasion. When addressing the regiment this day on parade, and recounting the gallant services it has performed, and which are inscribed on the colours presented to it, I forgot to take due notice of your own; and though it may be considered that in the discharge of this gratifying duty and in the few words of advice I have expressed in too high terms the opinion I entertain of the XX Regiment, I now distinctly assert as constable of this ancient fortress, where your regiment has been some time stationed, that, notwithstanding the various local temptations to which your young lads have been exposed, I have received the most favourable reports of their attention to the duties of the garrison, and of their discipline and subordination. From my own recollection, I also declare, that of the many distinguished regiments of the British army which I have had the honour to command, *this, the best and most distinguished*, is entitled to all the encomiums I may have bestowed upon it.[1] (Cheers.) I cannot, however, conclude without earnestly recom-

---

[1] On a previous occasion, at a service dinner, His Grace spoke of the regiment in similar terms; and added, to calm the startled company, that he bestowed such unqualified praise upon the corps, because it had won all its Peninsular honours with one battalion.

mending to the officers of the regiment, from the senior to the junior, if they wish to attain eminence or distinction in their profession, to follow the example afforded by their gallant commander. (Hear.) I have unfortunately mislaid or forgotten a record which I had prepared of his meritorious services, most of which were achieved on the same fields and in the same division that the XX acquired their renown; but he bears on his breast the approbation of his Sovereign, and I know sufficient to enable me to say, that the rewards and honours which have been conferred on him by his Sovereign and his country have been merited, that his example is worthy of imitation, and will, if followed by those under his command, lead to the same glorious career which he has pursued. I regret that my avocations elsewhere prevent me from enjoying the happy society which I see assembled round me, and I must, therefore, beg leave to withdraw, declaring that I shall always feel happy in promoting by any means in my power the well-being of the British army, or in assisting by my presence or advice any meeting having for its object the support or advancement of its discipline."[1]

His Grace, at the conclusion of his address, quitted the tent, and finally the Tower, amidst the acclamations of the assemblage.

---

[1] *United Service Journal*, 1840, vol. i, pages 120-121.

NOTE.—Of the officers who were present with the corps at the coronation of Her Majesty Queen Victoria, and at the presentation of colours by the Duke of Wellington, there now (1888) survive: Major W. N. Hutchinson, now General, Colonel of the 33rd, Duke of Wellington's, Regiment; Captain F. Horn, now General Sir F. Horn, Colonel of the XX; Lieutenant and Adjutant H. Crawley, now Lieutenant-Colonel, retired; Lieutenant E. Hill, afterwards Major 96th Regiment; Lieutenant L. D. Gordon, now L. D. Gordon-Duff, M.P. for Banff 1857 to 1861, Colonel of Volunteers; Ensign G. B. Crespigny (now de Crespigny) late Paymaster, School of Musketry at Hythe, Colonel in the army.—*Army and Navy Gazette*, 11th August, 1888.

CHAPTER XXVIII.

1838–1841.

March to Weedon and Manchester—Changes among the Officers—Inspections—Change of Stations—The First Railway Journey—Arrival at Dublin—Death of Captain Barlow—Retirement of Colonel Thomas, C.B.—Embarkation for Bermuda.

ON the 11th July, 1838, the regiment proceeded by march route to Weedon, viâ Barnet, St. Albans, Dunstable, Stratford, and Towcester. A detachment consisting of eight companies marched from Weedon to Manchester, under Major Sir Gaspard le Marchant, on the 16th of October. The headquarters and remaining companies left Weedon on the 22nd November and arrived in Manchester on the 1st December, and were quartered in Salford barracks.

During the years 1837-8, a great many changes occurred among the officers of the corps. Lieutenant-Colonels Green and Tovey retired. Captain Deshon was promoted Major, and Lieutenant Fred. Horn Captain. Majors le Marchant and Hutchinson, Lieutenants H. D. Crofton, Lord Mark Kerr, and Fred. C. Evelegh exchanged into the corps. Some of these names were for many years to be associated with the XX, some with one of the most glorious periods in its history, and one (General Sir Fred. Horn, K.C.B.) is still borne on its roll. Lieutenant H. Crawley was appointed Adjutant, vice Hollinsworth, who exchanged to the 56th Regiment.[1]

On the 29th January, 1839, the regiment was in-

---

[1] See Appendix.

spected for the first time since its arrival from India, by Sir Richard Jackson, commanding the Northern District. Sir Charles Napier inspected the regiment on the 29th May, and was pleased to express his satisfaction with the appearance and smartness of the men on parade.

On the 13th June, headquarters and two companies marched to Stockport, six companies to Ashton-under-Lyne, under Major McLean, and two companies under Captain Fred. Horn to Rochdale. The thanks of the Mayor and Corporation were voted to the XX, for its services in suppressing the Chartist disturbances, and in apprehending the ringleaders. On the 18th August, Sir Charles Napier inspected the detachment of eight companies, stationed at Ashton-under-Lyne under the command of Captain Horn. The establishment of the regiment was in this month fixed at eight hundred rank and file. Sir Charles Napier again inspected the regiment on the 27th May, 1840, previous to its embarkation for Ireland.

The headquarters of the corps, under Colonel Thomas, C.B., marched from Stockport to Manchester, on the 4th June, and was conveyed by rail to Liverpool. This was the first railway journey made by the corps. On the 8th June, the regiment went on board H.M. Ship "Vesuvius," and arrived at Kingstown the following morning, and marched to Dublin, being quartered in the Richmond barracks, and was here inspected on the 10th October, by Sir E. Blakeny, by whom it was highly commended. On the 12th December, the headquarters and two flank companies, under Major Croad, marched to Athlone, *viâ* Maynooth, Mullingar, and Ballymahon; two companies, under Captain Barlow, had preceded the headquarters on the

7th. On the 9th, one company, under Lieutenant Crespigny, marched to Maryboro'; one to Portumna, under Captain Lord Mark Kerr;[1] one, commanded by Major Smith, to Shannon Bridge; one to Bannagher, under Lieutenant Sharpe. Two companies, commanded by Captain Frazer, marched to Limerick on the 27th March, 1841, followed by Major Croad with the headquarters and flank companies, on the 2nd April.

From Limerick the regiment furnished detachments to the following towns and villages: Clare Castle, Tipperary, Toomevara, Silvermines, Pachawn, Portroe, Rathkeale, and Abbeyfeale.

Captain Barlow[2] died at Limerick on the 12th June, 1841, after a brief illness of a month's duration. He had previously been on detachment at Pachawn, and came to Limerick for change of air.[3]

The regiment was unexpectedly ordered to proceed to Cork for embarkation for Bermuda. Captain Horn and two companies marched on the 25th August, and two under Captain Frazer, on the 26th, followed by

---

[1] Lord Mark Kerr exchanged into the XX on the 28th December, 1838; he was promoted Captain (by purchase) on the 26th June, 1840, and Major on the 25th July, 1851. He left the XX when promoted Lieutenant-Colonel on the 30th December, 1853. Lord Mark Kerr commanded the 13th Regiment at the battle of Tchernaya, and at the siege of Sebastopol. In the Indian Mutiny he commanded the force at the relief of Azinghur, at the attack on and retreat from Fort Jugdespore. He was wounded in the latter affair. He took part in the Trans Gogra campaign, and commanded at the action of Toolespore. Lord Mark Kerr is now General, K.C.B., and Colonel of the Somersetshire Light Infantry.

[2] Captain F. C. Barlow had served in the XX since the 2nd July, 1824, when he came to it as an Ensign. He was promoted Lieutenant on the 25th October, 1827, and Captain on the 18th December, 1829. He was for some years with the regiment in India.

[3] His son, Captain F. W. Barlow, served in the XX from the 9th March, 1860, until he retired by the sale of his commission on the 3rd February, 1874. He was present with the 2nd Battalion in India, China, Japan, South Africe, and Mauritius; and at Bermuda with the 1st Battalion.

the headquarters on the 27th; the route lay through the towns of Bruff, Charleville, and Mallow. On the 31st August, the corps was concentrated at Cork, having been separated in detachments since December of the previous year.

Colonel Henry Thomas, C.B.,[1] retired from the regiment on the 6th September, 1841. This distinguished officer had commanded the XX for eleven years; he was succeeded by Major W. N. Hutchinson, who was promoted Lieutenant-Colonel.

Two companies, consisting of seven officers, and two hundred and twenty-eight men and fourteen women, commanded by Major Horn, embarked at the Cove of Cork, on board the ship "General Palmer," on the 11th of September, but were detained in harbour by adverse winds until the 16th. The headquarters and remaining companies, under the command of Lieutenant-Colonel Hutchinson, embarked on the 27th of September, and sailed on the evening of the 30th.

---

[1] See Appendix.

NOTE.—Lieutenant-Colonel Hutchinson introduced into the corps the first edition (1842) of the *Regimental Standing Orders;* these regulations were revised in 1860 by the late Colonel J. Cormick, and again on a recent occasion, to meet the requirements of existing army orders, otherwise they remain as originally published by Colonel Hutchinson.

Chapter XXIX.

1841–1853.

Arrival at Bermuda—Formation of a 2nd Battalion—Epidemic of Yellow Fever—Change of Stations—Arrival at Halifax, Nova Scotia—Embark for Quebec—Change of Commanding Officers—Amalgamation of the Two Battalions—Fire at Montreal—Complimentary General Order—Sail for England—Winchester and Plymouth—Active Service—Sail for Turkey.

THE chartered ship "Cornwall," with the undernamed officers on board, arrived at Bermuda on the 1st and disembarked on the 3rd November, 1841: Lieutenant-Colonel W. N. Hutchinson; Captains F. M. Frazer, H. D. Crofton, L. D. Gordon,[1] F. C. Evelegh; Lieutenants E. Brook, G. B. C. Crespigny, G. Steevens, H. O. de Crespigny, Sir R. Gethin, Bart.; Ensigns E. G. Hallewell,[2] G. F. Weller-Poley,[3] W. A. Eyre; Paymaster C. South, Quartermaster D. Bilham, Surgeon S. Tevan, M.D.

---

[1] Captain Gordon joined the XX as Ensign on the 25th July, 1834. He was promoted Lieutenant on the 28th July, 1838; Captain, 31st December, 1839; and Major on the 9th June, 1846. He served with the regiment in India, Bermuda, and Canada. Major Gordon retired by the sale of his commission on the 25th July, 1851. He has since assumed the name of Duff, in addition to that of Gordon.

[2] Ensign Hallewell's commission was dated 31st December, 1839. He was promoted Lieutenant on the 15th April, 1842. Lieutenant Hallewell was Adjutant of the regiment for five years. He was promoted Captain on the 29th December, 1848, and transferred to the 28th Regiment on the 17th December, 1850. Captain Hallewell served in the Crimean campaign as Deputy Assistant-Quartermaster-General to the Light Division, and in this position he was present at the battles of Alma, Inkerman, and during the siege of Sebastopol. He received the medal and clasps, created a Knight of the Legion of Honour, 5th class of the Medjidie and Turkish medal. He was promoted Brevet-Major 12th December, 1854; Lieutenant-Colonel, 2nd November, 1855; and Colonel, 2nd November, 1860. Colonel Hallewell was appointed Commandant of the Cadet College, Sandhurst, on the 1st April, 1864; and this position he held until his death, which occurred in 1869.

[3] G. F. Weller-Poley joined the XX on the 17th April, 1840; promoted Lieutenant on the 15th April, 1842; and Captain, 27th December, 1850. He retired on the 20th January, 1854.

The "General Palmer" disembarked Major Horn, and the following officers with the detachment, on the 9th November, 1841: Captain J. B. Sharpe; Lieutenants S. R. Berdmore, R. L. Lye; Ensigns J. G. L. Adlercron, W. P. Radcliffe; Adjutant R. B. Smith, Assistant Surgeon R. J. Cole, M.D.

The headquarters were stationed at Hamilton, and three companies at Ireland Island. On the 7th May, 1842, orders were received that the regiment was to be formed into two battalions; the service companies being denominated the 1st Battalion, and the Depôt, augmented to six companies, the Reserve Battalion. This was the third occasion of a second battalion being formed. The establishments were: 1st Battalion, five hundred and forty rank and file; Reserve, five hundred and forty rank and file; Depôt, one hundred and twenty rank and file; total, one thousand two hundred.

The "Java" transport, with the Reserve Battalion on board, arrived at Bermuda in the autumn of 1842. The following officers accompanied the battalion: Major F. Croad; Captains R. S. Murray, B. Newman, and P. Hennessy; Lieutenant H. Crawley (Acting Paymaster); Ensigns H. Murray, G. Tomson[1] (Acting Adjutant), J. R. Jackson, H. R. Cowell, and J. Pethebridge; Assistant Surgeon E. Howard.

A draft, consisting of three officers and twenty-seven men, under the command of Lieutenant Maurice Cane,[2]

---

[1] Ensign Tomson was promoted Lieutenant on the 9th October, 1843. He was Adjutant of the Reserve Battalion for two years, and was promoted Captain on the 30th December, 1853. Captain Tomson retired from the service on the 7th June, 1854.

[2] Maurice Cane's commission as Ensign was dated 9th August, 1839. He was promoted Lieutenant (by purchase) on the 7th September, 1841, and Captain on the 1st September, 1848. He retired in 1850, and subsequently became a partner in the banking firm of Cane & Sons, Dublin.

arrived at Bermuda on board the transport "Nuna," on the 28th November, 1842. An epidemic of yellow fever raged in Bermuda during the month of August and following months of 1843. The 1st Battalion was scattered about the islands in detachments. The two flank companies were encamped on Prospect Hill, two companies occupied a building in Devonshire Parish, one was sent to Tucker's Island, and a few men to a small island in Hamilton Harbour. The Reserve Battalion was encamped at the ferry, near St. George's (known in later days as the old ferry).

Notwithstanding these and other precautions, the battalions lost, between the months of August, 1843, and February, 1844, a large number of officers, non-commissioned officers, and men. The names of the officers who died are: Captain F. M. Frazer and Lieutenant Adlercron, at Ireland Island; Ensign Pethebridge and Captain Newman, at St. George's; Lieutenant and Adjutant Smith and Captain Brook, at Hamilton.

The 1st Battalion lost one hundred and six sergeants, rank and file; and the Reserve Battalion eighty-seven rank and file.

An exchange of stations between the two battalions took place on the 13th March, 1844, the First occupying St. George's, and the Reserve Hamilton and Ireland Island. On the 8th April, a draft of three officers and one hundred and thirty-five men, under Lieutenant Garstin,[1] arrived from the Depôt. On the 20th February, 1846, the establishment was augmented to two Lieutenant-Colonels; and a staff (with the exception of Paymaster) was sanctioned for the Reserve Battalion. This made the Reserve Battalion perfectly

---

[1] Lieutenant Garstin was promoted Captain, on the unattached list, on the 14th March, 1851.

separate and distinct from the first; hitherto both battalions were under the command of the Lieutenant-Colonel of the regiment.

On the 28th April, 1847, the 1st Battalion embarked on board H.M.S. "Vengeance," eighty-four guns, Captain Lushington, for Halifax, Nova Scotia. The numbers embarked were as follows: Officers, eighteen; sergeants, thirty; rank and file, five hundred and eleven.

The "Vengeance" arrived in Halifax harbour on the 4th and the regiment landed on the 5th of May. His Excellency Lieutenant-General Sir John Harvey, K.C.B., inspected the corps on the 7th, and spoke in terms of the highest praise of the state of the battalion, and of the manner in which it drilled.

Both battalions embarked on board H.M.S. "Belleisle" for Quebec on the 8th September, arrived there on the 21st, and proceeded thence by steamers to Kingston, Canada West, where the 1st Battalion arrived on the 25th, and the Reserve Battalion at London, Upper Canada, on the 29th September, 1847.

Lieutenant-Colonel Hutchinson exchanged with Lieutenant-Colonel A. T. Cunynghame into the Guards, and the command of the regiment devolved upon Lieutenant-Colonel Horn, who joined from the Reserve Battalion (stationed at London, C.W.), on the 19th June, 1849, and assumed the command of the 1st Battalion.

On the 1st April, 1850, the regiment moved from Kingston and London to Montreal in four divisions, under the command of Lieutenant-Colonel Horn, Major Crofton, Captain Berdmore, and Lieutenant-Colonel Cunynghame respectively, where they were finally amalgamated into one battalion of ten companies (one thousand men), under the command of Lieutenant-Colonel Horn. On the amalgamation the junior staff officers had to resign their appointments. Ensign Adams[1] was Adjutant of the 1st Battalion, and Ensign Padfield of the Reserve, but the latter being the senior staff officer, he became the Adjutant of the regiment. Major-General Sir A. Pilkington, K.C.B., succeeded to the Colonelcy of the regiment on the 25th November, 1850, vice Sir James Barnes deceased. Lieutenant A. Beatty died at St. Helens Island, Montreal, on the 2nd January, 1852.

On the 8th July, 1852, a disastrous fire broke out in Montreal, destroying one thousand five hundred houses. The regiment assisted in working the engines and protecting property to a large amount, and by its exertions succeeded in saving the barracks from destruction.

The following is an extract from the general order, published by the commander of the forces on the 9th July, 1852: "On several occasions the exertions of the XX Regiment have elicited the grateful acknowledgments of the inhabitants of Montreal, but on no previous occasion of fire was the steady, cheerful, and sustained efforts of the corps so conspicuously displayed." Major-General Sir A. Pilkington, Colonel of the regiment, died in February, 1853, and was succeeded by Major-General Sir William Chalmers, C.B., K.C.H.

On the 1st June, 1853, the regiment received orders to hold itself in readiness to embark for England. The following is an extract from the general orders, dated Montreal, 1st June, 1853: "The XX Regiment being about to embark for Great Britain, the Lieutenant-

---

[1] Ensign G. H. Adams joined the XX on the 14th April, 1846, and was appointed Adjutant on the 9th April, 1849. He was promoted Lieutenant (by purchase) on the 25th July, 1851. Lieutenant Adams exchanged to the 86th Regiment on the 13th February, 1852. He ultimately commanded the 86th (May, 1877, to November, 1881), and retired with the honorary rank of Major-General on the 19th November, 1881.

General commanding the forces cannot part with this highly distinguished corps without requesting the officers, non-commissioned officers, and soldiers to accept his thanks for their general good conduct during the five years they have been stationed under his immediate observation. Lieutenant-General Rowan will never cease to feel the warmest interest in the welfare of every individual composing the XX Regiment."

The regiment embarked at Quebec in the following order: Three companies, under the command of Major Crofton, on board the freight-ship "Thomas Arburthnot," on the 3rd June; three companies, under Captain Sharpe, on board the "Santipore," on the 9th June; headquarters and three companies, under Lieutenant-Colonel Horn, on the 10th June, on board the "Joseph Somes;" and two companies, under Captain Crespigny,[1] on board the "Emerald Isle," on the 24th June.

The several detachments landed at Southampton on the 1st, 5th, 7th, and 16th days of July, and proceeded to Winchester, where the regiment was stationed.

The undermentioned officers disembarked with the regiment: Lieutenant-Colonel Horn, Major Crofton, Captains Sharpe, Crespigny, and Lye; Lieutenants Tomson, Wood, Butler, Anstey, Dowling, Maycock, Hay, James, and Leet; Ensigns Lutyens, Peard, Dickens, and Warren; Captain and Paymaster South, Lieutenant and Adjutant Padfield, Quartermaster Bilham, Surgeon Maclagan, and Assistant-Surgeon Howard.

---

[1] Captain Crespigny was gazetted Ensign to the XX on the 29th July, 1836; he was promoted Lieutenant on the 20th July, 1839, and Captain on the 17th June, 1842. He retired to the unattached list on the 1st April, 1855, on which date he was appointed Paymaster. His name was subsequently changed to de Crespigny. He was Paymaster of the School of Musketry at Hythe from the date of its establishment, until the 15th August, 1881, when he retired with the rank of Colonel.

The establishment of officers at this time was thirty-eight. The Paymaster of the regiment, Captain C. South, retired on half pay on 11th October, 1853. This officer was born in the XX, and served in it for thirty-nine years. He joined the corps as Ensign on the 14th June, 1814; was promoted Lieutenant on the 17th of December, 1818. He received the thanks of the commander of the forces in Ireland on the 30th of April, 1818, for capturing and conveying into Sligo a smuggler, while in command of detachment on the west coast of Ireland.[1] He served with the regiment in St. Helena, and accompanied it to India; was Adjutant of the wing which was employed in the reduction of the hill forts in the Southern Mahratta country in the years 1824-27.

Lieutenant South was appointed Paymaster of the corps on the 23rd August, 1827, and he held this position until his retirement on half pay in October, 1853. He sailed with the brigade of Guards to the East as their Brigade Paymaster, and was present with the brigade in its services in 1854-55, and received the Crimean war medal, with clasps for Alma, Balaklava, Inkerman, and Sebastopol; also the Turkish medal.

On the conclusion of the war, Major South was appointed Paymaster of the Royal Academy, Woolwich, and he held this appointment until he was placed on retired pay with honorary rank of Lieutenant-Colonel on the 1st April, 1870, when he had completed, within a few days, fifty-six years' active service.

Lieutenant-Colonel South died suddenly in the

---

[1] *Hart's Army List*, 1874, pages 584, 585.

NOTE.—Colonel South was for many years Master of the regimental "Masonic Lodge, Minden, No. 63," and his portrait forms the frontispiece of the History of the Lodge.

library of the Royal Academy, in the year 1874, but the actual date does not appear in the official Army List.

Major-General Sir William Chalmers, having been appointed Colonel of the 78th Regiment, was succeeded in the Colonelcy of the XX by Major-General Henry Goodwin, C.B., dated 25th October, 1853. Major-General Goodwin died on the 26th December, and was succeeded by Major-General Nathaniel Thorn.

On the 13th January, 1854, three companies, under Major Crofton, proceeded to Plymouth, and occupied quarters in the Mill Bay barracks. On the 19th, four companies, under Captain Sharpe, went into quarters in Mount Wise and Granby barracks, Devonport, and detached Captain Crawley's[1] company to Dartmoor convict prison. The headquarters, under the command of Lieutenant-Colonel Horn, occupied St. George's Square barracks, Devonport, on the 26th January.

On the 23rd of March, the regiment received orders to prepare for active service. It was formed into eight service and two depôt companies; the establishment (one thousand men) was completed on the 31st March, but was increased to one thousand two hundred men in the following month.

The regiment moved into the Citadel, Plymouth, in the month of May.

The service companies of the corps were inspected by Major-General Sir Harry Smith, K.C.B., on the Hoe, Plymouth, on the 6th June, 1854.

---

[1] Henry Crawley passed from the Royal Military College to the XX as Ensign on the 11th October, 1827; he was promoted Lieutenant on the 11th June, 1830. Lieutenant Crawley was Adjutant of the regiment for three years (1838-41). On the 9th October, 1843, he was promoted Captain, and Major on the 11th May, 1855. Major Crawley served with the regiment in India, Bermuda, Canada, and in the Crimea from the 10th December, 1854, to the 16th July, 1855. He retired upon full pay on the 16th October, 1855, with the honorary rank of Lieutenant-Colonel.

The regiment embarked on board the P. and O. Company's steamship "Colombo," at the Royal Victualling Yard, Plymouth, on the 17th July, and sailed for Turkey, at two p.m., on the 18th. The details of the corps on this memorable embarkation are as follows:—Lieutenant-Colonel Fred. Horn (commanding); Majors H. D. Crofton and F. C. Evelegh; Brevet-Majors J. B. Sharpe and S. R. Berdmore; Captains R. L. Lye, G. Steevens, W. P. Radcliffe, W. W. Wood, C. R. Butler, and E. F. Anstey;[1] Lieutenants H. James, J. G. Hay, S. R. Chapman, E. Leet, G. Bennett, W. H. Macneill, G. S. Peard, M. T. Rotheram, and C. E. Parkinson; Ensigns G. Douglas, H. B. Vaughan, T. Parr, J. W. D. Lewis, and L. Kekewich; Paymaster G. Mosley, Lieutenant and Adjutant F. Padfield, Quartermaster D. Bilham, Surgeon E. Howard, Assistant Surgeon T. Wright, and forty-six sergeants, forty corporals, fifteen drummers, and eight hundred and sixty privates, or a total of nine hundred and ninety-one of all ranks.

---

[1] Captain Anstey was thirteen years in the regiment. He was promoted Captain on the 7th June, 1854. He was present at the battles of the Alma, Balaklava, Inkerman, and siege of Sebastopol, until the 18th June, 1855, when he retired.

CHAPTER XXX.
1854.

Voyage to the East—Varna—Crimea—The Disembarkation—March to the Alma—The Battle—Bivouac on the Field—March into the Interior—Cholera—Sebastopol—Commencement of the Siege—Heavy Fire on the Trenches—Battle of Balaklava—Attack on the 2nd Division—Casualties to 1st November.

AFTER a pleasant voyage the "Colombo" arrived at Malta on the 26th July, and sailed the following evening for Constantinople; on 2nd August she anchored in Becios Bay. Cholera appeared among the troops on board the "Colombo," and, two cases (Privates Towley and Levermore) having terminated fatally, the regiment was landed on the Asiatic shore, opposite to Bujukderé, on the 7th of August. The regiment again embarked on board the "Colombo," on the 30th of August, and sailed for Varna, proceeding thence on the 7th September to Baljik Bay, the rendezvous of the allied fleets.

At dawn on the 7th the "Colombo" sailed with the flotilla for the Crimea. Cholera still lingered with the corps, three men falling victims to it during the passage to the Crimea. On the evening of the 14th September the XX disembarked[1] (nine hundred and seventy-one all ranks) near Lake Saki. A lovely morning was

---

[1] Each officer carried a haversack containing 4½lbs. of cooked salt meat and biscuit, rolled great coat, blanket, wooden canteen, small ration of spirits, change of underclothing, and, of course, sword and revolver. Each man carried the same ration as the officer, great coat wrapped up into a kind of knapsack, inside of which was a pair of boots, socks, shirt, and forage cap; he also carried his canteen and a portion of the mess cooking utensils. In addition to his firelock and bayonet, he had a cartouche box with fifty rounds of ball for the Minié and sixty for the small bore. There were only thirty-five Minié rifles in the regiment.

followed by a cloudy, gloomy evening, and a wet night, during which the corps lay on the beach. Our men spent a miserable night, exposed to the drenching showers of rain (no tents had been sent ashore), with no other protection than that afforded by great coats and blankets saturated with moisture. Tents were issued on the following day (15th).

The XX formed part of the 1st Brigade, 4th Division.[1] At daybreak on the 19th of September, the regiment struck their tents and placed them on board the boats for conveyance to the ship appointed to receive them. At nine o'clock, with band playing and colours flying, the regiment commenced its march into the interior of the Crimea.[2] The night of the 19th was cold and damp, and the men were comfortless as they lay in the bivouac, rolled up in their coats and blankets.

About noon on the 20th of September, the army advanced on the Alma. The 4th Division, under Lieutenant-General Sir George Cathcart, was on the extreme left of the British line, and marched in echelon to the 1st Division to protect the left flank of the allied army from an attack by the enemy's cavalry. The XX was not actively engaged in the battle of the Alma, which took place on this day, and ended at five o'clock in the evening. The army bivouacked on the heights it had won. Colonel Horn commanded the 1st Brigade, 4th Division, and Lieutenant-Colonel H. D. Crofton

---

[1] The regiments of the 4th Division were the XX, 21st, 46th, 57th, 63rd, 68th, and 1st Battalion Rifle Brigade. In the Peninsular War the XX was also in the 4th Division.

[2] The march of the army was delayed by want of transport, and by the weak and sickly state of the men, many falling from the ranks with cholera. The XX would appear to be one of the few exceptions to the sickly state. Doctor Russell says the XX, 21st, and 1st Rifle Brigade were remarkably fresh and clean.

the XX, at the battle of the Alma, and until the 24th of September. On the 21st and 22nd, the regiment was employed in burying the dead and carrying the wounded to the ships.

At daybreak on the 23rd, the XX left the heights of Alma, marched into the beautiful valley of the Katcha,[1] and, on the following day, to Belbec, a distance of about six miles. Five men of the XX died at this village from cholera of a virulent type.

On the departure of the army, on the 25th of September, the 4th Division remained at Belbec to keep open the communications; on the 26th it pushed forward to Mackenzie's Farm, and descended thence to the Tchernaya. On touching the river on the 26th, the division, by a forced march, moved up the Khantor Pass to the plateau on the south side of Sebastopol, immediately confronting the "Great Redan." On the 30th September, Sir George Cathcart moved the division to the south-west of the ground afterwards known as Cathcart's Hill. The division was to support the left attack. Many a gallant soldier of the XX fell a victim to that scourge of the army, cholera.[2] Its ravages were accelerated by the exposure of the men, both by day and night, to all the variations of temperature. The regiment was still (3rd October) without tents, and the rations were often short; for instance, on the 26th and 27th of September, the regiment received no meat ration.

The siege of Sebastopol may be said to have commenced on the 10th of October, on which day ground

---

[1] In this valley delicious grapes, pears, and apples were plentiful; the ground was covered with crocuses and hyacinths, chiefly yellow and purple.

[2] Up to the 3rd October, the mortality of the army from cholera exceeded the casualties of the Alma; it was at the rate of 26 per cent.— *Times*.

was first broken, and the earthworks commenced. The XX was on duty in the trenches on the first day. Lieutenant Rotheram[1] was slightly wounded.

At half-past six a.m. on the 17th October, the allies opened a heavy cannonade on Sebastopol; a furious fire was sustained on both sides until evening, when it slackened considerably, and ceased entirely as the darkness fell. During this combat, Privates Wosley and Wyatt were killed; and Privates Langley, Riton, and Young were wounded.

A very heavy fire was directed against the trenches occupied by the XX on the 22nd October, by which two men were wounded. This slight loss was attributed to the excellence and solidity of the works.[2]

It was discovered, early on the morning of the 25th of October, that a strong Russian corps was moving into the valley of Balaklava, thereby threatening the rear of the allies' position, and interrupting the British communications with the town.

After defending the breast-work on Canrobert's Hill with rare valour against overwhelming numbers, and losing, in killed alone, no less than one hundred and seventy men out of one weak battalion, the little body of Turks which there had been left unsupported was at length driven in; and their comrades in the three half-battalions that had held the three easternmost of the redoubts on the line of the Causeway then withdrew in all haste, retreating at once on Balaklava. The 1st (His Royal Highness the Duke of Cambridge's) and the 4th Divisions were ordered to the scene of action at once, and arrived on the ground at 10-40 a.m. The

---

[1] Lieutenant Rotheram retired by the sale of his commission on the 15th October, 1855.
[2] *Times.*

4th Division, to which the XX belonged, was placed in advance of Balaklava, and in the centre of the British position.

After the cavalry charge, the 4th Division, together with two French regiments, advanced to operate against the right of the Russian position. About noon the XX, led by Colonel Horn, attacked and drove the Russians from the redoubt "Arabtabia," and re-captured the guns taken from the Turks in the morning. Private Lynch was killed. The fighting on this eventful day ceased at a quarter-past one, but the XX remained in position on the heights until relieved by French troops about five p.m.

On the 26th, the regiment supported the 2nd Division in repelling an attack of about four thousand Russians, who were driven back to Sebastopol with considerable loss.

Between the 27th October and 1st November, one drummer and four privates were wounded in the trenches.

CHAPTER XXXI.

The Battle of Inkerman.

THE following *précis* of the part played by the regiment at the battle of Inkerman will enable the action of its different fractions to be more readily understood. The 2nd Division, camped above the Home Ridge, under Major-General Pennefather, was attacked by the Russians about six o'clock on the morning of the 5th of November. The serious nature of the attack was not at first comprehended, and consequently only those men who had not been in the trenches on the previous night were ordered to reinforce the 2nd Division. Acting on this order, Colonel Horn with the left wing of the regiment marched to Inkerman. Colonel Horn's wing entered the fight on the left of the road, near the camp of the 2nd Division, and fought in the central parts of the field during the whole day. Two fractions of it became separated from the main body, and acted independently, under Lieutenants W. H. Dowling[1] and H. B. Vaughan, until near the close of the battle. At seven o'clock, all men remaining in camp, including those who had been on duty in the trenches on the previous night, were directed to proceed to

---

[1] Lieutenant Dowling had been on duty in the trenches on the previous night, but he marched to Inkerman with Colonel Horn. During the action he reminded the Colonel that although he had been in the trenches he was then present, and showing him his chako, which was pierced by a bullet, said, "Look, Colonel, the chances are a fellow ought to get off after that." From this moment he was not observed with the left wing. He and the volunteer party who were with him, in some way, became detached from Horn's wing, and will be found giving a good account of themselves in another part of the fight.

Inkerman. This order had been anticipated by Lieutenant-Colonel H. D. Crofton, who had already left camp with the right wing, and was marching straight to the Sandbag battery to support the Guards. Two companies were placed in position at the battery to strengthen its defences, and, after fending off the Russian attacks, charged down the steep slopes with the Guards and detachments of other corps. These companies were led by Captain W. P. Radcliffe.

The remaining companies of the right wing, under Lieutenant-Colonel Crofton, aligned on the right of the Coldstreams, and here came into communication with Sir George Cathcart, their own divisional commander, who happened to be at this point. At the request of the latter, or by his instructions, Colonel Crofton attacked a Russian column, broke it, and tumbled it down the hill, followed in pursuit, and again met Sir George Cathcart, who had also gone down the slope. Sir George now caused the survivors, together with the party under Lieutenant Dowling, that had become detached from Colonel Horn's wing, to be re-formed, and sent them against the Iäkoutsk Regiment, which now stood between him and the Guards. The survivors of this, the right wing, after carrying out Cathcart's orders, joined in part the Guards and in part the left wing, under Horn, which had assembled after the fight at the stone wall enclosure, near the camp of the 2nd Division.

The assembly sounded in the camp of the XX, about half-past six on the morning of the 5th of November, and at seven, the "left wing" (which included all men who had not been in the trenches on the previous night[1]), under the command of the

---

[1] Some men who had been in the trenches accompanied this wing.

officer commanding the corps, Colonel F. Horn, marched by the windmill towards Inkerman, which at this hour was covered by a fog, so dense that our men could not see fifty yards beyond until after mid-day. The wing came under fire near the camp of the 2nd Division; Colonel Horn deployed into line, and entered the conflict which was raging at this point.

As Mr. Kinglake's *History of the War* describes in great detail the services of the XX at Inkerman, we will freely quote from his invaluable work. Of Colonel Horn's wing, he says in volume v :—" Lord Raglan ordered an aide-de-camp, Captain Somerset Calthorpe, to bring forward the wing of the XX, and take it up at once to General Pennefather. This was speedily done. After moving up the Home Ridge by ground on the right of the post-road, Colonel Horn, with his men of the XX, there came under fire, and he at once deployed into line, then began to advance down the slope. The state of the atmosphere had by this time in some measure changed, and was clear enough to disclose a massive body of Russians pressing up through the brushwood, at a distance of about a hundred yards. The men of the XX delivered their fire, and thus manifesting their presence to the enemy's gunners on Shell Hill, drew upon themselves a storm of artillery missiles. Whilst still a good way off from the column they understood they were ordered to charge, they briskly worked their way forward under a powerful fire of both artillery and small arms, which was continually lessening their scanty numbers; but the obstacles interposed by rugged ground and thick brushwood soon distorted their line, and, by making a rapid movement impossible, precluded them from executing as yet what an Englishman means by a 'charge.' Thus circumstanced, they advanced firing. Before long, the exigencies of their hastened progress over obstructed ground had brought them into what one may call close skirmishing order. Their colours drew towards them some stragglers from other regiments, whom they welcomed into their fellowship. Presently they found that the enemy, whilst directly confronting them with his masses, was also overlapping their line on each of its flanks; and there was obvious room for question as to what in such case they should do; but in the absence of any direction proceeding from higher authority, it was judged that their right course must still be to 'force the enemy back down the hill,' and therefore fight on to the utmost against the troops straight in their front. There ensued a combat, maintained for some time by the industrious use of the firelock, and Colonel Horn's people at length had so nearly exhausted their cartridges as to be driven to the expedient of taking ammunition from the pouches of the dead. But a change of temper came on; and at the thought of the bayonet, these men of the XX seemed all to have but one will. Despite hostile masses on their flanks, they were glowing with that sense of power which is scarce other than power itself. To men of their corps, and to none other, had been committed the charge of a sacred historic tradition; and if they were to use the enchantment, they must not, they knew, endure that, in their time, its spell should be broken. The air was rent by a sound, which—unless they be men of the initiated regiment—people speak of as strange and 'unearthly.' After nearly a century from the day when their cry became famous, and forty years after the time when it last resounded in battle, these men of the XX once more had delivered their old 'Minden yell.'[1] Disregarding alike the force on their right and the force on their left, they sprang at the mass in their front, and drove it down the hillside. In pursuit, they inclined to the left, and were presently on the post-road. Following its course, they passed over the Barrier, and descended some hundred yards into the Quarry Ravine, but by that time they were in a desperate state, but, despite their forlorn condition, Colonel Horn's wing of the XX was never forced back to the crestwork. Sometimes losing, sometimes gaining ground, it remained fighting out in the front."

What remained of Colonel Horn's wing, after four hours' continual fighting in the central parts of the field, and in advanced positions, was slowly falling back, about noon, from the ground between the Barrier and the Kitspur, where it was joined by half a battalion of French Chasseurs. Colonel Horn fronted his men, the Chasseurs formed up on his right, and for some time they held their ground against two columns of the enemy. This combat was sustained by musketry fire alone: no resolute bayonet charges were undertaken. Colonel Horn was here temporarily disabled by a wound in his thigh, and was obliged, for a brief interval, to withdraw from the fight. Our men had exhausted their ammunition, and the French Chasseurs drew off to their right, but the Russians did not follow up their advantages, and this combat came to an end.

About two o'clock, in obedience to the orders of the Duke of Cambridge, Colonel Horn again advanced

---

[1] In his recollections (1857), Sergeant Campbell says, "that the companies at the Sandbag battery gave an unearthly yell that Russians never heard before or since."

with the remnant of his wing; it was exposed to artillery and musketry fire, but was not otherwise engaged. The battle was now waning, the Russians were drawing off and retiring into Sebastopol. Colonel Horn withdrew his wing and fell back to the stone wall enclosure near the camp of the 2nd Division, where he was joined by the other portions of the corps.

Lieutenant H. B. Vaughan marched to Inkerman with Colonel Horn's wing and carried one of the colours, but he was relieved from this post on reaching the camp of the 2nd Division. Vaughan took part in the victorious charge made by the wing, but, together with some men of the corps, became separated from the main body in the Quarry Ravine. The exploits of this little band and their leader are thus told by Mr. Kinglake in his fifth volume:—"Lieutenant Vaughan chanced to be with the first of the pursuing soldiery, and he found himself in command of about a score of men belonging partly to his own regiment—the XX—but partly also to the Guards and regiments of the 2nd Division. With the aid of a volunteer officer[1] (Lieutenant Johnson, of the Indian Irregular Cavalry), he formed up his men across the road, and moved steadily forward, pushing always before him the enemy's disordered troops. He was approaching the part of the Quarry Ravine where it makes a sudden bend in its course, when, on looking towards the crest straight before him, he saw a Russian light battery brought rapidly on to its edge; and presently he and his men were under its plunging fire. In a moment he saw what to do. Choosing out a few of the Guards and

---

[1] Attached to the XX.

other men armed with the Minié rifle, he bade them disregard altogether the enemy's infantry, sight their pieces for three hundred yards, and steadily shoot at the battery. He was so well obeyed by his marksmen—they knelt down and took aim with studious and deliberate care—that the battery, after firing another round, limbered up and made off in great haste. It was only on the approach of fresh columns that the now scattered fragments of Horn's victorious soldiery, and with them Vaughan's little band, began to fall back from the far advanced ground they had reached in the eagerness and heat of pursuit."

Vaughan's party, and other small fractions of different regiments, were forced to retire from the Quarry Ravine by a large and overwhelming column of fresh troops. Of this retreat and the incidents that followed, Mr. Kinglake says:—" Other knots of our soldiery became linked in retreat with the troops near Bellairs, bringing up their number to nearly, perhaps, two hundred; and amongst the accessions on the right—proper right of our line—was that score of men, under Vaughan, chiefly men of the XX, and Guardsmen, whom we saw doing venturesome service in an earlier stage of the battle. From time to time, after retreating a little way, Vaughan caused the men with him to turn and show front, and, there being amongst them a few who have some cartridges left, he was able to vex the assailants with occasional shots; but, of course, no such efforts as these could retard for even an instant the march of the heavy trunk column; and, indeed, at this time our interposed soldiery must have been doing the enemy more good than harm, because they screened him from artillery-fire. Suddenly, and with great joy, they found that they were retreating upon a strong column of red-capped soldiery drawn up in good order at a distance of no more than a hundred yards. This force was the battalion of the 7th Léger. The interposed distance was lessening every instant, and it soon became fit that, without another moment's delay, our people should cease to linger between the French and the Russians; for, whilst being themselves almost harmless for want of cartridges, they were screening the enemy from the fire of a strong battalion. Accordingly, the knot of our men, under Vaughan, with the rest of those forming the right—proper right—of the interposed English troops, fell back into the rear of the French column, and then, briskly re-fronting, formed line; but towards the centre and left, our men, though preparing to do the like, had become so weary, so sullen, so callous by this time to danger, that they were provokingly slow in their movements. They at length fell back into the rear of the French battalion, and there formed up in support as Vaughan's men on the right had already done; but their tardiness had already wrought mischief, for, by the time the front had been thus at last cleared, the head of the Russian column was so near that its soldiery, if so they should choose, might charge home, and offer cold steel without first having to suffer under more than one round of fire."

As soon as their front was clear, the French battalion (Vaissier's 7th Léger) poured one volley into the Russians, but, when ordered to charge, a panic seized the battalion, and, notwithstanding the efforts of their officers, they fell back in disorder, and forced their way through Vaughan's men, who were drawn up on the right of the line. A young French officer rushed out in front of the battalion and hoisted his cap upon the point of his sword. Vaughan sprang forward and stood by his side, Lieutenant Parkinson[1] followed his example, and a third officer did likewise. There the four stood steadfast, amidst a storm of musket balls, without being even once struck. The Russians saw the confusion, and seized the opportunity for charging the wavering battalion with loud cheers. But they suddenly stopped dead; they had at this moment been pierced in flank by Colonel Daubeney with some men of the 55th Regiment. This gave the French officers an opportunity of rallying their men. Someone near Vaughan cried out in French, "Drums to the front!" Both the drummers and buglers ran out boldly and sounded their "Double quick, charge." The whole line, English and French, pressed forward, and, after a moment's hesitation, the Russian column fell back from before them, pursued in anything but an orderly fashion by the exulting soldiery.

The foregoing pages will give some idea of the brilliant and ceaseless efforts of Lieutenant Vaughan's small party: never deterred by numbers, advancing or retiring as the exigencies of the moment demanded, with no fixed ground for their operations, fighting any and wherever the enemy was to be found, and so they continued until ordered to fall back to the place appointed for the re-assembly of the corps.

We must now recount the proceedings of Colonel Crofton and his wing, composed chiefly of those who had been in the trenches on the previous night.

The usual relief of the parties on duty in the trenches took place at four p.m., on the 4th of November, the

---

[1] Lieutenant, afterwards Captain, Parkinson served throughout the Crimean campaign and the Indian Mutiny, received the war medals, also the 5th class of the Medjidie and Sardinian Medal. He died of dysentery at Benares, on the 2nd of June, 1858.

XX furnishing one hundred and sixty men of the relieving body. There had been a continual succession of showers from the early morning, but, as the darkness set in, the rain fell in one unceasing torrent, and before an hour's duty was completed officers and men were wet to the skin. One portion of the detachment were in the trenches, and the other, under Captain W. P. Radcliffe and Lieutenant W. H. Dowling, were posted in extended order at some considerable distance beyond the advanced trench. The wing returned to camp about half-past five, on the morning of the 5th. These men had been exposed to rain and cold, and, within one hour of their return to camp, before they had an opportunity of changing their clothes or breaking their fast, asked that they might be led to the front on hearing that an attack was imminent. Lieutenant Dowling repeated the men's request, adding that he wished to accompany them, and, together with all those who happened to be with him, marched to Inkerman with Colonel Horn's party. Dowling and his men soon became separated from Horn's wing, and worked their way up to the Sandbag battery, there joining their own wing, which had entered the battle under Colonel Crofton.

Sir George Cathcart had given instructions that those who had been in the trenches on the previous night were to remain in camp, but, on learning the serious nature of the attack, he withdrew the detaining order, but he had previously been quietly disobeyed.[1]

About seven o'clock, Lieutenant-Colonel Crofton and the right wing marched in fours from camp; they were ordered to support the Guards, who were at this

---

[1] *Invasion of the Crimea*, vol. v, page 81.

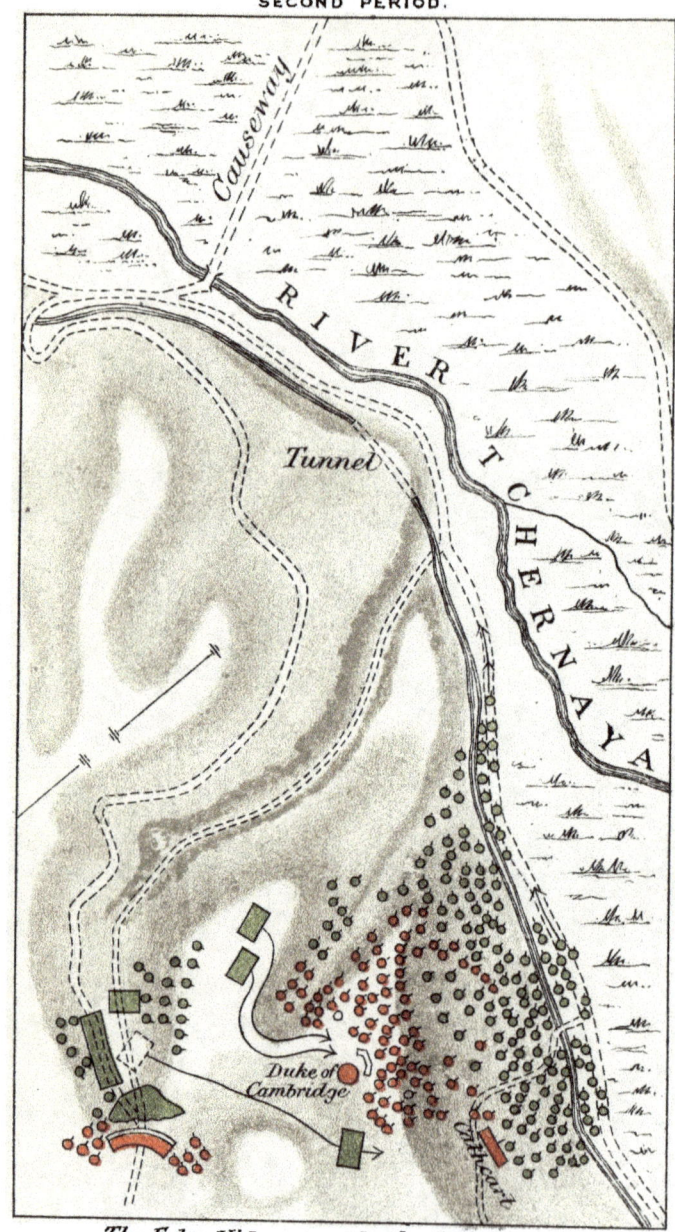

FIGHT ON MOUNT INKERMAN
SECOND PERIOD.

The False Victory won by the Guards and some companies of the XX, 46th, 68th and 95th regiments.
Kinglake Vol V, Chap VI, page 258.

time hard pressed. As the wing approached the Sandbag battery, Colonel Crofton gave the command "Front turn," which changed the formation to an advance in line, which was, however, of short duration, as Colonel Crofton halted the wing at the place where the Duke of Cambridge and his staff were standing. They were here ardently welcomed by Colonel Cunynghame,[1] who shouted "Hurrah! here comes the grand old Twentieth! you are much wanted." The Duke exhorted them to be careful how they fired, as his men were just in front. The wing again advanced, some companies joining in the defence of the Sandbag battery, and the others, under Colonel Crofton, aligning on the right of the Coldstreams, and were here brought into communication with Sir George Cathcart, their divisional commander.

The action of these few companies, in numbers not reaching perhaps one hundred men, is thus told by Mr. Kinglake :—" Passing now from our right towards our left, we come next to Colonel Crofton's wing of the XX, or to that fraction of it which had aligned on the right of the Coldstream, and was now divided by only a narrow space from the scene of the charge led by Torrens. Desiring, perhaps (as naturally he might), to act in conformity with the operations of Cathcart (his divisional chief), Crofton undertook to assail the battalion directly confronting him, but was wounded at an early moment. A staff officer chanced to ride up who proved to be Colonel Cunynghame, 'an old XX man.' Lieutenant Dowling, accosting him, said: 'Colonel, all our mounted officers are killed or wounded. Where shall we go?'

---

[1] Colonel Cunynghame was a Quartermaster-General to the 1st Division. He formerly commanded the XX.

Cunynghame, accepting[1] the leadership thus cast upon him by the chance of battle, caused the troops to form a well-knit line, marched them down to within a hundred yards of the enemy's column, and then, halting them, opened a fire which forced the battalion to yield. The halt of these XX men was not long maintained. When Cunynghame left them, they not only advanced in pursuit, but 'drove the Russians like sheep,' and were soon far below the crest, some getting down close to the spot where Cathcart sat in his saddle, and in this fortuitous way rejoining the commander of their own division." (Pages 246-7, vol. v.)

But a catastrophe was at hand; General Cathcart and his men were intercepted by a Russian column (the Iäkoutsk Regiment), which was now on the heights above them, from which they had so recently charged. The further action of this intercepted body is thus described by Kinglake:—" There were near him (Sir G. Cathcart), dispersed in the brushwood, some men, who, though busied like the rest of the troops in pursuit, could still be reached by his orders. They were only some fifty in number, but they belonged to the XX, a regiment of historic renown, which is famous for imparting its aggregate quality to the individual soldier. Cathcart gathered together the fifty men of the XX, and, with these formed rudely in line, undertook to move up against the overhanging body of some seven or eight hundred men which stood on the crest above him. In ascending to make their attack, these few 'Twentieth' men were obstructed by the varying abruptness of the acclivity; but, if aggregate strength

---

[1] The leading into action of Dowling's detachment by the late General Cunynghame is recorded in Hart's *Army List*.

was thus neutralized, the individual soldier toiled forward with a determination all his own, and the twenty or thirty men who formed the right of the line—Maitland[1] forced his horse along side of them—had not long been climbing the steep, when on the shoulder of the hill they emerged all at once from below into the close presence of the enemy. Then, panting after their effort, they sprang at the left of the column, the part directly confronting them, and the Russians there exposed to the onset began to break and give way without waiting for the thrust of the bayonet. But in the right-hand part of the column its troops stood their ground with more firmness, and did not fall back. Even there, however, the Russians, though turning round, still so far gave way to the English ascendant that they 'accepted the files.' Here, there, and in several places, they allowed some strong wilful assailant to tear his way in through their ranks, and every intruder thus received into the hostile mass fought hard, as may well be supposed, for life no less than for victory, using sometimes the butt end of the musket, sometimes a ready fragment of rock. From the vantage-height of his saddle, Maitland was able to see the combats thus maintained on his left. A column which endures this kind of invasion is commonly doomed; but here the disproportion of numbers was overwhelming; and, however formidable the intruding assailant might prove to any hapless Russian so planted or packed as to be within reach of his bayonet, the paths of blood he thus opened were after all so narrow, so few, and so far apart, that the body, in spite of such stabs, was able to

---

[1] Major Maitland, D.A.A.G., 4th Division, now General, on the retired list.

hold together; and one must infer, though no witnesses speak, that of the brave Twentieth men who thus engulfed themselves bodily in the depths of the column, a large proportion fell slain. Still, if Russian narrators speak truly, there were some, at least, of our soldiery who cut their way out through the column. The Russians, indeed, seemed to have thought that the main body of their assailants succeeded in cutting through. 'At this moment,' says General de Todleben, 'confusion began in the ranks' (Cathcart's ranks), 'but being quickly rallied, these brave troops made a supreme effort, and throwing themselves with desperation upon the Iäkoutsk Regiment, they succeeded in forcing its ranks, and cutting for themselves a way through the midst of our soldiers.'" (Vol. v, page 276.)

The gallant Dowling[1] was shot through the head, as he led his small band of heroes to the charge. It is very gratifying to be able to confirm General de Todleben's statement, that some of the XX did cut their way through the Russian column.

The following is an extract from a letter, sent by a sergeant of the XX to his friends in England; and by him, no doubt, intended only for the home circle, but fortunately for us it appeared in the *Times* of November 27th, 1854:—"We charged into a body of Russians, without any support, and it's the greatest miracle in the world how we ever came out again. The last words we heard from Sir George Cathcart were, 'Nobly done, Twentieth.'"

This is the last we are able to glean of this fragment of the corps; no doubt some found their way to the

---

[1] Lieutenant W. H. Dowling had been eleven years in the XX. He was with the regiment at Balaklava, the commencement of the siege of Sebastopol, and at Inkerman. He was Subaltern of the Grenadier company.

small stone enclosure, close to the camp of the 2nd Division, where the different groups and parties of the regiment seem to have met. That it suffered severely, in both killed and wounded, there can be no doubt. Colonel Crofton[1] was dangerously wounded (shot in the neck, right hand and wrist shattered, and contused knee) in the early part of the first attack; and Brevet-Major Sharpe was shot through the body at the same moment.[2]

We must now follow the fortunes of that fraction of Colonel Crofton's wing that remained at the Sandbag battery. These companies were under the command of Captain Radcliffe; part of his men were in the battery, and the remainder on the crest of the ridge. They had not been long here when the Russians made their crowning effort to carry the heights by hurling three thousand men of the Okhotsk Battalions against the defenders of the ridge and battery.

Of this struggle, Mr. Kinglake writes at page 230, vol. v:—"They began to roll up the line of our people ranged under the parapet, and already had fought their way on as far as the first embrasure, when some men of the Grenadiers, and some of the XX, and some too of the 95th, collected themselves for a blow, and then fell upon the intruding mass with such impetuosity as to

---

[1] Colonel Crofton served seventeen years in the corps. He commanded at the Alma, and, as we have seen, a wing at Inkerman. But his services passed unrecognised. This lamented officer was shot on the barrack square at Preston, on Saturday, the 14th of September, 1861, by Private McCaffery, 32nd Regiment. Colonel Crofton was in command of the Depôt Battalion. McCaffery stated that he did not intend to shoot the Colonel; he also shot the Adjutant. Both were heirs to Baronetcies.

[2] Major Sharpe joined the XX as Ensign on the 27th March, 1835. He was promoted Lieutenant 12th April, 1839; Captain, 7th September, 1841; and Brevet-Major on the 20th June, 1854. He was with the regiment in Bermuda and Canada, and was present at all the actions in the Crimea. Major Sharpe died at Scutari, on the 28th of December, 1854.

thrust it back out of the battery, and the rest of the column then bending under the power of the Scots Fusiliers, the whole force was overthrown and driven fast down the hill side."

Not satisfied with repelling the assaults of the enemy, the whole of Captain Radcliffe's men, together with the Guards and men of other regiments, charged over the hill and fell upon the Russians below; they would suffer no check from their officers, but pursued eagerly as long as the enemy could be reached and their ammunition lasted.

Mr. Kinglake, in page 255, vol. v, describes this scene as follows:—"All seemed to be flight and pursuit, Russian masses descending the steeps in headlong confusion—English soldiers tearing in full chase with a vehemence hard to control. At some points the Russians, when neared by their pursuers, made haste to throw down their arms and fall prostrate in the attitude of Oriental worship, calling piteously for mercy in the name of Christos! The rout seemed complete." And further, at page 258, goes on to say: "So now along the whole line, which had extended from Cathcart's on our right to where Champion's wing of the 95th thus charged on our left, the enemy was in hasty retreat."

During this charge, Captain Butler of the Grenadier company was wounded in the shoulder, but not before he had shot with his revolver four Russian soldiers.

Assisted by Captain Butler, Lieutenants Hay and James,[1] Captain Radcliffe collected all the men—about one hundred—within reach, irrespective of regiment,

---

[1] Henry James exchanged into the XX on the 7th April, 1848, and was promoted Captain on the 11th December, 1854. He served in the Crimean campaign, including the battles of the Alma, Balaklava, Inkerman, and the siege of Sebastopol, until the 9th August, 1855, when he retired by the sale of his commission.

and led them back towards the Sandbag battery. But here an unpleasant surprise awaited them; the heights they had so recently left in the full flush of victory were now held by a dense mass of Russians. Our men were without ammunition, so Radcliffe decided to lead them round by the side of the hill; for half a mile they had to run the gauntlet of an incessant, clinging fire of musketry. Many men fell here. They were soon rejoiced by the sight of a French regiment, which now came up and intervened itself between Radcliffe and his assailants; he then pushed on until he came to a boundary wall near the camp of the 2nd Division, where his men at once came under the fire of a Russian battery which, as can be imagined, caused considerable annoyance, until it was silenced by Collingwood Dickson's eighteen-pounders. In the meantime, the different fragments of the corps were being re-united. Colonel Horn and all that remained of his wing had come in; Vaughan and his small band, ordered in from the front, had found their way hither; and the few stragglers that had fought with Crofton and Dowling had again rejoined the corps.

The regiment received a fresh supply of ammunition, and was formed up preparatory to advancing in support of the troops still engaged. About this time Captain Wood[1] was slightly wounded.

The XX made their final movement against the enemy in this great battle by supporting the skirmishers, during which Lieutenant Bennett was wounded. The last casualty in the regiment on this eventful day

---

[1] Captain W. T. W. Wood exchanged into the XX on the 25th April, 1845, and was promoted Captain on the 20th January, 1854. He was present at the battles of the Alma, Balaklava, Inkerman (wounded), and the siege of Sebastopol. He retired by the sale of his commission on the 12th February, 1855.

occurred here, when a man of the corps was killed by a shell from one of the ships in the harbour.

Colonel Horn was the senior surviving officer of the 4th Division, and brought it out of action. Major Evelegh (who fought all day with Horn's wing) assumed the command of the regiment, and arrived in camp with it about five p.m.[1]

At Inkerman, fourteen officers and three hundred and forty men of the XX were engaged; they fought incessantly and against enormous odds during eight and a half hours. About one hundred and forty men were on duty in the trenches, under Captain G. Steevens and Lieutenant G. S. Peard.[2] The casualties of the XX exceeded those of any other corps, Guards excepted. They were as follows:—

	Officers.	Sergeants.	Drummers.	Rank and file.
Killed	1	2	1	27
Wounded	8	9	1	119
Missing	...	...	...	6
Total	9	11	2	152[3]

Of the wounded, four men died before the returns were made up, and by the 31st of December twelve had died at Scutari.

The following are the names of those who fell at Inkerman:—Lieutenant W. H. Dowling; Sergeants G. Boteel and J. Young; Drummer H. Wheeler; Privates T. Ashby, T. Berry, T. Bradford, S. Byford,

---

[1] The return of the Guards and XX from Inkerman is immortalised in Miss Thompson's celebrated picture.

[2] Lieutenant Peard joined the XX as Ensign on the 5th July, 1848, was promoted Lieutenant on the 24th March, 1854, and Captain on the 11th May, 1855. He was with the regiment at the Alma, Balaklava, and siege of Sebastopol. Captain Peard retired from the service on the 1st August, 1857.

[3] These numbers are taken from Lord Raglan's despatch, dated 23rd November, 1854, submitting corrected returns of the casualties at Inkerman.

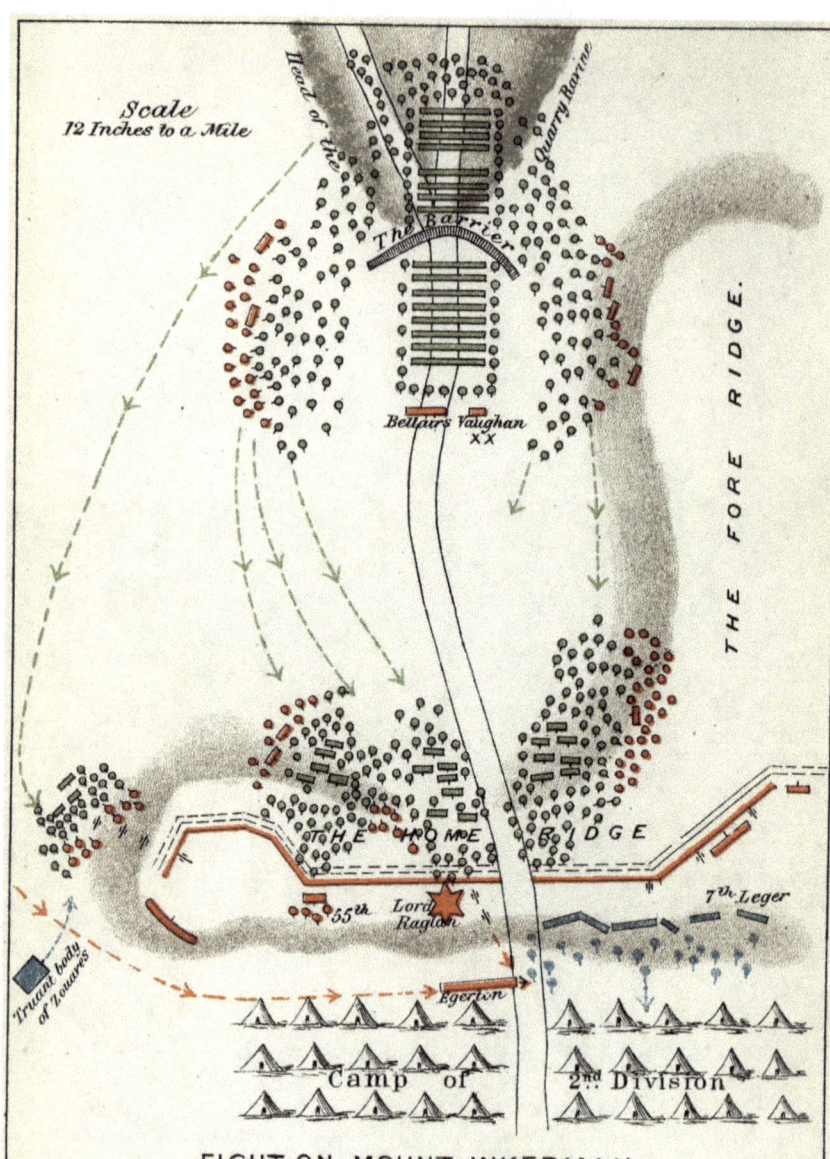

FIGHT ON MOUNT INKERMAN
Third Period.

The Enemy's advanced Forces breaking over the crest of Home Ridge, capturing the half of an English Battery, driving off the rest of its guns, surprising and forcing back a remnant of the 55th Regiment and causing the 9th Leger to retreat into Pennefather's Camp. The Enemy's great trunk column simultaneously advancing and crossing the Barrier.

Kinglake Vol V.

P. Carty, J. Clarke, J. Deffrey, P. Fallow, E. C. Hinton, J. Masterson, B. McDonough, T. McGovern, J. Merriday, H. Moles, P. O'Kelly, G. Pritchard, C. Payne, W. Perry, E. Poor, T. Rainbrin, J. Slater, G. Stebbins, H. Wallis, M. Whelan,[1] and J. Wood.

The following officers and non-commissioned officers were wounded:—Colonel F. Horn; Brevet-Lieutenant-Colonel H. D. Crofton; Brevet-Major J. B. Sharpe (died at Scutari, 28th December, 1854); Captains W. T. W. Wood and R. C. Butler; Lieutenant G. H. Bennett; Lieutenant and Adjutant F. Padfield; Ensign L. Kekewich[2] (carrying the colours); Colour-Sergeants J. Mathison (died 23rd December, 1854) and J. Whybrow[3]; Sergeants S. Gibson, G. W. Griffiths, A. Lawrie, J. Parker, A. Rule (was given the "Legion of Honour" by consent of the regiment), J. Rolph (died 15th December, 1854), and J. Smith; Corporals F. Best, J. Campbell, J. Grey, J. S. Langmaid, M. Magrane, W. O'Neill, J. Osborne, and G. Thorne.

Privates J. Hawkins, W. Hobday, H. Houghton, W. Love, M. Mullins, and J. Murray are the names of the six men reported as missing. There is no doubt they were taken prisoners, and were all, most probably, wounded. We know the fate of four of them. In the *Times* of January 4th, 1855, the subjoined letter was

---

[1] A party of the Light Company searching for wood in the month of March, 1855, found the skeleton of Private Whelan. They knew the remains to be his, as the braces and cap were marked with his number. The skeleton of a Russian soldier lay close by.

[2] Died at Corfu, of dysentery, 16th February, 1855.

[3] This non-commissioned officer was promoted Sergeant-Major in December, 1858. He served throughout the Crimean and Indian Mutiny campaigns. Was promoted Ensign, 10th April, 1860, and Lieutenant on the 10th October, 1864. He exchanged to the 58th Regiment, and was employed for many years in the Indian Barrack Department. He served in the 2nd Battalion Rifle Brigade for two years, and retired upon a pension with the rank of Lieutenant-Colonel on the 21st November, 1877.

published. It was written by a man of the XX, a a prisoner in the hospital, inside Sebastopol:—

"Sebastopol, November 23rd.

"I have got the opportunity of writing to let you know where I am. I was taken prisoner on the morning of the 5th. I was close to that battery on the hill, when the Russians advanced up to the battery. I was hit by a musket ball on the right ear; at the same time a stone or piece of shell hit me on the body and knocked me down. Before I could get up again I had my firelock taken from me, and was hit on the head, which left me insensible for a time. Seven or eight of them pricked me with their bayonets, and hit me with the butts of their firelocks; one was going to fire at me, but the others would not let him. They dragged my belt off, and took me over the bridge where their wounded were, till night. Then they took us close to the harbour on the right of the town, into a hospital. I am getting quite well now. The officers are very kind to us. We have 1lb. of bread, some soup with a little piece of meat in it, and a glass of tea per day. They say that they shall shift all that are able to go in a few days, but I do not know where. I saw John Hawkins the first night, but I have not seen him since; I think he must have died. Mullins of No. 1 is dead. There is me and Murray of No. 1. Will you let my friends know where I am?"

The name of the writer was not published. Of the four mounted officers, three had their horses shot under them, viz.: Colonels Horn, Crofton, and the Adjutant, Lieutenant Padfield.

The colours of the regiment were borne by Lieutenants Hay, Vaughan, Parkinson, and Ensign Kekewich.

Sergeant D. Loughland and four men[1] volunteered to carry the body of Sir George Cathcart off the field, which they did under a heavy fire. Sergeant Loughland received the medal for "Distinguished conduct in the Field." The four men were also decorated on the recommendation of the members of the deceased General's staff.

This ends our narrative of one of the most glorious days in the history of the corps.

Major F. C. Evelegh, Captains W. P. Radcliffe and R. C. Butler received Brevet promotion for "Distinguished conduct in the Field" at Inkerman; and Colour-Sergeant P. Geraghty[2] was promoted Ensign.

AN INKERMAN EPISODE.

ASSISTANT-SURGEON RICHARD WOLSELEY,[3] XX REGIMENT.

OF the many small groups that had been gathered together, after the charge of the Guards, XX, and others from the Sandbag battery, there was one

---

[1] Unfortunately the names of these men are not recorded in the Manuscript Records, and we have not been able to ascertain them with any degree of certainty. They were not published in any paper.

[2] Colour-Sergeant Geraghty was born in the XX at Cork, on the 30th May, 1818. He enlisted in the regiment on attaining the age of fourteen years, and was for twelve years a non-commisioned officer. Promoted to Ensign on the 5th November, 1854, he obtained his Lieutenancy on the 17th February, 1855. Appointed Adjutant of the regiment on the 16th November, 1855, and promoted Captain in the 2nd Battalion on the 10th September, 1858. Captain Geraghty served throughout the Crimean campaign, and in the Indian Mutiny, including the siege of Lucknow. Captain Geraghty was for many years Town Major at Kingston, Canada West. He retired from the service by the sale of his commission, and was subsequently appointed a Military Knight of Windsor. He died in the year 1877, but the date of his death has not been ascertained.

[3] A younger brother of General Viscount Wolseley. He was killed by a fall from his horse at Meerut on the 23rd December, 1886. At the time of his death he was Deputy-Surgeon-General.

endeavouring to reach its former position on the heights; but, during the ascent and as the fog lifted, they discovered that a Russian column (the same body that Dowling's fifty men had, but a short time before, so gallantly torn their way through) was standing between them and the crest they sought to reach.

At pages 276-7, vol. v, Mr. Kinglake thus describes their action:—"They had not yet moved far up the hill, when they found themselves directly confronted and fired upon by a part of the interposed battalion, which—because of the smoke and mist—our people had not before seen. These Russians were disposed in no order that well could be traced by the eye, but they formed a thick belt of infantry at a distance of only about twenty or thirty paces from our people. It chanced that with the English soldiery thus challenged no combatant officer was present; yet amongst them they had that kind of leader which the stress of the moment required. Assistant-Surgeon Wolseley, of the XX Regiment, had marched with Crofton's wing of the regiment. He was one who lived, heart and soul, under the dominion of the Christian faith; but the heraldic motto of his house was expressive, perhaps, of the tendencies handed down to him by his warlike ancestors, and the theory which it bade him remember was this one: 'Man to man is, and must be, a wolf.'[1] Unconsciously biassed, perhaps, by his inborn fighting propensity, he had contrived to persuade himself that the spot where his medical services would prove the most useful was—of all places on earth!—the Sandbag battery; and there, strange as it may seem, he had established his field hospital. When afterwards the

---

[1] *Homo homini lupus.*

hundred fell back, he had moved along with them, and was now one of those whose retreat appeared to be blocked by a part of the Iäkoutsk Battalion. He had come into action without his sword, but he uttered a self-inspiriting prayer for the welfare of his soul, without deigning to ask from God any mere prolongation of life; and when he had got his hold of a firelock—choosing one, by the blessing of Heaven, which had the bayonet fixed—he was a formidable antagonist for even the most pious soldier of Russia's orthodox Church. Here and there, some moments before, he had heard orders given or repeated; and they were all to the same effect, and all consistent with the dictates of his own soldiery instinct, he had one at least of the requisites for conducting a difficult enterprise,—that is, a clear, steadfast idea. Wolseley spoke a few words to the men within range of his voice, and told them what they now had to fight for was—not victory only, but—life. Then, the minds of his hearers being ripe, he gave them the word of command, 'Fix bayonets, charge, and keep up the hill!' The soldiery answered him with a burst of hurrahs, sprang forward to the charge, and in the next instant were tearing their way through the thicket of Russians. They suffered, it is believed, heavy loss in proportion to their scanty number (one-half); but they achieved their purpose, and came out at length on the southern or English side of the force which had undertaken to block their path."

CHAPTER XXXII.

1854-1855.

Day after Inkerman—Burial of Sir George Cathcart—The Siege of Sebastopol—The Great Storm—Hardships and Sufferings endured—The Regimental Arrangements—Working Parties commended—Armed with the Enfield—Attack of the 23rd March—Lord Raglan's Despatch—Assault of the 18th June—Operations during July and August—Assault of the 8th September—Death of Major Chapman.

ON the day after Inkerman, the regiment was employed in the sad and melancholy office of burying the dead and removing the wounded. In the afternoon it was present, under arms, at the burial of its late Divisional Commander, Lieutenant-General Sir George Cathcart.

From the 7th to the 14th of November, the siege dragged on; the monotonous cannonade was not broken by even an affair of outposts or a sortie from the town. In this period one man of the regiment was wounded.

On the 14th November, there occurred the "Great Storm." From six a.m. until midnight, a violent hurricane swept over the harbour of Balaklava and the camp of the allies. In the camp not a tent[1] was left standing, the air was filled with canvas, blankets, great coats, &c. Our men stood in groups in front of their levelled tents while rain and wind tore over them; exposed to cold and wet without the remotest chance of obtaining food

---

[1] There was, we believe, one single exception. Captain Radcliffe's tent withstood the gale, and afforded a friendly shelter to Lieutenant Peard and another officer who were brought into it sick.

or shelter until the storm ceased. About midnight, the wind veered round to the west and became much colder; this change was soon followed by a storm of sleet and snow. Men were starved to death by cold.[1] In volume vii, page 160, Mr. Kinglake thus describes the storm and the sufferings it inflicted upon the army:—
"In the evening of the 13th, after wild storms of rain, there set in a calm, which lasted until an hour before sunrise on the following day; but then over the open downs on the Chersonese, and the neighbouring coasts, harbours, and roadsteads, there swept on the 14th November a violent hurricane, accompanied by thunder and lightning, by heavy rain, hail, and sleet, and followed before the day ended by driving snow. The storm was a cyclone revolving upon a centre which passed from south to north at the rate of no more than some twenty miles an hour, but on this moving axis, the whirlwind flew round with a velocity said to have reached nearly a mile in the minute. Twenty-one supply and store ships were dashed to pieces. On shore, it tore up trees by the roots and unroofed houses. Into the camp of the allies the tempest brought unspeakable misery. The tents not only fell, but were many of them torn to pieces and swept away utterly, with all the things they contained; the hospital marquees presented so great a breadth of canvas to the rage of the blast, that, in spite of every effort to uphold them, they were almost the first tents to fall; and thus not only men fit for duty, but the wounded, the sick, and the dying became exposed all at once to the biting cold of the blast, and deluged with rain and sleet. The trenches were quickly flooded, no food, camp fires could not be

---

[1] "About six in each Division."—*Times*.

lighted, and no remedy for this miserable condition of things."

With the morning of the 15th came a bright, clear sky, and, though cold, hungry, and ankle deep in mud, the men's spirits were raised on once more beholding the sun. These hardships did not end with the storm, but had to be endured by our half-starved, ill-clad soldiers through a great portion of the intensely cold and dreary winter, which they spent in the trenches before Sebastopol.

Two men of the regiment were wounded in the trenches on the 22nd November. Private Cowie was killed on the 23rd, and four men were wounded on the 26th.

The incessant rains turned the trenches into dykes. The men were without shelter or protection from the cold, their threadbare, worn-out clothing affording no warmth. The constant exposure and hardships soon resulted in a large increase of sickness, and on the 28th of November cholera broke out, the average death rate for the army being sixty per day.[1]

At this period the siege was practically suspended, so far as the British were concerned; but there appears to have been apathy on both sides, as the Russians only fired one gun in every five minutes.

---

[1] *Times.*

NOTE.—Many were the contrivances adopted to ensure protection from the severities of the weather after the "Great Storm." The most successful of the enterprising builders were Captains Radcliffe and Macneill, if their own idea of comfort and the envy of others is to be taken as a measure of success. Their hut was constructed in this way. They dug a pit twelve feet long, eight feet wide, and four feet deep. After many futile efforts on the part of their faithful servants, wood to form the roof was "procured" from Balaklava. The beams were first covered with brushwood, followed by a layer of mud, which was covered with horses' skins, and which in their turn received a final coating of mud. A room perfectly wind and water-tight was the result, and occupied exactly a month in preparing.

The roads from Balaklava to the camp had become impassable from the depth of mud; horses and mules struggled under their burdens, but only to fall and die in this slough of despond. The XX, together with the other regiments of the 4th Division, suffered more from this cause than the rest of the army, as their camp was farthest from the source of supplies.[1]

The regiment was not supplied with tea, coffee,[2] or sugar during the last nine days of November, and for several days with only half rations of biscuit and meat, and on the 30th day of the month with only two ounces of meat (salt pork) per man.

The Russians made a sortie on the morning of the 2nd of December. In this affair Privates McCormack, Coulston, and Wilson were wounded. Private McCormack died on the following day.

Privates Davies and Pindar were wounded on the 4th of December, and Drummer Tickner on the 14th. Captain R. Leigh Lye[3] died in camp on the 10th of December.

Two very determined sorties were made on the night of the 21st and morning of the 22nd, in which three men were wounded. The enemy attacked the trenches on Christmas night, but were repulsed with loss. Private Drudge was killed, and Privates Doolan and Duggan were wounded. The Russian batteries always kept up a heavy fire on the trenches, but particularly at night.[4]

---

[1] *Invasion of the Crimea.*

[2] Up to this date, the green, unburnt berry had been issued.

[3] Richard Leigh Lye joined the XX as Ensign on the 3rd November, 1837; he was promoted Lieutenant (by purchase) on the 9th August, 1839; and Captain (by purchase) on the 30th December, 1845. He was present at the battles of the Alma, Balaklava, Inkerman, and the siege of Sebastopol to the date of his death.

[4] Lord Raglan.

The months of December and January were the worst of the siege. During the first six days of December, there were storms of wind and rain, and on the seventh the first hard frost set in; from this day and until the close of the month there were alternate storms of rain and snow, with bitter frosts. The weather on Christmas day, Lord Raglan described as being the worst he had ever experienced.

From the 1st to the 16th of January, there were heavy and continual falls of snow, accompanied by biting north-easterly winds, which drifted the snow into the trenches as fast as it could be cleared out by the unceasing efforts of the working parties. On the 16th, the thermometer fell as low as 10° Fahrenheit, and during the twenty-four hours never rose above 14°. This was the coldest day of the siege. A man of the regiment died in his tent from congestion of the brain, caused by cold; and there were in the regimental hospital one hundred and fifteen men.[1]

The privations of the regiment at this time were considerably lessened in their intensity, and the efficiency of the corps maintained[2] by the good arrangements made within it, and by the care exercised by the officers in all that concerned the welfare of those placed under them.[3]

The following is an extract from a letter written by a man of the regiment to his friends, who sent it to the editor of the *Essex Standard*, from which paper it was copied and re-published in the *Times* of the 25th of December, 1854:—"We have no firing to cook with,

---

[1] Doctor Howard, surgeon of the regiment.

[2] Colonel Hugh Smith, A.A.G., 4th Division.

[3] In one of the manuscripts so kindly placed at the disposal of the regiment by Mr. Kinglake, there is a note by the author commenting upon the excellence of the regimental arrangements.

but when we come across a tree we down with it for fuel. We are poisoned with vermin and dirt; the men are dying with cold and exposure; we are tenting it, and are in the open air twenty days out of the month watching the enemy, and there is every sign of our remaining in this position for the winter. Our officers are noble fellows, and they do all they can to alleviate the sufferings of the men."

There was a general improvement in the weather on the morning of the 17th of January, but from this date and until the end of the month, there were severe and sudden changes of temperature; storms of wind, rain, and snow following each other in quick succession. It was found more difficult to keep the trenches in good order than it had been during the sharp frosts of the preceding period: mud and melting snow were no sooner removed than the surface was turned into a smooth, slippery sheet of ice, that had to be broken at the cost of much labour to ensure a safe passage through the trenches. To perform this laborious but necessary work, and at the same time to watch with vigilance a crafty enemy, called for the highest qualities of the soldier. The official journal of the siege pays the regiment a compliment for their work at this time.

"18th January, 1855.

"The XX Regiment, under Captain Radcliffe, worked with energy, but the remainder very badly, and twenty-three men had to be checked pay in consequence."

From the 16th of January, the amelioration in the condition of the men of the regiment may be said to have commenced. Both from the public and private sources supplies of food became abundant, and warm clothing plentiful. The health of the men began to mend, and there was a steady decrease of the daily casualties from sickness and death.

February was an uneventful month for the XX, laying before Sebastopol. Being suitably clothed and well-fed, they were in a measure able to withstand the severities of the weather. During many days the ground was frozen too hard to admit of any work of construction being done in the trenches; in fact, the chief occupation was removing snow and keeping the trenches clear.

The regiment was armed with the Enfield rifle on the 1st of March.

On the night of the 22nd of March, the XX furnished working and covering parties for the trenches. The working parties were employed in thickening the parapets of the incomplete and unarmed batteries, "The advanced No. VII," and "The advanced No. VIII," under the directions of Captain Montagu, Royal Engineers, and Captain S. R. Chapman, XX (Acting Engineer). The covering party was commanded by Brevet-Major C. R. Butler. About half-past one on the morning of the 23rd, an unusually strong column of five hundred Russians, led by General Biruloff, advanced under cover of darkness, that could almost be felt, and favoured by a howling wind which prevented our men hearing their approach. This column surprised the covering party in the advanced trench, pushed forward to the redoubts where the parties were working, drove them out, and took Captain Montagu prisoner. The Russians remained for some little time in possession of the batteries, capturing seventy picks and fifty shovels. But the men of the XX had only thrown down their tools to take up their arms. Under the leadership of Captain Chapman,[1] they charged the Russians with the bayonet, and turned them out of the batteries. Ten Russians were killed and their bodies left in the trenches, and two of their wounded were taken prisoners. In this combat our men used the bayonet alone, not a cartridge was fired. Of it, Mr. Kinglake says, "It was fraught with good proof of the quality of our officers and men."

Brevet-Major Butler and Captain Chapman were highly commended for their distinguished gallantry by Lord Raglan, in his despatches of the 24th and 27th of March, and Captain Chapman was promoted Brevet-Major. Corporal Thady Halpin (afterwards sergeant) and Private John Gee nobly supported their officers on this occasion, and were awarded the medal and gratuity for "Distinguished conduct in the Field." Privates J. Grannell and J. Mearns were killed, and T. Murphy taken prisoner. The following were wounded:—Corporals H. Fisher (dangerously) and T. Halpin (severely); Privates M. Byrne (dangerously), P. Golding, P. Keating, J. Lewis, P. Rowe, J. Russell, and W. Witney. From this date casualties in the trenches were not of frequent occurrence. On the 23rd of April, Private S. Johnson was wounded; and on the 9th of May, Private T. Fernay was killed and P. Bray severely wounded. Lieutenant F. Parr[2] died in camp, on the 25th of March.

The men of the regiment improved both in health and spirits during May; the fine warm weather produced a marvellous change. The Adjutant of the regi-

---

[1] Lord Raglan's despatch.
[2] Lieutenant Parr joined the XX in January, 1854, and was promoted Lieutenant on the 8th December, 1854.

ment, Lieutenant Padfield,[1] was severely wounded on the 8th of June, during the storming of the Quarries by the regiments serving in the right attack. An attempt was made on the 18th of June to take the Redan by assault. The 57th Regiment formed the storming column, and the XX was to follow close up and fill in the ditch. The regiment paraded at midnight the 17th, and marched to the assigned position, at the right attack. Each man was provided with a pick and shovel, while two hundred carried gabions. The trenches were crowded with men of different regiments, who were not on duty, and who impeded the passage of the regiment to the front, and eventually forced the storming column from its true direction, causing it to leave the trenches at a point where it at once came under a slaughtering fire from the Redan. The 57th, joined by the covering party of riflemen, advanced towards the re-entering angle of the Redan, and—inclining a little to the left—established itself upon ground within thirty yards of the Artakoff battery. Lieutenant-Colonel Evelegh, Lieutenants Holmes and O'Neill were wounded. Lance-Sergeant D. Palmer, Privates McGorman and Paull were killed; and Privates Bryan, Barnes, Mulcahy, Jones, Rodgers, Russell, Simmonds, and Wood were wounded.

Colonel F. Horn was appointed to the command of a brigade from this date; and the command of the

---

[1] Lieutenant Francis Padfield had been seventeen years in the ranks, fifteen of which he had been a non-commissioned officer, and seven Sergeant-Major. He was in possession of the good conduct medal. He was promoted Ensign on the 7th April, 1848, and appointed Adjutant on the 22nd December, of the same year. He was promoted Lieutenant on the 6th June, 1854, and Captain on the 21st September, 1855. He was present at the battles of the Alma, Balaklava, Inkerman, and siege of Sebastopol. At Inkerman he was wounded and his horse was shot under him. On the 8th June, a musket ball passed through his hip. He retired from the service in consequence of his wounds.

regiment devolved upon Lieutenant-Colonel F. C. Evelegh.

The undermentioned men were killed and wounded in the months of July and August. From the 4th of August the siege was pressed with great vigour, the whole of our batteries pounding Sebastopol with a tremendous cannonade:—

	KILLED.	WOUNDED.
11th July	—	Private Thompson
12th ,,	Corporal Kavanagh	—
25th ,,	—	,, Folen
,, ,,	—	,, Perryar
30th ,,	—	,, Flaherty
12th August	—	,, Washington
13th ,,	—	,, Watson
15th ,,	—	Corporal Smith
18th ,,	—	Private Joyce
,, ,,	—	,, O'Neill
,, ,,	—	,, Whitmore
24th ,,	Private Lathom	,, Holmes
,, ,,	—	,, Wood
29th ,,	—	,, Eldridge

On the 1st day of September, Privates G. Jokes and E. Sharpe were killed.

The XX was on duty in the trenches on the night of the 7th of September, and remained there during the assault on the morning of the 8th, which failed through the supports not being brought up in time.

It was decided that the 4th Division should storm the Redan at five o'clock on the following morning, but the Russians evacuated and fired the city during the night.

Corporal P. Fuller, Privates Barry, Cates, Connolly, Joyce, and Reay were wounded in the trenches on the 8th. Brevet-Major S. R. Chapman[1] was also dangerously wounded in the knee during the attack on the 8th, and died on the 20th.

---

[1] Major Chapman joined the XX on the 10th February, 1852. He proceeded with the corps to the Crimea, and was present at the battles of Alma, Balaklava, and Inkerman. He was appointed Acting Engineer and attached to the "left attack" from the commencement of the siege on the 10th of October. Major Chapman served in the trenches, as Superintending Engineer, on forty-six days and forty-nine nights. On the 23rd March, as recorded in the preceding pages, he distinguished himself by his ready resource and gallant conduct. This was not a solitary instance. During the night of the 4th June, although not on duty, Major Chapman was in the trenches, near No. 14 Battery, when an alarm was raised; he at once called for volunteers, which were furnished by the 39th Regiment. With this party he advanced to the front, posted sentries, and afforded protection to the working parties. At the assault on the 18th of June, Major Chapman and Lieutenant H. Elphinstone, were orderly officers to Major-General Harry Jones, Commanding Royal Engineer during the siege operations. In what capacity he served at the attack of the 8th September, when he was wounded in the knee, is not stated. In a confidential despatch dated 16th September, 1855, Major Chapman was recommended for promotion, in recognition of the zeal and intelligence he had displayed during a long service at this eventful siege of three hundred and thirty-seven days. The career of this promising officer closed on the 20th September, when he died of the wound received on the last day of the siege. The remains of four officers of the XX are buried on Cathcart's Hill:—Brevet-Major S. R. Chapman, Captain R. Leigh Lye, and Lieutenants W. H. Dowling and Frederick Parr.

NOTE.—The foregoing particulars of Major Chapman's services are chiefly taken from the *Official Journal of the Siege Operations.*

Chapter XXXIII.

1855–1856.

The Kinburn Expedition—Deaths from Sickness during the Campaign—Honours bestowed on the Corps—Peace Proclaimed—The XX Quartered in Sebastopol—Embarkation for England—Arrival at Spithead.

FROM the fall of Sebastopol to the 4th of October, the regiment remained inactive, but on this day, under the command of Lieutenant-Colonel F. C. Evelegh, thirty officers and four hundred and seventy-four men embarked at Kazatch on board H.M.S. "Algiers," for Kinburn. The expeditionary force was commanded by Brigadier-General Spencer. The "Algiers," with the XX on board, anchored off Odessa on the afternoon of Monday, the 10th of October. Fort Kinburn is on the south side of the entrance to the Dneiper, and is situate on a long narrow spit of land; on the opposite or north side stands Fort Okzakoff.

The XX with the other regiments of the brigade landed without opposition on the 15th October. An intrenched camp was at once formed about four miles from the fort. Kinburn was bombarded by the fleet on the 17th of October, and, after a resistance of a few hours' duration, surrendered at five o'clock in the evening. From the 20th to the 23rd of October, the XX was engaged in making a reconnaissance as far as Patrausky. The expedition returned to the Crimea, and the XX disembarked at Kazatch on the 3rd of

November. Captain J. G. Hay[1] was promoted Brevet-Major on the 2nd November, 1855, in recognition of his services during the campaign.

From the date of its landing on the Crimea to the end of the year 1855, or in little more than fifteen months, the XX lost by death from disease and sickness nearly four hundred men. The privations of cold and hunger, overwork by day and night, and constant exposure, made our men an easy prey to cholera, diarrhœa, dysentery, fever, scurvy, and pulmonary complaints. From these and other causes (exclusive of wounds) there died :—

At sea, on passage to Scutari	30
,, ,, England	1
In the hospitals at Scutari, Kululu, Corfu, and Smyrna, between the 21st November, 1854, and 31st March, 1855	109
At these hospitals at other dates	10
On the Crimea, in 1854	66
On the Crimea, in the months of January, February, and March, 1855	121
From the 1st April to the 31st December, 1855	45
Total	382

In addition to the foregoing numbers, there died during the passage to the Crimea five men, at Malta two, and five in the Crimea, in 1856; bringing the total number of deaths from sickness alone to three hundred and ninety-four.[2]

---

[1] Major J. G. Hay joined the XX as Ensign on the 31st December, 1844; he was promoted Lieutenant on the 1st September, 1848, and Captain on the 29th December, 1854. He retired upon half pay. Major Hay was promoted Lieutenant-Colonel and retired from the service by the sale of his commission on the 20th April, 1866. His name is now Hay-Boyd.

[2] The Crimean casualties were taken from the nominal register of the regiment, which contains the names, description, and what finally became of every man who

These figures will give a vivid idea of the terrible sufferings endured by all ranks in the campaign on the Crimea. There was not a single desertion to the enemy from the XX during the war.

In the XX, it was not the custom to look for and search out individual acts of heroism or bravery, but what had been inculcated was this, that every man should act up to and verify the motto of the corps, "Omnia Audax."

The honours that were bestowed on individual officers, non-commissioned officers, and men were well earned, not by solitary acts of bravery, but in most cases by a long course of distinguished gallantry before the enemy.

In addition to the war medals, the following were decorated with the orders named:—

Companions of the Bath.—Colonel F. Horn and Lieutenant-Colonel F. C. Evelegh.

The Order of the Legion of Honour.—Colonel F. Horn, C.B., Lieutenant-Colonels H. D. Crofton and F. C. Evelegh, Major G. Steevens, Brevet-Major C. R. Butler, Colour-Sergeant A. Rule,[1] Sergeant J. Campbell, Private J. Brown.

---

joined the corps from the year 1820 to 1874. Great care has been exercised in collecting the information for this work. If necessary, the name, date, and place of death of every man could be given.

[1] Now Captain in the 49th Middlesex Rifle Volunteers (Post Office Volunteers). Captain Rule joined the XX in 1845, and soon attained the rank of Sergeant. He served in Bermuda and Canada with the regiment, and proceeded with it to the Crimea; was present at the battles of Alma, Balaklava, and Inkerman; wounded at the latter. He served throughout the whole of the siege of Sebastopol, and never missed a tour of duty in the trenches, except for fourteen days whilst recovering from the wound received at Inkerman. He was present at the sorties of the 12th January, 23rd March, the assaults of the 18th June and 8th September. He was frequently highly commended for skilful shooting. He accompanied the regiment to Kinburn, and returned with it to England in July, 1856. He was recommended on one occasion by Colonel Evelegh, C.B., "*as a most zealous, active, non-*

Medals for Distinguished Conduct in the Field.—
Colour-Sergeant P. A. Farrell[1]; Sergeant Thady
Halpin; Corporals J. Gee and J. Turner; Privates E.
Andrews, T. Catling, D. Connolly, J. Gipson, W.
Hennessy, P. Hules, D. Laughland, W. Mann, and P.
Sherlock.

French War Medal.—Colour-Sergeants George
Boxall, John Brown, and Jos. Moss; Privates J.
Brown, M. Callaghan, H. Gray, W. Hennessy, C.
Kirkham, and J. Lowe.

Order of the Medjidie.—Fourth class, Colonel F.
Horn, C.B.; Lieutenant-Colonels H. D. Crofton and
F. C. Evelegh; Brevet-Major R. C. Butler; fifth

---

commissioned officer in the trenches before Sebastopol. He was one of two men selected by the Captains of the regiment, and approved of by myself, as being worthy from his *excellent service* to wear the *Legion of Honour*. Sergeant Rule's name was frequently mentioned to me by officers in command of parties of the regiment in the trenches, as having performed his duty remarkably well." From Colour-Sergeant he was appointed Sergeant-Instructor of Musketry, and, on the formation of the Second Battalion in May, 1858, he was promoted Sergeant-Major, which position he held until his discharge from the service in 1866. As Sergeant-Major, his conduct and abilities merited and received the highest praise. In a farewell regimental order, Colonel Browne, commanding the battalion, held up his exemplary conduct, high character, and abilities as a soldier, as a fit subject for the emulation of the young soldiers in the battalion. The officers presented him with a cheque for £66. On the formation of the Post Office Volunteers in February, 1868, Sergeant-Major Rule was appointed Sergeant-Major, and rendered valuable assistance in raising the corps and bringing it to the high state of efficiency which it has attained. On resigning the Sergeant-Majorship of the Post Office Volunteers in 1873, he was appointed to a Lieutenancy in the corps by Colonel du Plat Taylor, and, at the general wish of the officers, he was on the 18th December, 1876, promoted Captain, although there were many qualified subalterns, senior to him in the regiment. The high reputation that Captain Rule gained as a marksman in the trenches before Sebastopol, he has still maintained. Sergeant-Major Rule was selected and appointed a "Yeoman of the Guard" by His Royal Highness the Duke of Cambridge, on the 12th March, 1866.

[1] Colour-Sergeant Farrell commanded a company or party at the battle of Inkerman, on the officers being wounded. For this and other acts of distinguished service, together with a long and meritorious career, he was recommended in July, 1856, by Colonel Evelegh, C.B., for the good conduct medal and annuity of £15, which were granted, and which he enjoyed until his death on the 11th July, 1886.

class: Captains S. Dickens and A. R. Warren; and Lieutenants C. E. Parkinson and H. B. Vaughan.

Sardinian War Medal.—Lieutenants C. E. Parkinson, H. B. Vaughan, and Colour-Sergeant J. Whybrow.

The memory of those who fell in the Crimea is perpetuated by a monument in Exeter Cathedral. It bears this inscription:—

THIS MEMORIAL
IS PLACED HERE
BY
THE OFFICERS,
NON-COMMISSIONED OFFICERS,
AND PRIVATE SOLDIERS,
OF
HER MAJESTY'S XX
OR EAST DEVONSHIRE REGIMENT,
AS A TOKEN OF AFFECTION
FOR THEIR COMRADES,
WHO LOST THEIR LIVES
IN THE SERVICE OF THEIR
COUNTRY,
DURING THE CRIMEAN CAMPAIGN
OF 1854 AND 1855.

The memorial consists of an upright slab of marble, resting on an ornamented base and surmounted by an arch of black marble, in the centre of which is the badge of the regiment. At the sides of the tablet are two private soldiers of the regiment, fully accoutred, resting on their arms.

Above the monument now hang the colours, which were presented to the regiment by the Duke of Wellington, in 1838, and which passed through the Crimean and Indian Mutiny campaigns.[1]

The XX was not engaged after the Kinburn expe-

---

[1] A picture of the monument and colours in the chancel of Exeter Cathedral was painted by Mrs. Hill, and presented to the officers of the 1st Battalion by her husband, Major E. Hill, who was in the regiment when the colours were presented by the Duke of Wellington in 1838.

dition. An uneventful winter had passed when the proclamation of peace was made known to the army by a salute of one hundred and one guns, on the 5th April, 1856.

The regiment quitted the hutments and moved into the town of Sebastopol on the 16th June, preparatory to embarkation.

One wing embarked on board H.M.S. "Brunswick," under Brevet Lieutenant-Colonel G. Steevens[1] on the 20th June; and the headquarters, under Lieutenant-Colonel F. C. Evelegh, on board H.M.S. "Centurion" on the 24th June.

The two divisions arrived at Spithead on the 17th and 18th July respectively, were at once landed, and proceeded to Aldershot by train.

---

[1] George Steevens was the son of Colonel Charles Steevens, a former commanding officer of the XX, and a distinguished Peninsular officer. He joined the XX as Ensign (by purchase) on the 3rd August, 1838. He was promoted Lieutenant (by purchase) on the 17th April, 1840, and Captain on the 14th April, 1846. He served with the regiment in Bermuda, Canada, and throughout the Eastern campaign of 1854-5, including the battles of Alma, Balaklava, and the siege of Sebastopol. He was promoted Major on the 16th October, 1855, and Brevet-Lieutenant-Colonel in the following year. He retired from the service on the 29th August, 1856. Lieutenant-Colonel Steevens died at Cheltenham on the 4th February, 1857.

CHAPTER XXXIV.

1856–1858.

Reviewed by Queen Victoria—Sergeant James Campbell—Banquet at Portsmouth—Colonel F. C. Evelegh, C.B.—Orders for Immediate Embarkation for India—Departure from Aldershot—Embarkation at Spithead—List of Officers—Landing at Calcutta—March to Benares—XX Posted to the 4th Division—Colonel Evelegh appointed Brigadier—Battles of Chanda—Ameerapore—Sultanpore—Arrival at Lucknow—The Siege—Storming of the Engine House—Capture of the Residency—Captain Warren—Lieutenant W. F. F. Gordon—Capture of Gao Ghat and Moosa Bagh—Officers mentioned in Lord Clyde's despatches—Raising of the 2nd Battalion—Field Operations—Sickness.

THE regiment was inspected at Aldershot, on the 31st July, 1856, by Her Majesty Queen Victoria and His Royal Highness the Prince Consort. Sergeant James Campbell was especially brought to the notice of Her Majesty, who was graciously pleased to decorate this distinguished non-commissioned officer with "The Legion of Honour," in the presence of all the officers, non-commissioned officers, and men of the XX.[1]

On the 5th August, 1856, the regiment proceeded from Aldershot to Portsmouth, where it was joined on the 17th by the Depôt from Parkhurst, Isle of Wight. The regiment was entertained at a public banquet, on the 16th September, by the citizens of Portsmouth,

---

[1] Sergeant Campbell was severely wounded at Inkerman, but on recovering from his wounds he rejoined the corps before Sebastopol. He was remarkable throughout the siege as a valiant soldier, one that could be depended upon under any stress of circumstances. On one occasion, with twelve men he held an advanced trench, although beset on all sides by swarms of the enemy. Sergeant Campbell was found medically unfit to accompany the regiment to India in 1857; he was subsequently transferred to the 2nd 10th Regiment, and for many years was garrison Sergeant-Major at Cape Town.

in honour of its services in the Crimean War. In compliance with orders received from the Horse Guards, a new Depôt was formed at Chichester, on the 23rd of October.

The order of the "Companion of the Bath" was conferred on Colonel F. C. Evelegh, the officer commanding the regiment, on the 29th of December, 1856.

On the 7th February, the regiment returned to Aldershot. On the 20th July, Colonel Evelegh received orders to hold the regiment in readiness for immediate embarkation for India, in consequence of the serious aspect of the revolt in that country. The depôt was at once recalled from Chichester, recruiting actively carried on, and the regiment formed into ten service and two depôt companies. On the 6th of August, the service companies marched from Aldershot to Farnborough, and were thence conveyed by train to Portsmouth, having previously been taken leave of in most flattering terms by H.R.H. the Duke of Cambridge and Major-General Lawrence, C.B. (commanding brigade), who bore high testimony to its good conduct and discipline. The embarkation took place the same day on board the "Champion of the Seas," which sailed from Spithead on the 8th in company with the sister ship "James Baines," the latter carrying the 97th Regiment. The "Champion of the Seas" carried a part of the 42nd Highlanders. The "James Baines" carried the other part.

The undermentioned officers embarked with the service companies:—Lieutenant-Colonels F. C. Evelegh, C.B., and G. M. Lys; Majors W. P. Radcliffe and C. R. Butler; Captains G. H. Bennett, C. E. Parkinson, W. S. Dickens, A. R. Warren, T. C. Lyons, B. G.

Dashwood,[1] G. E. Francis, and P. G. Hewitt; Lieutenants H. B. Vaughan, W. Mitchell, J. Little, E. A. Patrickson, F. G. Holmes, F. L. Edridge, T. S. McDonogh, J. Carden, W. F. F. Gordon, W. D. Nunn, Honourable A. E. Vereker, G. B. Duffin, and G. Gethin; Ensigns C. Fahie, O. T. Burne, S. Egan, R. Blount, T. H. Holbyn, F. G. Horn, and S. Johnstone; Lieutenant and Adjutant P. Geraghty; Quartermaster J. Aylett; Surgeon E. Howard;[2] Assistant Surgeons H. Kelsall, J. Munday, and F. J. Shortt.

On the 19th November, the regiment arrived at Calcutta after a favourable voyage of three months, during which no casualties occurred on board; and disembarked on the following day. It at once proceeded by march-route up the Grand Trunk Road to Benares,

---

[1] Captain Barrington G. Dashwood joined the army on the 13th February, 1852, and exchanged to the XX on the 9th March, 1855. He was promoted Captain on the 10th August, 1856. Captain Dashwood was present with the regiment at the battles of Chanda, Ameerapore, and Sultanpore, the siege and capture of Lucknow, the actions at Buxer-Ghat, Churda, and Fort Musjeidia. He retired from the service by the sale of his commission in April, 1862. Captain Dashwood died in London on the 31st May, 1885.

[2] Edward Howard was appointed to the XX as Assistant-Surgeon on the 29th April, 1842. He served with it five years in Bermuda, and in this period he gained a lasting reputation for his unremitting care and kindness to the sick during a visitation of yellow fever. He went with the regiment to Canada, and returned with it to England in 1853. He was promoted Surgeon on the 24th February, 1854. Surgeon Howard was with the regiment throughout the Crimean campaign, and was present at the battles of the Alma, Balaklava, Inkerman, and the siege of Sebastopol. These names will be sufficient to bring to the mind of the reader all that Doctor Howard must have done to allay the sufferings of the sick, the wounded, and the dying. He accompanied the regiment to India, and served throughout the Indian Mutiny campaign. Doctor Howard received the Crimean War medal and four clasps, the Turkish medal, the 5th class of the Medjidie, and the Indian Mutiny medal and clasp for Lucknow. He was promoted Surgeon-Major on the 29th April, 1862. During the regiment's service in India, Surgeon-Major Howard had to contend with several outbreaks of cholera. He returned to England with the regiment in March, 1867; and retired on a pension on the 22nd June, 1867, with the honorary rank of Deputy Inspector-General. Doctor Howard died at Minden-Wolfe, Bedford, on the 28th June, 1885.

where it was retained to form part of the Fourth Division, assembling under the command of Brigadier-General Franks, C.B., for service in the Jaunpore district. The division (composed of two batteries of artillery, the 10th, XX, and 97th Regiments, and a large Goorkha force under Rajah Pulwan Sing) was divided into three columns, of which one was given to Colonel Evelegh, C.B., who was subsequently appointed a Brigadier of the British infantry of the division, by warrant, dated 9th February, 1858. The force remained inactive until the 9th of February, when it was ordered to make a forward movement into the province of Oude, many large bodies of rebels having collected on the south-eastern frontier. On the 19th February, the division advanced from Singramao on Chanda, a village strongly intrenched, and occupied by a considerable force of the enemy under the celebrated Oude chief, Mehndie Hussein. After a short action, in which the skirmishers were principally engaged, the rebels were driven from their position with a loss of seven guns. The troops, after a few hours' rest at Rampara, continued their march to "Ameerapore," reached it late in the evening, and unexpectedly came upon a still larger body of the enemy under Mahomed Mehndie Hussein. A short running fight ensued, but with no decided results; the lateness of the hour and darkness of the night preventing any pursuit. Many of the enemy were killed, however, whilst the loss on our side was comparatively trivial. The XX bivouacked under arms for the night, on the field of action.

On the morning of the 23rd, the force made a rapid advance on "Sultanpore," a town of some extent situated on the banks of the Goomtee. Around this place were intrenched a body of rebels said to number

25,000 men, with twenty-five guns. After a hot and dusty march the force came up with the enemy at noon, and at once attacked his position, which was carried after a fight of two hours' duration. A feint was made on the enemy's front, while Brigadier Evelegh fell on their right rear and drove them out of the intrenchments. The loss of the rebels in this action was computed to amount to one thousand eight hundred men; twenty-one guns of various calibre were captured. Private Joseph Hay of the XX was killed. The Fourth Division continued its march unopposed to Lucknow, and arrived there on the 4th of March, in time to take part in the siege of that famous city.[1] In thirteen days the regiment had covered one hundred and thirty miles and fought three actions.[2] The siege was looked upon as one of great moment, and preparations for the struggle were actively carried on by both armies. The Commander-in-Chief's army amounted to 25,000 men, British and Native; on the other hand, the rebels had erected fortifications and batteries of immense strength, and made it known that they were resolved to fight step by step in defence of their capital. Offensive operations commenced on the 9th. Lord Clyde had determined not to make an assault or engage his troops in street fighting, until the defences had been considerably damaged and weakened by artillery fire. From the 9th to the 13th, the XX were in the trenches on the outskirts of the town. On the 11th, Sergeant A. Dempsey, Privates W. Bewsher, C. Buckley, F. Davy, C. Moseley, W. Porter, and J. Starman were wounded; on the 12th, Private W. Joyce; and Private J. Head on the 13th. On General

---

[1] *London Gazette*, 25th May, 1858. Lord Clyde's despatches.
[2] Malleson, page 338.

Frank's division devolved the honour of attacking the "Kaiser Bagh" and "Imambarra," which were justly considered to be the keystones of the enemy's position. The Kaiser Bagh consisted of a series of courts and buildings and constituted the citadel of the rebels.

On the 14th March, the XX, supported by some companies of the 38th, was ordered to advance. As the enemy on the approach of the British troops fled in the greatest panic, the regiment with other corps advanced to the Kaiser Bagh and occupied it almost without opposition.[1] The regiment was then ordered to see the "mess house" (32nd Regiment's mess house), "motee mahal," and other buildings "clear of the enemy." These buildings all lay between the Kaiser Bagh and the Gomtee river. Little or no opposition was offered until the force arrived before a large, square, loopholed building called the "engine house," with a number of horses and carriages outside. The building was immediately surrounded by the two leading companies of the XX, detached for this purpose, under Major Radcliffe, and a large number of the enemy, who were inside, were thus cut off. The remaining companies of the XX and 38th Regiments were stationed outside. In some way or another the detachment became divided, the greater portion under Captain Francis[2] entering the building by a narrow passage at one side, while the remainder under Major Radcliffe moved to the right. The latter party pursued some of the rebels into a large "Serai," with only one gateway for entrance or exit. In shape it was almost a square: the sides were divided into

---

[1] *London Gazette*, 25th May, 1858.

[2] Ensign Burne, who had been sent to these two companies with an order, accompanied Captain Francis's party.

small separate compartments, which were open on the side towards the court-yard; the rebels occupied some of these directly facing the gateway, and some in the far corner of the yard. These compartments enabled the enemy to bring a cross fire on anyone advancing across the court, while affording good shelter to their occupants. On arrival at the gateway, as there appeared to be a little hesitation on the part of the men, Major Radcliffe called to them to follow him, and made a dash across the court for the compartment immediately facing the gateway. Two men, Privates Lincoln and Hill, at once followed their officer. In the first dash, Hill was killed by a shot from the left side of the court, but Major Radcliffe, closely followed by Lincoln, managed to reach the compartment he was making for. As they rushed through the doorway of this compartment, which held three Sepoys, a shot fired from it grazed both Lincoln's shoulder blades, causing a slight wound only; at the same moment one of the Sepoys made a blow at Major Radcliffe's head with a tulwar, cutting through his "Solar Topee" and "Puggaree" to the skin, but the skin was not broken. Major Radcliffe cut the man down, but while doing so was wounded in the hand by a sword cut from the third Sepoy. Lincoln, in the meanwhile, had bayonetted the man, who had fired as they entered the compartment, and he now gave the finishing strokes to the two swordsmen. Lincoln in the struggle received a sword cut over the eye. After the first rush, the remainder of the yard was soon cleared by dropping small live shells into the compartments through holes in the flat roofs, and the detachment then moved on to assist in clearing the main portion of the "engine house" building. In the meantime Francis's party, pressing along the narrow passage before mentioned, in which they had two men killed, arrived at a small room filled with a motley collection of the enemy; cavalry, infantry, and artillery mixed together indiscriminately and armed with every conceivable weapon. A fierce interchange of volleys was now carried on through the open doorway, the men on each side watching their opportunity to deliver a hasty shot round the corner of the door without exposing themselves. This, however, could not go on for ever, and, after sometime, Captain Francis[1] ordered all his men to load; they then made a dash through the doorway, and, in spite of two XX men being shot and two cut down, they succeeded in effecting an entrance. The rebels thus caught fought desperately. The room was now crowded to its utmost with friend and foe. Our men, making free use of the bayonet, at last managed to clear more standing room for themselves, and soon the rebels, seized with panic, made a desperate attempt to escape, by flying from the small room into a large central apartment, filled with engines, cranks, pipes, furnaces, boilers, and other appliances of machinery. Just as they entered it, however, they were met by another body of rebels, who were trying to escape from Major Radcliffe's party.[2] This party,

---

[1] Colonel G. E. Francis joined the XX as Lieutenant on the 9th February, 1855. He served with the regiment in the Crimea from November, 1855, to July, 1856. He was promoted Captain on the 31st July, 1857. Captain Francis accompanied the regiment to India, and was present at the battles of Chanda, Ameerapore, Sultanpore, and the subsequent march on Lucknow. He served throughout the siege. His gallant conduct at the storming of the "engine house" is described in the foregoing pages. Captain Francis was Brigade-Major at Agra. He was promoted Major in the 2nd Battalion on the 22nd November, 1864, and Lieutenant-Colonel on the 2nd July, 1874. Lieutenant-Colonel Francis retired on a pension on the 10th May, 1878, and was granted the rank of Colonel.

[2] Major Radcliffe, after leaving the "Serai," was detained by a medical officer dressing his wounds, and could not accompany his party further.

whose earlier doings have already been described, had, after entering the main building, fought their way to the central apartment, driving the rebels before them. Caught now between the two parties of the XX, the rebels had no chance of escape; all were shot or bayonetted. At this juncture a fire broke out in the building, the beams and doorposts having become ignited from the constant discharge of firearms. The number of the enemy killed in these rooms amounted to three hundred, while fifty or sixty more, in endeavouring to escape, were killed by the companies of the XX and 38th Regiments stationed outside the building. The loss to the XX was[1] Privates T. Cox, J. Farsden, E. Halliday, C. Hill, and T. Webber, killed; and twelve men wounded, one of whom, Private Winstanley, died of his wounds. Private R. Nicholson was wounded on the 15th and died of his wounds.

On the 16th, the XX was attached to Sir James Outram's division, and took part in the capture of the residency, crossing the Goomtee by a bridge of casks opposite the Secunderbagh.[2] The residency was taken after a very slight resistance. In this affair eleven men were wounded. Five companies of the regiment took possession of and held the Chutter Munzil, Mhotee Mahael, and other palaces on the banks of the Goomtee.

On the 17th, the XX was engaged in driving the rebels from the buildings and houses in the Chandnee Chowk (main street); the street was held by five companies of the XX, and three of the 79th Highlanders.[3]

---

[1] This account of the storming of the engine house is taken principally from *Up among the Pandies*, by Lieutenant (now Colonel) V. D. Majendie, R.A., pages 214-218.

[2] *London Gazette*, 26th May, 1858.

[3] Sir James Outram's despatch, dated 22nd March, 1858.

The rebels showed in force in the streets running off the main street, and caused our men much annoyance by the musketry fire from the houses.

On the 18th, Captain Warren's[1] company captured a very fine brass nine-pounder loaded to the muzzle with grape.[2] Captain Warren was wounded in the cheek whilst leading his men to the charge.

Lieutenant Gordon, who was in command of a piquet in the street on this day, was ordered by Brigadier-General Douglas to clear the rebels out of the houses in his front. Lieutenant Gordon carried out this duty most effectually; he led his men into the houses, drove the rebels out, killing twenty-three of them.[3] Sergeant J. Buckley and twenty-three men were wounded. Three companies of the regiment, under Captain Bennett, formed part of a force which was commanded by Sir James Outram on the 19th. At half-past six a.m. the rebels were attacked and driven out of Gao Ghat; thence the troops proceeded without opposition through the suburbs towards Moosa Bagh.

---

[1] Captain A. R. Warren joined the XX as Ensign (by purchase) on the 12th March, 1852, was promoted Lieutenant (by purchase) on the 16th June, 1854, and Captain (by purchase) on the 1st May, 1855. He served with the regiment for one year (1852-53) in Canada, and in the Crimea from the 20th January, 1855, to the 19th July, 1856. He served throughout the siege of Sebastopol, including the assaults on the Redan of the 18th June and 8th September. For his services in the Crimea, he received the Crimean medal with clasp for Sebastopol, 5th class of the Medjidie, and Turkish medal. Captain Warren accompanied the regiment to India in August, 1857. He took part in the battles of Chanda, Ameerapore, and Sultanpore, siege of Lucknow, and the affairs at Mohan, Meangunge, Forts Churda, and Musjeidia. He was promoted Major on the 13th December, 1859 (by purchase). Major Warren retired from the service by the sale of his commission, on the 12th April, 1864. He is now Sir A. R. Warren, Bart., and Lieutenant-Colonel, commanding the 3rd Munster Fusiliers (formerly South Cork Militia).

[2] *My Diary in India*, vol. i, page 342; Malleson's *History of the Indian Mutiny*, vol. ii, page 404.

[3] Despatch of Major-General Sir James Outram, dated 22nd March, 1858; Malleson, vol. ii, page 404.

On reaching some open ground the enemy were found in great strength, and at once opened fire with two guns, but took to flight on the approach of our skirmishers. The cavalry followed in pursuit, and the artillery were sent back under charge of Captain Bennett and the three companies of the XX.[1]

For their services during the siege of Lucknow, the following officers were mentioned in the despatches of Lord Clyde, dated Lucknow, 26th March, 1858:—Brigadier-General Evelegh, C.B., commanding the 7th Infantry Brigade, was particularly thanked; Lieutenant-Colonel G. M. Lys, commanding the regiment; Major W. P. Radcliffe, and Ensign O. T. Burne, Brigade Quartermaster. The services of Captain G. Bennett and Lieutenant W. F. F. Gordon were brought to the notice of the Commander-in-Chief by Major-General Sir James Outram. Lord Clyde drew special attention to the services of two Highland regiments only, but in the last paragraph he says: "The subsequent attack on the Imambarra and the Kaiserbagh reflected the

---

[1] Sir James Outram's despatch, 22nd March, 1858.

NOTE.—Lieutenant W. F. F. Gordon was promoted Captain in this year. In 1865 he was severely mauled by a wounded tiger, and was lame for life from the injuries he received. Captain Gordon served in the XX until the 24th January, 1873, when he exchanged as Major into the 63rd Regiment, and eventually succeeded to the command of that corps. The following is an extract from the MS. Records of the 63rd Regiment:—"Lieutenant-Colonel W. F. F. Gordon, commanding 63rd Regiment, died whilst on leave at Barielly, on the 17th March, 1880, at the house of Major G. B. Wolseley, 65th Regiment, A.A.G. Lieutenant-Colonel Gordon, who came from the XX Regiment as a Major on the 24th January, 1873, held command of the regiment on several occasions, and his death was deeply regretted by all ranks. A party consisting of Major W. L. Auchinleck, five officers, and ten men went to Barielly, for the purpose of escorting his body to Umballa. At Barielly his remains were escorted to the railway station by the 2nd Queen's and 30th Regiments. He was buried at Umballa with the usual military honours, and a small monument marks the spot where his body was interred in the Umballa Cemetery. In a letter from the Horse Guards, His Royal Highness the Commander-in-Chief said "that Lieutenant-Colonel Gordon's death was a loss not only to his regiment, but to the service."

greatest credit on the regimental leaders of the 4th Division and the soldiers that followed them."

A second battalion was added to the regiment on the 28th of March, and was raised in Ireland: the depôt of the first giving two hundred men to form the nucleus of the new battalion, the command of which was conferred upon Lieutenant-Colonel W. P. Radcliffe, who, with many other officers appointed to it, left the first battalion for England.

Lieutenant J. Little died at Cawnpore on the 9th of April, and Captain C. E. Parkinson at Benares on the 2nd of June. Both these deaths were due to acute dysentery contracted during the siege of Lucknow. A monument to the memory of these officers was erected at Cawnpore.

From March until June the XX was nominally quartered in Lucknow, but was really employed nearly the whole of this period in constant and harassing expeditions against remnants of the rebel force in the surrounding country. Whilst stationed at Lucknow, the regiment was afflicted with much sickness; sixty-three men died of disease in the brief period of three months.

Chapter XXXV.

1858-1859.

March from Lucknow—Camp at Nawabgunge—Duties of the Field Force—Expedition to Mohan—Actions at Hussengunge, Meangunge, and Poorwah—Attack and Destruction of Fort Simree—Engagement at Berah—Instructions to Brigadier Evelegh—Defeat of the Rebels at Buxer-Ghat—Colour captured by Private Bray—Casualties—Anecdote of Colonel Evelegh—Return to Nawabgunge—Evelegh selected to Command a Special Field Force—Major Butler commands the XX—March to Churda—Attack on Fort Musjeidia—Night-March to Bankee—Surprise and Defeat of the Rebels—Two Companies with Colonel Christie's Column—Deaths since Landing—Evelegh leaves the Regiment—Lieutenant-Colonel Cormick succeeds to the Command—Lieutenant-Colonel Butler—Gondah.

ON the 10th of June the XX marched from Lucknow to Nawabgunge, situate between Cawnpore and Lucknow, where a standing camp had been established on an arid, sandy plain, about fourteen miles from the first-named city. The regiment formed part of the Nawabgunge moveable column, which consisted of the XX, 23rd, 53rd, and 80th Regiments, a battery of Bengal Horse Artillery, and a regiment of Sikh Cavalry; the whole being commanded by Brigadier General Evelegh, C.B. The camp at Nawabgunge was partly intrenched and partly protected by hackeries, or native bullock carts, which were interwoven so as to form a sort of hedge. An elephant and mule detachment was formed at Nawabgunge by Colonel Evelegh. It was composed of fifty men of the best shots in the corps, who were mounted on mules; they sometimes accompanied the cavalry and artillery, but generally preceded the column as scouts. The chief duty assigned to the Nawabgunge Field Force was to keep open the roads between Lucknow and Cawnpore, during the months of June, July, August, and September; active operations by the main body of the army under Lord Clyde were at this time suspended. The charge placed upon Brigadier Evelegh necessitated upon his part untiring vigilance, and upon the troops under his command constant and harassing marches by night and day during the heat of an Indian summer. At one o'clock on the morning of the 4th of August, the Brigadier left the camp at Nawabgunge, with two guns of the Bengal Artillery, one hundred and eighty men of the XX, mounted on elephants,[1] and three hundred Sikh Cavalry, for Mohan (a town standing on an eminence, about eleven miles distant), where it was reported the rebels were concentrating in force. The movements of the column were retarded by bad roads, so that, in place of reaching Mohan an hour before sunrise, as was intended, it did not come upon it until an hour after, and was consequently unable to fall on the enemy by surprise.

The column re-crossed the Sye at seven a.m., and breakfasted under a tope which commanded the bridge. At half-past ten a.m. the vedettes sent in word that the enemy were moving towards the right flank. To meet them, one company of the XX was sent forward in skirmishing order, while Colonel Evelegh, with the Sikhs and artillery, worked round their right flank. The enemy was checked in his advance by the skirmishers, and, on coming under the fire of the Bengal Artillery, retired *en masse*. Our men and horses were

---

[1] Each elephant carried five men.

exhausted by the exertions of the day and the extreme heat of the night, and as the rains had set in the Brigadier decided to return to Nawabgunge, where the force arrived at three a.m. on the 5th.[1]

The station of Mohan was attacked by the rebels on the 7th. Intelligence of this attack reached Colonel Evelegh at five a.m. on the 8th, and at six he started from Nawabgunge with three hundred Sikh Cavalry, two guns Bengal Artillery, carrying twelve men of the XX on the limbers. When about three miles from Mohan, Colonel Evelegh, leaving the direct route, turned off towards Hussengunge, a village between Mohan and Rassulabad, the occupation of which would cut off the rebels' line of retreat. On coming within a mile of Hussengunge, he perceived the rebels falling back on that place from Mohan. He immediately set off in pursuit with his small force, overtook the rebels, killed forty-five of their number, and captured one brass three-pounder, some elephants and camels. This affair was planned with great foresight, and executed with rapidity.[2] The force left Nawabgunge at six a.m., marched ten miles, fought an action, and returned to camp by half-past six on the evening of the same day.[3] In vol. iii, page 284, Colonel Malleson says, "This action had the effect of clearing the rebels from many of the districts of Unao and Mallaon." During September the Nawabgunge column was undisturbed, but on the 8th of October the XX took part in an action which was fought at Meangunge, by Brigadier Evelegh, in which the rebels had about two hundred and fifty killed, and

---

[1] Brigadier Evelegh's despatches, *London Gazette*, 16th November, 1858.
[2] Malleson's *History of the Indian Mutiny*, vol. iii, page 284.
[3] *London Gazette*, 14th November, 1858.

three guns captured. The regiment was a second time engaged at Poorwah on the 4th November.[1] At five o'clock on the morning of the 8th of November, Brigadier Evelegh's column, to which the XX furnished two hundred and forty men, left Poorwah for Morar Mow. It was difficult to gain access to this village, as the surrounding country was intersected with deep nullahs and salt pits. The cavalry drew the enemy's attention to both flanks, while the main body forced their way into the village, when the enemy fled, but with a loss of one hundred men killed, chiefly Sepoys, and two guns captured.[2]

The moveable column left Morar Mow, at six a.m., on the 9th November, for the Fort of Simree, which it was the Brigadier's intention to attack. The enemy's cavalry and infantry were observed after an hour's march from Morar Mow, but these retired on the approach of the column; their infantry, however, soon reappeared in force in a jungle, which lay in the line of march of the column. Brigadier Evelegh thereupon sent three companies of the 80th, and two of the XX to drive them out of the jungle, while another company of the XX was ordered to search a village in its vicinity.[3] The companies of the XX and 80th soon forced the rebels from their cover, and then moved to their right in support of a troop of cavalry under Lieutenant Chamberlain, which was at this time hard pressed by the main body of the enemy's infantry, who were

---

[1] Of the actions at Meangunge and Poorwah little or no information has been obtained. At page 286, vol. iii, Malleson says, "About the same time"—early in October—"Brigadier Evelegh defeated the rebels at Miánganj, between Lucknow and Cawnpore, took two guns, and put two hundred of them *hors de combat*.

[2] *London Gazette*, 4th February, 1859.

[3] *Ibid.*, 22nd February, 1859.

found to have taken up a position in a thick belt of jungle, and who were further protected by ground so broken as to be difficult even for infantry. The musketry fire of the XX and 80th, together with the fire of the guns, soon compelled the enemy to leave their shelter; they were then promptly followed by the XX and 80th, who pushed through the jungle in skirmishing order, and ultimately drove them from a hill, where they attempted to make a stand. The cavalry, artillery, and the detachments of the XX and 80th now fell back on the other portion of the column. This portion was commanded by Major Miller, of the 80th, and was stationed about two miles from the scene of Evelegh's fight. Miller's detachment was also engaged with the rebels, but his assailants fled on the approach of Evelegh's column.[1] The whole force was delayed here, as the Brigadier could not obtain reliable information as to the direct road to the fort. After the column had advanced about half a mile, the fort was discovered in the middle of a jungle, so dense that the walls could not be discerned at a distance of one hundred yards. The fort was shelled by the mortars; two companies of the XX were sent to take possession of a village, lying to the right of the jungle, while a third company protected the baggage. The remainder of the column attacked and captured the fort, inflicting great loss on the rebels. In this action the infantry endured great fatigue, skirmishing through jungles and over broken ground for three hours between seven a.m. and twelve noon. Of the XX, Private J. Wilson was killed. Two guns and twenty thousand rounds of ammunition were captured. Captain T. C.

---

[1] *London Gazette*, 22nd February, 1859.

Lyons commanded the detachment of the XX, and Lieutenant O. T. Burne was staff officer to Brigadier Evelegh, who mentioned both of these officers in his despatch.[1] The capture of this fortress and defeat of the rebels weakened their cause considerably; a large number of Talookdars came in and declared their allegiance, as also did the villagers; the Sepoys alone holding out. Before leaving Simree, Brigadier Evelegh caused the fort to be destroyed. The next engagement was fought at Berah. Whilst on the march on the 17th of November for the village of Ginwarra, the column passed through the village of Berah, and halted under some trees about three-quarters of a mile from the village, to allow the siege train ammunition to close up on the main body. The rebels suddenly appeared in force and commenced firing into the rear of the column from a cluster of trees, surrounded by a mud wall. They were now also in possession of Berah. Brigadier Evelegh turned about and attacked the mud-walled enclosure and the village simultaneously, forced the rebels to abandon both, and sent the Sikh Cavalry to pursue them. The pursuit was continued until the flying enemy unexpectedly came upon the rear-guard of Evelegh's column under Major Miller, of the 80th, whom the Brigadier had instructed to so order his march that he (Miller) could fall back, if necessary, to support Major Bulwer's (23rd Fusiliers) escort, which was convoying ammunition and a month's supply of provisions for the whole force.

Major Miller's detachment opened fire on the flying rebels, dispersing them in all directions. The enemy were at least five thousand strong at Berah, with four

---

[1] *London Gazette*, 22nd February, 1859.

guns, and were led by the celebrated Rana Bene Madho.[1]

Three of their guns were captured at the village, and one hundred and twenty men were killed. During the attack on Berah by the main body, a company of the XX, under Captain Lyons, carried by assault a village which the enemy had occupied in considerable numbers. For this service Captain T. C. Lyons was thanked by the Brigadier in his despatch. Captain J. J. S. O'Neill, the Brigade Major, was also mentioned as being "particularly useful."[2] In this affair Private P. Sherlock was wounded. The column completed its march and encamped at the village of Ginwarra the same evening.

After defeating the rebels at Berah on the 17th, Brigadier Evelegh was directed to advance to Peroo, on the Sye, in pursuit of Bene Madho. The Brigadier remained two days at Nuggur, and, on the 20th, he informed the Commander-in-Chief that he had done so, as he considered the position an admirable one, enabling him at the most opportune moment to strike the rebels under Bene Madho. On the 21st he received instructions from the Chief of the Staff, which forbade rest until Bene Madho was run to earth.[3] The instructions were repeated by Lord Clyde in a private note of the same date from Buch ran Wan, in which he also

---

[1] Lord Clyde's despatch, dated 25th November, 1858: "Bene Madho had actually the audacity to send in a Vakeel to know what terms he might now expect. This man made his appearance about the same time that an emissary arrived from Evelegh, carrying a despatch in a quill concealed about his person, in which the Brigadier gave an account of an action he had just been fighting with this very Bene Madho's Sepoys."—*My Diary in India*, vol. ii, page 315.

[2] *London Gazette*, 22nd March, 1859.

[3] "November 21st, Roy Barielly. Evelegh has received instructions from General Mansfield to follow Bene Madho, and not to lose sight of him for a moment—easy to give, but difficult to follow."—*My Diary in India*, vol. ii, page 328.

R

asked for information. At two o'clock on the following day, Lord Clyde received intelligence from the Brigadier that Bene Madho was endeavouring to get into Dhondiakhera, a stronghold on the Ganges, a place of great sanctity, where the fanatical zeal of his followers could be easily aroused.[1] The Commander-in-Chief effected his junction with Brigadier Evelegh at Nuggur on the 23rd, having made a forced march to do so. In his despatch of the 25th November, he says, "I accordingly joined Brigadier Evelegh at Nuggur on the 23rd instant, having marched sixty miles in three days, and have reason to congratulate myself on having done so, as the enemy had again mustered in considerable force at the stronghold at Dhondiakhera."

Lord Clyde commenced the attack at six o'clock on the following morning (24th). He deployed his infantry and thus brought them into touch with Evelegh's column on the right; his cavalry was ordered to move to the left and guns to the front.[2] Whilst these dispositions were being made, Brigadier Evelegh had commenced the attack by a heavy cannonade, which was soon followed by a continuous fire of musketry, our men at the same time advancing rapidly towards the enemy's stronghold. Bene Madho's troops were soon discovered to be flying in two directions, both up and down the Ganges: as the XX, who were on the right of our line, moved forward they inclined to their left, and thus met a large body of the rebels, and at one point drove some hundreds of them into the deeper parts of the river, where they were either shot or drowned. In this action the men of the XX distinguished themselves under the eye of the

---

[1] *My Diary in India*, vol. ii, page 329.
[2] *Ibid.*, vol. ii, page 330.

Commander-in-Chief. One man, in particular, Private P. Bray, of the light company, performed a gallant feat. He swam across the Ganges in pursuit of a Sepoy carrying the Queen's colour of the 54th Native Infantry, and eventually succeeded in capturing the colour after a desperate struggle in which he was severely wounded.[1]

The troops followed in pursuit of the rebels until midnight.[2] The loss of the rebels was immense. In this action (called Buxer-Ghat), Privates T. Barry, T. Giles, W. Friol, T. Sullivan, H. Arnold, and G. Marshall were killed; Sergeant G. Thorn, Lance-Corporal S. Mullett, W. Smithers, H. Stevenson, W. Hiller, and A. Flood were wounded. The defeat of the rebels at Buxer-Ghat was the death blow to the rebel cause in Oude; the Rana Bene was now a fugitive with a few personal followers.[3]

The XX returned to the camp at Nawabgunge on the 28th November. On the 29th, Brigadier Evelegh was selected to command a special service force, and

---

[1] MS. Records.

NOTE.—Private P. Bray joined the XX in January, 1849. Served throughout the Crimean campaign and was wounded before Sebastopol on the 9th May, 1855. He accompanied the corps to India, was present at the siege of Lucknow and all the actions in the mutiny. Bray was wounded at Buxer-Ghat and again at Muchlee Goan on the 13th April, 1859, when he received a sword cut wound on both hands. Private Bray was discharged with a good character on the 28th March, 1860. The captured colour is in the mess of the 1st Battalion.

[2] Lord Clyde's despatch, dated 25th November, 1858.

[3] Ibid.

NOTE.—The following anecdote was for many years current in the regiment. It was recently mentioned in a paper on the services of the regiment during the mutiny, which was read at the Young Men's Christian Association, Burnley, Lancashire, by George Tilling, watchmaker of that town, and formerly Sergeant in the XX:—At Buxer-Ghat a ball passed through Colonel Evelegh's topee (Indian helmet): coolly taking it off, and looking at the hole the bullet had made, the Colonel said with a smile, and at the same time looking towards the men close at hand, "Old Jack is not gone yet." Old Jack was a nickname by which the Colonel was known amongst the men.

joined Lord Clyde at Lucknow on this day. The Commander-in-Chief, in his despatch dated 18th January, 1859 (*London Gazette*, 24th March, 1859), states: "Finding on my arrival at Lucknow, on the 28th November, that I should be obliged to stop there a few days to make certain arrangements, and to meet the demands of the correspondence of the army, the brigade, which had latterly accompanied me, was not allowed to halt, but was pushed on at once under Brigadier Evelegh, C.B., to assist in the reduction of the Seatapore district. On the 2nd December, the Brigadier occupied the fort of Oomeriah after a sharp resistance; he remained there for three days, levelling it to the ground. This fort, owing to its position, had hitherto barred the north-west road from Lucknow, and had for a long time been a source of much inconvenience."

On the completion of this service, Brigadier Evelegh was directed to march on Fyzabad, and to take post at Gondah, where he would form a reserve to the columns moving northwards.

Captain T. C. Lyons was Brigade-Major to Brigadier Evelegh's brigade during these operations, and the XX was commanded by Major R. C. Butler. On the 4th of December, the regiment marched from Nawabgunge to Lucknow, and joined a brigade which was formed for service under the Commander-in-Chief, Lord Clyde.

Eight companies of the XX and the 2nd Battalion Rifle Brigade formed the European contingent to the brigade. This column marched at the rate of twenty miles a day to Fyzabad, where it crossed the Gogra, and thence in two marches reached Secrora, subsequently moving to Bareitch. On the 23rd December, the regiment left Bareitch, passed Nanparah on the

26th, and, after a march of twenty miles, attacked a large body of the rebels at Bargidia (otherwise Churda). After a slight resistance the enemy sought safety in flight, leaving their guns in the hands of the brigade.[1] They were pursued until the darkness set in. At ten o'clock on the following morning (27th), the force marched from camp, and, after passing through two jungles, they deployed on a plain, and advanced towards the fort of Musjeidia. Some companies of the XX and Rifle Brigade were sent out in skirmishing order about noon, and worked their way under the fire of the guns of the fort, until they came close up to its parapets; from the position thus gained they kept up such a steady fire, as soon cleared the Sepoys from the parapet and silenced the guns.[2] Our mortars shelled the place for three hours, and at four o'clock the firing had ceased and the rebels had fled from Musjeidia. The fort, which was small but very strong, was destroyed on the following day. In this action Privates T. Cunninghame, J. Day, and J. Dennis were wounded.

The brigade returned to Nanparah on the 29th, and on the 30th made a night-march to Bankee, where the rebels had assembled under the Nana. The night was intensely dark, there were no roads, and the guides were unreliable. The heavy guns were left at Nanparah in charge of a detachment of the XX. A wing, half the men being mounted on elephants, accompanied Lord Clyde to Bankee.[3] They left camp at Nanparah at half-past eight p.m. The column was guided in its course by a lantern placed on the back of the elephant

---

[1] *London Gazette*, 24th March, 1859.
[2] *Ibid.*, 24th March, 1859. *My Diary in India*, vol. ii.
[3] *My Diary in India*, vol. ii.

which carried the guides. Bankee was reached before sunrise. From the official account, we learn that "The enemy was surprised, and attacked with great vigour, driven through a jungle which he attempted to defend, and finally into and across the Raptee."[1] The brigade halted at Bankee on the afternoon of the 31st December.

Whilst the main portion of the regiment was serving in the force under the immediate direction of the Commander-in-Chief, two companies had been detached from Bareitch on the 21st December, and were posted to a column which was commanded by Colonel Christie, of the 80th Regiment.[2] This column marched up the left bank of the Sarjoo to Darmarpore, operating in conjunction with many other columns. Colonel Christie conducted a successful skirmish on the 23rd December, and captured two of the enemy's guns. He made a circuit to the north by Pudnaha, and rejoined the Commander-in-Chief on the 2nd January. From the date of its landing in India to the 31st December, 1858, the regiment lost from sickness alone two officers and one hundred and thirty men. The rebels were now almost powerless, and the campaign was virtually at an end.[3]

On the 17th January, 1859, the XX marched into Gondah (a town in Oude, sixty miles north of Lucknow). Large drafts of officers and men from England augmented the strength of the battalion at this date to thirty-two officers and one thousand and twenty-four men. Brigadier Evelegh, C.B., left for England on the 21st February, and retired from the

---

[1] *London Gazette*, 24th March, 1859.
[2] *Ibid.*, 24th March, 1859.
[3] Lord Clyde's despatch, dated 18th January, 1859.

service by the sale of his commission on the 28th October. (See Appendix.)

Lieutenant-Colonel J. Cormick was promoted from Major in the 2nd Battalion, and joined at Gondah on the 4th March, when he assumed the command. Major R. C. Butler[1] was promoted Brevet-Lieutenant-Colonel and Captain T. C. Lyons Brevet-Major (dated 26th April, 1859), in recognition of their services during the campaign.

---

[1] Lieutenant-Colonel Butler was sixteen years in the XX. He served throughout the Crimean and Indian Mutiny campaigns. For his distinguished conduct at Inkerman, where he was severely wounded in the shoulder, he was promoted Brevet-Major. Major Butler behaved with great gallantry at the attack on the trenches on the 23rd March, for which he was mentioned in despatches by Lord Raglan. He was present at the siege of Lucknow, and for some time commanded the permanent camp at Nawabgunge; and also the regiment in several of the actions fought in the winter of 1858. Lieutenant-Colonel Butler was an excellent officer and a brave soldier. As a Captain, he commanded the Grenadier Company. Although of great physical strength, his health was undermined by the two campaigns; and he retired from the service by the sale of his commission on the 15th December, 1859, and died shortly afterwards.

CHAPTER XXXVI.

1859-1867.

Death of Major-General Thomas, Colonel of the Regiment—Cantonments at Gondah—Building of Barracks—Convoys Plundered—Field Operations by Lieutenant-Colonel Cormick—Actions at Muchlee Goan and Khyber Jungle—Colonel Cormick's Despatch—Captain Vaughan's special Service Column—Defeat of the Rebels—Occupation of the Barracks at Gondah—Final Operations under Colonel A. Holdich, C.B.—Death of Lieutenants Holmes and Horn—Inspection by General Sir Hugh Rose—Change of Stations—Formation of a Field Service Column—Sir William Mansfield inspects the Regiment—Quartered at Calcutta—Preparations for the Return to England—Volunteering—Arrival at Plymouth.

MAJOR-GENERAL Henry Thomas, C.B., died in London on the 21st September, 1858, and the Colonelcy of the regiment was conferred upon Major-General Marcus Beresford, C.B., who was at this time in command of a division of the Madras army. General Thomas had commanded the corps for many years; he was a Peninsular officer of great distinction (for his services see Appendix).

The cantonments at Gondah had been destroyed by the rebels during the mutiny, and as the suppression of the rebellion became complete, the building of barracks for the men and bungalows for the officers was commenced. Great difficulty, however, was experienced in obtaining coolie labour, as the jungles, by which Gondah was surrounded, were infested by large bodies of the rebels under Bala Rao and other leaders. The Nana Sahib was supposed at this time to have found a temporary refuge in the Terai jungle. Supplies for the regiment, in transit from Fyzabad, were often plundered by the rebels.

This state of affairs could not be tolerated. Many efforts were made to bring the mutineers to battle, or to fall upon them in sufficient numbers as to have a wholesome and deterring effect on their depredatory and inconvenient courses; but these attempts had been defeated by the guides, who were always unreliable and often wilfully misleading.

A force, consisting of a wing of the XX, a squadron of Sikh Cavalry, and one battery of artillery, under Lieutenant-Colonel Cormick, marched to the village of Athona on the 7th of April, but the rebels had left before the troops reached the village. Colonel Cormick encamped his men until the 9th, when they returned to Gondah. On the evening of the 10th, Cormick again moved out from Gondah, with the same detachments as before mentioned. On the following evening the tents were pitched at Muchlee Goan. The baggage animals were sent out to feed, when some rebels endeavoured to effect the capture of an elephant. Two companies of the XX, under Captain F. L. Edridge, were ordered out. Captain Edridge advanced cautiously in skirmishing order, and surprised the rebels in a ravine, as they were partaking of their evening meal. The enemy made an attempt to resist, but after an ineffectual fire they fled into a dense jungle, keenly pursued by Captain Edridge and his skirmishers. It was now dark and Colonel Cormick recalled the companies. In this action twenty of the enemy were killed.

About ten a.m. on the 12th, Colonel Cormick broke up his camp and marched his force to Wuzurgung. On the next day he moved towards Gondah, *via* the Khyber Jungle, and the village of Magowa.

Between two and three thousand rebels were found in the jungle. They were again surprised and on this occasion in a very faulty position, having a marsh of considerable extent in their rear. Colonel Cormick advanced with the artillery and Jones's Sikh Cavalry: the enemy formed section squares, which were soon smashed by the grape and canister poured into them by the artillery; the Sikhs then charged and drove them into the water. A great many of the rebels were making good their escape by a ford on the right of our advance, under cover of a low range of hills; but Captain Edridge, who commanded the infantry column, had his right flank protected by a company in extended order on the crest of these hills, and this company cut off the enemy in their retreat, killing a large number of the fugitives. Captain Edridge pushed forward with the main body of his column and engaged the rebels still in the water, who were nearly all shot or drowned. On this day between three and four hundred were killed. Of the XX, Privates P. Bray and J. Walsh were wounded. Two stand of colours were captured by the Sikh Cavalry. From this date there was peace at Gondah.

Subjoined is an extract from the despatch[1] of Lieutenant-Colonel Cormick: "To Captain Edridge and the men of the XX great praise is due. Lieutenant Hon. A. Vereker acted as my orderly officer and rendered great assistance."

At this time Captain H. B. Vaughan was in command of a special field force, composed of three guns Bengal Horse Artillery, two companies of the XX, and one hundred and eighty men of Hodson's Horse. Vaughan attacked a body of the rebels at Bishowee Muddy on the 27th April. He failed to prevent their

---

[1] *London Gazette*, 25th July, 1859.

MAP OF THE COUNTRY AROUND LUCKNOW.

gaining the jungle, but with his cavalry and twenty-five men of the XX mounted on elephants he overtook and dispersed them on the banks of the river, killing seventeen of their number. An elephant, some horses, ponies, forty stands of arms, and a quantity of baggage were captured.[1]

Captain Vaughan[2] defeated the rebels a second time on the 5th May. On this occasion the colours of the 15th Native Infantry were captured. This engagement was favourably noticed by the Governor-General in Council in a despatch dated 29th May, 1859, but we have failed to obtain the particulars of it.

During the month of May, 1859, the regiment began to occupy by degrees the barracks which were being built for it at Gondah, having been up to this period (from its landing in 1857) under canvas. Colonel A. Holdich, C.B., who had joined the battalion in September of this year, was appointed a Brigadier, for the purpose of conducting the final operations against the rebels on the frontier.

On the 9th of November, six companies of the XX, under Lieutenant-Colonel Cormick, marched from Gondah towards the northern frontier of Oude, to take part in these operations. No fighting of any sort ensued, and the whole of the rebels and their leaders, to the number of about four thousand men, unresistingly gave themselves up. On the 24th

---

[1] *London Gazette*, 31st December, 1859.

[2] Captain Vaughan joined the XX in 1853. He served throughout the Crimean campaign, and was not absent from duty a single day, either with leave or from any other cause. At Inkerman he behaved with great coolness and intrepidity. He accompanied the regiment to India, and was present at the siege of Lucknow, and at all the actions fought during the campaign. Captain Vaughan was a dashing soldier, and a successful company leader; one in whom the men had the greatest confidence. He was promoted (by purchase) to an unattached Majority in 1870, and subsequently obtained the rank of Colonel. He died on the 26th June, 1885.

December this detachment returned to Gondah. Brigadier Holdich and the troops received the acknowledgments of the Governor-General in Council "for their excellent services," in a despatch dated the 1st of February, 1860. Lieutenants Holmes[1] and Horn[2] died at Gondah on the 17th of March, 1860. A monument was raised to their memory at Gondah. The regiment was inspected at Gondah, on the 14th December, by His Excellency Sir Hugh Rose, Commander-in-Chief; after a minute inspection, he expressed his satisfaction at the appearance of the battalion in the most flattering terms.

The following is an extract from a letter dated 21st January, 1861, on the inspection of the corps: "The field day was well conceived and excellent. His Excellency was much pleased with the appearance, evolutions, kits, barracks, and conduct of the regiment."

On the 9th April, 1861, the regiment was inspected by Major-General Campbell, who said in his confidential report that, "The men are a fine, smart, well-drilled, and well-behaved body of men, as good in quarters as they are in the field."[3]

A change of stations took place early in 1861. The regiment proceeded on the 9th of February, by march route, from Gondah to Gorruckpore, arriving there on the 20th. On the 4th February, 1862, the head-

---

[1] Lieutenant F. G. Holmes joined the XX on the 16th February, 1855, and was promoted Lieutenant on the 15th June of the same year. He served at the siege of Sebastopol, and was wounded at the assault on the 18th June, 1855. He accompanied the regiment to India, was present at the siege of Lucknow, and at every action in which the regiment was engaged during the campaign. At Morar Mow he was orderly officer to Brigadier Evelegh.

[2] Lieutenant F. G. Horn was a nephew of General Horn. He joined the XX on the 29th February, 1856, and was promoted Lieutenant on the 15th June, 1858. During the mutiny he took part in the affairs at Churda and Musjeidia.

[3] Adjutant-General's Office, Calcutta, 5th September, 1861.

quarters and one wing marched from Gorruckpore to Benares; and on the 29th of October the wing, which had remained at Gorruckpore, moved to Azinghur; this proved a very unhealthy station. On the 19th December, the date of departure from Azinghur, one hundred and sixty-five men were in hospital suffering from fever, and twelve men had died. In December, 1863, the regiment was quartered at Rorkee and Futteghur. In February, 1865, it moved to Dinapore. In September of this year, three hundred men were held in readiness to form part of a field force under Colonel J. Cormick, which was to be employed against some mountain tribes. The expedition was subsequently abandoned. On the 1st of November, His Excellency Sir William Mansfield, Commander-in-Chief, inspected the regiment, and expressed himself as highly satisfied with its drill and discipline. He said that he made it his especial duty to visit the regiment, to personally satisfy himself that it was worthy of the favourable reports that the various inspecting general officers had made on it. He was also the more anxious to see it, owing to the high enconiums passed on it by General Sir Hugh Rose, the late Commander-in-Chief in India, and he was happy to be able to say that Colonel Cormick and the officers, non-commissioned officers, and men deserved the highest credit for their drill, steadiness, and efficiency.

In January, 1866, the left wing, commanded by Captain W. D. Nunn,[1] moved to Calcutta, followed by

---

[1] Captain W. D. Nunn joined the XX as Ensign, on the 20th February, 1855, and was promoted Lieutenant on the 21st September, 1855, and Captain on the 29th July, 1859. He served with the regiment at the siege of Sebastopol and expedition to Kinburn—(medal with clasp and Turkish medal). He accompanied the regiment to India, and was present at the battles of Chanda, Ameerapore, Sultanpore, siege and capture of Lucknow, the actions at Mohan—(Orderly Officer

the headquarters and right wing, on the 17th February, under Major W. L. D. Meares. The regiment was now preparing to return to England after an absence of nine years. During the months of October and November, three hundred and thirteen men volunteered to continue their service in India, and were transferred to the selected regiments. On the 4th December, the headquarters—strength ten officers and three hundred and thirty-three all ranks—under Colonel J. Cormick, embarked on board the merchant ship "Patrician." The left wing—eight officers and one hundred and thirteen men—with Major W. L. D. Meares in command, embarked on board the ship "Beaumaris Castle" on the 18th December.[1]

The headquarters reached Plymouth and disembarked on the 27th March, and the left wing on the 8th April, 1867.

---

to Brigadier Evelegh), Hussengunge, Meangunge, Churda, Fort Musjeidia, and Bankee. Captain Nunn was promoted Brevet-Major on the 5th July, 1872, exchanged to the 2nd Battalion in November, 1872, and retired by the sale of his commission in July, 1875.

[1] During the homeward voyage a death occurred on each of these ships. On the "Patrician" there was also a birth. Charles Sutton, the eldest son of Colonel (then Captain) Edridge, was born on the 11th February, 1867. He is now a Lieutenant in the Liverpool Regiment.

Chapter XXXVII.

1867-1881.

Quartered at Plymouth—Detachment to Exeter Riots—Detachments at Bristol and Trowbridge—Removal to Aldershot—Death of Colonel Cormick—Change of Stations—Sent to Ireland—Inspection—Presentation of Colours by Lord Strathnairn—Change of Stations—Embark for Bermuda—Sir F. Horn, Colonel of the XX—Quartered at Halifax, N.S.—Embark for Cyprus—Change of Camps—Headquarters to Malta—XX Return Home.

AT Plymouth the regiment was quartered in the Mount Wise and Raglan barracks.

On the 8th April, 1867, two hundred men, under the command of Major Edridge, were suddenly ordered to proceed to Exeter to aid the civil authorities in the suppression of the Bread Riots.

The detachment left Plymouth at midnight, and for two weeks after its arrival in Exeter it had many irksome duties to perform. It returned to Plymouth on the 7th November, with the exception of I Company, which remained at Exeter under Captain J. Aldridge.[1] On the 11th November, D Company, commanded by Captain G. Gethin,[2] was sent to Bristol, and was reinforced by B and G Companies on the 23rd

---

[1] Captain Aldridge joined the XX as Ensign in June, 1857, was promoted Lieutenant (by purchase) 10th September, 1858, and Captain 12th April, 1864. He served in the Indian Mutiny campaign, took part in the actions at Churda and Musjeidia. He was with the 2nd Battalion in China and Japan. Captain Aldridge retired upon half pay on the 27th March, 1874. He joined the Queen's County Militia on the 28th March, 1874, and ever since has taken a zealous interest in all that concerns this regiment.

[2] Captain Gethin joined the XX on the 19th June, 1855, and was promoted Captain (by purchase) 13th December, 1859. He went to India with the regiment, served throughout the Indian Mutiny campaign, including the siege of Lucknow. He retired by the sale of his commission on the 13th September, 1870.

December, the whole being commanded by Major Edridge. In April, 1868, two of these companies moved to Trowbridge and one to Exeter. Whilst stationed at Devonport the regiment obtained over two hundred recruits, chiefly from the counties of Devon and Cornwall.

On the 26th May, 1868, the headquarters left Devonport, proceeding by sea to Portsmouth, and thence by rail to Aldershot, and was quartered in the east block, where it was joined by the detachments from Exeter and Trowbridge.

The regiment suffered a severe loss on the 10th of July, 1868, by the death of its commanding officer, Colonel John Cormick, who died after a brief illness (congestion of the lungs) of seven days.[1]

It is quite unnecessary to make any special reference to the efficiency of the regiment during Colonel Cormick's command. All that the reader may wish to know on that point he will find in the preceding chapter. But as Colonel Cormick devoted especial care and attention to the musketry practice, and encouraged it in every possible way, the figure of merit attained by the regiment will be of interest. The two last years of his command and the year after his death are quoted :—

	Order of Merit in the Army.
1867	First.
1868	Second.
1869	Second.

On the 17th May, 1869, the headquarters and five companies under Lieutenant-Colonel Cobbe (who had succeeded to the command on the death of Colonel

---

[1] See Appendix.

Cormick) marched to Great Bedwin, *viâ* Basingstoke and Newbury, and thence by train to Bristol, where they were quartered in the Horfield barracks. The remaining five companies under Major Meares marched to Portsmouth, and were conveyed by sea to Plymouth, being quartered in the Raglan and Mount Wise barracks. Lieutenant-Colonel D. L. Colthurst exchanged to the XX from the 17th Regiment. He joined the regiment at Bristol on the 14th of August, 1869. On the 7th December, 1869, the XX was placed under orders for service in Ireland, and left Bristol at eleven p.m. on the 9th for Plymouth, where it was joined by the five companies from Exeter, the whole embarking on board H.M.S. "Simoom" early on the morning of the 10th. The "Simoom" reached Kingstown and the regiment disembarked on the 12th December. The headquarters and five companies proceeded by train to Kilkenny, and five companies to the Curragh camp under Major Meares.

The Commander of the Forces in Ireland, General Lord Strathnairn, inspected the regiment on Saturday the 22nd January, 1870. His intention of making the inspection was intimated by telegraph; the message appointing twelve noon for the parade was received at quarter to twelve a.m. The regiment paraded under Captain Addison and Lieutenant Davies (Captain and Subaltern of the day), who were the only officers in barracks.[1]

In his official report on the regiment, his Lordship said the men were clean and well turned out, and the barrack rooms were clean and regular.[2]

---

[1] The other officers were hunting with the regimental beagles.

[2] Notwithstanding the short notice, the General made a close inspection, and mentioned in his remarks on the parade that he had noticed one man without a ball bag.

S

The presentation of new colours, to replace those given to the regiment in 1838 by the Duke of Wellington, had been deferred in consequence of the death of the lamented Colonel Cormick. General Lord Strathnairn,[1] who had consented to make the presentation, at the request of the late Colonel Cormick, decided that the ceremony should take place at Kilkenny on Wednesday, the 26th January, 1870. Lord Strathnairn, attended by Captain Hozier, A.D.C., arrived on the parade ground precisely at half-past one p.m., and was received with a general salute from the regiment, which was commanded by Major W. L. D. Meares, in the absence on leave of Lieutenant-Colonel Colthurst.

The old colours were trooped, the band playing "Auld Lang Syne." The new colours were then brought to the front, placed on a pile of drums, and consecrated by the Honourable and Very Reverend the Dean of Lismore, who officiated in the absence of the Bishop. His Lordship then presented the colours to Ensigns G. E. Kenworthy-Browne[2] and A. E. de la Poer,[3] who received them kneeling.

Lord Strathnairn, then addressing the regiment, said: "The emblems of honour which I have given into the keeping of the XX Regiment are the catechism of discipline—that military word which represents all the obligations of a soldier's duty; which makes him as resolute and forward in the field as he is peaceful and orderly in quarters; which unites him in good comrade-

---

[1] Better known as Sir Hugh Rose; he was raised to the peerage by the title of Baron Strathnairn in 1866.

[2] He was promoted Lieutenant in 1871, and Captain in 1879. Captain Browne retired from the service in September, 1881.

[3] Ensign de la Poer retired by the sale of his commission on the 14th February, 1871.

ship round his colours in action; which prompts him to save a wounded comrade, or to nurse him in sickness—that discipline which teaches him never to turn from an enemy, but to spare him when he is fallen; to hesitate before no sacrifice or hardship which duty calls for. While, on the one hand, your colours are the catechism of your duties, they are also, on the other hand, the history of your fame. And if ever a regiment had a right to value that history, it is the one which I have now the honour to address. Those brief records on your colours—they are but simple words, but they tell of battles and deeds of arms of imperishable recollection, which have decided the world's events in the pages of history. I do not ask the XX Regiment to do their duty by their colours. Why should I? They have for nearly two hundred years carried them from victory to victory in every quarter of the globe. But I do ask them to bear in mind, to cherish, to study, the many emblems of success which were carried this day through their ranks—that honoured list which began in Germany at Minden, and ended in distant India at Lucknow. Think of Minden, where your regiment lost so many men that your commander ordered them into the second line. Remember how the XX entreated that they might not retire from the first line, which had been the scene of their success—how they assured their General that their *spirit* would supply the place of their two hundred and fifty gallant comrades who had died for their duty. Remember that the great commander, the Duke of Wellington, who granted you the greater part of your emblems, would never allow a regiment to wear one except for an undoubted victory. So military was His Grace that he would not accept a drawn battle, or a retreat, however honourably and well conducted. It must be a real victory, on or beyond the enemy's ground. I return my expressive thanks to the XX Regiment for the distinction they have conferred upon me, and the gratification they have afforded me, in asking me to present them their new colours. And the honour is enhanced because it was the most illustrious of British commanders, the Duke of Wellington, who gave you your last colours in 1838,—a commander whose excellence we endeavour to imitate, but even the bounds of whose pre-eminence we cannot attain. May Heaven continue to this noble regiment the bright days of which, in its mercy, it has vouchsafed to them so many."[1]

The regiment then marched past, and the ceremony concluded. Major Meares and the officers of the regiment entertained Lord Strathnairn and a large company at luncheon, where the customary toasts were proposed. The men of the regiment were entertained at a dinner in honour of the day.

The officers present were Majors Meares, Edridge, Captains Vaughan, Aldridge, Laprimaudaye,[2] Addison,[3] Lieutenants Davies,[4] Jones,[5] Beaumont,[6] Gahan,[7] Ensigns Browne, de la Poer, and Waudby,[8] Lieu-

---

[1] From the Kilkenny *Moderator* of the 29th January, 1870.

[2] Retired from the service by the sale of his commission on the 15th February, 1871.

[3] Exchanged to half pay in October, 1871.

[4] Retired by the sale of his commission on the 12th July, 1870.

[5] Transferred as Captain to 56th Regiment, 26th August, 1870, and subsequently retired on half pay. He is now a Major in the Warwick Regiment.

[6] Lieutenant Beaumont was promoted Captain on the 1st January, 1875. In the following year he retired upon half pay, and died on the 3rd February, 1877.

[7] Staff Paymaster 51st Regimental District.

[8] Ensign Waudby was promoted Lieutenant on the 27th October, 1871, and Captain in the 2nd Battalion in 1878. He retired on half pay the same year in consequence of ill health, and died in 1881.

tenant and Adjutant Hussey,[1] Paymaster Gibbs,[2] Quartermaster McKay,[3] and Surgeon-Major Arden.[4]

The regiment remained at Kilkenny until July, 1870; during this time it had furnished detachments at the towns of Tipperary and Templemore.

On the 12th July, the headquarters and two companies proceeded to Cork; four companies to Camden Fort; two companies to Carlisle Fort; and two companies to Youghal.

On the 22nd May, 1871, the headquarters and the several detachments proceeded to the Curragh camp, where the regiment was stationed until the 5th January, 1872, when it moved to Dublin and was quartered in the Richmond barracks.

On the 18th and 19th of August, seven companies, under the command of Lieutenant-Colonel Colthurst,

---

[1] Lieutenant C. E. Hussey joined the XX as Ensign (by purchase) on the 20th March, 1859, and was promoted Lieutenant (by purchase) on the 10th June, 1862. He was appointed Adjutant of the 1st Battalion on the 7th August, 1866, and he held this appointment until the 21st December, 1870. He was promoted Captain on the 14th September, 1870. On resigning the Adjutantcy, Captain Hussey was specially selected to drill different regiments of militia in the south of Ireland. Captain Hussey embarked with the battalion for Bermuda in March, 1873. He was Fort Adjutant in Bermuda from the 20th August, 1874, to the 31st March, 1875, when a Brigade Major was appointed. From the 1st December, 1875, to the 31st August, 1880, he was Adjutant of the 8th Lancashire Volunteers (now 1st Volunteer Battalion Lancashire Fusiliers). Captain Hussey was aide-de-camp and private secretary to the Governor of Tasmania from the 1st September, 1880, to the 27th August, 1881. On the 1st July, 1881, he was promoted Major, and Brevet-Lieutenant-Colonel on the 21st June, 1887. Since 1881, Lieutenant-Colonel Hussey has served with the 2nd Battalion in India (his second tour of Indian service), and is now commandant at Deolalee.

[2] Major Gibbs was transferred in 1887 to a regimental district. He had served in the XX since 1857. He retired with the honorary rank of Lieutenant-Colonel, and died in 1884.

[3] Quartermaster McKay joined the XX in 1855. He was promoted Quartermaster in November, 1869, retired from the service with the honorary rank of Major in 1884, and died on the 3rd June, 1888.

[4] Surgeon-Major Arden was transferred to the regimental district at Galway. He subsequently retired from the service.

were sent to Belfast to aid the civil authorities in quelling riots between the Orangemen and Roman Catholics. On the 26th of this month, the headquarters moved from Dublin to Newry, and were here joined on the 1st of September by three companies from Belfast; one company had been sent to Monahan, and three to Armagh, on the suppression of the riots at Belfast.

On the 5th of October, 1872, Lieutenant-Colonel D. L. Colthurst[1] retired on half pay, and was succeeded in the command of the battalion by Major W. L. D. Meares.

The regiment embarked at Belfast on board H.M.S "Tamar," on the 5th of March, 1873, and sailed for Bermuda on the following day. After a pleasant voyage, the "Tamar" arrived at Bermuda on the 26th March, and the XX was quartered at St. George's, with a detachment of two companies at Ireland Island.

On the embarkation of the battalion, the Depôt companies were left at Newry. Towards the end of the month they proceeded to Bury, Lancashire, where they have since been located, and which is now the headquarters of the territorial district of the regiment.

On the 16th January, 1875, the headquarters marched from St. George's to Prospect Hill, and the detachment changed from Ireland Island to Boaz.

---

[1] Lieutenant-Colonel Colthurst's first commission as Ensign was in the 17th Regiment, dated the 20th July, 1847; he was promoted Lieutenant (by purchase) on the 17th November, 1848, and Captain (by purchase) on the 7th September, 1852. He served with the 17th Regiment in the Crimea from January to July, 1855, and took part in the assault on the Redan of the 18th June. He was promoted Major (by purchase) on the 27th May, 1860, and Lieutenant-Colonel (by purchase) on the 23rd January, 1869. Lieutenant-Colonel Colthurst exchanged into the XX on the 1st August, 1869. With the 17th Regiment he served in Canada and Jamaica. He received the Crimean and Turkish War Medals. Colonel Colthurst commanded the XX for three years. He was for many years member of Parliament for Cork County.

The battalion embarked on board H.M.S. "Tamar," on the 23rd of November, 1876, and sailed on the 24th for Halifax, Nova Scotia, arriving there on the 29th; it disembarked on the following day, and occupied the Wellington barracks. General Sir Frederick Horn was appointed Colonel of the XX, from the 45th Regiment, on the 17th March, 1876, in place of General Marcus Beresford, deceased. Sir Frederick Horn had spent the whole of his regimental career in the XX (see Appendix).

On the 10th May, 1878, Colonel W. L. D. Meares[1] completed five years' service in command of the battalion and was placed on retired pay with the honorary rank of Major-General. He was succeeded in the command by Major F. L. Edridge, who was promoted Lieutenant-Colonel on the 11th May.

On the 13th November, 1878, the battalion embarked on board H.M.S. "Orontes," and sailed for Cyprus, calling at Bermuda, Gibraltar, and Malta. The "Orontes" reached Cyprus on the 12th December; the battalion landed at Larnaca on the following day, and marched to the camp at Goshi, continuing its march the next day to Mathiati, where it was accommodated in huts. On the 21st February, 1879, four companies, under the command of Major J. J. S. O'Neill, left

---

[1] Major-General Meares joined the 98th Regiment as Ensign, on the 29th November, 1850, and was promoted Lieutenant (by purchase) on the 11th October, 1853. Lieutenant Meares served with the 98th Regiment in India, until his transfer to the XX on the 11th August, 1854. He served with the XX at the siege of Sebastopol, and the expedition to Kinburn. He was promoted Captain on the 16th October, 1855, and subsequently retired on half pay. Captain Meares was appointed to the 2nd Battalion in March, 1858, and served with it in China and Japan. On the 12th April, 1864, he was promoted Major (by purchase) and posted to the 1st Battalion, which he joined in India, taking command of the left wing at Futteghur. His service was continuous with the battalion from this date until his retirement.

Mathiati for Zügoh, five marches from the former place. These companies were employed in making the section lying between Zügoh and Salico, of the new main road from Limassol to Platras, the commissariat depôt at the foot of Mount Tröodos. On the 24th of April, five companies, under the command of Lieutenant-Colonel Edridge, marched from Mathiati to Larnaca and embarked on board H.M.S. "Himalaya" for passage to Malta. On arrival at Malta, Captain F. W. Birch[1] assumed the command of the wing until the arrival of Major O'Neill from Cyprus early in June.

On the 1st of May, the headquarters left Mathiati for Tröodos under Captain E. P. T. Goldsmith, and established the first camp on the summit of the Mount Tröodos (five thousand five hundred and ninety feet above the level of the sea), on the 5th May. The headquarters and five companies spent two summers (1879-80) at this camp. The camping ground was extended and cleared, good roads were made, an open-air theatre built, and many other improvements carried out. The health of the men was excellent. In the winter of 1879-80 the wing was encamped at Polymedia near Limassol. The headquarters and wing embarked from this place for Malta on the 6th of October, 1880, in H.M.S. "Tamar," arrived at Malta on the 10th, and went into barracks at Lower St. Elmo.

Owing to the reduction of the garrison of Malta by one regiment, the battalion was suddenly ordered to

---

[1] Major F. W. Birch joined the XX as Ensign on the 10th November, 1865; he was promoted Lieutenant on the 14th October, 1868, and Captain on the 10th February, 1877. He was Instructor of Musketry of the 2nd Battalion from the 6th August, 1875, to the 9th February, 1877. He was promoted Major on the 19th November, 1881. Major Birch was Adjutant of the 2nd Volunteer Battalion Lancashire Fusiliers from the 31st August, 1882, to the 31st August, 1887.

return to England, and it embarked on board H.M.S. "Himalaya" on the 15th January, 1881, under the command of Lieutenant-Colonel Edridge. Previous to embarkation the regiment was inspected by Major-General Feilding, commanding the infantry brigade, who was pleased to express himself in very flattering terms of its appearance on parade, and good conduct in garrison.

The "Himalaya" arrived at Queenstown on the 27th January, 1881; on the following day the battalion disembarked and was quartered in Cork barracks. The strength of the regiment on this date was twenty-seven officers, thirty-eight sergeants, and five hundred and eighty-two rank and file.

Chapter XXXVIII.

1881–1888.

The XX at Cork—Change of Title—Transfers from the Battalion—Stations in Ireland—Guards of Honour—Fermoy—Liverpool—Manchester—Inspection by H.R.H. the Duke of Cambridge at Manchester and Fleetwood.

THE unsettled state of affairs in Ireland in 1881 prevented both officers and men from obtaining the customary leave of absence granted on the return of a regiment from a tour of foreign service. On the 1st of July, 1881, the title of the regiment was changed from "XX" to the "Lancashire Fusiliers,"[1] but its numerical order in the army still continued to be the XX. In this year a great many changes took place among the men of the regiment: about one hundred were transferred to the first class Army Reserve, and two hundred were transferred to the 2nd Battalion for service in India. On the 3rd November, two companies were sent to garrison Haulbowline, Cork Harbour; and one company to Youghal on the 5th December. On the 25th January, the battalion was placed under orders to leave Cork. On the 27th, the headquarters and five companies proceeded to Templemore, two companies to Tipperary, and one company to Nenagh. Subsequently detachments were furnished to Newcastle, County Limerick, and to Scariff, County Clare, Roscrea, County Tipperary, and Carlisle Fort, Cork Harbour. Whilst stationed at Templemore, the regiment frequently furnished parties to aid the civil authorities at evictions, seizures of

---

[1] General order, No. 41, May, 1881.

cattle, and at different protection posts in the Counties Clare, Limerick, and Tipperary.

The duties in connection with evictions were fatiguing and harassing; the men frequently left barracks at midnight, and returned on the following afternoon.

Colonel F. L. Edridge[1] was placed on half pay on the 11th of May, 1883, on completing five years' service in command of the battalion. Colonel Edridge served twenty-eight years in the XX.[2] Since leaving the regiment he has commanded the XX Regimental District for five years. Colonel T. H. Clarkson succeeded to the command of the regiment on the retirement of Colonel Edridge. On the 15th August, 1884, a detachment (one hundred men) was sent to Camden Fort, under the command of Major Goldsmith.[3]

---

[1] Colonel Edridge joined the XX as Ensign on the 19th February, 1855. He served at the siege of Sebastopol and with the expedition against Kinburn. He was promoted Lieutenant (by purchase) on the 10th August, 1856, and Captain (by purchase) on the 7th August, 1857. Captain Edridge embarked with the regiment for India, landed at Calcutta, and marched to Benares, where he was left in command of a detachment of the regiment. Captain Edridge took part in the actions of Muchlee Goan and Khyber Jungle (see pages 265, 266). He returned to England with the regiment in March, 1867, and was promoted Major (by purchase) on the 3rd September, 1867. Major Edridge embarked with the regiment for Bermuda in March, 1873, and succeeded to the command on the 11th May, 1878. He commanded the regiment at Halifax, Cyprus, Malta, and in Ireland. Under orders of the Queen in Council he administered the government of Cyprus, and commanded the troops in that colony from the 6th September to the 20th November, 1879.

[2] The officers of the regiment presented Mrs. Edridge with a silver tea and coffee service as a memento of the Colonel's command, and as an acknowledgment of the sincere interest she had always shown in the women and children of the regiment.

[3] Major E. P. T. Goldsmith joined the 2nd Battalion XX as Ensign on the 11th February, 1862; he was promoted Lieutenant on the 11th July, 1868, and Captain on the 2nd July, 1875. With the 2nd Battalion he served in India, China, Japan, South Africa, and Mauritius; and with the 1st Battalion in Bermuda, Halifax, Nova Scotia, Cyprus, and Malta, his service abroad extending over a period of seventeen years. When Ensign he was Fort Adjutant at Yokohama for two years (1864-66), and he filled a similar position at Hong-Kong for over a year (1866-67). He acted as Adjutant to a wing of the 2nd Battalion in South Africa for eighteen months (1870-71). At St. George's, Bermuda, he was Garrison Adjutant for two year- (1873-75). During the greater part of the time he held this appointment,

In April, 1885, their Royal Highnesses the Prince and Princess of Wales visited Killarney and other places in the south of Ireland. On the 14th, they passed through Fermoy, the regiment furnishing the guard of honour. The band of the regiment (Lieutenant Goodlake in charge) was stationed at Killarney during the residence of the Royal party at Killarney House. At the conclusion of the visit to Ireland, their Royal Highnesses were pleased to express, through the Lord Lieutenant, their approval of the conduct and playing of the band at Killarney.

The regiment proceeded by wings from Fermoy to Queenstown, and embarked on board H.M.S "Assistance" on the 21st of September, 1885. The "Assistance" sailed the same day, called at Plymouth, and arrived at Chatham on the 24th; the battalion disembarked on the following day, and occupied the Chatham barracks. Owing to a reorganization of the corps of Royal Engineers, which produced larger requirements of barrack accommodation, the XX was ordered from Chatham to Manchester, where the headquarters, under Colonel Clarkson, arrived on the 24th of March. A detachment (eighty-six men), commanded by Major W. Glencross,[1] was sent to Weedon

---

Lieutenant Goldsmith was also Adjutant of the 1st Battalion (24th August, 1873—31st July, 1875). On the 21st July, 1875, he was promoted Captain. In addition to his duties as Captain in the regiment, he performed the duties of Regimental Paymaster for four years (1877-1880). Captain Goldsmith was promoted Major on the 1st July, 1881.

[1] Lieutenant-Colonel Glencross joined the 2nd Battalion XX as Ensign on the 16th April, 1858, and was promoted Lieutenant on the 5th May, 1859. On the 27th May, 1862, he was appointed Adjutant of the 2nd Battalion, and he held this position until the 11th June, 1866. He served with the 2nd Battalion in China, Japan, and India, and with the 1st Battalion in Burmuda. On the 31st January, 1870, he was promoted Captain. Captain Glencross was Adjutant of the 12th Lancashire Volunteers (now 2nd Volunteer Battalion Lancashire Fusiliers), from the 31st August, 1877, to the 31st August, 1882. He was promoted Major on the 1st July, 1881, and a Brevet-Lieutenant-Colonel on the 21st June, 1887.

on the 23rd March, 1886. From the 10th to the 13th of May, 1886, the regiment furnished guards of honour at Newsham House, near Liverpool, during the residence of Her Majesty Queen Victoria, for the opening ceremonies of the Liverpool Exhibition. The Manchester Royal Jubilee Exhibition was opened by their Royal Highnesses the Prince and Princess of Wales, on the 3rd and 4th of May, 1887. The regiment was on duty in the streets, and formed the guards of honour in the exhibition building, and at the railway stations on the arrival and departure of the Royal party. The Prince of Wales was pleased to express, to the officer commanding the regiment, his pleasure at the appearance of the regiment, which he had particularly noticed, and without wishing to make any invidious distinction, he indicated the guard then on duty (at the London Road Station) as deserving particular praise.

On the 11th of May, 1887, Lieutenant-Colonel James Smyth[1] succeeded to the command vice Colonel Clarkson,[2] whose period of service had expired.

---

[1] Colonel James Smyth was gazetted Ensign to the XX on the 2nd July, 1858, and was promoted Lieutenant on the 15th December, 1859, and Captain on the 24th March, 1869. Both these steps were obtained by purchase. He served with the 2nd Battalion in India, China, and Japan, and with the 1st Battalion in Burmuda and Malta. He was promoted Major on the 9th January, 1880, and Lieutenant-Colonel on the 9th June, 1884. He succeeded to the command on the 11th May, 1887, and was promoted Brevet-Colonel on the 9th June, 1888.

[2] Colonel Clarkson joined the 99th Regiment as Ensign on the 21st September, 1852; was promoted Lieutenant on the 14th August, 1854, and Captain on the 8th April, 1859. He served with the 99th Regiment in Australia from November, 1852, to June, 1856, and nine months with it in India. He was Adjutant of the 99th for two years, and of a Depôt battalion from the 16th January, 1857, to the 1st September, 1868. He was promoted Major on the 2nd September, 1868, appointed to the 63rd Regiment in January, 1873, and exchanged into the 2nd XX on the 26th March, 1873. He was promoted Brevet-Lieutenant-Colonel on the 23rd August, 1877, and succeeded to the command of the 1st Battalion on the 11th May, 1883.

On the 27th September, 1887, a detachment of one hundred rank and file proceeded to Leeds under the command of Captain E. Roderic Owen. On the occasion of the visit to Manchester of His Royal Highness the Field Marshal Commanding-in-Chief on the 30th September, the several guards of honour were furnished by the regiment.

On the 1st of October, the battalion took part in a volunteer review, which was held on the Salford Racecourse. This is the third occasion upon which the 1st Battalion was paraded with the 3rd Volunteer Battalion of the regiment.

At the conclusion of the review, the commanding officers were called to the front, and the Duke of Cambridge, addressing them, said: "I have great pleasure in making my inspection to-day. It was chiefly of volunteers, but I am glad to say—and I feel that you, too, will be pleased that it was so—that the volunteers were associated with a portion of Her Majesty's regular forces. The more they are so associated in their own sphere, the better it will be for both services." After a reference to the 13th Hussars, His Royal Highness said: "The XX Regiment turned out very well. They are a smart, well-drilled, very good corps."[1] At the conclusion of the review, His Royal Highness inspected the barracks, and said that the rooms were remarkably clean.

On the 14th of April, the detachment at Leeds was withdrawn, and one of similar strength sent to Fleetwood.

On the 19th of May, 1888, His Royal Highness the Duke of Cambridge inspected the detachment at the

---

[1] *Army and Navy Gazette*, October 8th, 1887.

hutments, Fleetwood. His Royal Highness saw the company in review order and then inspected the barrack rooms.

"At the conclusion of the inspection, His Royal Highness complimented the officer in command (Lieutenant H. A. Kinglake)[1] on the state of his detachment. He said the men were clean, smart, and well turned out; and that the barrack rooms were in very good order."[2]

As this work was being concluded, instructions were received from the Horse Guards directing the regiment to be held in readiness to proceed to Glasgow about the 11th day of February, 1889. The regiment has not been stationed in Glasgow since it was commanded by Wolfe.

---

[1] Hamilton A. Kinglake joined the XX at Halifax, Nova Scotia, on the 23rd January, 1878, as second Lieutenant. He was promoted Lieutenant on the 2nd December, 1879, and Captain on the 23rd May, 1888. Captain Kinglake retired upon half pay on the 15th January, 1889, when he was appointed Captain in the 3rd Battalion (Militia) Somersetshire Light Infantry.

[2] *Army and Navy Gazette*, May 26th, 1888.

THE SECOND BATTALION.

CHAPTER XXXIX.

1858-1863.

A National Emergency—Raising of the 2nd Battalion—Lieutenant-Colonel Radcliffe—Clonmel—Waterford—Tralee—Inspections—Presentation of Colours—Speech of General Lord Seaton—Curragh Camp and Dublin—Move to England—Aldershot—Portsmouth—Retirement of Colonel Radcliffe—Embarkation for India—Arrival at Calcutta.

THE demands of the Crimean war and the ravages which it had made in our army had hardly passed away when the great mutiny broke out in the Indian Sepoy army and among the natives of Bengal.

In the presence of this pressing national emergency, the Government decided to increase the establishment of the army by adding a second battalion to each of the first twenty-five regiments.

On the 3rd of March, 1858, the 2nd Battalion XX Regiment was brought into existence, and its establishment was fixed at eleven hundred and twenty-six of all ranks. The command of the battalion was conferred upon Major W. P. Radcliffe, an officer who had served with distinction in the Crimean and Mutiny campaigns. Major Radcliffe was promoted Lieutenant-Colonel on the 26th March, 1858, and left the 1st Battalion, together with many other officers who had been appointed to the 2nd, at Lucknow on the 31st of March.

The nucleus of the new battalion was formed by the transfer from the depôt of the 1st Battalion of one hundred and two men (instructions dated 2nd March,

T

1858), and one hundred men (authority dated 15th April). These two hundred and two transfers, under Captain Ord and Lieutenant Morshead, arrived at Clonmel on the 29th April, 1858. On the 12th May, 1858, the battalion, under Major J. Cormick, was inspected by Major-General Eden, C.B., commanding the Cork division, who expressed his satisfaction with the state of the battalion.

On the 24th June, recruiting parties were sent to London, Lurgan, and Plymouth. On the 25th of August, the battalion, under Major Cormick, moved from Clonmel to Waterford; and on the 22nd of the following month (September) proceeded by rail from Waterford to Killarney, and thence by march route to Tralee. The headquarters, under Major Cormick, arrived at Tralee on the 23rd, and the remaining portion of the battalion, under Brevet-Lieutenant-Colonel Campbell, on the 24th of September.

From the 27th April to the 5th October, 1858, one hundred and sixty-two recruits and twenty-eight trained soldiers (the latter transfers from other corps) joined the battalion. The recruits were chiefly raised by the staff of the battalion.

On the 5th of October, 1858, the battalion, under the command of Major Cormick, was inspected by Major-General Eden, C.B., commanding the Cork division, who again complimented the battalion on its appearance under arms, etc. A recruiting party was sent to Wellington, in Somersetshire, on the 26th December, 1858.

The battalion marched in two divisions to Killarney, and thence proceeded by rail to Clonmel, where the first division arrived on the 19th, and the second on the 20th of January, 1859.

Between the 6th October, 1858, and the 26th May, 1859, two hundred and forty-three recruits and nine transfers joined the battalion.

On the 26th of May, 1859, the battalion, under the command of Lieutenant-Colonel Radcliffe, was inspected at Clonmel by Major-General J. Eden, C.B., commanding the Cork division. At the conclusion of the inspection, the General addressed the regiment in these terms:—"Officers and men of the 2nd Battalion XX,—I am very much pleased with your appearance and with the general military bearing and moral character you have always preserved. The progress you have made in your drill is very creditable to Colonel Radcliffe and the officers of the regiment. I have never heard a complaint against any of the officers or men from the inhabitants of the towns where you have been located; and I regret that you are now to part from my divisional command, in which you have been placed thirteen months, the entire period since your formation. Wherever you are stationed, I shall always take a deep interest in your welfare."

On the 2nd of June, 1859, the battalion, under the command of Lieutenant-Colonel Radcliffe, proceeded by rail from Clonmel to Dublin, and was quartered at Richmond barracks. Major-General Gascoigne, commanding the Dublin division, inspected the battalion on the 6th of June, and made the following complimentary address:—"Men of the XX,—I wish to let you know what I have just said to your officers. Since I have been in command of this division, I have seen four or five second battalions, but none so good as this. I do not wish to speak disparagingly of the others, but I must say that I have not seen any so good, so steady, or so soldierlike, and it is very creditable to your officers, who I am sure have not been idle since your battalion was formed. You have now come to a garrison town for the good of the service, where you will see old soldiers from whom you may learn much good; but I would warn you against the temptations consequent upon a garrison town. I only hope you will maintain that good character which I have received of you from your last station."

The battalion was subsequently inspected by General Lord Seaton, G.C.B., who praised it, and expressed his concurrence with the official report made by Major-General Gascoigne, on the efficiency and good conduct of the battalion, which his Lordship expressed his intention of bringing to the notice of His Royal Highness the Field Marshal Commanding-in-Chief.

General Lord Seaton, G.C.B., commanding the Forces in Ireland, presented colours to the 2nd Battalion at Richmond barracks, on the 1st August, 1859. The battalion formed square, and his Lordship then addressed the regiment as follows:—"In presenting these colours at your request, Colonel Radcliffe, I may be allowed to observe that on entering the army I was appointed to the XX Regiment, that I served my first campaign with it, and continued to share with it for many years the active service on which the corps was engaged. Early friendships and attachments leave the strongest impressions and associations, and you may imagine that I feel it almost a right to be preferred on this occasion for the duty which you have proposed that I should undertake.[1] A day could not have been fixed upon more appropriate for the 2nd Battalion of the XX Regiment to receive colours

---

[1] See Appendix.

than the 1st of August, 1859, the centenary anniversary of the battle of Minden, where the XX (then called Kingsley's Stand) contributed to the splendid success of the day, and were particularly thanked by Prince Ferdinand of Brunswick for their conduct. After the Seven Years' War, the regiment was employed in America, and subsequently in the West Indian Islands, and then on the expedition to North Holland. In the general action in the defence of the position of the Zype, the XX repelled the attack of a strong corps, and the Commander-in-Chief, Sir Ralph Abercrombie, stated in his despatch that two battalions of the XX maintained the high reputation they had always borne. In Egypt, in 1802, the XX had the honour of attacking the French posts at Alexandria, which led to the immediate surrender of the place and the capitulation of the French army. The next service on which the XX was employed was in Calabria, where at the battle of Maida the regiment turned the right flank of the enemy, and decided the action. In Portugal, at Vimiera, the regiment was sharply engaged under Sir Arthur Wellesley; and on the retreat through Gallacia, in Spain, under the illustrious Moore, formed the rear-guard with the gallant 28th and 52nd, and reached Corunna in the best order, although they had the hardest work. In the campaign of the Duke of Wellington, in Spain and the south of France, the services of the XX were arduous and distinguished; and in the Crimea, and Hindustan, they are so recent and well known, that I shall only add that their discipline and good conduct at home have always been not less to be commended than their achievements abroad. With these examples, and with the orders of Wolfe amongst the records of the XX, the reputation which the regiment has always borne will, I am confident, be upheld and maintained by the Second Battalion."

His Lordship then handed the colours to Ensigns R. Fraser[1] and C. A. Vernon.[2] Colonel Radcliffe then thanked his Lordship in these words: "My Lord,— Allow me to offer you the thanks of the officers, non-commissioned officers, and private soldiers of the 2nd Battalion XX Regiment, together with my own, for the honour you have conferred upon us in presenting us with our first set of colours, the gift of Her Gracious Majesty. From the XX Regiment having had the honour at one time of claiming so distinguished an officer as yourself, as belonging to it and serving in it, we are doubly proud of receiving them at your hands. This day has been chosen for the ceremony of presentation, from its being, as you have mentioned, the anniversary and centenary of the battle of Minden, fought August the 1st, 1759, and in which the XX bore a most gallant and conspicuous part. It was, therefore, to be desired that the day should be particularly marked, that that *esprit de corps* so essential to the well-being and good conduct of a regiment, and so inseparable from all good regiments, might be increased and strengthened in our newly raised 2nd Battalion. Our ranks being mostly composed of young soldiers, we must necessarily be without much experience; time, however, will cure that; and I trust that, wherever we may be, at home or abroad, in quarters or in the field, by always remembering this day, and the honour we have received of being entrusted with those colours,

---

[1] Ensign R. Fraser joined the XX on the 30th April, 1858; he was promoted Lieutenant on the 29th July, 1859, and retired by the sale of his commission in July, 1867. He was with the 2nd Battalion in India, China, and Japan.

[2] Ensign C. A. Vernon was promoted Lieutenant 25th May, 1860, and retired in May, 1863.

we may endeavour to emulate and equal our older and more tried brothers in arms, and deserve, in the fullest sense, the name of British soldiers." The new colours were then trooped, the battalion marched past and the parade ceremonies closed. The customary Minden festivites were held with great spirit.

The XX and 30th Regiments marched from Dublin to the Curragh, *viâ* Blessington, on the 13th and 14th of September, 1859, under Major-General A. A. T. Cunyngham, C.B.

The battalion was inspected on the 1st October, 1859, by General Cunyngham. At the conclusion of the inspection, the General assembled the officers and said:—"Colonel Radcliffe, I beg to express my satisfaction at the exertions of yourself, and of all ranks under your command, for the honour of the name and number you bear. I feel convinced that, by a steady adherence in the same path, you will do credit to the responsible position with which you are entrusted, and honour to the Queen, your country, and the battalion you command. I have every reason to be satisfied with the proficiency they have gained, and it will be a pleasing task to report favourably of your regiment to my superiors. I beg you will express my sentiments to your battalion."

From the 26th May to the 1st October, 1859, one hundred and forty recruits and nine trained soldiers joined the battalion. On the 1st of November, 1859, the battalion, under the command of Colonel Radcliffe, proceeded by rail from the Curragh to Dublin, and occupied quarters in the Royal barracks.

On the 17th March, 1860, one hundred transfers from the depôt of the 1st Battalion joined the battalion. In the months of April and May, 1860, the regiment was inspected by General Sir George Browne, G.C.B., Major-General H. Blomfield, C.B., and Lieutenant-General Gascoigne, all of whom expressed the highest opinion of the efficient state of so young a battalion. The battalion proceeded in two divisions to the Curragh camp, on the 11th and 12th May, 1860.

After spending a year at the Irish camp of exercise, the regiment proceeded to Dublin, and embarked at the North Wall, on the 2nd May, 1861, on board the steamships "Preussicher Adler" and "Juverna," for passage to Bristol, and thence moved by train to Aldershot.

The battalion formed part of the 2nd Brigade at Aldershot, and was inspected by Brigadier-General W. G. Browne on the 3rd October, 1861, and on the 7th May, 1862. On both occasions the Brigadier expressed his approbation of the efficiency, and the good system of interior economy, which prevailed in the regiment.

The battalion, under the command of Lieutenant-Colonel Radcliffe, marched to Ascot on the 1st August, 1862, and was encamped on the Heath. On the following day it took part in a volunteer review before Lieutenant-General Sir J. L. Pennefather, K.C.B.

The regiment returned to Aldershot on the 4th August. On the 9th September, the battalion, under Colonel Radcliffe, Majors Dickens,[1] Lyons,[2] and

---

[1] Major W. D. S. Dickens was gazetted Ensign of the XX on the 19th August, 1851, and promoted Lieutenant on the 7th June, 1854, and Captain on the 20th February, 1855. He served with the regiment in Canada for two years (1851-1853), and in the Crimea from the 10th December, 1854, to the 19th July, 1856. Captain Dickens went to India with the regiment in 1857, and was present at the battles of Chanda, Ameerapore, and Sultanpore, the siege and capture of Lucknow. He was promoted Brevet-Major on the 20th July, 1858, and Major on the 28th October, 1859. He exchanged to the 31st Regiment on the 9th February, 1864. Major Dickens was promoted Brevet-Lieutenant-Colonel on the 26th March, 1869,

Captain Meares, marched in four divisions from Aldershot for Portsmouth. The various detachments marched *viâ* Woolmer, Emsworth, Petersfield, Havant, Westbourne, and reached Portsmouth on the 11th September, and were quartered in the Anglesea barracks.

Major-General Lord William Paulet, C.B., inspected the regiment on the 21st October, 1862. In a few words he expressed his satisfaction at the appearance

---

and Lieutenant-Colonel commanding the 31st Regiment on the 25th February, 1874. He retired upon half pay on the 15th March, 1879. On the 1st October, 1877, he was promoted Colonel, and Major-General on the 19th October, 1887. General Dickens received the Crimean medal and clasp for Sebastopol, Turkish medal, and the fifth class of the Medjidie. For the Indian Mutiny campaign he was awarded the medal and clasp for Lucknow.

² Major T. C. Lyons joined the 16th Regiment as Ensign (by purchase) on the 31st October, 1845, and was promoted Lieutenant (by purchase) on the 2nd November, 1849. He was Adjutant of the regiment for three and a half years; and served with it in South Africa three years (1848-1851), in the West Indies three years (1851-1854), and in Canada one year. On the 27th July, 1855, he was promoted Captain in the XX, and joined the regiment in the Crimea on the 21st February, 1856, when he was appointed to the command of the Grenadier company. Captain Lyons accompanied the XX to India in August, 1857. He commanded the marksmen of the regiment at the battles of Chanda, Ameerapore, and Sultanpore. He was present throughout the siege and capture of Lucknow (2nd to 22nd March, 1858). Captain Lyons took part in the affairs at Mohan, Morar Mow, Berah, capture of Simree, and action at Buxer-Ghat. He was Brigade-Major to the special field service column, under Brigadier Evelegh, which captured Fort Oomirah. Captain Lyons received the medal and clasp for Lucknow, was three times mentioned in despatches, and was promoted Brevet-Major for service in the field (26th April, 1859). He was promoted Major on the 16th November, 1860, in the 2nd Battalion. Major Lyons exchanged to the 87th Regiment on the 17th July, 1863. He was promoted Lieutenant-Colonel and succeeded to the command of that regiment on the 25th December, 1865. Colonel Lyons retired on half pay on the 22nd March, 1871. He commanded the Brigade Depôt at Preston from the 1st April, 1873, to the 18th December, 1875. He was Assistant Adjutant-General at the headquarters in Ireland from the 9th December, 1875, to the 12th October, 1877, and Quartermaster-General from the 13th October, 1877, to the 31st March, 1882. Colonel Lyons was nominated a Companion of the Bath on the 2nd June, 1877. On the 1st July, 1881, he was promoted Major-General. He commanded an infantry brigade at Aldershot for one year (1884-1885); and was appointed to the command of the western district (Devonport) on the 1st of April, 1885.

of the men, their steadiness under arms, and the state of the battalion generally. Lieutenant-Colonel W. P. Radcliffe, the officer who had raised the battalion and brought it to its high state of efficiency, retired on temporary half pay on the 12th June, 1863. He was succeeded in the command of the regiment by Lieutenant-Colonel H. R. Browne, from the half pay list.

The battalion embarked at Portsmouth in three divisions, for service in Bengal. One company, under Captain Meares, embarked on board the "St. Lawerence" on the 20th July, and arrived at Calcutta on the 11th November. The left wing, under Major Ord, embarked on board the "Conflict" on the 24th July, and reached Calcutta on the 29th October. The headquarters, under Lieutenant-Colonel Browne, embarked on board the "Blenheim" on the 25th July, and arrived at Calcutta on the 19th November, 1863.

CHAPTER XL.

1863-1868.

Ordered to China—Outline of the History of Japan—The Daïmios—Attack on the Legation—Landed at Hong-Kong—Detachment to Yokohama—The 67th Regiment—Headquarters to Japan—Cholera—Death of Captain Honourable A. E. P. Vereker—Review at Yokohama—Assassination of Major G. W. Baldwin and Lieutenant R. N. Bird—Their Characters and Services—Execution of the Murderers—Sir Rutherford Alcock—Letter to Colonel Browne—Approbation of Major-General Guy—The Field Battery—Inspection by General Guy—The Taku Forts—The Legation Guard—Embarkation for Hong-Kong—Letter of Thanks from Sir H. S. Parkes—Presentation of a Farewell Cup—Embarkation for South Africa—Stations.

ON its arrival at Calcutta, the battalion was at once placed under orders for service in China and Japan. To explain the cause of this sudden change of destination, it will be necessary to give an outline of the state of affairs in Japan at this date, and in bygone ages. For upwards of two centuries, Japan had been a sealed country to the rest of the world. With the exception of the Dutch, no European nation had any commercial intercourse with it since the expulsion of the Portuguese in 1639. One of its laws not only sanctioned, but commanded that, should any foreigner be found in the country, he was to be put to death. The state of Japan presented, in many respects, a similar condition to that of Europe in the feudal ages. The country was divided into provinces, or large districts, each being governed by a Japanese nobleman (called a Daïmio), who exercised within the limits of his province unlimited power, the Government only interfering on rare occasions.[1] These Daïmios had collected

---

[1] *Japan as it Was and Is*, by Richard Hildreth. Published at Boston, United States.

round them large bands of armed retainers or vassals, whom they supported and clothed in their uniforms, and who were ready to do their bidding on all occasions even if death was the result. To the Daïmios the advent of foreigners into their country, and the consequent spread of knowledge amongst their dependents and followers, was most distasteful; they foresaw the decline and ultimate downfall of their power and influence. Some of the most influential amongst them accordingly determined to expel the intruders and to deter others from coming to their country; and, in consequence of their intrigues, many foreigners were murdered on the public roads and in the streets of Yedo,[1] Yokohama, and Nagasaki. The Japanese Government invariably expressed the greatest concern that these outrages should occur, and offered every reparation in their power; yet they were not strong enough to resist the power of the Daïmios and bring the offenders to justice. These outrages culminated in a night attack on the British Legation at Yeddo, in which the English Minister, Sir Rutherford Alcock, narrowly escaped with his life.[2] The Minister addressed a serious remonstrance to the Japanese Government, in which he informed them that they would be held responsible for the outrage. The Shôgun (then the temporal ruler of Japan) declared that he was powerless to protect the Legation from further attacks, and that he could not be responsible for the lives of its inmates if they continued to remain in Yedo. Sir R. Alcock intimated that he would apply to his own Government for a British regiment to protect the lives and property

---

[1] The name of this town has since been changed to Tokio.
[2] Adam's *History of Japan*, vol. ii; and *Three Years in the Capital of the Tycoon*, by Sir R. Alcock.

of British subjects and guard the Legation from further insults.

The 2nd Battalion, which had just arrived at Calcutta for service in the Bengal Presidency, was, in consequence, ordered to Hong-Kong, a convenient port for the assembly of troops destined for Japan. The battalion embarked on board the "Nubia" on the 20th and 21st November, 1863, leaving a small detachment with the women and children at Dum Dum, a station about three and a half miles distant from Calcutta. The "Nubia" reached Hong-Kong on the 8th, and the battalion disembarked on the 9th of December, and was quartered on the Kowloon peninsula opposite to Hong-Kong. Two companies (one hundred and sixty-one men) embarked at Hong-Kong on board H.M.S. "Vulcan" on the 5th January, 1864, and were landed at Yokohama on the 23rd January. This was the first detachment or portion of a British regiment quartered in Japan.[1] The officers who accompanied it were Captains W. D. L. Meares (in command), R. Blount,[2] Lieutenants J. Smyth, F. W. Barlow, Ensigns D. O'N. Power, and E. P. T. Goldsmith.

The headquarters of the battalion, under the command of Lieutenant-Colonel H. R. Browne, embarked at Hong-Kong on the 25th and 28th of June, 1864, on the steamship "Chanticleer" and the sailing vessel "Queen of England," and landed at Yokohama on the 14th July. Previous to leaving Hong-Kong, cholera broke out in the regiment, which was sent into camp

---

[1] The 2nd Battalion XX was the first British regiment stationed in Japan. The second regiment was, by a remarkable coincidence, the 67th, a wing of which was there with the 2nd Battalion. The 67th had been the first second battalion of the XX; raised in August, 1756, it became the 67th in April, 1758.

[2] Captain R. Blount had served with the 1st Battalion in the Mutiny campaign. He retired as Major on the 19th April, 1878.

in consequence. Several men died in the camp at Kowloon. For about a month after the arrival of the battalion at Yokohama the disease spread rapidly, and notwithstanding all the efforts of the medical officers,[1] who were unremitting in their attentions, upwards of forty men died of the disease. None of the officers suffered, although their quarters were only separated from the men's by a few yards.

Captain the Honourable A. E. P. Vereker[2] died of smallpox at Yokohama, on the 12th October, 1864. On the 20th of October a review was held of the troops (British and Indian) forming the Yokohama garrison, under Colonel Browne. Some Japanese troops also took part in the parade, but performed their exercises separately. The review was witnessed by Sir R.

---

[1] Surgeon-Major P. M. Woodward, Surgeons R. A. Hyde and W. Hensman.

[2] Captain the Honourable A. E. P. Vereker joined the XX on the 2nd March, 1855, and was promoted Lieutenant on the 16th October, 1855. He was present at the siege of Sebastopol from the 3rd September, 1855, and with the expedition to Kinburn. He served with the Land Transport Corps from the 9th March to the 30th June, 1856. He went to India with the 1st Battalion, and commanded a section of marksmen at the battles of Chanda, Ameerapore, and Sultanpore. He took part in the siege of Lucknow and the affairs of Churda, Musjeidia, and Bankee (Acting-Adjutant). At the actions at Muchlee Goan and Khyber Jungle he was Orderly Officer to Colonel Cormick. In April, 1859, he was promoted Captain and joined the 2nd Battalion in Ireland, and he continued to serve with it until his death. A monument, which bears the following inscription, was erected to his memory:—

> SACRED TO THE MEMORY OF THE
> HONOURABLE A. E. P. VEREKER,
> CAPTAIN 2ND BATTALION XX REGIMENT,
> THE YOUNGEST SON OF
> VISCOUNT GORT,
> OF EAST COWES CASTLE,
> ISLE OF WIGHT.
> DIED 12TH OCTOBER, 1864.
> AGED 32 YEARS.
> SINCERELY BELOVED
> AND
> DEEPLY REGRETTED BY
> HIS BROTHER OFFICERS.

Alcock, Her Majesty's Envoy and Minister, and by the Japanese Viceroy and Minister, and other high officials, who had been sent from Yedo for this purpose. The object of the review was to impress the Japanese with a sense of our power, to strengthen the government, and to encourage those Daïmios who were favourably disposed to us. That it succeeded will be seen from the following extract from a letter addressed to Colonel Browne by Sir Rutherford Alcock. "It is something to have done this by the mere presence of such a force; and it is the best tribute to the soldierly qualities and efficient appearance of the troops under your command.[1] Of all the triumphs a soldier can win, none can be more satisfactory, or so entirely without alloy, as a moral victory such as has now been gained, thanks to you, your officers, and the men, who have thus peacefully, but most efficiently, upheld the interests and dignity of our country, at a time when both were in danger, and any evidence of weakness must have seriously compromised them."

Towards the end of November an event happened which cast a gloom, not only over the regiment, but over the whole of the civilised community at Yokohama. This was the assassination of Major G. W. Baldwin and Lieutenant R. N. Bird, of the 2nd Battalion, which was accomplished on the evening of the 21st of November, by two Japanese. The particulars can be thus briefly told. On the 20th of November, 1864, Major Baldwin and Lieutenant Bird started on horseback from the camp (which was

---

[1] The troops present were the 2nd Battalion XX, detachment 67th Regiment under Major Miller, a half battery Royal Artillery under Lieutenant T. Wood, a detachment 2nd Belooch Regiment under Captain Fairbrother. Several hundred Japanese were present, and took part in the review.

situated on the bluff overlooking the foreign settlement at Yokohama), for a few days' excursion to some of the places of interest to foreigners, and which were within the boundaries known as the treaty limits. The Buddhist idol Diabutsñ was the chief attraction.[1]

On the morning of the 21st, Baldwin and Bird were seen at the island of Euoshima by several European gentlemen, who endeavoured to persuade them to make one party, but as this arrangement would have prevented the officers from seeing the idol, they declined to alter their plans. After visiting Diabutsñ, they were slowly returning to Yokohama. Their route lay through a flat country, and along a broad alley planted on each side with tall trees of ancient growth. They continued on this road until it takes a sharp turn to the right, when it is narrowed into a footpath, on one side of which there stood a large tree, the trunk concealing a small seat of turf. Persons sitting in the tree could easily, without allowing their own presence to be known, see others approaching from whatever direction they might come. There was a third road, walled on either side, and covered with a thick growth of shrubs, leading from the alley to the sea, and from behind this wall a Japanese boy witnessed the murder. The boy was going on an errand, when he was spoken to by a couple of two-sworded men (samurai), who questioned him as to the distance they were from the image and the sea. On his return, the boy found the same men sitting on the turf seat in the tree. One of them warned him off, saying it would be dangerous to remain. The boy took to the road leading to the

---

[1] A colossal bronze image, about sixty feet high, and so large that five persons can stand in the two palms of the hands, and five more can sit across the joined thumbs.

shore, and hid himself in the bushes behind the earthen wall. From this position he perceived the two officers wending their way at an easy pace along the plain from Diabutsñ, the Major being a-head. When they reached the tree where the Japanese were sitting, and as the Major's horse was passing it, the two samurai, who had drawn their long two-edged swords, sprang out and cut him to the ground. They then attacked Bird, who had now rounded the tree, and they wounded him so severely that he, too, uttering a piercing cry, fell from his pony. Baldwin raised himself up, his face and clothes covered with blood, and staggered to the wall and attempted to get over it, but his merciless assailants rushed at him; another terrible shriek rang through the air, and all was still. The boy, too frightened to move, saw Baldwin (a tall man with dark hair) creeping on all fours to the spot where his friend lay. The boy told what he had witnessed to

---

NOTE.—Major Baldwin was the son of a veteran officer, who had fought in the South of France and at Waterloo, under Wellington; in all the battles of the Sikh War, of 1845-1846; and had died of wounds received at Chillianwallah. George Walter Baldwin was gazetted as Ensign to his father's regiment (31st) on the 4th of April, 1846, at the age of sixteen years. He was promoted Lieutenant (by purchase) on the 20th July, 1849, and Captain (by purchase) on the 31st October, 1851. Captain Baldwin landed in the Crimea on the 22nd May, 1855. He was present at the siege of Sebastopol, and at both the assaults on the Redan on the 18th June and 8th September. He received the Crimean medal and clasp; also the Turkish medal. Captain Baldwin served throughout the campaign in the North of China, in 1860, including the siege of Sinho, and the storming of Tangku (medal and clasp for Taku forts). He was promoted Brevet-Major on the 1st April, 1863, and Major on the 30th June, 1863. Major Baldwin exchanged from the 31st Regiment to the XX on the 9th February, 1864. He was a popular officer, and a man of artistic tastes.

Robert Nicholas Bird joined the XX as Ensign on the 30th August, 1859, and was promoted Lieutenant (by purchase) on the 2nd December, 1862. He was of a gentle and amiable disposition, greatly beloved by all his brother officers.

The graves of these officers are marked by monuments erected by their brother officers. The epitaph on each simply records the name, age, date, and cause of death.

U

the villagers, and they placed the bodies under a shed. These men stated that the two officers had lived for some hours, and that they heard them speak to each other.[1] The funeral, which was carried out with great ceremony, took place at Yokohama on the 24th November, and was attended by the whole of the 2nd Battalion. The Minister, Admiral, the whole of the foreign community, and many Japanese officials were also present.

The assassins of Major Baldwin and Lieutenant Bird were brought to justice. Two accomplices were executed in the Tobé (Japanese prison) on the 16th December; and the chief murderer, Shimiduz Seiji, was publicly executed (the 2nd Battalion being present) in Yokohama on the 28th December, 1864. Seiji confessed and gloried in his crime; he looked upon foreigners as the enemies of his race and country. The second murderer was executed on the 30th October, 1865.

Sir Rutherford Alcock, Her Majesty's Envoy and Plénipotentiary in Japan, left for England on the 24th December, having been recalled to advise the Government on the state of affairs in Japan. Previous to his departure, the Minister wrote (letter dated 22nd December) to Colonel Browne a flattering and sincere acknowledgment of his own and the regiment's services during a period of difficulty and danger, both to the foreign representatives in Japan, and to the

---

[1] An inquest was held on the bodies on the 22nd and 23rd November. The British Consul, Mr. C. A. Winchester, presided as coroner, and Captains G. Rochfort, C. Fahie, and J. Aldridge acted as jurors. They found that the murder was committed about four o'clock in the afternoon. From the doctor's evidence, it would appear that one wound inflicted on Lieutenant Bird would have caused almost instantaneous death.

Tycoon's (Shôgun)[1] Government. The letter concludes thus: "And essentially to the strength which the forces under your command, and the use that has been made of them, has finally given to the Tycoon's Government, menaced as it was, at no distant period, with destruction by the great faction of Daïmios who had conspired to close this port, drive foreigners out of the country, and revert to a policy of exclusion. I cannot take leave without expressing to you my personal sense of gratitude, for the loyal and effective support, which you have invariably given to me as Her Majesty's representative."

Further testimony and appreciation of the services of the regiment was made by His Excellency Major-General Guy, commanding the forces in China and Japan. The Major-General expressed his approbation of the conduct of the garrison of Yokohama, praised Colonel Browne for the care and ability with which he had conducted a difficult and detached command, and very favourably mentioned Ensign E. P. T. Goldsmith, for the manner he had performed the duties of Fort-Adjutant during this trying period.[2]

In the month of March, 1865, a half-battery of field artillery (two nine-pounders and one twenty-four-pounder howitzer), fully horsed and equipped, was raised from the ranks of the battalion. Lieutenants F. W. Barlow and D. O'N. Power,[3] Sergeants C. Richards, H. O'Connell, T. Curran, three corporals,

---

[1] At this time there were two rulers in Japan, the Mikado or spiritual governor, and the Shôgun who represented the temporal authority. In 1868, the Mikado was made the supreme and absolute ruler, in all matters whether temporal or spiritual.

[2] Letter dated Adjutant-General's Office, Hong-Kong, 15th March, 1865.

[3] Lieutenant Power was Adjutant of the battalion for many years. He attained the rank of Major, and retired from the service in 1881.

one bugler, and thirty-six men composed the half-battery. Under the able instruction of Lieutenant W. L. Hutchinson, Royal Artillery, they attained a high degree of efficiency, and were specially commended by Major-General Guy, C.B.

This is probably the first and only instance of a field battery, efficient and ready for active service, being formed in an infantry regiment.

The battalion was inspected on the 6th June, 1865, by His Excellency Major-General Guy, C.B., commanding the forces in China and Japan. The Major-General complimented the battalion generally, but marked with his approbation its interior arrangements, the cleanliness of the men, their steadiness under arms, and general appearance.

A detachment, consisting of one sergeant, one corporal, and nineteen privates, under the command of Lieutenant J. Smyth,[1] embarked at Yokohama on the 14th June, 1865, in H.M.S. "Leopard," for passage to the Taku forts, which had been taken from the Chinese in the campaign of 1860. This detachment garrisoned the forts until the 26th October, 1865, when they were handed back to the Chinese Government. From the 22nd August, 1865, to the 7th April, 1866, a guard (consisted of one sergeant, two corporals, one drummer, and twenty privates), for the protection of the British Legation at Yedo and Yokohama, was furnished by the 2nd Battalion. The men were selected for their good character, and were commanded by Lieutenant R. D'Arcy.[2] On their return to regimental duty, Sir H. S. Parkes, the Minister in Japan, wrote (letter dated 7th April, 1866): "I should not omit to

---

[1] See page 285.
[2] Died at Youghal on the 27th March, 1871.

communicate to you my entire approval of the manner in which Lieutenant D'Arcy and the non-commissioned officers and men under his command have discharged the duty of this special service. The behaviour of the men has been, in all respects, unexceptional."

The left wing, under the command of Major A. W. Ord, embarked at Yokohama, in H.M.S. "Adventure," on the 11th, and arrived at Hong-Kong on the 19th April, 1866. The headquarters, under the command of Colonel H. R. Browne, was conveyed from Yokohama to Hong-Kong, in the same ship, and disembarked at the latter place on the 27th May, 1866. Captain C. G. Rochfort,[1] Lieutenant C. H. Webster, and eighty-five men of all ranks remained at Yokohama.

The following is an extract from a letter (dated 16th May, 1866), addressed to Colonel Browne by Her Majesty's Minister in Japan, Sir H. S. Parkes:—"On the occasion of the departure of the 2nd Battalion XX Regiment from Japan, I cannot omit to contribute my testimony to the excellent services performed by that corps, during the time it has been stationed here; or to express the high estimation I have formed of the very able manner in which, throughout a period of nearly two years, you have fulfilled the duties of this peculiar and responsible command."

A copy of the despatch (in full) was forwarded by Sir H. S. Parkes to the Secretary of State for Foreign Affairs, and by him passed to the Secretary of State

---

[1] Captain Rochfort joined the regiment as Ensign on the 9th March, 1855, and was promoted Lieutenant on the 10th August of the same year. He served with the regiment in the Crimea from the 11th September, 1855, to the 19th July, 1856. When the 1st Battalion went to India, Lieutenant Rochfort was sent to the depôt for duty. He was promoted Captain on the 30th March, 1858, in the 2nd Battalion. Captain Rochfort retired from the service in March, 1869, and died at Dublin on the 1st of May, 1882.

for War (General Peel), and to His Royal Highness the Field Marshal Commanding-in-Chief, all of whom were pleased to give expression to the great pleasure and satisfaction afforded them by the Minister's report. The Commander-in-Chief's letter was published in general orders at Hong-Kong on the 7th November, 1866. In transmitting to Colonel Browne copies of the correspondence which had taken place, the Major-General commanding said, "that he most cordially concurred in the well-deserved eulogy on the efficiency and high state of discipline of the 2nd Battalion XX Regiment."[1] The battalion was inspected by Major-General Guy, C.B., on the 26th November, 1866. The result of the inspection was conveyed to the battalion in a letter dated Horse Guards, 20th May, 1867, of which the subjoined is an extract: "The state of the 2nd Battalion XX Regiment is highly creditable and satisfactory; and His Royal Highness has desired that the expression of high commendation may be conveyed to Colonel H. R. Browne, and the battalion under his command."

---

[1] A very gratifying evidence of the popularity of the regiment and the respect in which it was held by the European residents in Japan was the presentation of a farewell cup. It bears this inscription:—

FAREWELL CUP
PRESENTED TO
THE OFFICERS 2ND BATTALION XX REGIMENT
BY THE
COMMUNITY OF YOKOHAMA.

The object of the artist in designing the cup was to make it a memorial of Japan. The bas-relief on one side is a view of Fusiyama, which is looked upon by the natives as a "sacred mountain," and to which pilgrimages are made. The bas-relief on the other side illustrates a favourite game of Japanese officers on horseback, which consists of taking up a ball with a sort of racket, and throwing it at a hole in the end of the list. Dragons are introduced as national emblems on the handles. A picture of the cup appeared in the *Illustrated London News* for January, 1867.

On the 20th March, 1867, the battalion embarked at Hong-Kong, in the steamship "Golden Fleece." The headquarters and left wing, under the command of Colonel H. R. Browne, disembarked at Durban, Natal, on the 1st May, 1867, and marched to Pietermaritzburg, fifty-four miles inland. One company, under Captain Harcourt[1] and Ensign Goldsmith, was stationed at Durban. The right wing, under Brevet-Lieutenant-Colonel A. H. Cobbe,[2] was detached to

---

[1] J. Simon Chandos Harcourt is a descendant of Simon de Montfort, Earl of Leicester, and is the owner of Runnymede. Captain Harcourt exchanged into the XX on the 8th December, 1865, from the 51st Regiment. He was a singular instance of an officer obtaining his company in two years without purchasing a single step of rank. He served in the Crimea, and was present at the battle of the Alma (Crimean medal and clasp, and Turkish medal). He was invalided from the Crimea, having contracted a dangerous fever. Captain Harcourt served throughout the campaign in North China, including the action at Sinho and storming of Tangkee (medal and clasp for Taku forts). He served as aide-de-camp to Brigadier Staveley in the operations against the Taepings in the vicinity of Shanghai in 1862, including the intrenched town of Chepao, the stockade at Nasiang, the walled cities of Kading, Tsingpoo, the intrenched town of Najow, and the walled town of Cholin (mentioned in despatches). Captain Harcourt retired from the service in March, 1869.

[2] Lieutenant-Colonel A. H. Cobbe passed from the Royal Military College at Sandhurst into the 87th Regiment as Second-Lieutenant, on the 16th June, 1843. He was promoted Lieutenant (by purchase) on the 10th June, 1845, and Captain (by purchase) on the 21st July, 1848. He was Adjutant of the 87th for two years (1846-1848). On the 2nd November, 1855, he was promoted Major (by purchase). Major Cobbe was employed as Civil Engineer on the public works department in India from December, 1853, to April, 1857. On the breaking out of the mutiny he resigned his civil appointment. From the 1st May to the 23rd September, 1857, he was present at the siege of Delhi. During the siege he served as a volunteer extra aide-de-camp to Sir H. Burrand, in addition to performing his duty with the brigade. He received the medal with clasps for Delhi. Major Cobbe commanded a provisional battalion at Hong-Kong from May to December, 1860. On the 17th July, 1863, he exchanged into the XX, and was promoted Brevet-Lieutenant-Colonel on the 28th July, 1864. Lieutenant-Colonel Cobbe served with the 2nd Battalion in China, Japan, and South Africa. On the death of Colonel Cormick (10th July, 1868) he succeeded to the command of the 1st Battalion; and on the 31st July, 1869, he exchanged into the 17th Regiment, which he commanded until the 15th July, 1879. Colonel Cobbe commanded the 1st Infantry Brigade of the Kuram Field Force, at the storming of the Peiwar Kotal, when he was severely wounded. Mentioned in despatches (*London Gazette*,

British Kaffraria, landing at East London, and marching thence to Fort Beaufort, where it was stationed, distant about one hundred and twenty miles from East London.

4th February, and 7th November, 1879), awarded the medal and clasp, and nominated a Companion of the Bath. Colonel Cobbe was appointed to the command of a brigade in Bengal (July, 1879, to September, 1882). He was promoted Major-General on the 6th May, 1882; and was placed on the retired list with the honorary rank of Lieutenant-General on the 1st September, 1886. General Cobbe was granted the distinguished service reward. He is a Major-General in the Reserve of Officers.

NOTE.—The whole of the official details (Chapters XXXIX and XL) from 1858 to 1868 have been taken from the records of the 2nd Battalion, printed and published by Lieutenant F. W. Barlow.

CHAPTER XLI.

1869–1888.

G Company struck by Lightning—Change of Stations—The Mauritius—Complimentary Order by Major-General G. S. Smyth—Wing to South Africa—The Return Home—Service in Ireland—Colonel H. R. Browne exchanges to the 37th Regiment—State of the Battalion during his Command—Service in England—Ordered to Ireland—Mullingar—Colonel John Davis retires upon Half Pay—Under Orders for India—Numerous Detachments—Volunteers—The Embarkation—Arrival in India—Stationed at Mhow—Inspections by Generals Stewart and Hardinge—Retirement of Lieutenant-Colonel O'Neill—Change of Stations—Guard of Honour at Ajmere—Inspection by Sir R. Phayre—Death of Major Randolph and Captain Furlonger—Inspection by H.R.H. the Duke of Connaught—Move to Ahmednagar—Colonel Webster retires—Lieutenant-Colonel G. D. Wahab succeeds to the Command.

ON the 14th of October, 1869, a singular accident happened to the headquarter wing, at Fort Napier, Pietermaritzburg. The wing was on parade in column of companies, being inspected by Colonel Browne, when a thunderstorm broke over the parade ground, and G Company, commanded by Captain McNamee,[1] was struck by lightning. One man (Private R. Hill) was killed and seven men were injured. Many of the rifles were destroyed. This is perhaps a solitary instance of a company of soldiers being struck down by a flash of lightning.

In October, 1869, Major Ord assumed the command of the wing quartered at Fort Beaufort, British Kaffraria. Early in 1870, one company, under command

---

[1] Captain John McNamee joined the army as Ensign on the 2nd February, 1849; he was promoted Lieutenant on the 3rd August, 1855, and Captain on the 29th February, 1864. He was granted a pension and the honorary rank of Major on the 17th May, 1876.

of Captain W. F. F. Gordon, was sent to Keiskamma Hook from Fort Beaufort, followed by the remaining companies of the wing in May, the Government having decided to relinquish Fort Beaufort as a military station. In consequence of the reduction of the garrison of South Africa, the wing under Major Ord left Keiskamma Hook about the middle of June, and marched *viâ* King William's Town to East London, and there embarked on board H.M.S. "Himalaya" for conveyance to Mauritius, calling at Natal, where the headquarters under Colonel Browne were taken on board on the 30th June, having marched from Pietermaritzburg on the 21st. The battalion thus came together after a separation of over three years. The battalion landed at Mauritius on the 12th July. An epidemic of measles having broken out on the voyage from the Cape, the regiment on landing was placed in quarantine in the fort at the entrance to Port Louis harbour. At the expiration of three days, the restrictions of quarantine were removed, and the battalion occupied the several stations allotted to it. Headquarters and one wing under Colonel Browne were quartered at Mahbourg; four companies under Major Francis at the Line Barracks, Port Louis; one company under Captain H. Webster at the citadel; and a party of thirty non-commissioned officers and men commanded by Ensign Duncan formed the guard for the Government House at Reduit.

The battalion was scarcely settled in its various quarters when the strength of the garrison was reduced by half a battalion. On the 22nd December, 1870, one wing (fourteen officers and three hundred and twenty non-commissioned officers and men), under

Major G. E. Francis, embarked at Port Louis on board the hired steamer "Marsden," for passage to the Cape of Good Hope. The wing landed at East London on the 30th December, and marched on the following day to King William's Town, which was reached on the 2nd January, 1871.

During the summer of 1871 it was intimated that the battalion would return to England in the autumn. On the 8th of November, 1871, Major-General G. S. Smyth, commanding the forces in the Mauritius, published a very complimentary farewell order, in which he stated the high opinion he entertained of the battalion, the excellence of its discipline and interior arrangements, and the exemplary conduct of the men on all occasions. The headquarters, under Major Ord, embarked at Port Louis, on board H.M.S. "Tamar," on the 25th November, 1871. The "Tamar" called at East London on the 5th December, and took on board the wing commanded by Major Francis, which had been stationed at King William's Town since the 2nd January. The "Tamar" reached Queenstown on the 25th January, 1872, and the battalion disembarked on the 26th, and proceeded by rail to the following places:—Headquarters and three companies to Buttevant, three companies to Tralee, one company to Killarney, and one company to Kilmallock. The two depôt companies (two hundred and eighty men), which had been attached to the 1st Battalion since the 1st of April, 1870, joined the headquarters at Buttevant, on the 29th January, under Captains R. Blount and C. Fahie.[1]

---

[1] Conroy Fahie was gazetted to the XX as Ensign on the 29th March, 1855, and was promoted Lieutenant on the 30th March, 1858. He served with the 1st Battalion in the Crimea from October, 1855, to July, 1856; and in India from

On the 3rd February, 1872, a detachment (ten officers and three hundred and sixty-seven men), under the command of Colonel Browne, proceeded to Tralee to aid the civil authorities during the elections. It returned to Buttevant on the 13th February.

On the 1st of January, 1873, Colonel Browne exchanged to the 37th Regiment, having within a few months commanded the battalion for ten years. Colonel Browne[1] considered that there was only one standard

---

August, 1857, to the 4th July, 1861. In the Mutiny campaign he was present at the battles of Chanda, Ameerapore, Sultanpore, siege and capture of Lucknow, the actions at Churda and Fort Musjeidia, under General Lord Clyde; and those at Muchlee Goan and Khyber Jungle, under Colonel Cormick. He was promoted Captain on the 17th November, 1863. Captain Fahie served with the 2nd Battalion in Japan, China, and South Africa. He died at Preston on the 31st December, 1875.

[1] Colonel Browne's commission as Ensign in the 9th Regiment was dated 3rd April, 1846. He was promoted Lieutenant on the 19th September, 1848, and Captain on the 28th December, 1849. As Captain he served with the 9th Regiment in the Crimea from the 27th November, 1854, to the month of June, 1856, and was present at both the assaults on the Redan. He was aide-de-camp to Major-General Ridley for three months, and Brigade-Major for five months. For his services in the Crimea he was promoted Brevet-Major, appointed a Knight of the Legion of Honour, and received the Crimean medal, Turkish medal, and the fifth class of the Medjidie. He was promoted Lieutenant-Colonel (by purchase) on the 20th February, 1857, and was appointed to the 87th Regiment on the 15th November, 1859. In 1860, Lieutenant-Colonel Browne proceeded with Sir Hope Grant's expedition from India to China. He retired upon half pay on the 17th August, 1861, and was employed on particular service in Canada from the 13th December, 1861, to the 4th July, 1862. Colonel Browne exchanged from the half pay list to the XX on the 12th June, 1863, and commanded the 2nd Battalion for nearly ten years. His services with the battalion in Japan, China, and Natal, are fully described in the preceding pages. Colonel Browne exchanged to the 37th Regiment on the 1st January, 1873, and again to the 63rd Regiment on the 1st December, 1874. He commanded the brigade at Saugor from the 26th June, 1875, to the 7th July, 1880. On the 1st October, 1877, he was promoted Major-General; and served in the Afghan war of 1879-1880 as commander of a brigade of the Keeram division in the Zoimusht expedition. He was awarded the Afghan war medal. Major-General Browne commanded the troops in Jamaica and Barbados from the 1st January, 1884, to 31st March, 1885. He was promoted Lieutenant-General on the 1st January, 1885, and retired with the honorary rank of General on the 8th July, 1885. General Browne is a Lieutenant-General in the Reserve of Officers.

by which the efficiency of a regiment could be judged; and that was the number of well-drilled, self-confident soldiers that could be placed in the field at the shortest notice. During his command this was his guiding principle, and he never swerved in working to achieve his object. The battalion was a highly-trained and well-organised body when he succeeded to the command, and he did not permit it to fall from this state during the long term he was at the head of it. He practised the men in every possible contingency of actual warfare. One detail may be particularised, and will act as an illustration of the whole system. Occasionally the assembly sounded at night without previous notice. The battalion arose, dressed, paraded, and marched from the barracks, and by daybreak would have traversed many miles over a rough country, often crossing streams, etc. To the rifle shooting he devoted unremitting care and attention, and of the success attained in this most important part of the regimental instruction it will be sufficient to quote the order of merit gained by the battalion in the last three years of Colonel Browne's command:—

Year.	Order of Merit in the Army.	
1870	Second	
1871	First	Exclusive of India.[1]
1872	Seventh	

In the year 1872 the battalion furnished detachments at Tralee, Killarney, Waterford, and Clonmel; and in 1873 companies were sent to the lower Shannon Forts, Haulbowline, and Rocky Island, Cork Harbour.

---

[1] General Orders, No. 33 of 1871 and 1872, and 29 of 1873. In the year 1870 the 1st Battalion was the third best shooting regiment in the army.

The battalion was encamped at the Curragh[1] for the drill season of 1873, and returned to Buttevant on the conclusion of the exercises. On the 7th August, 1874, the regiment moved from Buttevant to Preston. In July, 1875, it exchanged stations to Manchester, and left the latter town on the 28th May, 1876, for Aldershot, and occupied the huts in A, B, and E lines, south camp. Whilst stationed at Aldershot, under the command of Colonel J. Davis, the battalion gained a great reputation for its smart and soldier-like bearing on all occasions, both collectively and individually. The battalion left Aldershot on the 24th July, 1877, for Portland, and it remained there until the 13th March, 1879, when it proceeded to Plymouth, where it frequently changed quarters between the Citadel, Millbay, and Raglan barracks.

On the 24th September, 1879, one wing (eight officers and two hundred and forty-seven men) embarked on board H.M.S. "Assistance" for passage to Jersey, where it remained until the 18th of the following month (October). The half battalion again embarked on board the "Assistance," and was conveyed to Devonport, where the headquarters were taken on board, for passage to Ireland; the whole being landed at Kingstown on the 24th October, 1879. Seven companies proceeded by rail to Mullingar and one company to Sligo. Two companies (three officers and one hundred and ten men) were sent from Mullingar to Boyle on the 19th November, 1879. The regiment, being joined by the detachments from Boyle and Sligo, moved to the Curragh camp on the 26th May, 1880.

---

[1] In the manuscript records at the headquarters of the 2nd Battalion and at the depôt, the Curragh summer exercises and the move to Manchester are not mentioned. The names of the officers who commanded detachments are also omitted.

Colonel J. Davis,[1] who had commanded the battalion since the 1st January, 1873, retired upon half pay on the 9th June, 1880; he was succeeded in the command by Lieuteuant-Colonel J. J. S. O'Neill.

In January, 1881, the battalion was placed under orders for service in India; the embarkation to take place early in the autumn. From this date (January) there commenced a perfect exodus of detachments, which the battalion was obliged to furnish. The details are as follows:—On the 13th January, two officers and fifty men were sent to Maryborough; one officer and forty-one men to Naas on the 18th May, and this party was increased by a similar number on the 2nd June; on the 15th June, two officers and fifty men proceeded to Tuam;[2] on the 1st July, two officers and seventy men were sent to Gort, and a party of similar strength to Ballinrobe; on the 30th July, one officer and thirty-five men went to Westport; and on

---

[1] Colonel John Davis joined the 35th Regiment as Ensign on the 13th February, 1852, and was promoted Lieutenant on the 20th June, 1854, and Captain on the 16th September, 1859. He served with the 35th Regiment in the Indian Mutiny (Shahabad campaign) and received the medal. Captain Davis exchanged to the 37th Regiment on the 26th November, 1860, and was promoted Major on the 21st August, 1866, and Lieutenant-Colonel on the 15th February, 1868. Lieutenant-Colonel Davis exchanged to the 2nd Battalion XX on the 1st January, 1873, and commanded it until the 9th June, 1880, when he retired upon half pay. He was appointed Colonel on the staff, and commanded the troops at Shorncliffe from the 1st April, 1881, to the 9th October, 1883. Colonel Davis was promoted Major-General on the 1st of August, 1883, and was appointed to the command of a brigade in Egypt on the 22nd January, 1884. General Davis commanded the 2nd Infantry Brigade at the battles of Teb and Tamai. His name was mentioned in the despatches published in the *London Gazette* on the 27th March, 3rd April, 11th April, and 6th May, 1884. He received the medal with clasp, bronze star, and was nominated a Companion of the Bath. General Davis served at Suakim during the Soudan expedition of 1885, and was awarded an additional clasp. He was transferred to the command of the infantry brigade at Malta on the 1st April, 1886, and to the Dublin district on the 1st January, 1888.

[2] Lieutenant J. E. V. Dennis died at Tuam on the 29th August, 1881. He joined the regiment on the 13th August, 1879, and was promoted Lieutenant on the 12th February, 1881.

the 1st August, two officers and one hundred and thirty-five men were despatched to Castlebar. Many of these parties were changed regimentally, to allow those originally sent to be exercised in musketry at the Curragh. To fill up the numbers required by a regiment placed on the Indian establishment, volunteers from other corps were hurried into the regiment. In the month of May, 1881, the battalion received ninety-seven volunteers from ten different regiments. In June, thirty-eight volunteers from the 1/5th Regiment, and twenty-four from the 55th Regiment, joined the battalion. On the 1st August, thirty-six volunteers came from the 59th Regiment.

In this way, and at a time when it was denuded of many of its best men, the battalion was made the receptacle of much that was undesirable, and it required the vigorous measures of a firm hand to purify it, when it reached its destination in India. In addition to the volunteers, two hundred men were transferred from the 1st Battalion, and one hundred and four from the depôt at Bury. The detachments rejoined head-quarters between the 22nd and 31st of August. The battalion, under the command of Lieutenant-Colonel J. J. S. O'Neill, was conveyed by rail to Cork, and thence by steamer to Queenstown, where it embarked on board H.M.S. "Malabar" on the 19th of September. The "Malabar" sailed on the 21st September, and arrived at Bombay on the 21st October, when the battalion disembarked and proceeded to Mhow, sending a detachment of two officers and one hundred and seventeen men to Asirgarh, and one consisting of two officers and one hundred men to Indore.

On the 15th December, 1882, the battalion was inspected by His Excellency General Sir Donald

Stewart, G.C.B., Commander-in-Chief in India, who was pleased to express, in a general order, the highly satisfactory state in which he found the regiment. Lieutenant-General Honourable A. E. Hardinge inspected the battalion on the 3rd November, 1883, and stated that he was much gratified with all he had seen, and that he would report very favourably on the battalion.

Lieutenant-Colonel J. J. S. O'Neill[1] having commanded the battalion for the prescribed period, he retired upon a pension on the 9th June, 1884, with the honorary rank of Major-General. Lieutenant-Colonel C. H. Webster succeeded to the command.

The regiment marched from Mhow on the 3rd November, 1884, for Nasirabad and Neemuch; the latter place was reached on the 20th November; three companies remained here, and the headquarters and the remaining companies continued the march, arriving at Nasirabad on the 9th December.

On the 18th October, 1885, one company was sent

---

[1] Colonel O'Neill joined the XX as Ensign on the 6th June, 1854, and was promoted Lieutenant on the 29th December, 1854. He served with the regiment in the Crimea from the 20th May, 1855, to the 19th July, 1856. He was wounded at the assault on the Redan on the 18th June, 1855. He took part in the expedition to Kinburn. Lieutenant O'Neill went to India with the regiment in August, 1857. He was musketry instructor of the regiment from the 4th December, 1857, to the 3rd June, 1858. Lieutenant O'Neill was present at the battles of Chanda, Ameerapore, Sultanpore, the siege and capture of Lucknow, the affairs of Meangunge and Berah. At the latter he acted as Brigade Major, and was thanked by Brigadier Evelegh for his services. He was also present at Buxer-Ghat, Musjeidia, and Churda. He was promoted Captain on the 6th June, 1858. Captain O'Neill received the Crimean medal and clasp for Sebastopol, Turkish medal, the medal for the Indian Mutiny campaign with the clasp for Lucknow. Captain O'Neill was District Inspector of Musketry in Bengal for five years, and Chief Inspector for one year and nine months. He was promoted Brevet-Major on the 5th July, 1872, and Major on the 5th October of the same year. He was promoted Brevet-Lieutenant-Colonel on the 29th April, and Lieutenant-Colonel on the 9th June, 1880. He is now a Major-General on the retired list.

v

to quell a riot at Ajmere. The telegraphic order gave but short notice, and the men were complimented by the Brigadier for the smartness and celerity with which they turned out. On the 18th October, two companies, under Captains R. G. Randall[1] and T. E. Bland, proceeded to Ajmere as a guard of honour and escort to His Excellency Lord Dufferin, the Viceroy. The troops present at Ajmere were commanded by Lieutenant-Colonel C. H. Webster. The battalion was inspected by Lieutenant-General Sir R. Phayre, K.C.B., on the 19th January, 1886. He intimated that he was much pleased with the appearance of the battalion on parade, with their steadiness under arms, and the precision of their drill.

Major Walter Randolph[2] died of enteric fever at Nasirabad, on the 9th October, 1886. His Royal Highness the Duke of Connaught, Commander-in-Chief of the Bombay army, inspected the battalion on the 20th January, 1887. The general efficiency of the battalion was favourably reported upon, particularly the marked improvement in the shooting. Captain Sidney Furlonger[3] died at Nasirabad, on the 17th September, 1887, of enteric fever.

On the 2nd February, 1888, the headquarters, under

---

[1] Now Major in the 1st Battalion.

[2] Walter Randolph was gazetted Ensign of the XX on the 8th February, 1870, and was promoted Lieutenant on the 28th October, 1871. He was Adjutant of the 2nd Battalion for two years, and Instructor of Musketry for two years and six months. He was promoted Captain on the 15th November, 1879; and was appointed Adjutant of the 3rd Battalion (Militia) on the 21st September, 1880. He was promoted Major, 24th September, 1884, and resigned the Adjutancy on the 2nd February, 1885.

[3] Captain Furlonger joined the regiment as Sub-Lieutenant on the 11th October, 1876, and was promoted Captain on the 18th May, 1886. He had been Adjutant of the 2nd Battalion for a short time.

the command of Colonel Webster, proceeded by rail *viâ* Neemuch to Ahmednagar, where they arrived on the 6th February. On the 3rd February, two companies, under Major Collingwood, left Nasirabad and arrived at Ahmednagar on the 6th. On the 4th February, two companies, under Lieutenant-Colonel C. E. Hussey, went from Nasirabad to Satara; and one company to Kirkee. Colonel C. H. Webster,[1] having completed four years in command of the battalion on the 8th June, 1888, retired with the pension of his rank. He was succeeded in the command by Lieutenant-Colonel G. D. Wahab.[2]

---

[1] Colonel C. H. Webster joined the XX as Ensign on the 2nd May, 1858; was promoted Lieutenant on the 16th September, 1859; and Captain on the 17th March, 1869; Major on the 1st July, 1879; Lieutenant-Colonel 11th May, 1883; and Colonel, 11th May, 1887. With the 2nd Battalion he served in China, Japan, Natal, Mauritius, and India; and with the 1st Battalion in Cyprus, and Malta.

[2] Lieutenant-Colonel G. D. Wahab was gazetted to the XX as Ensign on the 28th January, 1859. He was promoted Lieutenant on the 30th November, 1860; Captain, 5th January, 1870; Major, 1st July, 1881; and Lieutenant-Colonel, 24th September, 1884. Colonel Wahab served with 2nd Battalion in India, China, Japan, South Africa, and the Mauritius; and with the 1st Battalion in India, Bermuda, Canada, Cyprus, and Malta.

APPENDIX.

GUSTAVUS HAMILTON, VISCOUNT BOYNE.

GUSTAVUS HAMILTON was a son of Lodwick Hamilton, who was the younger son of Archibald Hamilton, Archbishop of Cashel, and brother of Lord Glenanly. His father had been Colonel in the army of Gustavus Adolphus, King of Sweden, and had been raised by that monarch to the dignity of a peer, in his kingdom. He was killed at sea on passage to Ireland.

Gustavus Hamilton was an officer of the army in Ireland, during the reign of King Charles II, and, on the accession of King James II, he was sworn a member of the Privy Council; but when King James violated the laws of the country, Colonel Hamilton withdrew from His Majesty's service, and was deprived of his commission by Tyrconnell. He raised one hundred horse, to oppose the entry of two companies of King James's troops into Enniskillen, on Sunday, 15th of December, 1688. On the 18th December, 1688, he was unanimously chosen Governor of Enniskillen. As soon as he was elected Governor, he raised troops of foot and horse for the defence of the town. These men, in January, 1689, increased to twelve companies of foot and two troops of horse, and was formed into one regiment, of which Gustavus Hamilton was appointed Colonel. He commanded during the siege of Enniskillen, the capture of Omah, and directed all the operations in the surrounding country. So brilliant were these victories, and so great the fear that they inspired in the party of King James, that Dublin itself was in a constant state of alarm and panic, from dread of an attack by the Enniskillen men, under Hamilton.

On the 23rd January, 1689, he addressed a letter to the Earl of Mount-Alexander, the nobility, and gentry in the north-east part of Ulster, calling upon them to resist the unjust laws and exactions of King James.

The services of Gustavus Hamilton during this critical period can be thus summarised: He kept free from the enemy the whole county of Fermanagh, from the Castle of Crom to Ballishanny, and that part of the County of Donegal that lies next the sea, from Ballishanny to Killabeg, which will be above fifty miles in length. Within these limits he raised for their Majesties' (William and Mary) service three regiments of foot, two regiments of Dragoons, and about twenty troops of horse. King William III highly approved of the gallant conduct of Gustavus Hamilton; and, in recognition of his distinguished services, nominated him to the command of the XX on the 1st June, 1689. Colonel Hamilton served in the campaign of 1690 under King William. He commanded the regiment at the battle of the Boyne, where he displayed great bravery, and had one horse shot under him. He served in the campaign of 1691, under General de Ginkell; distinguished himself at the head of the Grenadiers at the capture of Athlone by storm; was present at the battle of Aughrim, and at the siege of Limerick. On the deliverance of Ireland being completed, he was appointed a member of the Privy Council, Governor of Athlone, and Brigadier-General in the army, and received a grant of some of the forfeited lands. In 1702, he served in the expedition to Cadiz, and at the capture of the Spanish fleet at Vigo. In 1704, he was promoted to the rank of Major-General, and in 1706 he obtained permission to dispose of the Colonelcy of his regiment. He was a member of the Privy Council in Ireland during the reign of Queen Anne, also in the reign of King George I; and, in October, 1715, he was created Baron Hamilton of Strackallan; in 1717, he was advanced to the dignity of Viscount Boyne. He died on the 16th of September, 1723.

LIEUTENANT-GENERAL WILLIAM KINGSLEY.

WILLIAM KINGSLEY was, for many years, an officer in the Foot Guards, in which corps he acquired a reputation for personal bravery and attention to duty. Of his early career the particulars are meagre. He was promoted to the rank of Colonel in 1750, and was nominated Lieutenant-Colonel of the 3rd Foot Guards in 1752. He was appointed to the Colonelcy of the XX on the 22nd May, 1756. In 1757, he served with the expedition employed on the coast of France, under Lieutenant-General Sir John Mordaunt. Colonel Kingsley was promoted Major-General in January, 1758. He served in the Seven Years' War, under Prince Ferdinand of Brunswick, and greatly distinguished himself at the head of the 2nd Brigade of British infantry (the XX was one of three regiments in the brigade) at the battle of Minden, for which he was thanked in general orders by Prince Ferdinand. He continued to serve with the army in Germany until the following year, 1760. He was appointed Governor of Fort William on the 22nd March, 1760, and promoted Lieutenant-General in December of the same year. He died in November, 1769.

MAJOR-GENERAL JAMES WOLFE.

JAMES WOLFE, eldest son of Lieutenant-General Edward Wolfe, was born at the Vicarage, Westerham, Kent, on the 2nd January (N.S.), 1726. He entered the army as second Lieutenant in Colonel Edward Wolfe's regiment of marines, on the 3rd November, 1741. On the 27th March, 1742, he was transferred to Colonel Duroure's (12th) Regiment, with which corps he proceeded on active service, and arrived at Ostend on the 10th May, 1742. He was acting Adjutant of the 12th Regiment at the battle of Dettingen on the 27th June, 1743; was appointed Adjutant on the 2nd July, 1743, when only seventeen years of age; and was promoted Lieutenant on the 14th July of the same year. He was appointed to a company in Burrell's Regiment (4th) on the 3rd June, 1744. He served with the army in Flanders, under General Wade and the Duke of Cumberland, in 1743-4-5; and was appointed Brigade-Major on the 12th June, 1745. He returned to England with the troops that were withdrawn from Flanders in the summer of 1745, for the suppression of the rebellion, headed by the Pretender, Prince Charles Edward, and was present at the battles of Falkirk and Culloden. He accompanied the reinforcements which sailed for the Netherlands early in January, 1747.

The war of the Austrian Succession afforded him many opportunities to show the bravery and decision of his character. At the battle of Val or Laffeldt, when scarcely twenty years of age, he was publicly thanked by the Commander-in-Chief for his masterly exertions at a critical moment. In this action he was wounded, and had two horses shot under him. On the 5th January, 1749, he was gazetted Major of the XX Regiment, and Lieutenant-Colonel on the 20th March, 1750, and from this date he commanded the corps until 1758. He was appointed Quartermaster-General of the expeditionary force, under the command of Sir John Mordaunt, which was despatched against Rochfort, and received the brevet rank of Colonel on the 21st October, 1757, for his services. On the 23rd January, 1758, he was appointed Brigadier-General for service in America. He commanded the advance party on the attack of Louisbourg, which capitulated on the 27th July, 1758. The whole garrison (five thousand six hundred and thirty-seven men) were taken prisoners and sent to England, two hundred and forty pieces of ordnance and fifteen thousand stand of arms were captured, besides great stores of ammunition and provisions.

Wolfe was known and spoken of as the "Hero of Louisbourg." He was appointed Colonel of the 67th Regiment on the 21st April, 1758, on the 2nd Battalion XX Regiment being constituted the 67th. On the 12th January, 1759, he was gazetted Major-General, and appointed to the command of the expedition against Quebec. Undismayed by his repulse near the falls of Montmorenci, on the 31st July, and although suffering from a chronic malady and fever, he saw in this reverse the necessity of greater efforts, and conceived the bold design of drawing the French from their unassailable position by scaling the Heights of Abraham. At midnight on the 12th September the troops left the fleet and scaled the precipice, and by daybreak on the 13th were formed up on the Plains of Abraham, ready to receive the enemy. The English numbered four thousand eight hundred and twenty-six, with only one gun; and the French seven thousand five hundred and twenty men, besides Indians, and were well supplied with artillery. Montcalm attacked the English about ten a.m.

The first attack was repulsed, the Canadians becoming thoroughly disorganised. Wolfe placed himself at the head of the Louisbourg Grenadiers and the 28th, and while leading them on was shot in the wrist, but, wrapping his handkerchief round the wound, he continued at the head of his troops. His bright uniform rendered him conspicuous, while he exposed himself in front of the Grenadiers. He had just given his order for the whole British line to charge, when he was again dangerously wounded, but, in spite of pain and weakness, he still persevered. The French could not withstand the bayonets and musketry of the British infantry, and when Montcalm fell, they gave way in every direction. Wolfe had received a third and mortal wound in the breast. When no longer able to stand, his only concern was lest his men should be disheartened by his fall. "Support me," he whispered to an officer near him; "let not my brave soldiers see me drop. The day is ours; keep it." He was then carried to the rear, and when those who attended him reached a small redoubt, he desired them to lay him down. "The mourning group thought their beloved commander was already lifeless, when the cry was heard, 'They run—they run!' Like one suddenly aroused from heavy sleep, Wolfe demanded, with great earnestness, 'Who—who run?' 'The enemy, sir,' he was answered; 'they give way everywhere.' Thereupon the expiring hero, summoning all his fleeting strength, rejoined: 'Go, one of you, my lads, to Colonel Burton; tell him to march Webb's regiment with all speed down to Charles River, to cut off the retreat of the fugitives from the bridge.' He then turned upon his side, and his last words were :—

'Now God be praised; I die in peace!'

Thus, in his three-and-thirtieth year, died—

'Wolfe, upon the lap
Of smiling victory, that moment won.'"[1]

The feeling of the country, on the receipt of the despatches announcing the surrender of Quebec and the death of Wolfe, is thus described by Horace Walpole :—"The incident of dramatic fiction could not be conducted with more address to lead an audience from despondency to sudden exultation, than accident prepared to excite the passions of a whole people. They despaired, they triumphed, and they wept, for Wolfe had fallen in the hour of victory! Joy, curiosity, astonishment, were painted on every countenance; the more they inquired, the higher their admiration rose. Not an incident but was heroic and affecting." Every town and village in Great Britain blazed with bonfires and illuminations.

Of the many panegyrics[2] written on the life, character, and death of Wolfe, we prefer that which appears in the volume of his orders issued when in command of the XX. This volume was published in 1780. The eulogy runs :—"By nature formed for military greatness; his memory retentive, his judgment deep, his comprehension amazingly quick and clear, his constitutional courage not only

---

[1] *Life of Wolfe*, page 586.

[2] Wolfe's biographer observes :—"It is a remarkable fact, that the truest estimates of Wolfe's character are presented in novels. In the *Virginians*, notwithstanding some confusion of time and place, we see much of the man as he lived and moved ; also, in the pages of *Chrysal*."—*Life of Wolfe*, page 488.

uniform and daring, perhaps to an extreme, but he possessed that higher species of it, strength, steadiness, and activity of mind, which no difficulties could obstruct nor dangers deter. With an unusual liveliness, almost to an impetuosity of temper, not subject to passion; with the greatest independence of spirit, free from pride. Generous almost to profusion, he condemned every little art for the acquisition of wealth, whilst he searched after objects for his benevolence; the deserving soldier never went unrewarded. Inferior officers experienced his friendly generosity. Constant and distinguishing in his attachments, manly and unreserved, yet gentle, kind, and conciliating in his manners, he enjoyed a large share of the friendship, and almost the universal goodwill of mankind; and, to crown all, sincerity and candour, a true sense of honour, justice, and public spirit seemed the inherent principles of his nature, and the uniform tenour of his conduct. He betook himself early to the profession of arms, and with such talents, joined to the most unweary assiduity, no wonder he was singled out as a most rising military genius; even so early as the battle of Val or Laffeldt, when scarce twenty, he exerted himself in so masterly a manner, at a very critical juncture, that he got the highest encomiums from the great officer then at the head of the army. During the whole war, he went on without interruption forming the military character; was present at every engagement, and passed undistinguished. Even after the peace, while others lolled in pleasure's downy lap, he cultivated the arts of war, and introduced (without one act of inhumanity) such regularity and exactness of discipline into his corps, that so long as the six[1] British battalions on the plains of 'Minden' are recorded in the annals of Europe, so long will 'Kingsley's' stand amongst the foremost of that day. Of that regiment, he continued Lieutenant-Colonel, until the Minister who roused the sleeping genius of his country called him into higher spheres of action. He was early in the most secret consultations for the attack of Rochfort; and what he would have done there, and what he afterwards did at Louisbourg, are recent in every memory. He no sooner returned thence, than he was appointed to command the important expedition against Quebec. There his abilities shone in the brightest lustre. In defiance of numberless unforeseen difficulties from the nature of the situation, from the great superiority of numbers, the strength of the place, and his bad state of health, he persevered with unwearied diligence, prac-

---

[1] 12th, XX, 23rd, 25th, 37th, and 51st Regiments.

tising every stratagem of war to effect his grand purposes. At last, alone in opinion, he formed and executed that great, that dangerous, yet necessary plan, which drew out the French to the fatal defeat, and will forever dominate him the conqueror of Canada. But there tears will flow; there, when within the grasp of victory, he first received a ball through his wrist, which immediately wrapping up, he went on with the same alacrity, animating his troops by precept and example; but, in a few minutes after, a second, and then a third fatal ball through his body, obliged to be carried off to a small distance in the rear, where roused from fainting in his last agonies by the sound of 'They run,—they run;' he asked eagerly, 'Who run?' and being told the French and that they were defeated, he said, 'Now God be praised, I die in peace,' and almost instantly expired."

Burial of Wolfe.

Sunday, November 17th, at seven in the morning, His Majesty's ship "Royal William" (in which the hero's corpse was brought from Quebec to Portsmouth) fired two signal guns for the removal of his remains. At eight the body was lowered into a twelve-oar'd barge, towed by two others, and attended by twelve more to the point, in a train of gloomy, silent pomp, suitable to the melancholy occasion; grief closing the lips of the barges' crews; minute guns firing from the ships at Spithead to the time of landing at Portsmouth point. The ceremony continued one hour. The 41st Regiment was ordered under arms before eight, and being joined by a company of the Royal Regiment of Artillery, marched from the parade to the bottom of the point to receive his remains. At nine the body was landed and put into a hearse, attended by a mourning coach, and proceeded through the garrison. The colours on the forts were hoisted half-mast high, the bells muffled rung in solemn concert with the march, minute guns were fired on the platform from the entrance of the corpse to the end of the procession. The company of Royal Artillery led the van, with arms reversed, the corpse followed, and the 41st Regiment followed the hearse, their arms reversed. The body was thus conducted to the Land Port gates, where the artillery opened to the right and left, and the hearse proceeded through them on its way to London. Though many thousands assembled on this occasion, not the least disturbance happened; nothing was heard but the murmurs of broken accents in praise of the ever-to-be-admired hero. At night, on the 20th, his remains were deposited in the family vault under the Parish Church at Greenwich.

The following resolution was unanimously passed in the House of Commons on Wednesday, November 21st, 1759: " That an humble address be presented to His Majesty, most humbly to desire that he will be graciously pleased to give directions that a monument be erected in the Collegiate Church of St. Peter, Westminster, to the memory of the ever-lamented late Commander-in-Chief of His Majesty's land forces, on an expedition against Quebec, Major-General James Wolfe, who, surmounting by ability and valour all obstacles of art and nature, was slain in the moment of victory, at the head of his conquering troops, in the arduous and decisive battle against the French army, near Quebec, fighting for their capital of Canada, in the year 1759; and to assure His Majesty this House will make good the expense of erecting the said monument." At the same time it was resolved " that the thanks of the House be given to the Admirals and Generals employed in this glorious and successful expedition against Quebec."

On the 4th October, 1773, the national monument was uncovered. It stands near the north transept of the Abbey Church, and occupies a large space in St. John the Evangelist's Chapel, facing the ambulatory. A large oval tablet in the centre of the sarcophagus contains the inscription:—

TO THE MEMORY OF
JAMES WOLFE,
MAJOR-GENERAL AND COMMANDER-IN-CHIEF
OF THE BRITISH LAND FORCES
ON AN EXPEDITION AGAINST QUEBEC,
WHO, AFTER SURMOUNTING BY ABILITY AND VALOUR
ALL OBSTACLES OF ART AND NATURE,
WAS SLAIN, IN THE MOMENT OF VICTORY,
ON THE XIII OF SEPTEMBER, MDCCLIX,
THE KING AND PARLIAMENT OF GREAT BRITAIN
DEDICATE THIS MONUMENT.

Epitaph on General Wolfe.

(From Sim's edition of Mickle's *Poems*.)

Briton, approach with awe this hallowed shrine,
And if a father's sacred name be thine,
If thou hast mark'd thy stripling's cheeks to glow,
When war was mentioned, or the Gallic foe;

If shining arms his infant sports employ,
And warm his rage—here bring the warlike boy.
Here let him stand, whilst thou, enrapt, shall tell
How fought the glorious Wolfe,—and how glorious fell!
Then, when thou mark'st his burning ardours rise,
And all the warrior flashing in his eyes,
Catch his young hand, and, while he lifts it here,
By Wolfe's great soul the future Wolfe shall swear
Eternal hate against the faithless Gaul—
Like Wolfe to conquer, or like Wolfe to fall!
What future Hannibals shall England see,
Raised and inspired, O gallant Wolfe! by thee.

GENERAL THOMAS CARLETON.

THOMAS CARLETON was a younger brother of Sir Guy Carleton, Lord Dorchester, being the fourth son of Christopher and Catherine (*née* Ball) Carleton, of Newry. He was born in 1732, and like his elder brothers entered the army, his first commission (Ensign) bearing date 12th February, 1755. He was promoted Lieutenant in the XX on the 27th December, 1755; appointed (by Wolfe) Adjutant of the corps, 26th February, 1756, and promoted Captain 27th August, 1759. Captain Carleton was present with the corps at the battle of "Minden," and the other engagements of the "Seven Years' War." In July, 1772, he was promoted Brevet-Major. He accompanied the regiment to Canada in the spring of 1776, and on the 8th May was appointed Quartermaster-General of the army in that province. Major Carleton was promoted Brevet-Lieutenant-Colonel on the 31st of July, 1776, and Lieutenant-Colonel of the 29th Regiment on the 22nd July, 1777. During the pursuit of the Americans in the autumn of 1776, Colonel Carleton commanded the advance guard of between three and four hundred Indians.[1] He accompanied Burgoyne on his expedition in 1777, but returned to Canada in August, as Sir Guy Carleton required the services of his Quartermaster-General, preparatory to handing over his command, his successor being daily expected.

Campbell, in his *Annals of Tyrone County*, says:—"In the spring

---

[1] Hadden's *Journal*, page 19.

of 1778, Lafayette was stationed in Albany. In March he went up to Johnstown, from which place he wrote to Colonel Gansevoort a letter, dated March 6th, 1778. This letter was enclosed in a letter from Colonel Livingston of the same date, of which the following is an extract: 'Enclosed you have a letter from Major-General Marquess de Lafayette, relative to Colonel Carleton, brother to General Carleton, who has for sometime been in this part of the country as a spy. The General apprehends he has taken this route by way of Oswego, and begs you'll send out such parties as you may judge necessary for apprehending him.' The following is the letter of Lafayette: 'Sir,—As the taking of Colonel Carleton is of the greatest importance, I wish you would try every means in your power to have him apprehended. I have desired Colonel Livingston, who knows him, to let you have any intelligence he can give, and to join to them these I have got by a tory about the dress and figure of Carleton. You may send as you please, and everywhere you'll think proper, and do every convenient thing for discovering him. I dare say he knows we are after him, and has nothing in view but to escape, which I beg you to prevent by all means. You may promise, in my name, fifty guineas in hard money, besides all money, etc., they can find about Carleton, to any party of soldiers or Indians who will bring him in alive; as everyone knows now what we send for, there is no inconvenience to scatter them in the country, which reward is promised in order to stimulate the Indians.—I have, etc., (Signed) DE LAFAYETTE.'"

Colonel Carleton was not apprehended, but the value of his services can be estimated by the anxiety of the American Generals to effect his capture. In 1778, Lieutenant-Colonel Carleton had command at Montreal; he continued to serve in Canada till September 22nd, 1782, when he obtained Sir Frederick Haldimand's permission to go to New York, where Sir Guy Carleton was serving as Commander-in-Chief of the British forces in America. When the province of New Brunswick was created in 1784, Colonel Carleton was appointed its first Governor; and he arrived at St. John's, the seat of his new government, on the 21st November, in that year. Colonel Thomas Dundas, a member of the Board of Commissioners for deciding upon the claims of American Loyalists, in writing about the country to the Earl Cornwallis from St. John's, New Brunswick, 28th December, 1786, says:—"Mr. Carleton, by his own attention and firmness, assisted by a well-chosen Council, has established good government." On the 2nd of May, 1783, Colonel Carleton married

Harriet, daughter of Van Horn, of New York, and widow of Captain Edward Foy, of the Royal Artillery, by whom he had issue a son, William, and two daughters. He became Lieutenant-Colonel of the 5th Regiment 26th September, 1788; Major-General, 12th October, 1793; Colonel Commandant of the 2nd Battalion of the 60th, 6th August, 1794; Lieutenant-General, 1st January, 1798; and General, 25th September, 1807. He died on the 2nd February, 1817, aged eighty-five years.

LADY HARRIET ACLAND.

DURING the great civil war between England and her American colonies, few circumstances attracted more attention at the time than the adventures of Lady Harriet Acland—wife of Major Acland, XX Regiment—whose affectionate solicitude for her husband's safety, endurance of hardship, and courage in the face of peril, made her the idol of General Burgoyne's unfortunate army, the theme of praise in the poets' corner of many an old periodical, and the heroine of a deep, though now forgotten, interest.[1] It should be borne in mind that, though figuring in the scenes about to be narrated, she was a woman of delicate form, gentle nature, and high birth.[2]

Lady C. Harriet C. Fox-Strangeways, third daughter of the first Earl of Ilchester, was born on the 3rd January, 1750, and married at Redlynch Park, Somersetshire, in November, 1771, John Dyke Acland, of Pixton. Lady Harriet accompanied her husband, whose regiment with ten other corps, all so weak that they mustered only some seven thousand bayonets, began the campaign of that year under Lieutenant-General Sir Guy Carleton, and, in common with the troops, she endured the most severe extremities of cold, wet, and hunger, while traversing a vast extent of wild country, till the Americans raised the siege of Quebec, made a precipitate retreat, and, from the various posts occupied by them in Canada, were driven over the frontier into the United States. After this, her husband's regiment was stationed in the pleasant little Isle Aux Noix, at the north end of the beautiful Lake Champlain, where they passed the winter.

---

[1] *Magazine of American History*, January, 1880, and *Lippincott's Magazine*, October, 1879.

[2] General Gates, U.S. Army, in writing to his wife, said of Lady Harriet, "She is the most amiable, delicate piece of quality you ever beheld."

When, in the spring of 1777, the XX under Lieutenant-Colonel Lind was selected to form part of the expedition commanded by General Burgoyne for the reduction of Ticonderoga, and to force his way to Albany, Lady Harriet resolved to accompany her husband on board the armed flotilla; but, as a severe engagement was expected, he insisted on her remaining at the Isle Aux Noix until the affair was decided, and they parted with mournful forebodings. After a pleasant voyage down the lake, the troops landed at Crown Point, whence the march began. The flank companies—Grenadiers and Light Infantry—of the corps composing the expedition being now under the command of Major Acland, he was employed without intermission on outpost duty, in skirmishing, and harassing the rear of the retiring Americans; and so incessant was the perilous work that his officers and men never had their uniforms off, but slept in their bivouacs booted and belted. At the battle of Hubbardton, Major Acland was wounded in the thigh.[1] Lady Harriet, who had been all this time with the other ladies of the army at the Isle Aux Noix, became so filled with alarm and anxiety, that, despite the arguments of those around her, she resolved to proceed to the front to rejoin her husband at all hazard, and become his nurse.[2] Amid tempestuous weather, though the season was summer, by a proffer of a large reward, she prevailed upon four boatmen to take her across the lake to a point near the place where her husband lay wounded. She discovered Major Acland in a poor American log-house, and there tended and nursed him until he was well enough to rejoin the army.

At Fort Edward, a village then consisting of twenty log-huts on the eastern bank of the Hudson, she purchased, or had constructed, a kind of vehicle, which was fashioned by two artillery gunners out of an old tumbril or ammunition cart, and in this impromptu carriage she resolved to follow throughout the campaign the fortunes of her husband, who could by no entreaties prevail upon her to remain in the rear, or in a place of safety. During a halt at this time, their tent was set on fire, by a Newfoundland dog upsetting a candle, during the night when they were asleep.[3] "An orderly sergeant of the Grenadiers," states an old magazine, at great personal hazard, saved both their lives, by dragging them out of the burning tent. Everything they had with them was destroyed. As our troops

---

[1] *Anburey*, vol. i, page 295.   [2] *Ibid.*, vol. i, page 332.
[3] *Ibid.*, vol. i, page 359.

advanced, the Americans retreated; the country became a wilderness full of obstructions; and the formation of no less than forty new bridges, with the repair of others, became necessary; while one, formed of logs, was two miles in length, to enable the army to cross a morass.[1]

Yet on toiled our stubborn British infantry, in their quaint, old-fashioned regimentals, with square skirts buttoned back, their pipe-clayed breeches and black leggings, long queues and kevenhuller hats; while the keen American riflemen, and treacherous Indian, with war-paint, plume, and hunting shirt, used by turns the tomahawk, the knife, and the bullet, as they hovered on their flanks. On the 30th July, General Burgoyne halted on the banks of the Hudson, in the heart of the revolted provinces, where he was deserted by the Indians and the majority of the Canadian volunteers. Difficulties surrounded him on every side; the haversacks of the soldiers were empty, and starvation menaced them daily, till the middle of September, when the Hudson was crossed. On the 19th the battle of Freeman's Farm was fought, when Major Acland again led the flank companies into action. Lady Harriet remained in a small hut, which she had discovered in rear of the field, the terrors of which she could see at a little distance. During the whole engagement, the poor wife, in her hut, heard the din of the cannonading and the musketry; she had seen the wounded and the dying borne past her, or crawling to the rear. A thousand episodes of horror and affright had been before her. She knew that the post of her husband, as leader of the flank companies, was one of the greatest risk, and every moment she had the terrible expectation of seeing him brought in wounded, maimed, it might be a shattered corpse. Lady Harriet had the mortification to see, ere long, the hut in which she had taken shelter crowded to the door with wounded and suffering soldiers, sent there by the surgeons for attendance; and a climax was nearly put to her misery, when two Grenadiers of the XX, the old regiment of "Wolfe" and "Kingsley," bore in between them one whom she supposed to be her husband, but who proved to be Major Harnage, of the 62nd, severely wounded and covered with blood.[2] On the 7th of October, ensued the engagement—battle of Bemus Heights—before the retreat to Saratoga, when sixteen thousand Americans, under Major-General Gates, surrounded Burgoyne's little force, consisting of only three

---

[1] *Political and Military Episodes*, page 268.
[2] He survived, and was Colonel of the 104th Regiment in 1782.

W

thousand five hundred men, famine stricken, worn out with toil, incessant fighting, and being now without horses or baggage. Lady Harriet, without a tent or hut, and bivouacked on the bare ground, among the sick and wounded, was a spectator of that hopeless conflict. Major Acland at the head of the Grenadiers covered the left wing of the British. He sustained a fierce attack from a vast column of Americans, whose great extent of front enabled them to engage the whole line of our Hessian Infantry. The 24th Regiment, advancing as a support, had in the end to give way; and in the dusk of the autumn evening Lady Harriet, who had all day been hovering near the field, learned that the troops were falling back on all sides, that Brigadier Frazer was expiring of a mortal wound, that Sir F. C. Clark, Burgoyne's favourite aide-de-camp, had been wounded by his side, and that her husband had been severely—rumour said mortally—wounded and taken prisoner. She passed the night among the discomfited troops, with the dead and the dying, in the vicinity of that disastrous field.[1] Next day, Lady Harriet hastened to General Burgoyne, and implored him "to afford her such assistance as would enable her to pass over to the enemy's camp, that she might join her wounded husband, and to obtain the permission of General Gates for this purpose."

Though her patience, fortitude, and tenderness were not unknown to Burgoyne, he was surprised and perplexed by this proposal, and at such a time, for the suppliant was in a situation requiring for herself the most tender care; moreover, she had been for many days and nights drenched by the autumnal rains in the open bivouac, and had frequently been without food and the common necessaries of life; and for a delicate woman, on the eve of becoming a mother, to leave the camp at night, to pass through a hostile district swarming with discontented Indians, Canadian deserters, lawless Colonists, and desparadoes of every kind, seemed to him "an effort above human nature."

We will continue the narrative in General Burgoyne's own words:—
"The assistance I was enabled to give her was small indeed, I had not even a cup of wine to offer her; but I was told she had found, from some kind and fortunate hand, a little rum and dirty water. All I could furnish to her was an open boat and a few lines, written upon dirty and wet paper, to General Gates, recommending her to his protection."[2]

---

[1] Anburey, vol. i, page 379.
[2] *Political and Military Episodes*, page 298; *State of the Expedition*, pages 127, 128.

Mr. Brudenell, the Chaplain, readily undertook to accompany her, and with one female servant, and the Major's servant—a private of the XX who had a wound, which he received in the last action, in his shoulder—she rowed down the river to meet the enemy.[1] The night was cold and miserable, and in the dark the little craft was rowed down the Hudson by Mr. Brudenell and the soldier. On reaching the enemy's advanced post the sentinel would not allow the boat to pass, or to come ashore. In vain the Chaplain urged that he was a man of peace and the bearer of a flag of truce; told them who his companion was and her purpose; but apprehensions of treachery made the officer commanding the outpost obdurate; and so for eight hours her sufferings and anxiety were prolonged. At daybreak she was permitted to come ashore, but in a most deplorable condition.[2] The American officer was touched by her appearance, and instantly conducted her to General Gates, who received her with all the politeness and humanity her merits, character, and rank deserved, and through the lines of the American army, amid thousands of curious eyes, she was led with respect to the tent where her husband was lying wounded. All her sufferings were then rewarded, and she nursed him with all the tenderness which seldom fails in producing a happy result, when ministered by the loving hands of wife or mother. Four days after Lady Acland left the British camp, Burgoyne surrendered, and the army agreed to lay down their arms at Saratoga. Major Acland was released in December, 1777, and at once proceeded with his wife to New York, where a son was born early in the next year, and whence they returned to England.

Lady Acland's son John succeeded his grandfather as eighth baronet, in 1785, but died the same year. The daughter, Elizabeth Kitty, received a portion of the family estates at her brother's death; and on the 26th April, 1796, she married Henry George, second Earl of Carnarvon. She died 5th March, 1831, leaving two sons and three daughters; one of her grandsons is the fourth or present earl.[3] Lady Harriet Acland died 21st July, 1815, after thirty-seven years of widowhood.

---

[1] Stanhope's *History of England*, vol. vi, page 275; and Anburey, vol. i, page 404.

[2] *Political and Military Episodes*, page 298; and Anburey, vol. ii, page 57.

[3] Burke's *Peerage and Baronetage*.

MAJOR-GENERAL ROBERT ROSS.

ROBERT ROSS, the descendant of an ancient family, was born in 1774, at the family seat Rosstrevor, County Down. He was the son of a soldier, and we find that an ancestor, Colonel Charles Ross, was killed at Fontenoy in the year 1745. Robert Ross was educated at Trinity College, Dublin, but before he had completed the customary course he adopted the military profession, and received his first commission as Ensign in the 25th Foot on the 1st of August, 1789, when only fifteen years of age. He was promoted to a Lieutenancy in the 7th Fusiliers on the 13th July, 1791; and on the 19th April, 1795, obtained his company in the same corps. On the 23rd December of this year he was gazetted Major (by purchase) in the 2nd Battalion 90th Regiment, from which he retired to the half pay list. On the 5th August, 1799, he exchanged from half pay to the XX Regiment, with which he continued to serve until promoted Major-General. Major Ross's first active service with the regiment was in Holland. At the intrenchments at Krabbendam his gallantry was conspicuously displayed, and he was severely wounded whilst bravely defending the earthworks. His wounds incapacitated him from further service in this campaign. He accompanied the regiment to Minorca in 1800, and was appointed to command the flank battalion of Light Infantry.

On the 1st of June, 1801, Major Ross was promoted Brevet-Lieutenant-Colonel for service in Holland. In 1801 he proceeded to Egypt with the regiment, and took part in all the operations before Alexandria, until the final surrender of the French. Lieutenant-Colonel Ross succeeded to the command of the XX in September, 1803; and, in October, 1805, proceeded in command of the regiment to Naples with the expedition under Sir James Craig. The expedition proved a failure, the troops evacuated the Neapolitan territory, and the XX were landed in Sicily. Major-General Sir John Stuart organised and landed an expedition in Calabria early in the following July, and the battle of Maida ensued on the 4th of July. Colonel Ross disembarked the regiment at daybreak on the 4th, and hurried to the scene of action. Their exploits at Maida are fully described in the account of that victory. The Adjutant-General to the army under General Stuart met Colonel Ross and explained to him the state of the battle. Ross caught its spirit in an instant:[1] his manner of bringing the XX into action was the event of the day. It has been generally conceded that no one more prominently contributed to the defeat of the French than Colonel Ross. For his services at Maida he received a gold medal, and was appointed aide-de-camp to the King with the Brevet rank of Colonel in the army.

Colonel Ross returned to England with the regiment in October, 1807. In July the following year he proceeded in command of it to Portugal, landed with the headquarters after the battle of Vimiera, and marched with the regiment to the frontiers and took possession of fortresses evacuated by the French under the articles of capitulation. On the completion of this duty he joined the army under Sir John Moore. Colonel Ross commanded the XX during the retreat on Coruña: the regiment formed part of the reserve, and often the rear-geard.

For steady discipline and patient endurance under great privations, sufferings, and hardships, the XX was an example to the army, and the credit is due to its commanding officer. His system was humane and consistent; he warned and guarded his men from temptations, considered and provided (often from his private purse) for their comfort, he encouraged them by his lofty example, and never failed to praise their efforts. In addition to the many skirmishes and engagements during the retreat, he commanded the XX at the battle of Coruña, and afterwards brought it to England. When Colonel Ross had completed and reorganised the regiment, it joined the expedition to Walcheren, where it was decimated by fever, and returned to England in September, 1809, a mere shadow of the regiment that had left a few months previously. For a second time within twelve months Colonel Ross filled the ranks of the XX, but it was not till after prolonged residences at country stations, that the effects of the Walcheren fever had entirely disappeared. In the autumn of 1812, the XX again sailed for the Peninsula, landed at Lisbon, and marched to the frontiers of Portugal.

On the 4th of June, 1813, Colonel Ross was promoted Major-

---

[1] *Narratives of the Great War*, page 247.

General, and appointed to the command of the Fusilier Brigade in the 4th Division, in which brigade the XX was serving. At the battle of Vittoria (21st June, 1813) he commanded the brigade, and also in all the subsequent battles and engagements (except Toulouse) of the war. His foresight, energy, and intrepid constancy[1] probably saved the army from surprise and destruction at Roncesvalles, on the 25th of July, 1813.[2] At the battle of Sauroren he greatly distinguished himself. He repulsed several desperate attacks, had two horses shot under him, and was specially mentioned in the Duke of Wellington's despatches.

Through the Chancellor of the Exchequer, Wellington bore testimony, "that General Ross's brigade distinguished themselves in the Pyrenees beyond all former precedent."[3] The following letter,[4] from General Ross to a near relative, deals with the fighting in the Pyrenees:—

"Heights above Eschalar, in the Pyrenees,
"August 3rd, 1813.

"My dear Ned,—Since my last, I have neither eaten the bread of idleness, nor has the grass grown much under my feet. On the 18th ultimo, having completed matters for our friends the Dons, towards carrying on the siege of Pampeluna, we withdrew from that place, and marched towards the frontier, taking post near Roncesvalles, famous for feats in the days of chivalry. Our division (Sir Lowry Cole's), with two other brigades and some Spaniards, occupied that and some neighbouring posts. Soult having been sent to wipe off the disgrace of Vittoria, bringing with him strong reinforcements, attacked us on the 25th, and, after a hard day's fight, by dint of superior numbers, obliged us to retire—which was safely effected, not without bloody noses—to the neighbourhood of Pampeluna, on the morning of the 27th. In the business of the 25th our (the XX) loss was considerable. Old Wallace, Bent, Oakley, Crockat, Walker, Smith, (all of whom I believe you know,) Champagné, and Thompson, wounded. Buist, the Adjutant, killed, with one hundred and thirty (sergeants, rank and file) killed and wounded.

"On the following day, Soult made his grand effort for the relief of Pampeluna, at about eleven o'clock, attacking the right and left of

---

[1] *History of the Peninsular War*, vol. iii, page 273.

[2] See General Bainbrigge's narrative.

[3] Speech of the Chancellor of the Exchequer, in the House of Commons, 14th November, 1814.

[4] Published in the *United Service Journal*, page 412, 1829.

the position held by our division. His attack was conducted with great vigour, but without success; our push with the bayonet, where the enemy gained a post, was irresistible. At length, finding himself foiled in every attempt, after a very considerable loss, not less, certainly, than from two to three thousand men, he retired, and on the 30th was in full retreat. From that to the 2nd, our pursuit was equally hot; the number of prisoners taken will probably amount to three or four thousand. The total loss of the French, from the period of re-entering Spain until the 2nd, when they returned to France, is estimated to be from sixteen thousand to seventeen thousand men; add to which the complete *cow* under which their army is, being twice defeated, and latterly under the command of their very best General, sent for the express purpose, with fresh troops, to thrash us. The latter proceedings are more glorious, and in their consequences more eventful, than the brilliant business of the 21st of June, at Vittoria. Poor Falls, my aide-de-camp, was wounded on the 28th, not, I trust, dangerously. On the 1st and 2nd we were at them again. We (XX) have lost, killed and wounded altogether, two hundred and sixty-three (sergeants, rank and file). I am perfectly well."

At the battle of Orthes, on the 27th of February, 1814, General Ross, with his brigade, five times carried the village of St. Boës, and as many times pushed the battle beyond it, until he was severely wounded and carried from the field. In his despatch announcing the defeat of the French at Orthes, the Duke of Wellington said, "I have to express my warmest approbation of the exertions of the gallant General Ross, of whose services I was unfortunately deprived very early in the battle."

In a private letter, of which the following is an extract, General Ross informs his correspondent of the events of the day, and tells in simple language of the affectionate attachment of his wife, and how she hastened through danger and privations to the side of her wounded husband. The incident stands in strong resemblance to the devoted heroism of Lady Harriet Acland, in the campaign of Saratoga:—

"St. Jean de Luz, March 12th, 1814.

"My dear Ned,—You will be glad to find that the hit I got in the chops is likely to prove of mere temporary inconvenience. I am doing remarkably well, and trust in two or three weeks to be again equal to the fight. My letter to Eliza, which she sent to you, will have reached you I hope in time to quiet your apprehensions respecting me. She is now at my elbow, having on the receipt of mine mounted her mule, and in the midst of rain, hail, mud, and all other accompaniments of bad weather, set off from Bilbao for this place, which she reached early on the fifth day, a distance between eighty and ninety miles, over snowy mountains and bad roads. Her anxiety and spirit carried her through, enabling her to bear fatigue without suffering from cold or bad weather. Our little boy is left at Bilbao with his nurse; he is an uncommon fine fellow, and would hold hard fight with the *King of Rome*. He and his establishment are to join us as soon as the weather admits of movement by water. I was wounded early in the affair of the 27th, so that I personally could be but little acquainted with the proceedings of the day, which were highly advantageous to us."[1]

General Ross was not sufficiently recovered from his wounds to take part in the operations subsequent to the battle of Orthes, which was his last act of service in the Peninsular war, and here also ended his personal connection with the XX. On the conclusion of the war with France, in April, 1814, England was at war with the United States. The Government decided to send an expedition to Chesapeake, and the Duke of Wellington was desired to select a General to command. His Grace chose General Ross, and, although scarcely recovered from the wounds received at Orthès, he accepted the appointment.

On the 1st June, he embarked on board the "Royal Oak," seventy-four-gun ship, commanded by Captain Dax, and sailed the same day for America. General Ross landed his troops (four thousand five hundred in all, including marines), and, marching direct upon Washington, arrived on the 24th of August in front of the Heights of Bladensberg, a village situated on the eastern branch of the Potomac, about five miles from Washington. The American army (nine thousand men), under General Winder, was drawn up in order of battle to receive them. The bridge, which was the key to the enemy's position, was defended by a flotilla and all the enemy's artillery, under Commodore Barney. Led by Ross, the British carried the bridge, Barney was wounded, taken prisoner, and fifteen guns were captured. Ross then attacked the first line of the Americans and tumbled it back on the second: before either could recover he sent the whole of his force against them with the bayonet. This charge was irresistible; the enemy at first yielded, and then

---

[1] Published in the *United Service Journal*, page 414, 1829.

fled in one confused mass from the field. The defeat was complete. General Ross had one horse shot under him. After allowing his troops a brief rest, he marched on Washington, and entered the city about eight p.m., as the shades of night were falling. As they passed the straggling outskirts of the town, a volley was fired from the windows of two houses. Ross narrowly escaped being shot, and his horse was killed. The houses were forced and the men who had fired made prisoners.

In a private letter General Ross says:—"So unexpected was our entry and capture of Washington, and so confident was Madison (President of the States) of the defeat of our troops, that he had prepared a supper for the expected conquerors; and when our advanced party entered the President's house they found a table laid with forty covers. The fare, however, which was intended for *Jonathan*, was voraciously devoured by *John Bull*, and the health of the Prince Regent, and success to His Majesty's arms by sea and land, was drunk in the best wines, Madison having taken to his heels and ensured his safety on the opposite bank of the river by causing the bridge to be broken down."[1]

The following gratifying testimony of the ability and character of Ross appears in the despatch of Admiral Sir Alexander Cochrane:— "On combined services, such as we have been engaged in, it gives me the greatest pleasure to find myself united with so able and experienced an officer as Major-General Ross, in whom are blended those qualities so essential to promote success where co-operation between the two services becomes necessary; and I have much satisfaction in noticing the unanimity which prevails between the army and navy."

General Ross paid the greatest respect to private houses and property in the captured city, but ordered the destruction, by fire, of the capitol, senate house, house of representatives, arsenal, dockyard, treasury, president's residence, and the great bridge across the Potomac. Competent authorities have computed the value of the property thus destroyed at two million pounds sterling. Very considerable difference of opinion has been expressed as to whether these severities were not too rigorous, but as this contingency was definitely provided for in his instructions, the Commander-in-Chief was necessarily exonerated from blame or censure. A member of the House of Commons stated "that he regretted that General Ross had

---

[1] *United Service Journal*, 1829.

been selected as the individual to execute the plans of vengeance (destruction of Washington) of the Government."[1] The success of the attack on Washington was all the more creditable to General Ross as he was enjoined by his instructions "not to attempt anything that *might be attended* with the want of success."[2]

In *The Art of War*, at page 385, Baron de Jomini says, "The world was astonished to see a handful of seven or eight thousand[3] Englishmen making their appearance in the midst of a State embracing ten millions of people, taking possession of its capital and destroying all the public buildings—results unparalleled in history."

The operations against Washington had so important an effect with the Americans that they were the more inclined to peace, and thus free England from a war which was irritating and difficult when the forces of France had to be opposed. The thanks of both Houses of Parliament were unanimously voted to General Ross for the capture of Washington, and the regiments employed received permission to have *Bladensberg* enscrolled on their colours.

General Ross left Washington on the 27th of August, and turned his attention to the city of Baltimore, which he intended to attack. The fleet, with the troops on board, anchored off North Point, about thirteen miles from the city, on the 11th of September.

On the following day (12th) all the troops and marines, numbering about four thousand men, disembarked and marched towards Baltimore. The route lay through an impenetrably wooded country, and riflemen might be concealed in every thicket, invisible except to the eye of an Indian. General Ross and Admiral Cockburne were both with the light troops in front of the column. At a sudden turning in the road a corps of the enemy was observed, whose right was supported by a wood which lay on our left; into this wood the enemy's right extended. A fire was opened simultaneously upon our advance by these troops, and by half a dozen rifles in a copse to our right. It was here that the gallant Ross received his mortal wound; the ball passed through his right arm into his breast. The advancing soldiers knew their General had been struck down, as his horse, with an empty saddle, dashed passed them a few moments later, and they passed the dying hero, as he lay under a tree, his life blood welling

---

[1] *Proceedings of the House of Commons*, 14th Nov., 1814.
[2] Private letter from General Ross to his wife. This letter is in the possession of his grandson, Captain John Ross, of Bladensberg, Coldstream Guards.
[3] The correct number was four thousand five hundred.

away.[1] He was carried to the boats at North Point, but expired before they were reached.

The last moments of this distinguished soldier are thus described by Admiral Cockburne in his despatch to Vice-Admiral Hon. Sir Alexander Cochrane, dated H.M.S. "Severn," 15th September, 1814. They show what a noble, unselfish man he was; not a thought of his own pain and sufferings, but all for those whom he was leaving. "It is with the most heartfelt sorrow I have to add that in this short and desultory skirmish my gallant and highly valued friend the Major-General received a musket ball through his arm into his breast, which proved fatal to him on his way to the waterside for embarkation. Our country, sir, has lost in him one of its best and bravest soldiers, and those who knew him, as I did, a friend most honoured and beloved; and I trust, sir, I may be forgiven for considering it a sacred duty I owe to him to mention here that whilst his wounds were binding up, and we were placing him on the bearer, which was to carry him off the field, he assured me the wounds he had received in the performance of his duty to his country caused him not a pang; but he felt alone anxiety for a wife[2] and family dearer to him than his life, whom in the event of the fatal termination he foresaw, he recommended to the protection and notice of H.M. Government and the country."

Sank to rest,
By all his country's wishes blest.

According to an officer who was present at Baltimore, "The death of General Ross, in short, seemed to have disorganised the whole plan of proceedings, and the fleet and army rested idle, like a watch without its mainspring."[3] The body of the General was placed

---

[1] An officer who was present says, "It is impossible to conceive the effect which this melancholy spectacle produced throughout the army. All eyes were turned upon him as we passed, and a sort of involuntary groan ran from rank to rank, from the front to the rear of the column."—*Narrative by an Officer*, pages 174, 175.

[2] Mrs. Ross had a presentiment that she never would see her husband again. She felt his being sent to America acutely. The General's letters from America were chiefly devoted to comforting and consoling her. He concludes one by saying, "This war cannot last long, we then meet *never* again to separate." On both sides the letters are couched in terms of the warmest affection.

[3] *Narrative of the Campaign at Washington*, page 200, by an Officer, who served in the Expedition. London, 1821. By some authorities, the authorship of this work has been assigned to the late Chaplain General, Rev. Mr. Gleig. Mr. Gleig served at Washington and Baltimore as a subaltern in the 85th Regiment.

on board H.M.S. "Tonnant," and conveyed to Halifax, Nova Scotia, where it was accorded a public funeral on the 30th of September. A monument was raised to his memory by the officers of the garrison.

If General Ross's services in America can be measured by the rejoicings of the enemy over his death, they were indeed great. On the news being known the most enthusiastic exultations were manifested in Baltimore; at least a dozen men claimed the honour of having shot him, and the same number of rifles were exhibited as the identical weapon from which the fatal ball had been fired.[1]

At the opening of Parliament on the 8th of November, 1814, in the speech from the throne, the Prince Regent referred to his distinguished services, and the loss the country had sustained by his fall. His Royal Highness had ordered the insignia of a Knight Commander of the Bath to be forwarded to General Ross, but his decease previous to their arrival caused them to be returned; with considerate kindness the Prince ordered them to be delivered to his widow, and at the same time commanded that the family designation should henceforth be *Ross of Bladensberg*.[2] This distinction is unique, and was the best conceivable way of transmitting to posterity the name and services of a distinguished commander. Memorials have

---

[1] A monument was erected on the spot where General Ross fell, to the memory of the man who shot him. It bears the following inscription:

ERECTED BY THE FIRST MECHANIC VOLUNTEERS
TO THE MEMORY OF
AQUILA RANDALL, AGED TWENTY-FOUR YEARS,
WHO DIED
IN BRAVELY DEFENDING HIS COUNTRY AND HIS HOME.

On a third side—

IN THE SKIRMISH WHICH OCCURRED AT THIS SPOT
BETWEEN THE ADVANCED PARTY
UNDER MAJOR RICHARD K. HEATH, OF THE 5TH REGIMENT M.M.,
AND THE FRONT OF THE BRITISH COLUMN,
MAJOR GENERAL ROSS, THE COMMANDER OF THE BRITISH FORCES,
RECEIVED HIS MORTAL WOUND.

A Subaltern's Furlough, by E. T. Cooke, Lieutenant 45th Regiment, London, 1833.

[2] In addition to the family designation being ordered to be Ross of Bladensberg, the following augmentation was made at the same time to the family arms:—Additional crest or badge: General's arm, with laurel wreath round it, issuing from a mural crown, grasping the broken flag of the United States. Addition to coat of arms: Same issuing from the embattled coat of arms of the family, grasping the broken flag of the United States. Additional motto: Over the additional crest "Bladensberg."

been raised in the United Kingdom to his memory by the nation, the division of the army that he had commanded, and by the XX.

In seconding a resolution for the national monument, a member of the House of Commons[1] did justice to his character in a few but appropriate terms: "In private life his goodness of heart, coupled with a peculiar kindness and urbanity of manner, secured the regard and esteem of all who knew him. Never was an officer so universally and sincerely lamented by those under his command. He possessed the happy skill of conciliating by his disposition, and instructing by his example: his military knowledge was great, for it was the result of practice and constant experience, whilst his foresight and example in the field were such as to excite the enthusiasm and reverence of those whom he led to victory."

In the national monument, which is tabular, there is little to admire. Britannia is represented weeping over the tomb of the departed warrior, on which an American flag is being deposited by a nude figure of Valour, while Fame descends with a wreath of laurels to crown the hero's head.

The officers, naval and military, of the Chesapeake army, together with the noblemen and gentlemen of the County Down, subscribed the sum of £2,337; from this amount a monument was raised at Rosstrevor; it is a granite column, and forms a very prominent landmark on entering Carlingford harbour.[2]

A third honourable and sincere memorial of affectionate sorrow was erected in the Parish Church, Rosstrevor, by those who had had the privilege of serving under his command in the XX. Influenced by sentiments similar to those which unite the members of a family with their parent, the officers, non-commissioned officers, and privates joined together to testify and record their feelings of esteem and regret for their late commanding officer.

General Ross has been compared to many illustrious soldiers, notably, Wolfe, Moore, and Desaix (called by the Arabs over whom he ruled the "Just Sultan," and by Napoleon pronounced the truest and most disinterested soldier of Republican France); but in these pages we prefer to trace and record the many phases of character, and incidents of service, which are in close resemblance to those of the "Immortal Wolfe."

---

[1] *Proceedings of the House of Commons*, 14th November, 1814.

[2] The caretaker of this monument was for many years Andrew Robb, a veteran soldier of the XX. He had served in the campaigns in Holland, Egypt, Calabria, and the Peninsula under General Ross. Robb died in 1856 or 1857.

Both these distinguished officers served in the XX, with an interval of rather more than forty years between them, as Major and Lieutenant-Colonel Commanding, in the last-named position for eight and ten years respectively; and both, by their superior ability, splendid example, and judicious practice, trained the regiment in that system of discipline, and nurtured that *esprit de corps*, which have raised the XX so high in the annals of British infantry. Wolfe and Ross were XX officers in something more than name, and never failed to remember the regiment by which they had been aided to rise to high commands. Ross, like Wolfe, died young, on the field of battle, at a critical moment, and on American soil; they both had one glorious fault, namely, an excess of courage.

The following particulars of General Ross's family are not without interest. General Ross married Elizabeth, daughter of Walter Glascock, Esquire; this heroic lady survived her husband many years, and died on the 12th of May, 1845. Of their five children, the eldest, David Ross, of Bladensberg, was born 24th September, 1804; and married, firstly, Sarah, only daughter of William D. Delap, Esquire, and secondly, in 1843, the Honourable Harriet M. Skeffington, by whom he had three sons—Robert S. Ross, of Bladensberg; John F. G. Ross, of Bladensberg, Coldstream Guards; and Edmund J. T. Ross, of Bladensberg, Royal Engineers.

FIELD-MARSHAL LORD SEATON, G.C.B., G.C.M.G., G.C.H.

JOHN COLBORNE was born in 1777. He was the son of a Hampshire gentleman (S. Colborne, Esquire, of Lyndhurst), and was educated at Christ's Hospital and Winchester. He joined the XX as Ensign on the 10th July, 1794, and was promoted Lieutenant on the 4th of September of the following year. Lieutenant Colborne proceeded with the corps to Holland in August, 1799, and took part in the battles of Krabbendam, the night-march to and capture of Hoorn, and at both the battles of Egmont-op-Zee. On Captain Powlett being wounded at the first action fought at Egmont, on the 2nd of October, he was selected during the action by Lieutenant-Colonel Philip Bainbrigge, the officer commanding the regiment, to command the Light Company. On the 12th January, 1800, he gained his Captain's commission. In the month of June, 1800, Captain Colborne accompanied the XX on the expedition to Belleisle, and was stationed with it at Minorca. His next active employment was in Egypt, where he took part with the corps at the attack on the forts at Alexandria. After a three years' sojourn at Malta, he embarked with the regiment for Naples. Captain Colborne fought with the corps at Maida, and was appointed, on the death of Captain McLean, to the command of the Light Company.[1] Colonel Kempt, who commanded the Light Battalion, sent Captain Colborne and his company to follow the enemy and gain information. He overtook the rear of the French column, which was marching in great confusion, but finding that he was entirely without support, Captain Colborne was compelled to fall back on his battalion.[2] At the end of the year 1806, he was appointed Military Secretary to General Fox, commanding the forces in Sicily and the Mediteranean; he afterwards acted in a similar capacity to Sir John Moore in Sicily, Sweden, Portugal, and Spain, this service ending only with the death of Sir John at the battle of Coruña. On the 21st January, 1808, he was promoted Major. In September, 1808, the XX under Colonel Ross was detailed to receive Fort Lalippe from the French and to escort the French troops to Lisbon. Major Colborne accompanied the regiment as bearer of the flag of truce, and an autograph letter from General Kellerman to the French Commandant.[3] This appears to have been his last act of official service with the corps, although for many years he fought in the same fields with it. He was Military Secretary to Sir John Moore during the Coruña retreat, and at the dying request of that illustrious commander, he was promoted Lieutenant-Colonel,[4] and was shortly afterwards nominated to the command of the 52nd Light Infantry.

Lieutenant-Colonel Colborne joined Wellington's army at Jaracejo, in 1809, and was sent to La Mancha, to report on the operations of

---

[1] *Reminiscences of My Military Life*, pages 47, 48.

[2] *History of the Great War*, page 251.

[3] *History of the Peninsular War*, vol. i, page 100.

[4] From the *Life of Sir J. Moore* (vol. ii, page 228), by his brother, this partial account of the death scene is taken. "I have made my will, and have remembered my servants; Colborne has my will and all my papers." As he spoke these words, Major Colborne, his Military Secretary, entered the room. He addressed him with his wonted kindness; then, turning to Anderson, said, "Remember you go to Willoughby Gordon (Secretary to H.R.H. the Duke of York), and tell him that it is my request, and that I expect he will give a Lieutenant-Colonelcy to Major Colborne; he has long been with me, and I know him to be most worthy of it."

the Spanish armies. He was present at the battle of Ocana. In the campaigns of 1810 and 1811, he commanded a brigade in Sir Rowland Hill's division, and was detached in command of it to observe the movements of General Regnier, on the frontier of Portugal. He also commanded a brigade at Busaco, Badajoz, Albuera, and Ciudad Rodrigo. At the latter place he was severely wounded whilst leading the stormers of the Light Division against the redoubt of Francisco. He commanded the 2nd Brigade of the Light Division at the battles of Nivelle and Nive, and during the campaign of the Basque Pyrenees. At the battle of Orthes and Toulouse he led the 52nd Regiment. Colborne acquired a great military reputation in the Peninsular campaigns. Napier describes him as a man capable of turning the fate of a battle, and one whose military judgment was seldom at fault.[1] In action he was cool, resolute, and full of resource. At the battle of Nivelle he was ordered (contrary to his own judgment) to attack the signal redoubt. Three times at the head of the 52nd did he assault it. Covered by the steepness of the hill from the enemy's fire till within forty yards of it, when the rush was made; but on each occasion they were stopped short by a ditch thirty feet deep, protected by palisades. Resorting then to a ruse, he held out a white handkerchief and summoned the commandant, pointing out to him how his work was surrounded, and how hopeless his defence. The garrison surrendered, having had only one man killed, whereas Colborne had lost two hundred men of the 52nd.[2] In 1814, he was appointed aide-de-camp to the Prince Regent, and Millitary Secretary to the Prince of Orange, Commander-in-Chief of the British Forces in the Netherlands. He was promoted Colonel on the 14th June, and nominated K.C.B.

Colonel Sir John Colborne commanded the 52nd at Waterloo, and here his chief feat was performed.

In the evening of this hard-fought day, but still long enough before sunset to leave time for winning, and even completing a victory, Napoleon made his grand effort.

Still holding that farm—La Haie Sainte—which his soldiery had wrested from the allies, he directed two columns of the Imperial Guard[3] (of which one was led by Ney) against the right centre of Wellington's line-of-battle; and, when these columns came up to within striking distance, the action reached its true crisis.

---

[1] *History of the Peninsular War*, by General Sir W. Napier, vol. ii, page 337.
[2] *Ibid.*, vol. iii, page 337.
[3] Not "the old" but the "Moyenne Garde."

APPENDIX. 353

It is only, however, of the column encountered by Colborne that we here have to speak in more than a cursory way. When closely approaching the crest, this column had before it at first troops only undertaking the task of sheer defence, and it forced back some companies of a regiment on Colborne's left. Then Colborne, instinctively feeling that, his left being thus uncovered, he could operate more effectively by assailing the assailants than by any efforts of sheer defence, led forward his single battalion (extended in line) against the serried mass of the Imperial Guard, then also advancing to meet it; and, when so near his huge quarry as to be able to undertake the manœuvre, Colborne neatly "brought round the right shoulder" of a part of his line; and, whilst meantime not sparing the enemy's front, poured also a shattering fire into the left flank of the close, thick-set column. The column, thus doubly assailed by a single battalion, stopped, reeled, then fell back in confusion, pursued for a while by Colborne with his victorious 52nd.

The other column of the Imperial Guard encountered resistance of a different kind not connected with Colborne's operations, but it was signally vanquished, and forced to retreat in disorder.

Occurring as it did in the sight of a large proportion of Napoleon's army, this double overthrow of the Imperial Guard, long victorious on the Continent of Europe, might well be taken to heart by the quick-witted troops of the French, ever swift to discern and appreciate a turning crisis in battle; whilst also—taking place at a time when other signs also pointed to the same conclusion—it showed the English Commander that now his moment had come. He ordered a general advance of his infantry line, and moved cavalry flank-wise to the part of the field from which he intended to launch it.

Colonel Colborne meanwhile had advanced so far in pursuit that his regiment became somewhat isolated, and having before him fresh bodies of Napoleon's infantry that seemed to show a stout front, he brought his men to a halt. But one was at hand who in many a battle had learnt to divine the true mood of "the enemy" during moments of crisis. A rider came trotting down to where the 52nd stood halted—a rider unattended by aides-de-camp, yet being no other than Wellington. He spoke some words simple and few to one who was only the chief of a single battalion, but words—if you think of the sequel—that sound as though fraught with victory, with the doom of Napoleon, with a peace (as between the great nations) strong enough to endure through an epoch of scarce less than forty years. The words, as we learn, were but these:—"Go on, Colborne,

X

they won't stand." There yet was hard work to be done by tired men and jaded horses, but he who spoke the words seemed to know, and this indeed proved to be true, that the crisis of the battle had passed. The fact of Colborne having originated the decisive movement is abundantly confirmed.[1]

It is acknowledged by French authorities, and it brought him great renown. Sir J. Colborne commanded a brigade on the march to Paris. On the conclusion of peace he was appointed Governor of Guernsey, where he was the means of reviving the Elizabeth College, which had fallen into decay. On the 27th May, 1825, he was promoted Major-General. In 1830 he was appointed to the command of the forces in Canada, and was subsequently created Governor-General, as well as Commander-in-Chief. Having suppressed the Canadian Rebellion, Sir John Colborne returned to England in 1838. He was promoted Lieutenant-General on the 28th June, honoured with the Grand Cross of the Bath, and raised to the peerage as Baron Seaton in the following year. He was appointed Lord High Commissioner of the Ionian Islands from 1843 to 1849, and there he had during the revolutionary mania of 1848 to deal with the demands of a people continually disaffected. On the 24th March, 1854, he was appointed Colonel of the 2nd Life Guards, and promoted General on the 20th June. Lord Seaton commanded the forces in Ireland from 1854 to 1860. The honours and distinctions conferred on him were the Grand Cross of the Bath and of Hanover, and of St. Michael and St. George. The order of Maria Theresa of Austria, of the Tower and Sword of Portugal, and of St. George of Russia. The Waterloo medal; the gold cross and three clasps; the silver medal with five clasps. On the 1st April, 1860, he was promoted Field-Marshal.

Lord Seaton combined a singular charm of manner with a great modesty and hatred of pretence. He is an example of an officer rising by his own merits to the highest rank in his profession without the aid either of friends or influence. The first twelve years of his military career belong to the XX. In those days the regiment was the only training school for young officers. Colborne first acquired a reputation as an excellent regimental officer, and thence he rose and added to it in every position in which he was placed. He ever held the XX in affectionate remembrance. At the presentation of colours to the 2nd Battalion, on the 1st August, 1859, he said, "In presenting

---

[1] Siborne's *Waterloo*, vol. ii, pages 177-179.

these colours at your request, Colonel Radcliffe, I may be allowed to observe, that on entering the army, I was appointed to the XX, that I served my first campaign with it, and continued to share with it for many years the active service on which the corps was engaged. Early friendships and attachments leave the strongest impressions and associations, and you may imagine that I feel it almost a right to be preferred on this occasion for the duty you have proposed that I should undertake." The command in Ireland was Lord Seaton's last employment. He passed away peacefully, at Torquay, on the 17th April, 1863, aged eighty-six years. This account of his career cannot be more fittingly closed than by the subjoined extract from the obituary notice which appeared in the *Times* of the 18th April, 1863:—"He was of the race of heroes who fought in the mightiest wars of modern times, who through those wars made England glorious, and maintained her independence, and who have left us an example which is part of our heritage—part of our life."

SURGEON ARCHIBALD ARNOTT.

ARCHIBALD ARNOTT, M.D., joined the army as Hospital Assistant on the 14th April, 1795, and was appointed Assistant Surgeon of the 11th Light Dragoons on the 25th December, 1796; promoted Surgeon of the XX Regiment on the 23rd August, 1799. He proceeded to Holland with the corps; was present at the storming of the intrenchments at Krabbendam, and at both the actions fought at Egmont-op-Zee. His next service with the XX was at Minorca, thence he went to Egypt; was present at the storming of the Forts at Alexandria. On the reduction, in 1802, of the regiment by one battalion, Doctor Arnott was placed on half pay, but was restored to active employment in the 1st Battalion on the 17th May, 1803. He served with the regiment in Malta, Sicily, Calabria, and was present at the battle of Maida. He was with the regiment in Portugal, being present at the battle of Vimiera, and in the retreat on Coruña. After a brief stay in England, he accompanied the XX on the Walcheren expedition, where the corps was decimated by fever, from the effects of which the regiment required two years' home service to recover. In 1812, Doctor Arnott again accompanied the XX to Portugal, serving in Lord Wellington's campaigns until the end of the war, including the battle of Vittoria, all the actions in the Pyrenees, in which the XX took part, and the battles of Nivelle,

Nive, Orthes, and Toulouse. He served with the XX in Ireland from 1814 to 1819, embarking for St. Helena in the latter year. At St. Helena, there occurred the most remarkable and eventful incident of Doctor Arnott's career; this was his professional attendance on the Emperor Napoleon during his last illness. He was called in to see the Emperor (having been previously consulted by Professor Antommarchi, the Corsican physician) about half-past ten on the night of the 1st of April, 1821. The room was perfectly dark, and he could barely distinguish the form of Napoleon as he lay on his camp bed.[1]

From this date he saw the Emperor daily, who always conversed with him in a friendly and affable manner. On the 14th of April, Napoleon presented the *Life of Marlborough* through him to the officers of the XX ;[2] and on the 19th made his celebrated denunciation of the British Government.[3] The Doctor's professional ability, kind and gentle manner, soon secured for him the full confidence of Napoleon; the good opinion of the illustrious patient was strengthened by the daily interviews, and ripened into a warm personal attachment and sincere esteem, which were respectfully reciprocated by Doctor Arnott. A few days previous to his death, Napoleon gave a very interesting testimony of his respect for Dr. Arnott. He desired that a valuable gold snuff-box might be brought to him, and having with his dying hand, and last effort of departing strength, engraved upon its lid with a penknife the letter "N," he presented it to him.[4] On the 3rd of May, he gave instructions that, should he become insensible, no English physician but Arnott was to touch him.[5] Doctor Arnott was present at the death of Napoleon, which occurred at forty-nine minutes past five in the afternoon of the 5th May. The Emperor bequeathed to Arnott the sum of six hundred Napoleons, and the British Government granted him a gratuity of five hundred pounds. Surgeon Arnott went with the XX to India in 1822, and retired upon half pay on the 25th of December, 1826, having completed thirty years' service, twenty-seven of which were passed in the XX. The following particulars of Doctor Arnott's life subsequent to his leaving the regiment are taken

---

[1] *Last Moments of Napoleon*, F. Antommarchi (Corsican physician to the Emperor), vol. ii, pages 60-70.
[2] *Ibid.*, page 96.
[3] *Ibid.*, pages 115, 116.
[4] *Gentleman's Magazine*, vol. xliv, page 324; and *Reminiscenees of My Military Life*, page 62.
[5] *Last Moments of Napoleon*, vol. ii, page 148.

from the obituary notices which appeared in the daily papers at the time of his death. Doctor Arnott was almost the last survivor of those whose names will be handed down to posterity in connection with the events of the last days of Napoleon. He had a rich fund of recollections and anecdotes of the period. These would have been read with interest, but, except a clear and distinct *Account of the last Illness, Decease, and Post-mortem Appearances of Napoleon*,[1] published in 1822, he could never be induced to commit them to print, being reluctant to mingle publicly in the keen and painful controversy of the time, although never concealing his opinion in private conversation. From the sphere of public duty Dr. Arnott retired to his native parish, and there, on his patrimonial estate of Kirconnel Hall, spent the evening of his days beneficially to the neighbourhood and honourably to himself; universally respected for his exemplary conduct in private life, and for the attention with which he discharged the duties of a magistrate and landlord. He sought in all ways to be useful to the community, his overflowing kindness, amiable manners, and readiness at every call to exert, gratuitously, his professional skill for the relief of the afflicted, endearing him alike in the halls of the rich and in the cottages of the poor. Few men have enjoyed a larger share of the affection and esteem of their contemporaries, or have left behind them a more pleasing impression upon the minds of survivors. Doctor Arnott died at Kirconnel Hall, Dumfriesshire, on the 6th of July, 1855, in the eighty-fourth year of his age.[2]

MAJOR-GENERAL HENRY THOMAS, C.B.

HENRY THOMAS was gazetted Ensign on the 1st April, 1798, and promoted Lieutenant on the 29th of December of the same year, and Captain on the 10th December, 1805. He accompanied Sir James Craig's expedition to Malta and Naples in 1805, and was attached to Sir James Kempt's Light Battalion. Proceeded with the army which took possession of Sicily; served there four years, and was present at the capture of the islands of Ischia and Procida. He joined the 3rd Battalion of his regiment (27th) at Escallio, in the north of Portugal, in April, 1813; and, having command of the Light

---

[1] A pamphlet of thirty-nine pages, a purely professional work.
[2] *Gentleman's Magazine*, vol. xliv, page 324.

Company, he was actively employed previous to and at the battle of Vittoria, investment of Pampeluna, battle of Roncesvalles, and battles of the Pyrenees, Heights of Linzoain, heights above Pampeluna, storming of the French position on the 30th July, and pursuit of the enemy until the 6th of August, 1813, passage of the Bidassoa and heights above Vera. In command of the Light Companies of the right brigade 4th Division, he commenced the battle of Nivelle by an attack upon the French advanced redoubt. In storming their main position, his horse was killed under him; he then attacked and drove the enemy out of the village of St. Pèe. On the 26th August, 1813, he was promoted Major, and was next engaged in the affairs at Garret's House, near Bayonne, on the 10th and 13th of December, when the army was put in motion to repel the enemy's encroachments on our winter position. Major Thomas commanded the aforementioned Light Companies at the battles of Orthes and Toulouse. On the day previous to that upon which the last-named battle was fought, he took possession of the bridge over the river Ers and the village Croix d'Orade, which had been captured by a charge of the 18th Hussars. Next morning he covered the advance of the divisions upon Mount Blanc, and subsequently masked the flank movement of the columns to turn the right of the enemy, and also the advance of the division until it crowned the heights: horse killed under him. He then drove in the enemy's skirmishers, and, at the conclusion of the battle, commanded the outposts of the division.

After the termination of the Peninsular war, he embarked at Bordeaux for Canada with the 1st Battalion 27th Regiment, and was present at all the operations on Lake Champlain, and covered the retreat from Plattsburg to Montreal. He returned to Europe, was present at the capture of Paris, and served in France with the army of occupation. He received the gold medal and clasps for Nivelle, Orthes, and Toulouse, and the silver war medal with three clasps for Vittoria, Pyrenees, and Nive. Major Thomas was promoted Lieutenant-Colonel on the 21st January, 1819, and exchanged from half pay to the XX in February, 1827. He served with the regiment in India and at home until he retired upon half pay on the 6th September, 1841, having commanded the corps for eleven years. New colours were presented in 1838 to the regiment, when commanded by Colonel Thomas, and a reference to Chapter XXVII will furnish the reader with the opinion of the greatest soldier of the age—Field-Marshal the Duke of Wellington—both on the regiment and its commanding officer. Colonel Thomas was member of Parliament for Kinsale from 1835 to 1841. He was promoted Colonel on the 10th January, 1837; Major-General, 9th November, 1846; and Lieutenant-General, 20th June, 1854; and on the 25th July, 1854, he was appointed Colonel of the corps. As a general officer he commanded the Belfast district from 1853 to 1858, and whilst holding this command he induced a large number of men—desirable soldiers—to volunteer from the Militia battalions of the County Down for service in the XX, to fill the vacancies caused by the war. General Thomas never lost his interest in the corps, nor in any individual officer, non-commissioned officer, or man belonging to it; in him they always found an earnest and able advocate. Full of years, this distinguished officer died on the 21st of September, 1858.

CAPTAIN HENRY HOLLINSWORTH, MILITARY KNIGHT OF WINDSOR.

IN the year 1798, Henry Hollinsworth, a boy of about eleven years of age, joined the XX. His extreme youth did not prevent his accompanying the regiment on active service in the following year, for we find he was present at the attack on the intrenchments at Krabbendam, and at both actions at Egmont-op-Zee. From Belle-isle and Minorca he proceeded to Egypt, and there passed through his second campaign in 1801, being present at the surrender of the forts at Alexandria. With the regiment he moved to Malta, and, after three years' residence on the island, proceeded to Naples in 1805, thence to Sicily and Calabria, took part in the battle of Maida, the reduction of Scylla, and the town of Reggio. Arriving in England in January, 1808, he left it in a few months for Portugal, was present at the battle of Vimiera, the capitulation of Elvas, advance into Spain and retreat on Coruña, and battle of Coruña. Served with the corps in the expedition to South Beveland (Walchern), returned to England in the autumn of 1809, and enjoyed the comparative rest of service at home until 1812, when he accompanied the regiment to Portugal, participating in its marches and fatigues, the battle of Vittoria, fight at Roncesvalles, all the actions in the Pyrenees, and the battles of Nivelle and Nive. He was promoted to Sergeant-Major in the autumn of 1813; and at the battle of Orthes, when leading a charge of the regiment at the village of St. Boës, was severely wounded in the right thigh.[1] Incapacitated by his wound from further service in this campaign, he rejoined the regiment in Ireland in 1814, and embarked with it for Saint Helena in 1819. He was on duty over the Emperor Napoleon, and took part in the funeral ceremonies, and was employed in guarding the tomb until 1822, when he left with the regiment for Bombay. Sergeant-Major Hollinsworth was promoted to Ensign and Adjutant on the 3rd of December, 1825, and Lieutenant on the 29th May, 1828, still retaining the appointment of Adjutant.

He returned to England with the corps in 1837, after fifteen years' service in India. On the 27th of April in the following year he exchanged into the 56th Regiment, with Lieutenant (afterwards Colonel) Crofton. Joining his new corps in Jamaica, he was employed in the Quartermaster-General's and Barrack departments, until he left the island for England, in 1840, in charge of invalids, calling at Bermuda, *en route* for released convicts. In 1841 he retired upon half pay. On the recommendation of Lord Fitzroy Somerset (afterwards Lord Raglan), the General Commanding-in-Chief appointed Hollinsworth's eldest son Ensign in the 54th Regiment, and subsequently promoted him Captain in the 10th Regiment; and he fought at the battle of Sobraon, and was shot whilst leading his company at Moultan, and lies at the side of Van Agnew and other gallant officers in the citadel of that fortress.[2] In consideration of his meritorious services, the Secretary of State for War (Lord Hardinge) appointed Lieutenant Hollinsworth Staff Officer of Pensioners for the eastern Wales district (Cardiff). At the date of this appointment he had passed the prescribed limit of age, and was unable to pay "the difference." That gratitude was not withheld by fixed and narrow rules, enhanced the value of the appointment. Lieutenant Hollinsworth remained at Cardiff until 1847, when he was removed to a similar office at Roscommon. Here he witnessed all the agonies of the Irish famine. On the 28th June, 1850, he was promoted Captain on the unattached list, and retired after serving over six years as Staff Officer of Pensioners.

---

[1] Hart's *Army List*, 1863.

[2] His third son (George) joined the ranks of the XX, and reached the rank of Sergeant. He purchased his discharge in 1872, and settled in Canada. He is now Major of the 42nd Regiment of the active Militia, and is Sessions' Clerk in the House of Commons, Ottawa. The regiment is indebted to Major Hollinsworth for kindly placing his father's papers at the disposal of the compiler of this work.

On the 24th January, 1852, in recognition of his long and faithful services, Her Majesty Queen Victoria selected Captain Hollinsworth from a list of numerous candidates, and nominated him a Military Knight of Windsor. As the Crimean war entered into its second year, militia regiments were embodied for service at home and in the colonies; and although a Military Knight of Windsor and a veteran who was enjoying a well-earned repose, Captain Hollinsworth volunteered his services, which were accepted, and, by permission of Lord Palmerston, he undertook the duties of Paymaster of the 2nd West York Militia, and with this regiment he served a year at Gibraltar. In the XX, Captain Hollinsworth served forty years, and of this long period he was abroad with the corps twenty-eight years and four months. He was Sergeant-Major for twelve years, and Adjutant for the same length of time. Captain Hollinsworth was present at every action or engagement (Toulouse excepted) in which the XX took part between the years 1799 and 1814; and received a medal with nine clasps.

This veteran officer died at Windsor Castle on the 14th September, 1865, at the age of seventy-eight years; and was buried on Monday, the 18th September, in the catacombs of the Royal Chapel of St. George, Windsor Castle, by a detachment of the Grenadier Guards.

GENERAL SIR FREDERICK HORN, K.C.B.

FREDERICK HORN was born at Mansfield, Nottinghamshire, on the 21st of June, 1805. He was appointed, by purchase, Ensign in the XX on the 26th January, 1826; promoted Lieutenant, by purchase, on the 17th April, 1828. He served with the corps in India from the 23rd May, 1826, to the 30th May, 1831, and again for a second tour from the 9th May, 1834, to the 6th January, 1837. He returned to England *viâ* overland route[1] in this year, and was promoted Captain, by purchase, on the 16th June, 1837; was present with the regiment at the coronation of Her Majesty, and at the presentation

---

NOTE.—In 1823, Captain Hollinsworth prepared for the War Office and the Regiment the manuscript records; the regimental copy is still preserved in the Mess of the 1st Battalion. In the same year, he resuscitated the regimental Masonic lodge, which had been established in the corps in 1748, the first master being Lord George Sackville. The chapter, warrants, plate, regalia, etc., were unfortunately lost during the Indian Mutiny.

[1] This journey occupied seven and a half months.

of colours by His Grace the Duke of Wellington, at the Tower, on the 7th July, 1838. Captain Horn accompanied the regiment to Ireland in 1841, and was promoted Major, by purchase, on the 7th September.

Major Horn commanded the detachment of the corps on board the ship "General Palmer," during the passage to Bermuda. On the Reserve Battalion being formed he was appointed to the command, and was promoted Lieutenant-Colonel on the 14th April, 1846, and posted to the Reserve, as commanding officer. With the exception of six months, in the year 1843, Colonel Horn served with the corps in Bermuda uninterruptedly, from 9th November, 1841, to the 11th May, 1847; he was also with the regiment in Canada from the 12th May, 1847, to the 6th July, 1853. Colonel Horn succeeded to the command of the 1st Battalion on the 19th June, 1849, and returned to England with it in 1853. On the 20th June, 1854, he was promoted Brevet-Colonel; and on the 18th July proceeded with the corps to the Crimea. At the battle of Alma he led the right brigade of the 4th Division, and continued in command of the brigade until the arrival from England of Brigadier-General Goldie, on the 24th September, when he resumed his command of the corps.

Colonel Horn commanded the XX at the battle of Balaklava, and re-capture of the redoubt "Arab Tabia" and guns from the Russians, which they had taken from the Turkish force that morning (25th October). He commanded the XX at the battle of Inkerman on the 5th November, 1854; in this great fight he was twice wounded, had a horse shot under him, and brought the 4th Division out of action (mentioned in despatches, *London Gazette*, 2nd December, 1854). Colonel Horn was present throughout the siege operations against Sebastopol, and in the trenches at the assault on the 18th of June, 1855, and the fall of the town. He continued at the head of the XX until the 18th of June, 1855, when he was appointed to the command of a brigade in the Highland Division, with the rank of Brigadier-General. Brigadier-General Horn was nominated a Companion of the Bath on the 5th July, 1855, and received the distinguished service pension of £100 per annum for his services in the campaign.

Brigadier-General Horn remained in the Crimea until the withdrawal of the army in July, 1856; received the Crimean medal with clasps for Alma, Balaklava, Inkerman, and Sebastopol, Sardinian and Turkish medals, officer of the Legion of Honour, and third class of the Medjidie. General Horn commanded the brigade at Malta from the 30th October, 1856, to the 1st November, 1861.

The command at Malta was the last active employment of General Horn; his subsequent promotions and honours were as follow:—Promoted Major-General, 13th October, 1860; nominated a Knight Commander of the Bath, 2nd June, 1869; promoted Lieutenant-General, 18th January, 1870; appointed Colonel of the XX, 17th March, 1876; promoted to the rank of General on the 2nd June, 1877. A long and distinguished career on the active list of the army was closed on the 15th December, 1880, on which date he was placed on the retired list. Sir Frederick Horn's services in the XX can be thus briefly summed up:—They extended over a period of fifty-four years, twenty-one of which he served with the corps abroad; he commanded (Reserve Battalion over three years, and 1st Battalion seven years) ten years under almost every condition of circumstance that can fall to the lot of an officer, in Bermuda, Canada, England, and the Crimea. Under his command, during times of peace, the XX maintained the highest reputation; and its war services in the eastern campaign are fully described in the chapters devoted to that epoch. In one respect, Sir Frederick Horn stands alone from all the distinguished officers who have been in the XX. He joined the corps as an Ensign, passing through all the grades and sharing its fortunes all over the world, until he reached General officer's rank, and eventually became the Colonel of the corps.[1]

COLONEL FREDERICK C. EVELEGH, C.B.

LIEUTENANT FREDERICK C. EVELEGH exchanged into the XX on the 18th January, 1839. He was promoted Captain, 12th March, 1841, and Major, 30th December, 1853. He served with the regiment in Bermuda for six years, and in Canada from May, 1847, to the 31st October, 1852. Major Evelegh sailed with the XX for Turkey on the 18th July, 1854; he was present at the battles of the Alma and Balaklava. He went to Inkerman with Colonel Horn's wing on the first alarm on the morning of the 5th November, and fought with that wing during the whole day. As senior officer (the command of the 4th Division having devolved upon Colonel Horn and Lieutenant-Colonel Crofton having been dangerously wounded),

---

[1] General Thomas commanded the corps as Lieutenant-Colonel, and subsequently became its Colonel.

he brought the XX out of action. For his distinguished conduct in the field at Inkerman, he was promoted Brevet-Lieutenant-Colonel (dated 12th December, 1854). Lieutenant-Colonel Evelegh served throughout the siege of Sebastopol. He was present with Sir John Campbell's brigade (storming column) at the attack on the Redan, on the 18th June, when he was slightly wounded.[1] He again succeeded to the command of the corps in the field, on Colonel Horn assuming the command of the brigade at the death of Sir John Campbell. Lieutenant-Colonel Evelegh, for the third time, commanded the corps on an eventful day (8th September), and from this date he became its commanding officer, Colonel Horn being appointed to the command of a brigade with the rank of Brigadier-General. During the siege, Colonel Evelegh did not miss a single tour of duty as field officer in the trenches. In this respect, he stands alone among all field officers of the 4th Division (eleven regiments). On special and trying occasions, Colonel Evelegh commanded the confidence of both officers and men; and the men of the 4th Division have been known to express their feeling of willingness to be led by him.[2]

The general officers[3] by whom the 4th Division was commanded at different periods of the war, without exception, entertained and expressed the highest opinion of his abilities as a soldier; and his conduct throughout the siege met, not only with their approbation, but frequently their highest commendation.[4] Another and greater authority, the late Field-Marshal Lord Strathnairn, has recorded this statement: "I was unacquainted with Colonel Evelegh until the late campaign in the Crimea. Taking great interest in the siege of Sebastopol, I made myself acquainted with the trenches, French and English; and, in doing so, heard from English Engineer officers their encomiums of the extreme care which Colonel Evelegh took of the defence of his trenches, and of the assiduity with which he patrolled and examined his outlying piquets." As second and often (when Colonel Horn was in brigade command) in command of the corps during the winter of 1854-5, his anxious care and untiring energy alleviated in no small degree the sufferings of the men, to

---

[1] Lord Raglan's despatch, dated 19th June, 1855.
[2] Colonel Hugh Smith, Assistant Adjutant-General, 4th Division.
[3] Sir George Cathcart, Sir John Campbell, Sir Henry Bentinck, Major-General C. A. Windham, Sir R. Garrett.
[4] Colonel Hugh Smith, Assistant Adjutant-General, 4th Division.

which was attributed their efficient state under unparalleled circumstances. Colonel Evelegh commanded the regiment at the attack and capture of Fort Kinburn. During the Crimean campaign his name was twice mentioned in despatches. He brought the regiment to England, and under his command at Aldershot and Portsmouth the corps gained, for smartness and perfect discipline, the approbation of the Generals under whom it served; and of His Royal Highness the Duke of Cambridge, on its departure from Aldershot, on the 6th of August, for embarkation for India. The regiment arrived in India, marched from Calcutta to Benares, and was posted to the 4th Division, commanded by Brigadier-General Franks. Colonel Evelegh was appointed a Brigadier in the division, and commanded a brigade at the actions of Chanda, Ameerapore, Sultanpore, and at the siege and capture of Lucknow. After the fall of Lucknow Brigadier Evelegh was frequently sent out in command of columns against the rebels threatening the city. On the 11th June he proceeded with his brigade to Nawabgunge, where a permanent camp was formed.

The arduous task of keeping open the communications between Cawnpore and Lucknow, a distance of forty miles, during an Indian summer and the rainy season, was assigned to the Brigadier. This service he carried out with unqualified success, and his falling on the rebels at a considerable distance from his own base, at a period of the year when European troops were not actively employed, had the best effect, and he was praised and congratulated by Sir Hope Grant accordingly (13th August, 1858).

In the months of August and October, he defeated the rebels at the following places, Mohan, Hussengunge, Meangunge, and between the 3rd and 18th of November at Poorwah, Morar Mow, Fort of Simree, and Berah. He successfully pursued the Rana Bene Madho, but only by following his own course and disregarding the instructions he had received, and thus led to the destruction of the enemy at Buxer-Ghat (at which he took an important part), which ended the rebellion in the Biswara district.

Brigadier Evelegh returned with his brigade to Nawabgunge, but on arrival there, on the 29th November, was ordered to leave his command and proceed at once to Lucknow. Lord Clyde paid Evelegh the compliment of selecting him to command a special service force, which he had himself intended to command, for the reduction of certain forts in the Setapore district.

On the 2nd December, the fort of Oomeriah was taken after a

stubborn resistance. This and several other strongholds were destroyed, and the district cleared. The force finally crossed the Gogra and halted at Gondah. The particulars of the different actions are fully narrated in the chapters devoted to the Indian Mutiny campaign.

During this campaign Brigadier Evelegh proved himself to be a daring, energetic, and skilful commander. His name was fifteen times mentioned in despatches in India, and he was twice thanked by the Governor-General in Council. For his services in the Crimea he received the war medal and four clasps, order of the Companion of the Bath, the Legion of Honour, and the Turkish medal; and for his services in India the silver medal and clasp for Lucknow.

Colonel Evelegh left the regiment on leave of absence on the 9th of February, 1859, and retired from the service, by the sale of his commission, on the 28th October of the same year. This step was regretted by none more than by the men of the XX—the soldiers who had submitted to his stern rules of discipline—who had trusted him implicitly, and whom he led to victory. As Colonel Evelegh's retirement was sincerely regretted in the corps, it also caused disappointment to distinguished officers who were anxious to see merit acknowledged and good service rewarded. Writing at a later date, Lord Strathnairn gives expression to this feeling:—"Colonel Evelegh commanded a brigade of all arms, in Oude, which fought many actions, and did admirable service, and so high was the opinion which I entertained of him, as an officer, from my knowledge of him in the Crimea, that I always looked forward, should I have the chief command in India, to give him the first brigade at my disposal; and I was very much disappointed, on account of the good of the service, and non-reward of merit, to find, when I was honoured with the chief command, that he had left the army."

GENERAL SIR W. P. RADCLIFFE, K.C.B.

WILLIAM POLLEXFEN RADCLIFFE was born at Warleigh, near Plymouth, on the 2nd December, 1822. He was educated at Winchester, and joined the XX as Ensign (by purchase) on the 12th March, 1841, and was promoted Lieutenant (by purchase) on the 2nd August, 1842. Lieutenant Radcliffe embarked with the regiment for Bermuda, and served with it there from 1841 to 1847, and five years in Canada (1847-1853). He was promoted Captain (by purchase) on the 25th July, 1851, and was appointed to the command of the Light Company. Captain Radcliffe proceeded with the regiment to the Crimea on the 18th July, 1854, and served with it in the Eastern campaign until the 13th August, 1855. He acted as aide-de-camp to Colonel Horn (in command of a brigade) at the battle of the Alma, and was present with the regiment at Balaklava. On the night previous to Inkerman he was on outpost duty in front of the advanced trench; he went into action on the following morning with Colonel Crofton's wing, and commanded two companies at the Sandbag battery (see page 213). For his distinguished conduct at the battle of Inkerman he was promoted Brevet-Major (dated 12th December, 1854). Major Radcliffe served throughout the siege of Sebastopol until the 13th of August, 1855, when he was ordered to England to take command of the Depôt companies at the Isle of Wight. During the siege, Major Radcliffe was conspicuous for that ready resource and tact in the management of men which makes the soldier work under all conditions of hardship and distress with cheerfulness, and face danger with a calm resolution.

On the 18th January, 1855, when the sufferings of our men before Sebastopol had reached the acutest stage, it is recorded[1] that the men under his command worked well and with energy, but that those of other corps had their pay stopped. Major Radcliffe took part in the assault of the Redan on the 18th of June. After his return to England he did a vast amount of good work at the regimental depôt, in procuring a good class of recruits, to fill the gaps made in the regiment by the prolonged campaign in the Crimea. He was promoted Major in the regiment on the 29th of August, 1856.

After a brief stay in England, he embarked with the regiment as senior Major on the 6th of August, 1857.

Landing at Calcutta on the 20th November, he marched to Benares, and subsequently took part in the operations conducted by Brigadier Franks, including the battles of Chanda, Ameerapore, and Sultanpore, also the final march on Lucknow. He was present with the regiment at the siege of that city, and on the 14th March, 1858, when the Kaiser Bagh had been so easily disposed of, he led two companies of the regiment against the walled enclosure known as the "Engine House." The detachment became divided, and Major Radcliffe, with a few men, forced an entrance into a Serai in which

---

[1] *Official Journal of the Siege.*

some rebels were hiding. After a sharp encounter the rebels were killed, but not before Major Radcliffe and Private Lincoln were severely wounded and Private Hill was killed.[1] Whilst the regiment was fighting before Lucknow it was decided by the Government to increase its establishment by one battalion. Major Radcliffe was selected to raise and organise the new battalion; he was promoted Lieutenant-Colonel on the 26th March, 1858, and left the 1st Battalion on the 31st of the same month, to join the 2nd Battalion in Ireland. On his arrival from India in 1858, Lieutenant-Colonel Radcliffe assumed the command of the 2nd Battalion at Tralee. His command was marked with unqualified success, and the young battalion was praised by every general officer by whom it was inspected. He was promoted Brevet-Colonel on the 12th March, 1863; and, on the 12th June, he retired on temporary half pay.

Colonel Radcliffe was unemployed until the 1st January, 1873, when he was appointed Inspector-General of Musketry at Hythe, and this important position he held until the 30th April, 1878. Colonel Radcliffe was promoted Major-General on the 21st November, 1876, his commission being subsequently antedated to the 28th October, 1868. Major-General Radcliffe commanded the Eastern District (Colchester) from the 1st October, 1878, to the 31st March, 1882, when he resigned the command, having attained Lieutenant-General's rank on the 9th March. The honours and rewards conferred on General Radcliffe were as follows:—He was appointed a Companion of the Bath on the 13th March, 1867, and Knight Commander of the Bath on the 29th May, 1886. He was awarded a distinguished service pension on the 8th September, 1881. Sir Pollexfen Radcliffe was placed on the retired list on the 1st April, 1887, with the honorary rank of General. He is also a Lieutenant-General on the reserve of officers. He received the Crimean medal with four clasps, the 5th class of the Medjidie, Sardinian war medal, Turkish medal, and the Indian Mutiny medal and clasp for Lucknow.

---

[1] For an account of the attack by Major Radcliffe and Privates Hill and Lincoln on the Serai, see pages 244, 245. Like many other gallant feats, this passed unnoticed. On the 5th September, 1888, Colonel Evelegh, C.B., writing of the storming of the Engine House, said: "I did not see the affair myself. Lys was in command of the regiment—I of the brigade. I believe it was one of the, if not the, *most creditable* for the regiment of all the numerous affairs that took place during the mutiny. Radcliffe ought to have had a V.C. for it."

COLONEL JOHN CORMICK.

JOHN CORMICK joined the 40th Regiment as Ensign on the 27th August, 1841; he was promoted Lieutenant (by purchase) on the 25th October, 1842, and Captain (by purchase) on the 12th July, 1850. Captain Cormick exchanged into the 18th Regiment on the 10th January, 1851. He served in the Gwalior campaign under Lord Gough, and was present at the battle of Maharajpore on the 20th December, 1843. He took part in the campaign in Burmah, in 1852-3, including the capture of Mantaban, Rangoon, and Prome. Captain Cormick landed with his regiment (18th) on the Crimea in December, 1854, and served throughout the siege of Sebastopol, except when incapacitated by his wounds. He was severely wounded (shot through the thigh), at the attack on the cemetery, on the 18th June, 1855. For his gallant conduct on this occasion he was mentioned in despatches, promoted Brevet-Major, and received a gratuity equal to twelve months' pay. He was promoted substantive Major on half pay on the 18th September, 1857, and in March, 1858, he was posted to the 2nd Battalion XX Regiment, which was about to be raised.

Major Cormick did excellent service in the early days of the 2nd Battalion. He was promoted Lieutenant-Colonel (by purchase) on the 24th December, 1858, on the retirement of Colonel Evelegh, C.B. Lieutenant-Colonel Cormick joined the 1st Battalion at Gondah, in February, 1859. He conducted the final operations against the rebels in the country surrounding Gondah, and commanded at the actions of Muchlee Goan and Khyber Jungle. He was promoted Brevet-Colonel on the 24th December, 1863.

Colonel Cormick received the bronze star for Maharajpore, the medal and clasp for Burmah, the Crimean war medal and clasp for Sebastopol, the Turkish medal, the fifth class of the Order of the Medjidie, and the Indian Mutiny medal. A reference to Chapter XXXVI will show that under his command the battalion maintained its high reputation both in the field and in garrison. Colonel Cormick died at Aldershot on the 10th July, 1868, from congestion of the lungs. His death was deeply regretted in the regiment, where his worth was understood and appreciated. During his command, the regimental benevolent fund, known as the "Commanding Officers' Fund," was established, and he aided it by considerable contributions from his private purse. By his will he bequeathed to the officers of the regiment one hundred pounds, to the sergeants fifty pounds, and to the men one hundred pounds. The latter was placed in the "Commanding Officers' Fund." His loss was not only regretted by those under his command, but also by those under whom he had served. The following letter from the private secretary and aide-de-camp of Field-Marshal Lord Strathnairn expresses his Lordship's opinion of the loss sustained by the regiment and the service:—

"45, Lower Brook Street, Grosvenor Square,
"London, 16th July, 1868.

"Sir,—Lord Strathnairn has heard with very sincere regret of the death of Colonel Cormick, and he cannot allow such a sad event to pass without expressing to the XX Regiment his feelings of respect for that lamented officer, and his sympathy with the regiment in the loss which they have sustained. When Commander-in-Chief in India, Lord Strathnairn had frequent occasion to praise Colonel Cormick and the regiment for its high state of discipline, so well worthy of its antecedents. It was, therefore, with especial pleasure and pride that his Lordship anticipated presenting new colours to this distinguished regiment, and he feels great regret at the untimely event which has thrown such a gloom over the regiment, and deprived the service of a good and gallant officer.—I remain, sir, yours faithfully,

"(Signed) O. T. BURNE, Major, Aide-de-Camp.
"The Officer Commanding
"1st Battalion XX Regiment."

The regiment marked the respect in which it held its late Commanding Officer by erecting to his memory, and also to the memory of Colonel G. Bennet,[1] who had been second Lieutenant-Colonel during Colonel Cormick's command, a tablet in Exeter Cathedral, which bears this inscription:—

COLONEL J. CORMICK,
DIED 10TH JULY, 1868.
COLONEL G. BENNET,
DIED 7TH NOVEMBER, 1867.
THIS TABLET IS ERECTED BY THE
OFFICERS, NON-COMMISSIONED OFFICERS, AND PRIVATES
OF THE XX REGIMENT,
IN TESTIMONY OF THEIR ESTEEM FOR THESE THEIR COMMANDING OFFICERS
AND OF SORROW AT THEIR LOSS.

---

[1] Lieutenant-Colonel Bennet had served with the regiment in the Crimean and Indian Mutiny campaigns. He was severely wounded at Inkerman. Lieutenant-Colonel Bennet retired upon half pay in 1867, and died shortly afterwards.

COLONEL SIR OWEN TUDOR BURNE, K.C.S.I., C.I.E.

OWEN TUDOR BURNE, son of the Reverend H. T. Burne, M.A., of Grittleton, Wilts, was born at Plymouth, on the 12th of April, 1837. He received a home education. After passing through Sandhurst, he obtained, at the early age of eighteen years, an Ensign's commission (15th May, 1855) in the XX. After a few months' service with the Depôt at the Isle of Wight, he joined the regiment at the Crimea on the 14th of March, 1856, having been detained four months at Malta, *en route*. Ensign Burne returned to England with the corps; but his home service was of short duration, as he embarked for India on the 6th of August, 1857, and landed at Calcutta on the 20th of November. As Ensign and Lieutenant, he served on the staff of Brigadier Evelegh, C.B., throughout the campaign. From the 8th January to the 9th of April, 1858, he was Staff Officer to Brigadier Evelegh and Brigade Quartermaster. He took part in the battles of Chanda, Ameerapore, and Sultanpore, and in the siege and capture of Lucknow. During the siege, he performed an act which was thus alluded to in later years by Sir Hugh Rose, when Commander-in-Chief in India: "When the 7th Brigade was stationed at the Chas Bagh, the communications of the brigade were broken by the unsteadiness of some Nepalese regiments; the brigade was for some time in considerable danger, had the enemy profited by the critical state of affairs and made a bold attack. Brigadier Evelegh sent Ensign Burne to the left, to endeavour to find the advanced posts of the XX, as there was heavy firing in their direction; this he did and returned with the report. The Brigadier then desired him to ascertain the state of affairs on the right, where the Nepalese were supposed to be. It was nearly dark when he started on this second duty, the ground over which he was to pass was unknown to him, and was occupied by the enemy, and the fire very heavy. He forded the canal with the water up to his chest, and made his way alone for about a mile, through the part of the city occupied by the enemy. He then came on some Nepalese troops, who were holding a position known as 'Bank's House.' He found these troops unsteady, and no British officer present; after seeing them properly posted, he again started, directed only by the sound of Enfield rifles. Passing in the dark through a considerable portion of the town, he came on some advanced sentries of the 42nd Regiment, who took him to their piquet. He found the officers ignorant of their position, and anxious for information. After giving and obtaining all that he could, he set out on his return, and reached Brigadier Evelegh with his report, having lost the direct way in the darkness of the night. The Brigadier was thus enabled to make proper arrangements for the security of his brigade. Brigadier Evelegh reported this service to Brigadier-General Franks, who recommended Ensign Burne to the Commander-in-Chief for a prospective Brevet-Majority, but His Excellency decided that he could not recommend him, as he was then an Ensign of only three years' service."

This daring feat thus passed unrewarded, notwithstanding the recommendations of the divisional and brigade commanders, and the expressed opinions of Captain Wood, 42nd Regiment, and Major A. B. Johnson, Brigade-Major. He also took part in the storming of the Engine House. For his services at Lucknow his name was mentioned in the despatches of the Commander-in-Chief. On the 10th of April he was promoted Lieutenant. Lieutenant Burne was Brigade-Major of the Lucknow column from the 10th of April to the 9th June. On the removal of the column to the camp at Nawabgunge, he was appointed staff officer to Brigadier Evelegh, and this appointment he held up to the 13th November.

Lieutenant Burne was present at the affairs of Mohan, Hussengunge, Meangunge, Poorwah, Morar Mow, Fort of Simree, and actions at Churda and Buxer-Ghat. On the 10th of September, he was appointed Adjutant of the corps. He served in the final operations on the Oude and Nepaul frontiers, including the actions at Muchlee Goan and Khyber Jungle.

In the corps his name has been handed down as a popular and successful Adjutant. The regiment was inspected by Sir Hugh Rose, Commander-in-Chief in India, at Gondah, on the 14th December, 1860. In his confidential report he wrote of the Adjutant: "A considerable share of the creditable state of the regiment is due to this promising officer, whose really high qualifications and gentlemanlike manner and conduct render him a valuable acquisition to the service."

So strong was the impression made upon the Commander-in-Chief that he appointed Lieutenant and Adjutant Burne his military secretary on the 17th September, 1861. This is the first and probably only occasion on which this or any similar important office was held by a subaltern officer, and it was gained by merit alone. Lieutenant Burne's departure from the regiment evoked a feeling of universal regret, but, as can be easily imagined, this feeling was shared by none more than the officer then in command, Colonel J. Cormick, who wrote to Lieutenant Burne in the following terms:—

"Gondah, 4th October, 1861.

"I received your resignation of the Adjutantcy this morning. I cannot sufficiently express how much I regret your leaving the regiment. I say nothing about your zeal and attention to your duties as Adjutant, for that is well known by all who have been in the regiment with you, but appreciated by none more than myself; but I always did admire your *esprit de corps*, which, combined with your holding the Adjutantcy, I have no hesitation in saying, conduced most materially in keeping the regiment in such an efficient state."

Lieutenant Burne resigned the Military Secretaryship on the 30th of October, 1862, owing to an expression of opinion by the Field-Marshal Commanding-in-Chief, that the Indian Military Secretary should be a field officer. In a letter from the Adjutant-General to the Goverment of India, dated 15th October, 1862, Sir Hugh Rose thus explains the cause of Lieutenant Burne's resignation:—"It is solely on account of the expression of the wishes of H.R.H. the Field Marshal Commanding-in-Chief that the office should be held by a field officer that Lieutenant Burne, the late Military Secretary, gives up the office, and His Excellency is in the highest degree satisfied with Lieutenant Burne's ability, zeal, and trustworthiness."

He was immediately appointed (31st October, 1862) aide-de-camp and private secretary, which post he held until the expiration of Sir Hugh Rose's term of command in India on the 23rd March, 1865.

Lieutenant Burne was promoted Captain on the unattached list, on the 9th of August, 1864, and in the XX on the 12th September, 1865, having in the meantime received the rank of Brevet-Major, dated 24th January, 1865. Major Burne was aide-de-camp to the Commander-in-Chief in Ireland from the 1st July, 1865, to the 5th November, 1868, officiating as Military Secretary during several important months of this period. At this time the Fenian conspiracy had to be dealt with, and on its termination he was thanked by Lord Strathnairn in these words: "Major Burne, first aide-de-camp, has afforded the Commander of the Forces the same useful assistance throughout the Fenian agitation which his Lordship has invariably received from him since he has served on his staff." Major Burne was further thanked by the Earl of Kimberley, then Lord-Lieutenant of Ireland, for his invaluable services as officiating military secretary for many months during the Fenian disturbances of 1866. On the

13th January, 1869, Major Burne was appointed private secretary to the Earl of Mayo, Governor-General and Viceroy of India. He was with the Earl when assassinated at Port Blair, Andaman Islands, on the 8th February, 1872. As in previous positions, his tenure of office enhanced his reputation. Of him, the acting Governor-General wrote (30th April, 1872) in an official minute: "I have before me a memorandum showing all the details of Lord Mayo's Indian journey. For this I have to thank Major Burne, Lord Mayo's private secretary and friend, of whom I shall take this opportunity of saying that he was not only the best private secretary that I ever saw or heard of, but that during the last three years he had performed with great ability and rare discretion, as the confidential assistant of the Viceroy, a greater amount of public business of a most difficult and delicate kind than has fallen to many men in India."[1] In a despatch, dated 15th March, 1872, the Government of India also bore this testimony: "We are aware that Lord Mayo was entirely satisfied with the zealous and efficient manner in which his officers worked for him. The duties of private secretary especially are of a most arduous and delicate nature, and we gladly give our personal testimony to the singular ability, discretion, and zeal with which they have all along been discharged by Major Burne."

Soon after the arrival in India of Lord Mayo's successor, the Earl of Northbrook, Major Burne returned to England. The Indian papers, without exception, referred to his retirement as a national loss, and the references were made, generally, in terms carefully and avowedly underdrawn, from deference to Major Burne's own modest and retiring character. The secretaries to the Government of India, previous to his departure from India, presented Major Burne with an elegant vase, bearing on one side, "In memory of Lord Mayo's Viceroyalty," and on the other, "Presented to Major Owen Burne, etc." Major Burne's connection with the XX ceased on the 15th May, 1872, when he was placed on half pay. He was political aide-de-camp to the Secretary of State for India from the 1st August, 1872, to the 15th October, 1874; and, in addition, during the last months was assistant political secretary, namely, from the 16th April to the 15th October, 1874. Major Burne was promoted Brevet-Lieutenant-Colonel on the 23rd July, 1874.

---

[1] In the *Times* of the 11th March, 1872, an extract from Major Burne's diary was published. It was pronounced a clear and graphic account of the death of Lord Mayo, told with extraordinary minuteness.

Lieutenant-Colonel Burne was specially selected (16th October, 1874) by the Marquis of Salisbury, on account of his political and military knowledge, to be secretary of the secret and political department of the India Office, one of the most important positions under Her Majesty's Government. He was allowed by the Field-Marshal Commanding-in-Chief to reckon this appointment as service towards promotion. Lieutenant-Colonel Burne accompanied the Earl of Lytton to India as private secretary, and this office he filled for two years (13th April, 1876—13th April, 1878). This was a special service appointment, made by the Marquis of Salisbury with the unanimous consent of the Council of India, Colonel Burne being allowed during his period of absence to retain his permanent appointment at the India Office.

He was created a Companion of the most exalted Order of the Star of India in May, 1872; Companion of the Order of the Indian Empire in January, 1878; and Knight Commander of the Star of India in July, 1879. On the 23rd July, 1879, he was promoted Colonel. In January, 1887, Sir O. T. Burne was appointed by the Queen to be a member of the Council of India.

THE ORIGIN OF THE XX.—COUNTY TITLES.

THE XX was raised in the city of Exeter, but during the first hundred years of its existence it was only once (1754) stationed there, being generally abroad or in Ireland. Up to the year 1782 it was known by the name of the Colonel who for the time commanded it, notwithstanding that the number was inscribed on the colours in gold Roman characters in the year 1751.[1] In the year 1782 it was designated the XX or East Devonshire Regiment.[2] The territorial appendage was conferred to assist the recruiting service and to strengthen the connection with the county which gave it birth. That any considerable number of Devonshire men joined the colours seems doubtful. In 1754, Wolfe calculated that it would take the whole winter to replace a hundred men who had volunteered for service in America. In 1796, when the regiment returned from the

---

[1] Royal Warrant by King George II, dated 1st July, 1751.
[2] Royal Warrant by King George III, dated 31st August, 1782.

West Indies, numbering less than four score men, recruiting in Exeter was a failure, and the regiment had to march northwards in consequence.

In the eighteenth century, the woollen and serge industries flourished in Exeter, and gave employment and good wages to the majority of the population. Hence one and the chief reason for the paucity of recruits. Of the officers, many belonged to Devonshire families, and county names can be traced to a comparatively recent period. The Devonshire connection was warmly cherished. Monuments to the officers and men who have fallen in the service of the country, and the colours around which they fought and fell, are in the cathedral of Exeter. In 1873, the regimental depôt was established at Bury, in Lancashire; and from the 1st of July, 1881, the regiment became the "Lancashire Fusiliers," but retained its place in the army as the Twentieth Regiment. Vain regrets are useless, and would be entirely out of place in this work. The old spirit still lives in the corps and cannot be affected by change of name or title. In its present county and under the present organisation it has four auxiliaries:—One Militia Battalion (3rd Lancashire Fusiliers, commanded by Colonel Thomas Hale) and three Volunteer Battalions: 1st Volunteer Battalion, headquarters at Bury, commanded by Lieutenant-Colonel T. P. Young; 2nd Volunteer Battalion, headquarters at Rochdale, commanded by Lieutenant-Colonel T. R. Phillipi; 3rd Volunteer Battalion, headquarters at Salford, commanded by Lieutenant-Colonel F. Haworth.

The most cordial relationship exists between the two forces: the volunteers evince the keenest interest in all that concerns the parent corps.

That the efforts of the regiment towards establishing friendly relations with its new county have not been altogether unattended with success is vouched for by the many expressions of regret on its departure from Manchester. There was one graceful allusion to the regiment, which, from the high character and position of the gentleman who pronounced it, must be inscribed in these pages. On the 16th January, 1889, Lieutenant-Colonel Glencross and the officers of the regiment entertained at supper a number of ladies and gentlemen.[1] During the supper, Oliver Heywood, Esquire, the High Sheriff of Lancashire, asked permission to address the company. He

---

[1] Previous to the supper a concert had been given on behalf of the funds of the Salford Royal Hospital.

APPENDIX. 377

said: "Out of the fulness of the heart the mouth speaketh, and he felt that he could not allow the present occasion to pass without expressing the regret of those present and his own sorrow at the approaching departure of the regiment. The unfailing courtesy and genial hospitality of the XX would never be forgotten; they have entwined the red rose of Minden with the red rose of Lancashire."

THE ORDERS OF WOLFE.

THERE is in the 1st Battalion a small octavo volume[1] of one hundred pages, composed chiefly of regimental orders, published by Lieutenant-Colonel James Wolfe, when commanding the XX. They are all directed to improve the discipline and professional training of the regiment. They all appeal to the soldier's sense of honour, and tell him that by any irregularity, however trifling, he casts a reflection and stigma upon his regiment. The friendship, personal protection, and indulgence of the commanding officer is held out to the good soldiers. In matters of drill and instruction, the orders enter into the most minute detail. Vigilance and exact attention to duty were constantly impressed (and on occasions enforced) upon the officers. It is impossible, however interesting they might prove, to republish the whole or even a fraction of these orders.

But there is one set, under whose precepts the men of "Kingsley's" fought at Minden, and in the battles of the Seven Years' war. These have been handed down to succeeding generations as containing all that a soldier of the XX should be when before the enemies of his country. They are entitled, *Instructions for the XX Regiment* (in case the French land), given by Lieutenant-Colonel Wolfe, at Canterbury, 15th December, 1755.

"Whosoever shall throw away his arms in an action, whether officer, non-commissioned officer, or soldier (unless it appears they are damaged so as to be useless), either under pretence of taking up others that are of a better sort, or for any other cause whatsoever, must expect to be tried by a general court-martial for the crime. If a sergeant leave the platoon he is appointed to, or does not take upon

---

[1] A second edition, published in 1780. It was presented to the regiment by Sir T. N. O'Brien, K.C.M.G., Governor of Newfoundland. Sir Terence had served in the XX.

him the immediate command of it in case the officer falls, such sergeant shall be tried for his life as soon as a court-martial can be conveniently assembled. Neither officer, non-commissioned officer, or soldier is to leave his platoon, or abandon the colours, for a slight wound; while a man is able to do his duty, and can stand and hold his arms, it is infamous to retire.

"The battalion is not to halloo or cry out upon any account whatsoever, although the rest of the troops should do it, until they are ordered to charge with their bayonets; in that case, and when they are upon the point of rushing upon the enemy, the battalion may give a warlike shout and rush in.

"Before a battle begins, and while the battalion is marching towards the enemy, the officer commanding a platoon is to be at the head of his men, looking frequently back upon them to see that they are in order, the sergeant in the meanwhile taking his place in the interval, and the officers are not to go to the flanks of the platoons till they have orders, or a signal to do so, from the officer commanding the battalion, and this will only be given a little before the action commences.

"If the battalion should be crowded at any time, or confined in their ground, the Captain or officer commanding a grand division may order his centre platoon to fall back till the battalion can extend itself again, so as to take up its usual ground.

"All the officers upon the left of the colours are to be on the left of their platoons. The Captain of the piquet is to be on the left of his piquet, and the Ensign in the centre.

"Every grand division consisting of two companies, as they now are, is to be told off in three platoons, to be commanded by a Captain, a Lieutenant, and an Ensign, with a sergeant to each; the rest of the officers and non-commissioned officers are to be distributed in the rere to complete the files, to keep the men in their duty, and to supply the places of the officers or the sergeants that may be killed or dangerously wounded.

"Every musketeer is to have a couple of spare balls, an excellent flint in his piece, another or two in his pouch, and as much ammunition as he can carry.

"A soldier that takes the musket off his shoulder, and pretends to begin the battle without order, will be put to death that instant:—the cowardice or irregular proceedings of one man is not to put the whole in danger.

"A soldier that quits his rank, or offers to flag, is to be instantly put to death by the officer that commands that platoon, or by the officer or sergeant in rere of that platoon; a soldier does not deserve to live who won't fight for his King and country. If a non-commissioned officer or private man is missing from an action, and joins his company afterwards unhurt, he will be reputed a coward and a fugitive, and will be tried for his life.

"The drummers are to stay with their respective companies, to assist the wounded men.

"Every officer and every non-commissioned officer is to keep strictly to his post, and to preserve all possible order and obedience; the confusion occasioned by the loss of men, and the noise of artillery and musketry, will require every officer's strict attention to his duty.

"When the files of a platoon are disordered by the loss of men, they are to be completed afresh with the utmost expedition, in which officers and non-commissioned officers in the rere are to be aiding and assisting.

"Officers are never to go from one part of the battalion to another without orders, upon any pretence whatsoever.

"The eight companies of a battalion are never to pursue the enemy, without particular orders so to do; the piquet and grenadiers will be detached for that purpose, and the battalion is to march on in good order to support them.

"If the firing is ordered to begin by platoons, either from the wings or from the centre, it is to proceed in a regular manner till the enemy is defeated; or till the signal is given for attacking them with the bayonet.

"If we attack a body less in extent than the battalion, the platoons upon the wings must be careful to direct their fire obliquely, so as to strike upon the enemy; the officers to inform the soldiers of their platoons before the action begins, where they are to destroy them.

"There is no necessity for firing very fast; a cool well-levelled fire with the pieces carefully loaded, is much more destructive and formidable than the quickest fire in confusion.

"The soldiers are to take their orders entirely from the officers of the platoons, and they are to give them with all possible coolness and resolution. If a battalion in the front line should give way, and retire in disorder towards the second line, and towards that part of it where we are posted (according to the present order of battle), every other platoon, or every other company, is to march forward a little, leaving intervals opened for the disordered troops to go through, and after they are gone by the battalion forms into front and moves forward to take post in the first line from whence the broken battalion retired.

"If a battalion upon either flank gives way and is defeated, the piquet or grenadier company, wherever it happens to be, is to fall back immediately, without any confusion, and protect that flank of the regiment.

"The misbehaviour of any other corps will not affect this battalion, because the officers are determined to give the strongest proofs of their fidelity, zeal, and courage, in which the soldiers will second them with their usual spirit.

"If the order of battle be such (and the country admit of it) that it is necessary to make breaches in the enemy's line for the cavalry to fall in upon them, the grand divisions of the regiment are each to form a firing column of three platoons in depth, which are to march forward and pierce the enemy's battalion in four places, that the cavalry behind us may get in amongst them and destroy them. In such an attack only the first of the three platoons should fire, immediately present their bayonets, and charge. These four bodies are to be careful not to run into one another in their attack, but to preserve the intervals at a proper distance.

"All attacks in the night are to be made with the bayonet, unless when troops are posted with no other design than to alarm, harass, or fatigue the enemy, by firing into their outposts or into their camp.

"If intrenchments or redoubts are to be defended obstinately, the fire is to begin in a regular manner, when the enemy is within shot, at about two hundred yards, and to continue till they approach very near; and when the troops perceive that they endeavour to get over the parapet, they are to fix their bayonets, and make a bloody resistance.

"All small parties that are intended to fire upon the enemy's columns, or marches upon their advance guard, or their rere, are to post themselves so as to be able to annoy the enemy without danger, and to cover themselves with light breastworks of sod, behind the hedges, or with trees, or walls, or ditches, or any other protection; that if the enemy returns the fire it may do no mischief. These parties are to retire to some other place of the same kind, and fire in the same manner, constantly retiring when they are pushed.

"But when a considerable detachment of foot is posted to annoy the enemy upon their march, with orders to retire when attacked by a superior force, the country behind is to be carefully examined, and some parties to be sent off early to post themselves in the most advantageous manner to cover the retreat of the rest; this is always to be done in all situations when a considerable body is commanded to retire.

"If an intrenchment is to be attacked, the troops should move as quick as possible towards the place—not in a line, but in small firing columns of three or four platoons in depth, with small parties between each column, who are to fire at the top of the parapet when the columns approach, to divert the enemy's fire, and to facilitate their passing the ditch and getting over the parapet, which they must endeavour to do without loss of time.

"It is of little purpose to fire at men who are covered with an intrenchment; but by attacking in the manner above mentioned one may succeed.

"If the seat of war should be in this strong enclosed country, it will be managed chiefly by fire, and every inch of ground that is proper for defence disputed with the enemy, in which case the soldiers will soon perceive the advantage of levelling their pieces properly; and they will likewise discover the use of several evolutions that they may now be at a loss to comprehend. The greater facility they have in moving from place to place and from one enclosure to another (either together or in separate bodies), without confusion or disorder, the easier they will fall upon the enemy with advantage, or retire when it is proper so to do, sometimes to draw the enemy into a dangerous position, at other times to take possession of new places of defence that will be constantly prepared behind them.

"If the battalion attacks another of nearly equal extent, whose flanks are not covered, the grenadiers and piquet may be ordered to detach themselves and surround the enemy, by attacking their flank and rere, while the eight companies charge them in front. The grenadiers and piquet should, therefore, be accustomed to these sort of movements, that they may execute their orders with a great deal of expedition.

"If the battalion is to attack another battalion of equal force, and of like number of ranks, and the country quite open, it is highly probable that, after firing a few rounds, they will be commanded to charge them with their bayonets, for which the officers and men should be prepared.

"If the centre of the battalion is attacked by a column, the wings must be extremely careful to fire obliquely. That part of the battalion against which the column marches must reserve their fire, and if they have to put two or three bullets in their pieces, it must be done. When the column is within about twenty yards they must fire with a good aim, which will necessarily stop them a little.

"This body may then open from the centre, and retire by files towards the wings of the regiment, while the neighbouring platoons wheel to the right and left, and either fire, if they are loaded, or close up and charge with their bayonets.

"If a body of foot is posted behind a hedge, ditch, or wall, and, being attacked by a superior force, is ordered to retire, the body should move off by files, in one or more lines, as perpendicular as possible to the post they leave, that when the enemy extend themselves to fire through the hedges, the object to fire at may be as small as possible, and the march of the retiring body as quick as possible.

"The death of an officer commanding a company or platoon shall be no excuse for the confusion or misbehaviour of that platoon, for while there is an officer or non-commissioned officer left alive to command, no man is to abandon his colours and betray his country.

"The loss of the Field Officers will be supplied (if it should so happen) by the Captains, who will execute the plan of the regiment with honour.

"If the battalion should have the misfortune to be invested in their quarters (or in a post which they are not commanded to defend) by a great superiority they have but one remedy, which is to pierce the enemy's line or lines in the night, and get off. In this case the battalion attacks with their ranks and files closed, with their bayonets fixed, and without firing a shot. They will be formed in an attack suited to the place they are in.

All possible means will be used, no doubt, to surprise them; but if they are found in arms, they are to be vigorously attacked with the bayonet. It is needless to think of firing in the night, because of the confusion it creates, and the uncertainty of hitting any object in the dark. A column that receives the enemy's fire, and falls immediately in amongst them, must necessarily defeat them, and create a very great disorder in the army.

"The men should consider that they are upon the point of entering into a war for the defence of their country against an enemy who has long meditated the destruction of it; that a drunken, vicious, irregular army is but a poor defence to a state; but that virtue, courage, and obedience in the troops are a sure guard against all assaults; that the troops that are posted in this country are designed to repel the enemy's first attempt; and that they should be in readiness to execute their part with honour and spirit, and not give themselves up to every excess, and to every irregularity in times like these; both officers and soldiers should exert themselves in every part of their duty, and show their countrymen that they deserve their esteem and consideration; and they should endeavour in a particular manner to recommend themselves to His Majesty, and to the Captain-General, for their zeal, fidelity, and valour."

EXTRACT FROM A MINDEN LETTER.

The following is an extract from a letter written by Lieutenant John Thompson, XX Regiment, in the hospital of Minden, on the 18th August, 1759. The original letter and an umbrella (the latter taken from the pocket of a French officer on the field of Minden) were presented to the officers of the 1st Battalion on the 24th August, 1869, by Mr. R. E. Thompson, of Kenfield, the representative of the Thompson family:—

"Hospital at Minden, August 18th, 1759.

"Dear Sir,—Agreeable to promise and inclination, I take the earliest opportunity of paying my respects to yourself and the good family at Pethem, this being the first day my health would admit of so long a letter. My wounds, I thank God, are, by report of my surgeons, now in a good way, but by no means free from great pain at times both day and night: insomuch that my surgeons cannot prevent frequent attacks of fever, which consequently raises inflammation. When I reflect on the miraculous escape (which is and will be every hour of my life) that my friends and self had by coming out of the field alive, it fills me with a just sense of the power and goodness of the great God above. I shall attempt by giving you a sketch of the proceedings of that day, notwithstanding I am certain a much abler pen than mine must fall greatly short, as no words can sufficiently paint the horrors and shocking sights which were every moment presented to the eyes of the living. At one in the morning of the glorious 1st of August, we received orders to turn out accoutred with all speed. The regiment was under arms in less than eight minutes— our tents left standing and baggage unpacked. Notwithstanding all this, a very few thought of an action, as we had often been alarmed in the same way. Exactness is always highly necessary. We marched towards Minden about two miles, found many regiments preparing, and the English on their march. At length the scene appeared; a battery of six guns began to play on the camp we had left. Very smartly we proceeded about a mile further, joined the Brunswick troops of infantry and our own and got into a regular line of battle march. Everything was still quiet before us until we got half a mile further; when we discovered the enemy with the greatest advantage over us, being already formed in battle array ready to receive us. On the immediate sight of us, they opened a battery of eighteen heavy cannon, which, from the nature of the ground (which was a plain), flanked this regiment in particular every foot we marched. Their cannon was ill-served at first, but they soon felt us, and their shot took place so fast, that every officer imagined the battalion would be taken off before we could get up to give a fire; notwithstanding we were then within a quarter of a mile of their right wing, and absolutely running up to the mouth of their cannon; in front, I had heads, legs, and arms taken off, flying into the front, a fire every moment; my right hand file of men, not more than a foot from me, were all by one ball dashed to pieces and their blood flying all over me. This, I must confess, staggered me not a little, but on my receiving a contusion in the bend of my right arm by a spent musket shot, it steadied me immediately. All apprehensions of hurt vanished; revenge and the care of the company I commanded took place, and was *then* much more at ease than at *this* time. By this time, we were within two hundred yards or less of them, and plainly perceived that the Fusiliers, Stewart's, and Napier's regiments were engaged. All this time their right wing was pelting us both with small arms, cannon, and grape shot.

"Just at this time I got wounded, after having been hit three times before by spent balls. But this seared me like red-hot iron, found myself fainting, and quitted the regiment, after having called for a fresh officer, but found no one to supply my place, several being (gone off) badly wounded or already dead. I had got four rods in the rear, but I heard the battalion fire, which pleased me so much in my agony that I stood stupefied, looking on them; many poor soldiers passing, begging me to come off. After a few moments I recovered my senses, and found I had no further business there, and made the best of my way, which was slow enough, over about a mile of common, where the balls came as thick as in front. By this time a soldier of the regiment, slightly wounded in the leg, came up, offering me his assistance; while supporting me his left leg was carried away by a cannon ball, the wind of which fairly turned me round but did not hurt me otherwise. The poor man is since dead. The common was strewed with dead and wounded men and horses. On the leeward side of those horses, quite dead, lay wounded soldiers that could not get any further, to shelter them from the small shot. The action came on in such hurry that we did not know where to look for the surgeons. Captain Parr and self walked three miles in this condition before we could get the blood stopped; at last we fortunately met my Lord George Sackville's coach and a surgeon he had in reserve for himself, which he need not have had, as there was no danger of his being hurt, as you will soon find out by the *vox populi*. We have little or no intelligence here, but find the enemy are intrenching by Hesse-Cassell, and the Duke alone at their heels. At least 10,000 of them have deserted. George is with me, to whom I owe my life from his great care before I came here, being two nights in a barn. I hope to have the satisfaction to hear from you soon, the more letters from a family the greater comfort. To whom as well to other friends I beg my best respects.

"From Sir,
"Your obedient servant,
"(Signed) THOS. THOMPSON.

"I hope the nation is now satisfied, as there was plenty of blood for their money."

LETTER FROM FIELD-MARSHAL LORD SEATON, G.C.B., TO MAJOR-GENERAL P. BAINBRIGGE.[1]

THIS letter was written to correct an inaccurate statement which appeared in Cannon's *Historical Records* of the XX (published 1850), as to the officer who commanded the 1st Battalion from the 10th September to the 6th October, 1799, and in the actions which were fought on and between the dates mentioned:—

"Deer Park, Honiton, Devon,
"December 5th, 1850.

"My dear Bainbrigge,—In respect to the queries contained in your letter of the 30th November, I think I can give you a more accurate statement of the movements of the XX and the officers in

---

[1] Eldest son of Brevet-Lieutenant-Colonel Bainbrigge, who was shot at the head of the 1st Battalion at the second battle of Egmont-op-Zee on the 6th October, 1799.

command from the 10th September to the 6th October, 1799, than appears in the records which you have inspected.

"Your father joined the XX at Preston, in June or July, before the formation of the two battalions.

"Lieutenant-Colonel Smyth and Major Ross were wounded on the 10th September, removed on the following day to the Helder, and did not join again till the return home of the battalion. Your father took the command of the 1st Battalion, after Colonel Smyth was wounded, and continued in the command of it till the day he was killed, on the 6th October.

"On the advance from the Zuype, on the 2nd October, he desired me to take the command of the Light Company, after Powlett was wounded.

"Several companies were slightly engaged about four or five p.m. in the sandhills. On the 3rd, the brigade marched into Egmont-op-Zee, the enemy having abandoned it in the morning.

"The action of the 6th was brought on, accidentally, by the advance of the Russians, with the intention of occupying certain posts in front of Beverwycke, and the movement of Sir R. Abercromby, to support them, when they were repulsed. The French followed up their success, and advanced in great force towards Egmont.

"The two battalions of the XX marched from their quarters about two p.m. Your father rode by the left, and spoke to me as he passed to take the command of the 1st Battalion; we were advancing in line towards the smoke, but not under fire. He had been at Alkmaar in the morning with several officers, not supposing that the brigade was likely to move. He must have been shot half an hour after he was at the head of the battalion. *Some of the companies on the right charged into the enemy's line, and were mixed with the French corps at the close of the evening. Captain Chalmers mentioned to me that he had in hands a French General for a short time.*

"All the regiments after dark were in great disorder. The French withdrew at night, leaving their posts in front of Beverwycke.

"Captain Power commanded the 1st Battalion on the retreat from Egmont-op-Zee to the Zuype, on the 7th and 8th October, till its arrival in England.

"We have not met for a long time. I hope you and your family are quite well.

"Believe me,
"Yours very sincerely,
(Signed) "SEATON."

GENERAL BAINBRIGGE'S NARRATIVE OF RONCES-VALLES AND SAUROREN.

THIS brief account of the battle of the Pyrenees, and of the events immediately antecedent, was written from memory by him at the request of his children about forty years since. General Bainbrigge lost his arm in that engagement when in the XX Regiment.[1] The following corps composed the 4th Division in 1813, commanded by Lieutenant-General Sir Lowry Cole, G.C.B.:— Right Brigade (Major-General Anson): 40th (1st Battalion), 48th (1st Battalion), and 27th (3rd Battalion) Regiments. Centre Brigade (Colonel Stubbs): Portuguese, 11th and 23rd Regiments of line, 7th Regiment Cacadores. Left Brigade (Major-General Ross): 7th and 23rd Fusiliers, XX Regiment, and one company Brunswick Oel Rifles. A weak provisional battalion composed of the 2nd Queen's, 53rd Regiment, one company 60th Rifles, a brigade of twelve-pounders, King's German Legion.

MARSHAL SOULT'S EXPEDITION TO RELIEVE PAMPELUNA.

About the middle of the month of May, 1813, the divisions of the allied army quitted their winter quarters. The officers and men were all delighted at the prospect of once more leaving Portugal, and this proved to be their final adieu. From St. Jas de Piscara, the headquarters of the 4th Division, where my regiment had been cantoned, we descended the Douro to Almendra at the confluence of the Coa, and crossed the Douro to the province of Trasos Montes, using a sort of ferry boat, which was secured by a rope with pulleys slung across the river from bank to bank, and by the aid of which we were drawn over the rapid foaming torrent.

The division halted at Terre del route Corvo, part of our brigade being left to assist in dragging the guns up the steep bank, which after much labour and perseverance was accomplished before night. A liberal supply of tents had been provided for this campaign, a decided improvement on the old system of bivouacking. We met no enemy until we reached the river Esla, where our Light Dragoons had an affair, and captured an advanced cavalry piquet. We crossed the Esla by means of a pontoon bridge, thence traversing Leonard

---

[1] General J. H. Bainbrigge was a younger son of Colonel Philip Bainbrigge, who was shot at the head of the XX at Egmont-op-Zee on the 6th October, 1799.

Castile to the river Ebro. It might in truth be deemed an excursion of pleasure; to me it was so; and I pass over several trifling affairs in which we were engaged, the particulars of which I forget. The decisive battle of Vittoria was fought on the 23rd of June, 1813. After witnessing with deep interest Sir Rowland Hill's attack on the heights on the enemy's extreme left, where Colonel Cadogan of the 71st Highlanders was killed, our division passed the Zadora at the bridge of Nanclares, and the ground vacated by us was occupied by the Household Brigade of cavalry; we lay down under a bank by the river side, which covered us from the fire of a French battery. The round shot passed without doing any harm, but the shells from their howitzers pitched close, and a tedious half hour was beguiled in watching them explode; several of our men were hit by the splinters. At length our Portuguese Brigade was ordered to stand up and charge the battery; the guns were captured, and with them the colours of the 100th French regiment of the line. We then stood to our arms and advanced across the plain, sometimes in line, sometimes in column, but the enemy abandoned every position as we approached, before we could close with him, and as evening advanced his retrograde movement assumed the character of a total rout. The 4th Division did not enter Vittoria, but, leaving the city on the left hand, we pursued the retreating enemy, without halting, until it was quite dark.

The regular roads were impassable for troops, being literally choked up with guns, carriages, wagons, and baggage of every description. This very tempting booty was passed untouched by any of us, but it was not long before it was taken possession of and plundered by the Spaniards in our rear, or by camp followers and stragglers. I have heard it asserted, on good authority, that upwards of one million sterling, in money and bills, was carried off by these people, and consequently lost to the victorious army as prize money. Silver coin in dollar (chiefly) was so plentiful for the first few days in our camp, that I recollect ten dollars (or five-franc pieces) being offered in exchange for a guinea or a bill of exchange on the agents. At daylight on the 22nd, we resumed our march; the 3rd, 4th, 7th, and Light Divisions followed the touch of the main body of the French army on the road to Pampeluna; and Sir Thomas Graham, with the left wing of the allies, pursued General Foy's corps towards St. Sebastian and Bayonne.

Few prisoners were taken, because the whole material of the French army having been abandoned at Vittoria, nothing remained to obstruct their retreat, which gave them the advantage in marching, and it behoved them to be quick in their movements, for they had no ammunition but such as was left in the pouches of the soldiers. The garrison of Pampeluna having been hastily completed by four thousand men, King Joseph hurried through the pass of Roncesvalles and halted at St. Jean Pied de Port, where he established his headquarters. Here the corps of the French army were reorganised and newly equipped, preparatory to taking the field again under the direction of Marshal Soult, who, having been commissioned by the Emperor as his Lieutenant, hoped to retrieve the reputation of the once invincible army, by forcing the allies to recross the Ebro and establishing his line on that river. On arriving near the walls of Pampeluna, Lord Wellington ordered the 7th Division, together with a corps of Spaniards, to commence the investment of that fortress, whilst he, with the remaining three divisions, pushed on towards Tafalla, in expectation of intercepting General Clausel's corps, which had been prevented joining the French army previous to the battle of Vittoria, by the rapidity of our advance from Portugal, and now the overthrow and retreat of the King cut off this corps from the main army, and its present position was extremely critical. Clausel, an experienced General, well acquainted with the country and the population of this part of Spain, obtained due information of our near approach; he consequently directed his course on Tudela and Zaragossa, abandoned some of his artillery, and, by incessant marching night and day, he succeeded in eluding his pursuers, and subsequently crossed the mountains by the pass of Iacca, and joined Marshal Soult at St. Jean Pied de Port in time to take part in the expedition to raise the blockade of Pampeluna. The 4th Division, forming part of the investing force, was then ordered to advance to the frontier. On arriving at Roncesvalles about the 20th July, we encamped near the villages of Espinal and Viscaret. Major-General Byng's brigade of the 2nd Division, Colonel Campbell's Portuguese brigade, and General Morillo's Spanish corps were at that time posted in our front; the 3rd Division was stationed at Olaque, a day's march in our rear. The 7th and Light Divisions had been sent far away to our left, to Vera, to cover the siege of St. Sebastian. Lord Hill watched the frontier about Mayor and in the valley of Bustan. The blockade of Pampeluna was now entrusted entirely to the Spaniards.

On the morning of the 24th July, Major-General Robert Ross, commanding our brigade, viz., 7th, XX, 23rd Regiments, and a company of Brunswick Oels riflemen, sent his aide-de-camp, Lieutenant Thomas Falls, of the XX, accompanied by an officer of General Morillo's staff, from Espinal to ascertain whether artillery could pass from Roncesvalles to Zindour by the mountain road to Maya and Val Carlos, where Campbell's Portuguese were in bivouac; two Spanish regiments were at that time in front with a strong piquet occupying an old redoubt. The following notes, taken by my friend Lieutenant Falls, are interesting, and go to show how much was owing to the untiring energy and activity of the late lamented "Major-General Robert Ross." I have always been of opinion that to him chiefly credit is due for preventing a surprise on the morning of the 28th July, and preserving the allied army from a terrible disaster:—"On returning from Espinal to the front the sentries told me they had obtained a man who appeared very cautiously moving along the front, feeling his way towards our line of sentries. I gave directions for him to be sent to the Major-General under an escort. On my arrival at Espinal to report my observations on the state of the roads, as well as on the manner the position appeared to me to be guarded, the General showed me a piece of soiled paper that had been sent to him by someone unknown, on which was written in Spanish, 'A good Spaniard begs to inform the officer commanding the advanced post that he will be attacked by a very powerful force to-morrow morning at half-past eight o'clock.'

"From the circumstance also of the spy having been sent in, and with a view of getting the XX and the 7th Fusiliers into the pass, the General told Brigade-Major Westcott and myself that he had determined in his own mind to push these two regiments forward, and give them some time to take a little rest, so as to enable them to be ready for any sudden work that might occur.

"The 23rd Fusiliers were to remain at Espinal, and not to move until they saw a white table-cloth hoisted on a sergeant's pike as a signal, when they were to move forward, and the baggage was to be packed and brought to the place where it had been proposed to form a camp, from the favourable report I had made of the ground compared with the filth of Viscaret, where a vast number of French soldiers had congregated after the battle of Vittoria, and died of typhus fever, heaps of their old clothing were still lying in the gardens adjoining. The monthly muster was to take place at five p.m., and commanding officers were then called upon to direct their men to lie down and take rest, so as at two o'clock in the morning we should march to the pass. I secured the Padrone of my quarter and placed a sentry at his window, and then lay down in my cloak before his bedroom door, having ascertained that he knew the very intricate pathway to the pass. We started at the appointed time; the road was very narrow and difficult to traverse, being intersected by fallen beech trees, so that we did not arrive at the top until seven o'clock. The whole of the position had the appearance of perfect quietness; the men in Colonel Campbell's camp were undressed, as we could observe with our glasses; they were certainly not on the *qui vive*, so that we concluded that the warning of our approaching attack was without the least foundation. The General and I then rode to the Spanish piquet in the old redoubt (or field work thrown up on the occasion of some previous war); we got into the midst of this piquet of a hundred men at least, without having been challenged or of any of them being aware of our presence, though sentries were posted, and on General Ross remonstrating with the officer in command on his extreme negligence, he excused himself by observing 'Two battalions of the regiment of Toledo were in his front.' It turned out, however, on further inquiry, that these two battalions had moved off in the course of the preceding night, and without any intimation having been given to this piquet, or to the regiment belonging to General Byng's brigade posted in a dell to their right towards Roncesvalles. As everything appeared so perfectly quiet, the General desired me to write a brigade order on one of my cards, viz., 'Camp equipage and bullocks with ammunition to close up, and the whole of the brigade to encamp on the plateau near the springs.' I then gave the order to hoist the signal agreed upon, and was proceeding to send the order by the first available officer I could meet with of the brigade, when I heard the General's voice calling me back. He said, 'The enemy are this instant attacking Byng; tear up your card and write another order':—viz., 'The whole of the ammunition mules to close up; all spare mules to be sent up also with rum and biscuit; baggage to be packed and kept in readiness to move off to the position in the rear. Guides to be instantly secured in the village to point out the way to Major-General Anson's brigade, and to the Portuguese brigade of the 4th Division.'"

The light companies of our own brigade now moved forward under Major Rose, of the XX, and became quiet spectators of the attack going on against General Byng, on the extreme right. The XX got into position and then piled arms; the 7th Fusiliers were still labouring slowly up the mountain to join us, and the Light Companies in front had been ordered to lie down, when a sergeant of the Brunswick Oels company came near and said that he observed dust rising above the trees of the forest below us, towards Val Carlos. Not long after we could distinctly observe parties of the enemy in advance feeling their way through the brushwood towards our front. About this time General Ross rode to our front and ordered the left wing of the XX to stand to their arms and to follow him up another path near the ascent of the mountain; the right wing with the colours remained below, but we moved forward to a place where our front was more contracted with thick copsewood on either flank. We lost sight of the left wing: they advanced some distance on a sort of table land above, when suddenly, in an undulation of the ground, they found themselves in the presence of a French column, the 6th Regiment Legère, and in distant windings of the road to Val Carlos, glimpses of the French army were obtained in full march. No time was to be lost—decision was necessary—General Ross instantly ordered the wing to the right about, except the rear company, and he called on Captain Tovey, whose dauntless and impetuous spirit prompted him to seize this opportunity to distinguish himself, marched his company deliberately up to the French column, and gave the word to charge. Nobly did this little band of heroes obey their officer's command. They closed in upon their adversaries, who, for the moment, appeared paralysed by this sudden and unexpected assault. Many of their front ranks fell. One of our men bayoneted the French Colonel Commandant, and his bayonet broke off short at the socket by the violence of the pitch he gave after the thrust. In the confusion which followed, Tovey ordered his company to retire "double quick," and, strange to say, the majority of the men made good their retreat. The right wing stood ready to receive the pursuing enemy at the narrow part of the ridge below, having a dense thicket on either side. When the retreating wing and the stragglers of Tovey's company had passed, closely pursued by the French, their drums beating the "*Pas de charge*," their officers vehemently leading on their men, we opened a deliberate and deadly fire, which checked their onward course.

I do not think that one of their men who may have succeeded in getting past our line ever returned to tell the tale. No prisoners were taken that day to my knowledge. Before the true cause of the retrograde movement could be accounted for, I was standing close to Major Bent, who commanded the Grenadiers, wondering what dire misfortune had happened, when Colonel Wade, Sir Lowry Cole's aide-de-camp, rode up and said: "My dear Bent, I entreat you on no account to yield an inch of this ground, or Byng and the Spaniards yonder will be cut off." Bent replied: "You know us, and may rely on our doing all we can." He did know us right well, for he had been our Adjutant, and he it was who taught me to mount guard. He perceived that all was right and, with a smile on his handsome countenance, galloped off.

The promise was fulfilled; we held our ground until our ammunition was expended, and then we were relieved by the 7th or 23rd Fusiliers (I am not sure which). Poor Bent (who was afterwards killed while commanding the regiment at the battle of Orthes) and two Lieutenants, Champagné and Crokat, were all severely wounded and carried off the field; leaving me at the close of this struggle and most important combat in command of the Grenadier company of one of the most distinguished of regiments—a proud position to be in for so young an officer. The wounded who could bear removal were immediately sent to the rear; several of the officers contrived to reach Vittoria, but Lieutenant-Colonel Wallace, a fine old veteran soldier, died on the way. Having obtained a fresh supply of ammunition and the usual allowance of ration, rum and biscuit, we lighted fires and tried to make ourselves comfortable. These fires were kept burning all night, and after our departure; the object was to deceive the enemy, who thought we remained in position. Amongst others we had a very melancholy duty to perform here: a grave was dug beneath some stunted oaks, and the body of our Adjutant (Frank Buist) was laid in it, wrapped in his military cloak. We all regretted poor Buist, for he was a kind-hearted man, and he left a widow and family of young children to mourn their loss. (This bereavement I had been early taught to feel myself, and I can sympathise with those whose fathers fall in battle.) The wounded who were too much hurt to be capable of being removed from the ground were collected and placed near the fires; small cards were then pinned on their jackets, having a few words written on each in French, consigning them to the mercy of our gallant enemy. This appeal was strictly attended to.

As soon as it became sufficiently dark to screen our movements from the French sentries, the brigade was ordered to fall in silently, leaving a piquet with instructions to keep the men as much as possible walking about in front of the fires so as to attract the notice of any patrols of the enemy who might be on the lookout. We commenced our retreat from the Lindouz, the mountain where we bivouacked after the action, and a memorable night-march it was.

A fog came on towards the evening of the 25th, whilst we were still engaged, and it hung on the mountains several hours after the sunrise next day; this enabled us to pursue our march unseen; and fortunate it was for us it was so, for, loaded as English soldiers always are, it would have proved no easy matter to ascend the very steep Mendichure Pass with a bold enterprising enemy like the French pressing on our rear, and the number of wounded multiplying, in fact difficulties appearing at every step. It became pitch dark as soon as we entered the beech wood, above the village of Espinal, and men frequently fell into deep holes or stumbled over roots and boughs of trees, and unavoidably tripped up others in their fall. These accidents, though trifling in themselves, caused infinite confusion and many tedious and vexatious halts. I find a difficulty in attempting to describe my feelings at the moment when the order was issued to fall in preparatory to the brigade moving off the ground. Wounded men knew they were to be left behind; poor fellows, they resigned themselves to their cruel fate without murmuring, contenting themselves with bidding farewell to their comrades, and sending kind messages to their friends at home. The reflections produced in my mind on this occasion were rendered still more painful by the long dismal howling of the wolves, scared from their usual haunts by the day's tumult in these wild and unfrequented regions. Instances of true friendship unquestionably exist in every corps on active service, yet I am inclined to think, when fighting becomes habitual, that self then becomes a predominant principle; the satisfaction naturally experienced in having escaped one's self prevents the mind from dwelling long on the misfortunes of others. On getting into the Roncesvalles road a little before daybreak, we had well-nigh fallen into a scrape with the cavalry piquet belonging to the rear-guard of Major-General Byng's column, also in full retreat. We halted to enable our own piquet and the stragglers to come up; when this had been effected, we formed in sub-divisions at half-quarter distance and moved on again, the cavalry of General Byng's rear-guard being instructed that now they might look out for a real enemy and no mistake.

The French skirmishers came up with us at noon, and a squadron of light cavalry joined in the attack on our divisional rear-guard under an officer of the 48th Regiment; they experienced rather a rough reception and kept at a respectful distance during the remainder of the retreat. The rear-guard then joined the division which had got into position beyond the town of Linzoain. We were in march along this ridge in course of the evening, when Sir Thomas Picton met us. One of our men who knew Sir Thomas recognised the gallant General at a distance, and exclaimed, "Here comes old Tommy; now boys, make up your minds to fight." Sir Thomas held a folded umbrella in his hand; he rode up to Major Westcott, and in his usual blunt manner asked "Where the devil are you going?" "The division is retreating, sir, by Sir Lowry's orders," was the reply. "Then he's a d——d fool." Halt your brigade instantly, the 3rd Division is coming up. He passed on to find Sir Lowry Cole, who happened to be with the rear-guard at that moment. This sudden halt turned out fortunate for us; it had the effect of checking the enemy's advance. The French General might feel unwilling to fight until the cause of this halt had been ascertained; he might have been deceived as to our real strength; his infantry were up and his cavalry and artillery all through the passes. A vigorous attack therefore must have proved very hurtful to us, to say the least, and if successful, which I think it would have been, our line of retreat was so encumbered with baggage, strings of mules laden with commissariat stores, and other hindrances, that the consequences would have been ruinous. We remained in this position till about midnight; in the meanwhile, Sir Thomas Picton had seen enough to satisfy himself that further retreat was necessary, and coincided with Sir Lowry Cole's view of affairs. As soon as it became dark, therefore, we were put in full retreat for the heights covering the approach to Pampeluna. We passed the 3rd Division, which now took the rear; and Sir Thomas Picton, as senior officer, took command of the entire force, which, including Spaniards and Portuguese, could not number less than 16,000 men. Nothing particular occurred during this march. The 4th Division proceeded down the valley of the Zubiri to about six or seven miles distance from Pampeluna, when it wheeled to the right and we moved along a mountain ridge, which stretches between the valley of the Zubiri and that of the little river Lanz, and screens the view of the level ground between it and Pampeluna. The 3rd Division passed on to the valley of Huarte and occupied the heights about that place. Whilst we were marching to take up our position, we had an opportunity of witnessing a novel sort of charge executed by a Spanish regiment belonging to the force investing the fortress of Pampeluna. A numerous party of the enemy's tirailleurs endeavoured to establish themselves on a hill occupied by the Spaniards; near our line of march, they ran vigorously at the French, who gave way as they approached; and our men declared that in the hurry they had neglected to fix their bayonets. They had a practical lesson afforded them next day on the use of that weapon, for Sir Lowry Cole, seeing the importance of retaining the hill, sent the 40th Regiment down to give them support; and this regiment remained in position there all night.

In the action on the ensuing day, it was conspicuous for many brilliant charges with the bayonet. Evening had set in when Lord Wellington had joined the retreating army. I can never forget the joy which beamed in every countenance when his Lordship's presence became known; it diffused a general feeling of confidence through the ranks. From that moment we had none of those dispiriting murmurs on the awkwardness of our situation, etc., etc., so common in our army whenever a retreat was ordered; now we talked of driving the French over the frontier again as a matter of course. Soon after reaching our halting ground, and after the companies had piled arms, Lord Wellington rode up to the head of the regiment, and, dismounting, took a spy-glass which was offered to him by one of our officers. He continued some time silently surveying the dark line of French troops moving along the brow of a hill, until Major-General Ross remarked that "this time Soult certainly meditated an attack." Without taking his eye from the glass, he replied, quickly, "It is just probable that I shall attack him." These words being overheard and repeated, we already felt confident of victory, only regretting that of necessity a night must intervene.

Lord Wellington, if I recollect rightly, was dressed in his usual grey frock coat, buttoned close up to the chin, and his little cocked hat, covered with oil skin, without a feather. There is certainly something peculiarly striking in the appearance of this great General: his quick glancing eye, prominent Roman nose, pointed chin, and compressed lip; altogether he impresses one with the idea of a more than ordinary man, and there can be no doubt that he does possess very largely that decision of character so essential in a commander. From Roncesvalles, the French army followed closely our line of march, until we turned from the right from the valley of the Zubiri, to take up our position on the Lanz; then their 1st Army corps, under General Clausel, wheeled also to the right and formed in position on a mountainous ridge, parallel with ours, their right extending to the village of Sauroren, in the valley of the Lanz, which they occupied in force. There was a deep valley or ravine between us, thickly studded with pine trees and bushes. In a direct line the two armies could not be more than five hundred yards apart, and the sentries of the piquets were within speaking distance. The two armies had so frequently been in the presence of each other, and accustomed to the same honourable system of warfare, that sentinels were seldom, if ever, molested on their posts; many harassing duties and alarms were thus avoided.

The mountains presented a picturesque and animating scene, and as fuel was to be had for the mere labour of cutting, the bivouac everywhere resounded to the stroke of the bill-hook, fires were soon lighted, and water being within reach, our men commenced cooking their lean ration beef. The evening was calm and sultry, and it was a luxury to be enabled to stretch one's self on the sweet-scented thyme, so common in those mountains, and disencumbered of trappings, canteen, and haversack, the latter, however, very scantily provided. Though greatly fatigued after a long and tiresome day's march, I well recollect on this occasion I felt no disposition to sleep. I lay down to ruminate over the strange events of the last three days, and listening with more than interest to the *qui vive* of the French sentries. I had watched the quick promotion of several officers of my own standing in the army, whose regiments were in the Peninsula before we went out the second time, and now my dreams were all for advancement, to be placed on a par with them. With the light-heartedness of two-and-twenty, I was raised in my own estimation, in consequence of the command of the fine Grenadier company having devolved on me; many of the old hands of this splendid company (as it landed in the Peninsula) had served with my honoured father[1] in Holland. They looked on me, the son of one of their old commanders, with more than ordinary interest, and evinced a general readiness to serve me. I was not unmindful of their regard, but felt greatly attached to them for their kindness. In the course of the night we were visited by one of those terrific thunderstorms, so often remarked as the harbinger of victory to our army in Spain. It is remarkable that a similar tempest preceded the crowning victory of Waterloo. On the night before the battle of Salamanca, also a violent storm with vivid lightning occurred. Many of our cavalry troop horses took fright, broke away from their picket stakes, and galloped madly over the half-sleeping soldiers; many of them strayed into the enemy's lines, and several of these horses were recognised next day ridden by French staff officers. The rain now fell in torrents; in a few

---

[1] Colonel Philip Bainbrigge.

minutes all our fires were totally extinguished, the loud peals of thunder echoed back from rocks and ravines, became one continued roar, the lightning was so vivid that its flashes illuminated the surrounding hilly and wooded country, exhibiting in all their wretchedness the thoroughly drenched soldiers of both armies; many of them might be seen huddled together in small parties; others, rolled in their blankets or great coats, were apparently sleeping soundly, unconscious of the raging tempest. This, I apprehend, is a true picture of what frequently occurs when troops are "on bivouac," and it was exposed to view on this occasion by the vivid flashes of lightning. A splendid sunrise succeeded the midnight storm, and made amends for our comfortless nights; the men soon forgetting their troubles in the all-exciting employment of getting ready for the coming battle. The dress of several of our men, having undergone a change since last parade, caused a good deal of merriment amongst their comrades; these men had possessed themselves of some French Tirialleurs' trousers, and they considered this a fitting opportunity of wearing them. Our old threadbare greys had been terribly torn in the last hard work in the mountain passes. I remember when searching with a party for one of our wounded men (a fiddler), who fell amongst the bushes where we made our stand on the 25th, observing several dead bodies with bare legs, and now the mystery was solved. It is remarkable how quickly men slain in action are stripped, not by the soldiers, I imagine, but by the heartless camp followers, who make a trade of plundering the dead.

Bad men are never wanting in any army; these fellows quit their ranks on any trifling pretence, and take care to stop behind for the sake of plunder. Uniformity in dress cannot be adhered to in the field, before an enemy; our men had their clothes patched with cloth of all colours, anything they could get. The grand object of Marshal Soult's expedition was the relief of Pampeluna, which since the retreat of the French army, after the battle of Vittoria, had been invested, and now it was blocked by a Spanish force under the command of Counte de Brisfal.

The Marshal commenced the battle on the 28th July, by sending a column of infantry, preceded and flanked by numerous skirmishers, down the valley on our left. The river Lanz flows through this valley, with the Argea, a larger stream, near the little town of Villalba. Pampeluna stands on the Argea, about two miles lower down. Soult had calculated probably on being able, by a rapid movement, to turn our left, and then open communication with the fortress, by a road running parallel with the stream. An immense convoy of stores of all kinds and provisions followed the French army for the supply of the place, the whole of which fell into our hands a few days afterwards. At present circumstances seem to favour the attempt; if our brigade had been forced, and not stood its ground, the enemy would have encountered only a trifling opposition from the Spaniards, and he knew this well. The French Marshal had observed shortly before he put his troops in motion, reconnoitring between the village of Sauroren and the foot of our position, no British troops being discernible beyond our left; he was probably not aware of the near approach of another division to join us at this very critical moment.

Lord Wellington had reckoned on the junction of the 6th Division at an earlier hour; their march had been retarded by the thunderstorm. The delay was fatal to the French. The French army had been newly clothed and appointed since the battle of Vittoria, and though their greatcoats were worn over their uniforms, they nevertheless made a splendid appearance. Their columns swept down the valley at a rapid pace, exposed to a sharp fire from the 7th Portuguese Cacadores, under Lieutenant-Colonel O'Toole. This was an exciting time, one which I shall not readily forget. Thoughtless, no doubt, as young men usually are, yet I could not repress the idea that this day might prove my last on earth, and when the whizzing of passing bullets became more frequent, I think I had fully made up my mind to be hit. I have long been convinced that a man is not the worse soldier for being religious; indeed, I have heard of many proofs to the contrary; and I am willing to believe at a time like this (now described) I did commend the keeping of my soul to Almighty God, for I had been taught to think of the soul's inestimable value, and always to respect religion, by the precepts and example of an affectionate and truly pious mother. Such feelings, however, at such a moment, can be but transient. The excitement caused by the passing scene engrosses attention, and all idea of personal risk (if it ever had any place) is banished from the mind, and a calm succeeds as at an ordinary "Field Day." Such, at least, was my experience. We did not wait long before our turn arrived. The Cacadores were very hard pressed, and the XX received orders to advance to their support.

The Colonel pointed to a chapel on the hill side overlooking Sauroren; we formed into sub-divisions of companies, right in front, and closed up to half distance. Just as I expected to be ordered to halt my company, for the regiment to deploy into line, Lieutenant-

Colonel Wauchope desired me to file off the Grenadiers to the right, saying, "You will enter the wood, and do your best to check the advance of the enemy's column now entering it from the other side of the valley." In giving this order to me, I have always thought the Colonel committed an error; the regiment could ill afford to spare its best company, though reduced in numbers by its exertions and losses on the 25th. On arriving at the edge of the wood, I passed through the line of our Light Company, telling Lieutenant Fitzgerald that I had instructions to proceed on and feel for the enemy. When half way down the hill, I first met the French advance party. I fancied they were taken by surprise, but soon perceived that I had to contend with old soldiers who knew their work thoroughly. We at once commenced firing, and I retired slowly up the hill, inclining to my right, files a little extended and defending every stone and tree; the enemy stretched out to his right and left, and increasing rapidly in numbers, were turning both my flanks. About this time I brought down one of the enemy myself; observing him stationed in a bush very close to me, I took a musket from the man next to me, aimed deliberately and fired; he disappeared, and I saw no more of him. I doubt whether these men were Tirailleurs, though they were acting as light infantry, for the one I fired at wore a bearskin cap, like Guards; they were some of the finest looking soldiers I ever saw. My men gradually closed into the centre, and we expected to be quickly surrounded, for our enemies were gathering thick. Branches cut by bullets from the trees were falling fast around us. However, we still presented a bold front as we retired slowly upwards. On reaching the edge of the wood we found to our great joy. not an enemy, but a strong detachment belonging to Major-General Byng's brigade (the 27th or 48th, I did not ascertain which). Here I rallied my men, and, being well together, I determined on advancing again without communicating with the supporting detachment. The enemy fell back before us. Shortly after this advance, I received a musket shot through the elbow of my left arm, another ball struck me in the side, lodging in my back. It is possible the same bullet did all the mischief, as both wounds were received at the same time. I continued with my men as long as I was able to stand, when, becoming faint from loss of blood, I gave over the command of the company to a sergeant; and a corporal assisted me to the rear and placed me under the first bit of rising ground we came to, where I was sheltered from the enemy's fire. After this the company was forced up the hill again, then, uniting with the detachment before mentioned, the whole charged. The enemy turned when they heard the cheer, and both parties went down the hill together: in several instances friends and foes tumbling neck and heels over each other. The casualties were few, because our soldiers had been cautioned not to follow too far; when all was over, the few men who were left of this once fine company re-joined the regiment. My servant fortunately escaped, and in the course of the evening he joined me by desire of Major-General Ross; he related to me the last particulars, amongst other things that in the charge he had seen a Frenchman actually bayoneted fast to a tree. This must have been accidental, for there was nothing savage or cruel in our mode of warfare, quite the contrary. To revert to the period when I was detached with the Grenadiers, the company's column in the valley of the Lanz had proceeded downwards a considerable distance; then it was that the Portuguese skirmishers of the 6th Division were first observed coming over the brow of the mountains, on the opposite side of the river. We could not tell who they were, but did not remain long in suspense, for they commenced a straggling fire on the enemy in the valley below. The 1st Brigade of the 6th Division issuing from the foot of the mountains forded the Lanz a little above the village of Oricana, and immediately formed across the valley, extending their right to the extreme left of the 4th Division, and, blocking the road, presented a barrier to the further progress of the French column. In the valley, another brigade of the same division formed on the right bank of the stream. When it is taken into consideration that a well-sustained musketry fire was now directed into the closed ranks of the enemy's advancing column from three sides at once, an idea may be formed of the consequent slaughter. The marvel is that any escaped. Marshal Soult now became convinced of the impossibility of breaking through our line of defence; and though the contest was continued for some time longer, I believe it was with the sole view of extricating the army from the difficulty. His gallant soldiers fought nobly, and did their best to win this battle for him; and they displayed a discipline and devotion very rarely met with in any army. On our side the action was fought chiefly by the 4th and 6th Divisions, and was severest where Ross's brigade was stationed. On both sides of the chapel, opposite Sauroren, the army made a succession of desperate efforts to establish themselves on our position, but no sooner did the attack columns approach, and the dark moustached countenances of the men with their broad-topped chacoes appear

AA

through the smoke, than loud hurrahs made the forest ring again; and regiment after regiment, as opportunity offered or occasion required, charged with the bayonet, and forced them back in confusion, for no time was allowed them to recover breath, after the exertion of ascending the steep. Many a brave man fell this day by the bayonet; the ominous British cheer told what was coming and might have had some effect in checking the desire for a collision, but probably, in all corps, there are certain desperate fellows impelled by an impulse they cannot control, who run on to meet inevitable death. I must not omit to mention that the different regiments composing our brigade were separated from each other and acted independently; they did not form an unbroken line, owing, I presume, to the strong nature of the ground, and the extent of front which we were required to keep. In one of the enemy's desperate assaults on our right, a Portuguese regiment of Campbell's brigade was over forward and gave way. The French followed up this advantage with their usual cries of "*en evant, en evant,*" and penetrated so far as to oblige General Ross to fall back. What an anxious moment this must have been, though I have been informed the result of the battle was never considered doubtful. The General's horse was killed under him, and Lieutenant Falls, his aide-de-camp, was wounded. I think Falls had been previously wounded near the chapel. Many instances of hand-to-hand conflicts occurred, the circumstances attending which I am unable to narrate. The 27th and 48th Regiments united attacked the enemy, who had obtained a temporary footing on the position, and, charging with their accustomed gallantry, recovered it. Lord Wellington, from the rocky eminence in the rear, had watched the combat, and was fully aware how much the Fusilier brigade had been outnumbered, and was not unmindful of it. He was heard to express repeatedly his warm admiration of their steady conduct. At the close of the action they were withdrawn. Major-General Byng took their place in front with his brigade. The 6th Division having moved considerably up the Lanz towards Sauroren, the French withdrew to their original position; thus ended the battle of the 28th July, 1813. It is called the battle of the Pyrenees. Another victory was gained near Sauroren on the 30th of the same month, and more fighting occurred before the enemy finally quitted the Spanish territory; yet the combat of the 28th decided the fate of the expedition to relieve Pampeluna and to recover the line of the Ebro. The result of that day's fighting was unexpected, and worked powerfully on the mind of Marshal Soult. Immediately after the conflict he determined on sending back his train of artillery to France, and thus probably saved it from capture. The fighting, while it lasted, was unquestionably severe, and I have heard it termed "bludgeon work." Our old fellows performed their duty nobly, each individual exerting himself with energy, as though the fate of the battle depended on his own prowess. This is the way the old "Two Tens" were accustomed to fight; mortal men could do no more.

The old XX was jocularly termed in the division the "*Young Fusiliers*," a compliment unquestionably; but at that period the regiment was composed of hardy old veterans, men inured to war in Holland, in Egypt, and Calabria, in the Coruña retreat. Although composing part of the rear-guard, it lost fewer men by straggling than any other corps in Sir John Moore's army. On its return to the Peninsula in 1812, it was at the particular request of Sir Lowry Cole incorporated with the 4th Division and brigaded with the Fusilier regiments, "The men of Albuera." The XX was unfortunate in losing so many field officers:—Lieutenant-Colonel Wallace and Lieutenant-Colonel Wauchope were killed in the Pyrenees; Major Rose in leading the stormers of the division in the breach of St. Sebastian; and Major Bent fell at the head of the regiment at the battle of Orthes, all within a few short months. To revert to the period of my being wounded, I may add that I lay for a considerable time on the spot to which I had been removed until a Portuguese medical officer, attached to the commissariat, came accidentally to the same place. He was mounted on a pony, and pitying my forlorn situation assented to the request that he should accompany me to the village in our rear; this kind-hearted man helped me to get into the saddle, and, leading the way, took me to the town of Villalba. I had no difficulty in procuring a quarter, the inhabitants having fled in terror, abandoning their homes for fear of a sortie from the garrison of Pampeluna. Several medical officers had established themselves in the place, and were examining and dressing the wounds of such as arrived there from the field of battle. I took possession of a room with a nice bed in it; and at night Major-General Ross came to see me. With his usual liberality, he threw his purse on the bed, desiring that I should take what money I required. This was the last time I had the happiness of seeing my much esteemed General, an officer beloved by every soldier who served under him. At the termination of the war with France, he was selected to command an expedition sent direct from the army to America; and he was killed near Baltimore, after a career of victory, very deeply regretted by all his friends and the nation at large. In him the army lost one of its brightest ornaments, for he was endowed with uncommon talent for military command, and was a brave and accomplished soldier. Sir Philip Bainbrigge, my brother, who was in the Quartermaster-General's department, joined headquarters from a reconnoissance at the close of the action; on inquiry he learnt that I was wounded, and contrived to find me out in the course of the night. He urged my speedy removal from Villalba, because another battle might be fought next day, and sorties from the fortress of Pampeluna were frequent. He provided me with a horse to carry me to the baggage camp, which was two leagues on the other side of Pampeluna, and, as I said before, General Ross sent my servant from the regiment to take care of me. Weak and suffering as I was it would have been far pleasanter to remain where I lay, but the bare idea of risking being made a prisoner, in the event of a successful sortie, enabled me to make the exertion necessary, and in the morning I commenced the journey: my shattered arm tied up in a sash, and my servant leading the horse. The baggage was reached in the course of the same day; here I found my own mule and baggage all right; but as there was no surgeon to examine my wounds, I decided on proceeding to Vittoria at once, which place I reached in five days more. At Vittoria I had the satisfaction of meeting the three officers of my own company, who had been wounded a few days before me. We were lodged together in the same house. My arm, from some unaccountable mistake, was not amputated until the 12th August; mortification had commenced, yet through the mercy of God, the skill and unremitting attention of Staff-Surgeon Berry, and aided by a naturally vigorous constitution, I recovered. By the end of September, I was enabled to mount my horse and proceeded to Bilbao and embarked in October, on board a return transport for England. My wounds opened afresh on the voyage, which proved a most tempestuous one of five weeks. There happened to be no medical chest on board; and my only attendant (a sailor lad) manufactured a sort of adhesive plaster, to prevent the stump of the shoulder from protruding. Thus terminated my connection with the XX Regiment and that glorious Peninsular army. In simple justice to the conduct of our chivalrous enemy, I gladly avail myself of the opportunity of recording that when the French army evacuated the Spanish territory, our wounded men left behind us on the Heights of Lindouz were retaken; and they had been treated

APPENDIX. 405

with the most marked attention by the French surgeons; our men said they had been frequently complimented by French officers for the gallantry displayed by the regiment on the 25th July in the pass of Roncesvalles. The fact is, the enemy were astonished at the devotion they witnessed on that day, and no doubt it had the effect of making them more cautious how they advanced against us through the mist. In this short expedition of ten days the French, by their own showing, lost 15,000 men; our loss for the same period was above 6,000. On my arrival in England, on the recommendation of Major-General Ross, I was appointed to a company in the 2nd Battalion 41st Regiment. At the peace the battalion was reduced, and I was subsequently rewarded with Brevet rank for service in the field, having assisted in earning four badges for my regiment. I own that I feel disappointed in not obtaining a decoration, medals having been profusely bestowed on the Waterloo army. I am of opinion that a medal is the most appropriate reward for service in the field—one which I feel convinced would be most prized by a soldier. It would go far to show that the man had fought his country's battles, and that his scars and mutilated limbs were not the consequence of mere accident; and though I have no reason to complain individually for not having been rewarded, yet this omission caused General Sir William Napier to conclude his graphic history of the Peninsula campaigns with the quaint remark: "Thus the war terminated, and with it all remembrances of the veteran's services."

(Signed) J. H. B., Bt.-Major (unattached).
1841.

P.S. 1850.—The foregoing narrative was written several years ago for my children, who wished me to detail the circumstances attending the loss of my arm. Since that period our kind and considerate Queen (God bless her) has commanded a medal to be struck with clasps to record the battles of the Peninsula. True it is that few of the old veterans survive to receive this long-wished-for mark of their Sovereign's approval of past services; nevertheless, the justice of their claim to honourable distinction is at length conceded, and they are now, though diminished in numbers, enabled to meet their more fortunate comrades of Waterloo and India on terms of equality as regards military decorations. I have received four clasps, one Vimiera, two Corunna, three Vittoria, four Pyrenees, the only badges earned by the regiment during the period of my service; but, in my opinion, the regiment deserved an additional badge for Roncesvalles. It was specially mentioned in the published despatches, as having distinguished itself in defending the pass, and I repeat that the stubborn gallantry of Ross's brigade, more particularly the XX, in resisting the first impetuous attack, saved the army. As Ensign in the XX the regimental colours (with the *old Minden Rose*) were in my keeping through the entire Corunna retreat, always in the rearguard; after the battle of the 16th January, in a pitchy dark night we marched down to the beach to embark. Owing to a mistake of the naval officer in charge of the boat, the two Ensigns with the colours and about a dozen men were taken on board a wrong transport, at day light, without affording us the means to remove to our headquarters' ship, and probably fearing capture, for the enemy had brought several of their guns to bear upon the shipping, the Captain most improperly cut his cable and stood out to sea. Stormy weather in the Bay of Biscay detained us many days, and I did not see the regiment again until its arrival at Portsmouth two or three weeks afterwards. Poor Colonel Ross was delighted beyond measure to possess his colours again.

LETTERS OF CAPTAIN J. KINCAID, RIFLE BRIGADE, AND LIEUTENANT-COLONEL G. TOVEY,

On the charge of No. 6 Company, XX Regiment, under the latter officer, at Roncesvalles.

THESE letters appeared in the *United Service Journal* of 1839. They form part of a correspondence which was published in that journal during 1839-40, on the subject of the bayonet as a weapon. In proof of the value of the bayonet in close quarters, Captain Kincaid, Rifle Brigade, instanced the charge of Captain Tovey's company at Roncesvalles, and called upon the latter to pronounce upon its authenticity. To this circumstance we are indebted for the extremely interesting and modest reply of Colonel Tovey.

Another correspondent (Steel) mentioned the charge of the Light Company of the XX, at Maida, and stated that he had seen a man of the XX kill, with the bayonet, three Frenchmen, in as many minutes.

CAPTAIN KINCAID'S LETTER TO THE EDITOR.

"When Soult advanced into the Pyrenees, in 1813, with the intention of relieving Pampeluna, the pass of Maya (I think it was) was held by the 4th Division. I forget whether my informant told me that an outpost had been surprised, but certain it is, their division was very much surprised one fine morning, to find the rugged ground in front of their encampment occupied by the enemy, who, without any ceremony, began blazing into their tents. Such things cannot occur without exciting especial wonder. The soldiers, half dressed, began hurrying to arms, women and donkeys screaming, staff officers madly galloping about, ordering and expecting impossibilities. The balls came flying thicker and faster from the enemy's rapidly-increasing numbers, and the moment was fraught with disaster, when a gallant centurion, a choice spirit of the old XX, at once came forth in character; his hundred bayonets quickly rallied at his call, and needing no order, with an enemy in front and disorder among his friends, he at once gave his own orders, 'Fix bayonets, trail arms, double quick, forward!' In five minutes there was not a living Frenchman in the field. Their skirmishers fled before him, and, in the sight of their division, he with his single company, with desperate and reckless charge, dashed into the head of a whole column of French infantry which had already gained the heights, overthrew them, and sent their whole mass rolling headlong and panic-stricken into the valley below. It was one of the most brilliant feats of the war. It gave his division time to form and to commence that orderly and splendid retreat which terminated on the victorious field in front of Pampeluna. George Tovey, where are you? for I have scarcely seen, scarcely exchanged two words with you, since these glorious days departed. Twenty-six years have rolled over my head since this tale was told me by a brother officer of yours; the details may, therefore, be faulty, though substantially correct. I call upon you, as the hero of it, to inform the world whether you ever saw a British bayonet used; for if you brought your gallant band from that triumphant fray with bloodless weapons, you have been woefully belied. Lieutenant-Colonel George Tovey, I say, come forth! for if you do not, by my pen I swear that I will continue telling tales of the same kind against you, until I kindle such a flame in your cheek as may set fire to your scarlet coat, and make a hole in your half pay, which it can ill afford; for though the illustrious Wellington rewarded you, at the moment, with a Brevet-Majority, it was all that the miserable policy of the rulers of that day, at home, permitted him to bestow. Men of minor note have since been exhibiting their pictures in panoramas and print-shop windows, while all the public has ever seen or heard of you is, when some hungry hotel-keeper at Cheltenham, or elsewhere, finds Lieutenant-Colonel tacked to your name and sticks it in the newspaper as a lure for others, not knowing or caring who George Tovey is. This must no longer be; and again I say, come forth, and for the honour of your bayonet answer for your charge! You may not thank me for the call, but I know the public will, for drawing aside the curtain which has so long hung between them and you.

"(Signed) J. KINCAID."

Captain Kincaid's letter was successful in bringing forth Lieutenant-Colonel George Tovey. The following is his reply:—

"Mr. Editor,—In the last number of your journal there is a letter from the gallant rifleman (Captain Kincaid), who, during the last French war, had so many opportunities of appreciating the value of a British soldier. As there are one or two trifling inaccuracies, and I have been, besides, called upon by name to pronounce upon the authenticity of the bayonet encounter he has related, I shall do so as briefly as possible. In the first place, the 4th Division, on the 25th July, 1813, did not occupy the pass of Maya; they were between it and Roncesvalles. Secondly, the division had been expecting an attack that morning, and the XX were lying in column by their arms. It was daylight when a German sergeant of the Brunswick Oel Corps, who had been out in front, came in haste to tell us that the enemy were close upon us, and that they had made the Spanish piquet (who were posted to give us intelligence) prisoners without firing a shot. The left wing of the XX was moved instantly to form upon some strong ground in the direction they were coming; and, while doing so, the enemy's light troops opened so galling a fire that Major-General Ross, who was on the spot, called out for a company to go in front. Without waiting for orders, I pushed out with mine, and, in *close order and double quick*, cleared away the skirmishers from a sort of plateau. They did not wait for us, and, on reaching the opposite side, we came so suddenly on the head of the enemy's infantry column, who had just gained a footing on the summit of the hill, that the men of my company absolutely paused in astonishment, for we were *face to face* with them, and the French officer called to us to *disarm;* I repeated *bayonet away, bayonet away,* and, rushing head-long amongst them, we fairly turned them back into the descent of the hill; and such was the panic and confusion occasioned among them by our sudden onset, that this small party, for such it was compared to the French column, had time to regain the regiment, but my military readers may rest assured that it was required to be done in *double quick*. The enemy had many killed, and the leading French officer fell close at my feet, with two others, *all bayoneted*. The company, with which I was the only officer present on this occasion, did not amount to more than between seventy or eighty men, and we had eleven killed and fourteen wounded. I appeal to those of the 4th Division who witnessed this affair, whether I have arrogated to myself more than this handful of British soldiers are entitled to. I have now responded to the call of the brave Rifleman, and followed up his random shot by a *bayonet thrust;* and as it is, in all probability, my last, either in the field or in print, I shall conclude by strongly advising our young soldiers to receive with caution the lucubrations of theorists, when opposed to the practical essays of the Duke of Wellington and other great commanders, who have figured in history since the first invention of the bayonet.

"(Signed) GEORGE TOVEY, Lieutenant-Colonel.
"Stanmore, 16th October, 1839.

"N.B.—A powerful man of the name of Budworth returned with only the *blood-soiled* socket of the bayonet on his piece; and he declared he had killed away until his bayonet broke; and I am confident, from the reckless and intrepid nature of the man, that he had done so."

CANADIAN AFFAIRS.

THE number of officers of the XX who have taken a conspicuous part in the early and critical periods in the history of Canada, and during the American War of Independence, is very remarkable.

It is unnecessary to make but a passing mention of the services of Wolfe at Louisbourg and Quebec, which terminated with his life on the Plains of Abraham. Wolfe's advance guard up the Heights of Abraham was commanded by Lieutenant-Colonel Hon. W. Howe, who had served six years in the XX under Wolfe. This officer subsequently commanded a division of the army whose headquarters were fixed at Philadelphia.

The founder and first Governor of the province of Nova Scotia was Lieutenant-Colonel Hon. Edward Cornwallis, XX; and the first Governor of New Brunswick was Lieutenant-Colonel Thomas Carleton, who had served over twenty-one years in the regiment. Lieutenant-Colonel John Parr was Governor of Nova Scotia for nine years (1782-1791).

Lord George Germain, to whom his contemporaries and history

assign the questionable distinction of sharing the responsibility for the loss of the American colonies, commanded the regiment for some years. The Earl of Shelburne, who took a very prominent part in attacking the Government, of which Lord George Germain was a member, for their mismanagement of American affairs, and particularly in regard to their instructions to the commanders of the army in America, served in the XX during Wolfe's command.

Major Acland commanded the Grenadiers of Burgoyne's army, and commenced the battles of Hubbardton, Freeman's Farm, and Bemus Heights. The advance guard (composed of Indians so long as they remained with army) was led by Major T. Carleton; this officer was also Quartermaster-General to the army at Montreal and New York, under Sir Guy Carleton. The Canadian rebellion of 1838 was suppressed by Sir John Colborne, and lastly, although it does not come within the limit of this notice, Major-General Robert Ross fell at the head of the army at Baltimore.

INDEX.

Abercromby, Major-General, 44
Abercromby, Sir Ralph, 102, 103, 104, 105, 106, 386
Aberdeen, 29
Aboukir Bay, 109
Abraham, Heights of, 328
Abraham, Plains of, 328, 409
Ackland, Brigadier-General, 115, 125
Acland, Lady Harriet, 90, 335, 336, 337, 338, 339, 343
Acland, Major J. Dyke, 84, 88, 90, 335, 336, 337, 338, 339, 410
Adams, Ensign G. H., 189
Adams, Captain-Lieutenant L. F., 104
Addison, Captain A. C., 273, 276
Adlercron, Ensign J. G. L., 186
Adlercron, Lieutenant J. G. L., 187
"Adventure," H.M.S., 309
Aghrim, Battle of (*see* Aughrim), 5, 6, 326
Ahmednagar, 323
Aix-la-Chapelle, Treaty of, 30
"Ajax," Ship, 124
Ajmere, 322
Albany, 334, 336
Albemarle, Earl of (*see* Bury), 36
"Albion," Ship, 166
Albuera, Battle of, 352
Alcock, Sir Rutherford, 300, 303, 306
Aldershot, 238, 239, 240, 272, 296, 297, 318, 365, 369
Aldridge, Captain J., 271, 276, 306
Alemtejo, 12, 13, 15
Alexandria, 109, 110, 111, 113, 340, 351, 355, 359
"Alfred," Ship, 141
Algeciras, 18
"Algiers," H.M.S., 233
Alma, Battle of the, 195, 196, 362, 363, 367
Almanza, Battle of, 12
Almendra, Town of, 142
Ameerapore, Battle of, 242, 365, 367, 371
Americans, 82, 83, 84, 86, 88, 89
Amherst, Major-General, 40
Amöneburg, Castle of (*see* Brucker-Muhl), 75
Anburey, Ensign T., *Travels and Letters from Cambridge*, 88
Ancient Irish Fencibles, 109
Andrews, Private E., 236
Annals of Tyrone County, 333

Anson, General Sir W., 176
Anson, Major-General, 387, 391
Anstey, Lieutenant E. F., 190
Anstey, Captain E. F., 193
Antigua, 11
Antoin, 27
Antommarchi, Professor, 167, 356
Antwerp, 28
Aquitain, Regiment of, 73
Arabtabia, Redoubt, 198, 362
Arauntz, 157
Arbonne, Village of, 156
Arden, Surgeon G., 277
Ardvoirlich, 33
Armagh, 278
Army and Navy Gazette, 286, 287
Arnold, Private H., 259
Arnott, Surgeon Archibald, 167, 168, 169, 355, 356, 357
Artakoff Battery, 230
Artillery, Bengal Horse, 251, 252, 253, 266
Aschaffenburg, 24, 25
Ascot, 296
Ashby, Private T., 216
Ashford, 107
Ashton-under-Lyne, 182
Asirgarh, 320
Asle, Captain, 9
"Assistance," H.M.S., 284, 318
Astorga, 130
Atalosti, Pass of, 146
Athlone, 182
Athlone, Siege of, 3, 4, 5, 326
"Atlas," Ship, 124
Aughrim, Battle of (*see* Aghrim), 5, 6, 326
Austrian Succession, War of, 327
Aybar, Town of, 143
Aylett, Quartermaster J., 241
Azinghur, 269

Baacum, Village of, 106
Badajoz, 13, 16, 352
Bagnara, Town of, 122
Bailey, Lieutenant, 66
Bainbrigge, Lieutenant-Colonel P., 101, 104, 106, 350
Bainbrigge, Lieutenant-General P., 58, 385, 404
Bainbrigge, Lieutenant J. H., 148

INDEX.

Bainbrigge, General J. H., 387
Balaklava, Town of, 222, 225
Balaklava, Valley of, 197
Balaklava, Battle of, 198
Baldwin, Major G. W., 303
Baljik Bay, 194
Ballinasloe, 5
Ballinrobe, 319
Ballishanny, 326
Baltimore, City of, 162, 346, 347, 348, 403, 410
Bambibre, 130, 131
Banff, 32
Bankee, Action at, 261, 262
Bareitch, 260
Barker, Ensign T., 41
Barlow, Captain F. C., 182, 183
Barlow, Lieutenant F. W., 301, 307, 312
Barnes, Sir James, 189
Barnes, Private, 230
Barney, Commodore, 344
Barnham Downs, 100, 101
Barry, Private, 231
Barrymore, Lord, 14
Barton, Ensign R., 41
Basingstoke, 37, 273
Bateman, Captain-Lieutenant, 99
Battenkill, 85
Batteroux, Major, 17
Bayonne, 156, 157, 358, 388
Beatty, Lieutenant A., 189
"Beaumaris Castle," Ship, 270
Beaumont, Lieutenant A. E., 276
Beckwith, Lieutenant-Colonel (*see* Brigade), 42, 48, 56, 59, 63, 164
Beckwith, General Sir G., 164
Belfast, 278, 359
Belgaum, 171, 172
Bellairs, Lieutenant, 205
Belle Isle, 108, 351, 359
"Belleisle," H.M.S., 188
Bemus Heights, Battle of (*see* Stillwater), 89, 337, 410
Benares, 241, 250, 269, 365, 367
Benevente, 129, 130
Bengal, 298
Bennett, Lieutenant G., 193, 215, 217
Bennett, Captain G., 240, 248, 249
Bennett, Colonel G., 370
Bent, Captain James, 114
Bent, Bt.-Major, 145, 157, 159, 160, 342, 392, 393, 403
Berah, Action at, 256, 257, 365
Berdmore, Lieutenant S. R., 186
Berdmore, Captain, 188, 193
Beresford, Major-General M., 264, 279
Bermuda, 183, 185, 186, 187, 278, 279, 360, 362, 363, 366
Berry, Staff-Surgeon, 404
Berry, Private T., 216

Berwick, Duke of, 12
Best, Corporal F., 217
Betanzos, 134
Beverwycke, 386
Bewsher, Private W., 243
Bidache, 157
Bidassoa, River, 154, 358
Bilbao, 344, 404
Bilham, Quartermaster D., 185, 190, 193
Birch, Captain F. W., 280
Bird, Lieutenant R. N., 303, 304, 305, 306
Biruloff, General, 228
Biscay, Bay of, 406
Bishowee Muddy, Action at, 266
Biswara, District, 365
Bladensberg, Battle of, 344
Blakeny, Sir E., 182
Bland, Captain T. E., 322
Blandford, 37
"Blenheim," Ship, 298
Blennerhasset, Lieutenant, 99
Blessington, 295
Bligh, Brigadier-General, 29, 30
Blomfield, Major-General H., 296
Bloomer, Ensign, 99
Blount, Ensign R., 241
Blount, Captain R., 301, 315
Boaz Island, 278
Bombay, 170, 320, 360
Bompard, Attack on, 97
Bordeaux, 161, 358
Boswell, Lieutenant, 56, 66
Boteel, Sergeant G., 216
Boutchiere, Lieutenant, 28
Boxall, Colour-Sergeant G., 236.
Boyd, Major C., 99
Boyd, Major Hay (*see* Hay), 234
Boyle, 164, 318
Boyne, Battle of, 2, 326
Boyne, Viscount, 5
Brabourne Lees, 124
Bradford, General Sir T., 176
Bradford, Private T., 216
Bray, Private P., 229, 259, 266
Brigade, Beckwith's (*see* Beckwith), 48, 74
Bristol, 35, 271, 273, 296
"Britannia," Ship, 117
Brook, Lieutenant, 126
Brook, Lieutenant E., 185
Brook, Captain E., 187
Browne, General Sir G., 296
Browne, Brigadier-General W. G., 296
Browne, Lieutenant-Colonel H. R., 298, 301, 302, 306, 307, 309, 310, 311, 313, 314, 316, 317
Browne, Ensign G. E. Kenworthy-, 274, 276
Brown, Private J., 235, 236
Brown, Lieutenant, 56
Brown, Colour-Sergeant J., 236

INDEX. 413

Brucker-Muhl, Battle of (*see* Amöneburg), 75
Brudenell, Reverend Mr., 339
Brunswick, Prince Ferdinand of, 47, 49, 50, 51, 52, 53, 56, 57, 59, 61, 62, 63, 68, 71, 74, 76, 327
Brunswick, Hereditary Prince of, 51, 59, 61, 62, 63, 64, 65, 66
Brunswick Oel Corps, 146, 387, 392
"Brunswick," H.M.S., 238
Brussels, 28
Bryan, Private, 230
Buckingham Palace, 176
Buckley, Sergeant J., 248
Buckley, Private C., 243
Budford Heath, 38
Budworth, Private, 409
Buffs, The, 131
Buist, Lieutenant and Adjutant F., 145, 146, 342, 393
Bulwer, Major, 256
Bunbury, Lieutenant-General Sir H. (*Narrative of the Great War with France*), 101, 103, 109, 118, 119, 120, 121
Burgoyne, Lieutenant-General Sir John, 81, 83, 85, 87, 90, 91, 92, 333, 336, 337, 339
Burmah, Campaign, 369
Burne, Reverend H. T., 371
Burne, Ensign O. T., 241, 244, 249
Burne, Lieutenant O. T., 256
Burne, Major O. T., 370
Burne, Colonel Sir O. T., 169, 371, 372, 373, 374, 375
Burrel's Regiment, 30
Burton, Colonel, 329
Bury, Lancashire, 278, 320, 376
Bury, Viscount (*see* Albemarle), 32, 33, 35, 36
Busaco, Battle of, 352
Butler, Captain C. R., 190, 193, 214, 217, 219
Butler, Bt.-Major C. R., 228, 229, 235, 236
Butler, Major C. R., 240, 260
Butler, Lieutenant-Colonel C. R., 263
Buttevant, 315, 316, 318
Buxer-Ghat, Battle of (*see* Dhondiakhera), 258, 259, 365, 372
Byford, Private S., 216
Byng, Major-General, 389, 391, 393, 394, 400, 402
Byrne, Private M., 220

Cacadores, 7th Regiment, 147
Cadiz, 9, 10, 326
Cadogan, Colonel, 388
Cahill, Surgeon, 93
Calabria, 100, 116, 340, 355, 359, 403
Calcabellos, 131, 132
Calcutta, 241, 269, 298, 299, 301, 365, 367, 371
Callaghan, Private M., 236
Calthorpe, Captain Somerset, 201
Cambarros, Village of, 130

Cambridge, United States, 92
Cambridge, H.R.H. the Duke of, 197, 203, 209, 240, 286, 287, 365
Camden Fort, 277, 283
Campbell, Major-General, 268
Campbell, Sir John, 364
Campbell, Colonel, 389, 391
Campbell, Brevet-Major, 106
Campbell, Lieutenant-Colonel, 125
Campbell, Lieutenant Donald, 171
Campbell, Sergeant James, 203, 235, 239
Campbell, Corporal J., 217
Canada, 82, 328, 332, 333, 334, 335, 354, 358, 362, 363, 367
Canada, Affairs of, 409
"Canada," H.M.S., 108
Cancalle Bay, 46, 47
Cane, Lieutenant J., 41
Cane, Lieutenant M., 186
Cannanore, 170
Cannon, Richard (*see Historical Records*), 385
Canterbury, 36, 37, 175, 377
Cape of Good Hope, 315
"Captain," H.M.S., 108
Carano, Village of, 115
Carden, Lieutenant J., 241
Cardiff, 360
Carleton, Sir Guy (*see* Dorchester, Lord), 80, 81, 333, 334, 335, 410
Carleton, Captain Thomas, 44
Carleton, Major Thomas, 80, 82, 409, 410
Carleton, General Thomas, 333, 334
Carlingford Harbour, 349
Carlisle, 29, 34
Carlisle Fort, Cork Harbour, 277, 282
Carlyle, Thomas, *Frederick the Great*, 27, 49, 61, 66, 69
Carnarvon, Earl of, 339
Carrickfergus, 2
Carty, Private P., 217
Cashel, 3
Cassel, 59, 61, 71, 74
Castelamare, 115, 116
Castlebar, 320
Castleton, 84
Castro Gonzalo, Bridge of, 129
Catalonia, 13
Cates, Private, 231
Cathcart, Lieutenant-General Sir George, 195, 196, 200, 208, 209, 210, 212, 214, 219
Catling, Private T., 236
Caulfield, Lieutenant, 97
Cavan, Major-General Lord, 105
Cawnpore, 250, 251, 252, 365
"Centurion," H.M.S., 238
Ceuta, Fortress, 17, 18
Chalmers, Major-General Sir W., 189
Chalmers, Captain, 386

414   INDEX.

Chamberlain, Lieutenant, 254
Chamblée, 80, 81
Champagné, Lieutenant-Colonel F., 99
Champagné, Lieutenant, 145, 342, 393
Champion, Major, 214
"Champion of the Seas," Ship, 240
Chanda, Battle of, 242, 365, 367, 371
"Chanticleer," Ship, 301
Chapman, Lieutenant S. R., 193
Chapman, Captain S. R., 228, 229
Chapman, Bt.-Major S. R., 232
Charlemont, Colonel Viscount, 8
Charlton, Lieutenant, 93
Chasseurs, 203
Chatham, 284
Chatham, Earl of, 92
Cheltenham, 165, 407
Chesapeake, 344
Chesapeake, Army, 349
Chichester, 240
China, 299
Christie, Colonel, 262
Christ's Hospital, 350
Chrysal, 329
Churda, Action at, 261, 372
Cintra, Convention of, 126
Ciudad Rodrigo, 128, 352
Clark, Sir F. C., 338
Clarke, Private J., 217
Clarkson, Colonel T. H., 283, 284, 285
Clausel, General, 143, 155, 389, 396
Clayton, Brigadier, 19
Clephane, Lieut.-Colonel D., 101
Clinton, Sir H., 90
Clinton, Lieutenant, 171
Clonmel, 290, 291, 317
Close, Lieutenant, 106
Clyde, General Lord, 243, 249, 252, 257, 258, 260, 261, 365
Coa, River, 142, 387
Cobbe, Lieutenant-Colonel A. H., 272, 311
Cochrane, Admiral Sir A., 347
Cockburne, Admiral, 346, 347
Codrington, Colonel, 11
Coimbra, 141
Colabah, 170, 171
Colbert, General, 132
Colborne, Lieutenant John, 104
Colborne, Captain John, 121
Colborne, Major John, 127
Colborne, Sir John (*see* Seaton, Lord), 350, 352, 353, 354, 410
Colborne, S., Esquire, 350
Colchester, 124, 136, 137, 138, 139, 368
Cole, General Sir Lowry, 142, 149, 158, 176, 342, 387, 392, 395, 396, 403
Cole's Brigade, 119
Cole, Assistant-Surgeon R. J., 186
Collings, Ensign J., 41

Collingwood, Major C. G., 323
"Colombo," Ship, 193, 194
Colthurst, Lieutenant-Colonel D. L., 273, 274, 277, 278
Columbine, Colonel V., 8
Colville, Captain Hon., 98
Compère, General, 118, 119
"Conflict," Ship, 298
Connaught, H.R.H. Duke of, 322
Connell, Ensign, 87
Connolly, Private D., 236
Connolly, Private, 231
Connor, Lieutenant C., 148, 159
Conroux, General, 155
Constantino, 133
Conway, Lieutenant-General, 38, 70, 75, 76
Cook, Lieutenant, 87
Cooper, Ensign, 93
Coote, Major-General, 109, 110
Cotton, Admiral Sir Charles, 123
Corfu, 234
Cork, 12, 19, 80, 108, 166, 183, 184, 277, 281, 282
Cork, Cove of, 139, 141, 162, 166, 184
Cormick, Major John, 290
Cormick, Lieutenant-Colonel John, 263, 265, 266, 267, 269, 270
Cormick, Colonel John, 184, 272, 273, 274, 369, 370, 373
"Cornwall," Ship, 185
Cornwallis, Earl, 334
Cornwallis, Major Hon. E., 28
Cornwallis, Lieutenant-Colonel Hon. E., 32, 409
Cornwallis, Major-General Hon. E., 38
Corsican Rangers, 117, 118
Coruña, 129, 136, 141, 341, 359, 406
Coruña, Battle of, 135, 341, 351
Coruña, Retreat on, 129, 341, 351, 355, 403
Cosby, Colonel, 20
Coulston, Private, 225
County Titles, 375
Cowell, Ensign H. R., 186
Cowie, Private, 224
Cowley, Captain, 56
Cox, Private T., 247
Craig, Lieutenant-General Sir James, 114, 115, 116, 340, 357
Crawford, Ensign, 56
Crawley, Lieutenant-Colonel H., 180, 181, 186, 192
Crespigny, Lieutenant G. B., 183, 185
Crespigny, Captain G. B., 190
Crimea, 194, 195, 233, 234, 235, 362, 369, 371
Croad, Major, 175, 182, 183, 186
Crofton, Lieutenant H. D., 181
Crofton, Captain H. D., 185
Crofton, Major H. D., 188, 192, 193

INDEX. 415

Crofton, Lieutenant-Colonel H. D., 195, 200, 207, 208, 209, 213, 215, 217, 218, 235, 236, 360, 363, 367
Crofts, Lieutenant, 93
Croix d'Orade, Village of, 160, 358
Crokat, Lieutenant W., 145
Crokat, Captain W., 169, 342, 393
Crosdale, Lieutenant D., 41
Crown Point, 83, 336
Culloden, Battle of, 29, 30, 327
Cumberland, Duke of, 27, 29, 34, 37, 327
Cunningham, Private T., 261
Cunynghame, Colonel A. T., 188, 209, 210
Cunynghame, Major-General A. T., 295
Curragh Camp, 277, 295, 296, 318, 320
Curran, Sergeant T., 307
Cyprus, 279, 280

Daïmios, 299, 303, 307
Daken, Doctor, 177
Dalrymple, Sir Hew, 127
Dalton, Lieutenant, 99
D'Arcy, Lieutenant R., 308, 309
Darmarpore, 262
Dartmoor, 192
Dashwood, Captain B. G., 241
Daubeney, Colonel, 207
Davies, Lieutenant, 273, 276
Davies, Private, 225
Davis, Commodore, 20
Davis, Colonel John, 318, 319
Davy, Private F., 243
Dax, Captain, 344
Day, Private J., 261
De Bay, Marquis, 14
De Broglio, Marshal, 50, 51, 52, 54, 61, 63, 68, 69, 70, 71, 72
De Castrides, Marshal, 65
De Contades, Marshal, 50, 51, 52, 53, 54, 55
De Crespigny, Colonel G. B., 180
De Crespigny, Lieutenant H. O., 185
De Fonblanque, *Political and Military Episodes*, 91
De Fronteira, Marquis, 13, 14
De Ginkell, General, 3, 4, 5, 7, 326
De Grammont, Duke, 25
De la Poer, Ensign A. E., 274, 276
De Leda, Marquis, 17, 18
De Montandre, Marquis, 12
De Noailles, Marshal, 24
De Norman, Brigadier, 65
De Segur, Lieutenant-General, 66
De Todleben, General, 212
De Villadarius, Marquis, 11
Deal, 101, 102, 137, 175
Deffrey, Private J., 217
Delap, William D., Esquire, 350
Delaune, Captain W., 41
Dempsey, Sergeant A., 243

Dennis, Lieutenant J. E. V., 319
Dennis, Private J., 261
Denshire, Lieutenant, 56
Dent, Ensign, 56
Derby, 29
Desaix, Marshal, 349
Deshon, Captain, 174, 175
Deshon, Major, 181
Desnouettes, General Lefebre, 129
Des Vaux, Lieutenant C., 104
Devizes, 37
Devonport, 192, 272, 318
Dinapore, 269
Donegal, 326
Dettingen, Battle of, 25, 26, 42, 327
Dhondiakhera, Battle of (see Buxer-Ghat), 258
Diabutsñ, 304
Dickens, Ensign W. S., 190
Dickens, Captain W. S., 237, 240
Dickens, Major W. S., 296
Dickson, Colonel Collingwood, 215
Diemel, River, 61, 62, 63, 68, 71
Dobson, Captain, 99
Dodd, *History of Gibraltar*, 21, 23
Don, Major-General G., 102
Don, General Sir G., 57
Donegal, Colonel the Earl of, 8
Doolan, Private, 225
Dorchester, Lord (*see* Carleton, Sir Guy), 333
Douglas, General, 2
Douglas, Brigadier-General, 248
Douglas, Ensign G., 193
Douro, 142, 387
Dover, 34, 35, 37, 137
"Dover," Ship, 141
Dowling, Lieutenant, 29th Regiment, 90
Dowling, Lieutenant W. H., 190, 199, 208, 209, 212, 215, 216
Down, Lord, 46
Drewry, Ensign, 106
Drudge, Private, 225
Dublin, 2, 164, 166, 182, 277, 278, 291, 295, 296, 325
Duff, Lieutenant-Colonel L. D. Gordon- (*see* Gordon, L. D.), 180
Dufferin, Earl of, 322
Duffin, Lieutenant G. B., 241
Duggan, Private, 225
Dughe, Lieutenant W., 41
Du Muy, Chevalier, 61, 62
Dum Dum, 301
Dumonceau, General, 103
Dunbar, Colonel, 36
Duncan, Ensign, 314
Dundas, Colonel T., 334
Dundee, 32
Dunne, Captain J., 41
Durban, 311

416 INDEX.

Duroure, Colonel, 327
Dykes, Lieutenant F., 41

Earle, Colonel T., 8
East London, 312, 314, 315
Ebro, River, 142, 388, 402
Eccles, Captain-Lieutenant, 99
Echallar, Action at, 149
Eden, Major-General, 290, 291
Edridge, Lieutenant F. L., 241
Edridge, Captain F. L., 265, 266
Edridge, Major F. L., 271, 272, 276, 279
Edridge, Colonel, F. L., 280, 281, 283
Edridge, Lieutenant C. S., 270
Edridge, Mrs., 283
Edwards, Bryan (*History of the West Indies*), 98
Edwards, Lieutenant W., 41
Egan, Ensign S., 241
Egmont-op-Zee, Battles of, 105, 106, 350, 355, 386
Egypt, 100, 109, 110, 111, 112, 340, 351, 355, 359, 403
Eighteenth Hussars, 358
Eighteenth Regiment, 369
Eightieth Regiment, 251, 254, 255
Eimbeck, Town of, 71, 72
El Burgo, 134, 135
Eldridge, Private, 231
Eleventh Light Dragoons, 355
Eleventh Regiment, Portugal, 387
Elvas, 13, 15, 126, 127, 128, 359
Embden, Town of, 47
"Emerald Isle," Ship, 190
Engine House, 244, 367
England, Lieutenant and Adjutant J., 41
Enniskillen, 325
Eschalar, Heights of, 342
Esla, River, 129, 142, 387
Espinal, 144, 389, 390, 394
Essex Standard, 226
Estremos, 13, 126, 127
Euoshima, Island of, 304
Evelegh, Lieutenant F. C., 181
Evelegh, Captain F. C., 185
Evelegh, Major F. C., 193
Evelegh, Lieutenant Colonel F. C., 230, 231, 233, 235, 236, 238, 240
Evelegh, Colonel F. C., 242, 363, 364, 365, 368
Evelegh, Brigadier F. C., 249, 251, 252, 253, 254, 255, 256, 257, 260, 262, 371, 372
Evina, Village of, 135
Exeter, 1, 35, 40, 99, 100, 271, 272, 273
Exeter Cathedral, 237, 370, 375, 376
Eyre, Ensign W. A., 185

Fahie, Ensign C., 241
Fahie, Captain C., 306, 315
Falkirk, Battle of, 29, 327

Fallow, Private P., 217
Falls, Lieutenant T., 148, 343, 390, 402
Falmouth, 136
Farnborough, 240
Faro Lighthouse, 122, 123, 124
Farquhar, Captain, 87
Farquhar, Captain W., 99
Farquharson, John, 33
Farrell, Colour-Sergeant P. A., 236
Farsden, Private J., 247
Faulkner, Lieutenant R., 41
Favell, Ensign, 106
Feilding, Major-General, 281
Fenton, Captain J., 99
Fermanagh, 326
Fermoy, 139, 140, 166
Fernay, Private T., 229
Fifth Division, 152
Fifth Regiment, 12, 14, 15, 17, 22, 320
Fifteenth Hussars, 131
Fifteenth Native Infantry, 267
Fiftieth Regiment, 109
Fifty-first Regiment, 55
Fifty-second Regiment, 128, 133, 351, 352
Fifty-third Regiment, 251, 387
Fifty-fourth Regiment, 360
Fifty-fourth Native Infantry, 254
Fifty-fifth Regiment, 207, 320
Fifty-sixth Regiment, 360
Fifty-seventh Regiment, 230
Fifty-eighth Regiment (French), 155
Fifty-ninth Regiment, 320
Filcher, Colonel, 59
Filcher, General, 65
First Division, 152
Fisher, Corporal H., 229
Fitzgerald, Colonel, 21
Fitzgerald, Colonel J. Foster, 170
Fitzgerald, Lieutenant, 149, 400
Fitzroy, Major-General Lord C., 102
Flaherty, Private, 231
Flanders, 8, 29, 327
Flank Battalion, 108
Fleetwood, 286, 287
Fletcher, Sergeant John, 152
Flood, Private A., 259
Folen, Private, 231
Fontenoy, Battle of, 27, 28, 42, 340
Foot Guards, 22, 23
Forbes, Major-General Lord, 140
Fort Anne, U.S., 84
Fort Augustus, N.B., 32
Fort Beaufort, South Africa, 312, 313, 314
Fort des Bains, 109, 110, 111
Fort Edward, U.S., 85, 336
Fort Kinburn, 365
Fort Lalippe, 127
Fort Simree, Capture of, 365, 372
Fort Triangular, 111

… INDEX. 417

Fortieth Regiment, 149, 369, 387, 396
Forty-first Regiment, 98, 331, 405
Forty-second Regiment, 240, 371
Forty-eighth Regiment, 148, 387, 394, 402
Forty-ninth Regiment, 95
Fourth Division, 149, 152, 155, 195, 196, 197, 198, 216, 225, 231, 242, 243, 250, 342, 358, 362, 387, 389, 395, 401, 403, 406, 408
Fourth Regiment, 327
Fox, General, 351
Fox, Right Hon. Charles, 92
Foy, General, 388
Foy, Captain E., 335
Francis, Colonel (U.S.A.), 84
Francis, Captain G. E., 241, 244, 246
Francis, Major G. E., 314, 315
Frankfort, Regiment of, 156
Franks, Brigadier, 242, 365, 367, 372
Fraser, Ensign R., 294
Frazer, Brigadier, 81, 83, 86, 338
Frazer, Captain F. M., 183, 185, 187
Frearson, Captain, 56
Freeman's Farm, Battle of, 86, 89, 337, 410
Friol, Private W., 259
Fuller, Corporal P., 231
Furlonger, Captain S., 322
Fusilier Brigade, 153, 342, 402
Futteghur, 269
Fyzabad, 260, 264

Gahan, Lieutenant M. C., 276
Galway, 5, 6
Galway, Earl of, 12, 13, 14
Galway, Regiment of, 14
Gambling, Sergeant Seth, 152
Ganges, 258, 259
Gansevoort, Colonel, 334
Gardener, Lieutenant J., 41
Garstin, Lieutenant, 187
Gascoigne, Major-General, 291, 292, 296
Gaskill, Lieutenant, 93
Gates, General H., 335, 337, 338
Gee, Lieutenant-Colonel, 28
Gee, Private J., 229
Gee, Corporal J., 236
"General Palmer," Ship, 184, 186, 362
Geraghty, Colour-Sergeant P., 219
Geraghty, Lieutenant P., 241
Germain, Lord George (*see* Sackville), 85, 92, 409, 410
Gethin, Lieutenant G., 241
Gethin, Captain G., 271
Gethin, Lieutenant Sir R., 185
Ghent, 24, 27
Gibbs, Paymaster, 277
Gibraltar, 16, 17, 19, 22, 23, 42, 79, 124, 279, 361
Gibson, Sergeant S., 217
Gilbert, Lieutenant, 93

Giles, Private T., 259
Ginwarra, Village of, 256, 257
Gipson, Private J., 236
Girod, Colonel, 127
Glascock, Walter, Esquire, 350
Glasgow, 31, 32, 33, 34, 287
Gleig, Chaplain General, 347
Glencross, Lieutenant-Colonel W., 284, 376
Godfrey, Lieutenant E. L., 159
Gogra, River, 260, 366
"Golden Fleece," Ship, 311
Goldie, Brigadier, 362
Golding, Private P., 229
Goldsmith, Ensign E. P. T., 301, 307, 311
Goldsmith, Captain E. P. T., 280
Goldsmith, Major E. P. T., 283
Gondah, 260, 262, 263, 264, 265, 266, 267, 268, 366, 369, 372, 373
Goodenough, Captain E., 41
Goodlake, Lieutenant H. S., 284
Goodwin, Major-General H., 192
Goomtee, 242, 244, 247
Goorkhas, 242
Gordon, Captain L. D. (*see* Duff, L. D. Gordon-), 185
Gordon, Lieutenant W. F. F., 241, 248, 249
Gordon, Captain W. F. F., 314
Gorruckpore, 268, 269
Gort, 319
Goshi, 279
Gough, Lord, 369
Gozo, 114
Graham, Lieutenant-General Sir T., 137, 142, 388
Granby, Marquis of, 60, 62, 68, 69, 71, 76
Grand Vizier, 112
Grannell, Private J., 229
Grant, Sir Hope, 365
Grant, James (*Adventures of an Aide-de-Camp*), 121, 122
Gravesend, 47
Gray, Private H., 236
Graydon, Vice-Admiral, 11
Great Bedwin, 273
Green, Lieutenant M., 41
Green, Colonel, 172, 173, 174, 175, 181
Greenwich, 332
Grenadiers, 5, 63, 84, 86, 88, 90, 213, 361, 392, 400, 401, 410
Grenadiers, Battalion of, Maxwell's, 48, 49, 62, 63, 64
Grenadiers of France, 73, 74
Grey, Captain, 44, 56, 66
Grey, Corporal J., 217
Griffen, General, 64
Griffiths, Sergeant G. W., 217
Grove, Lieutenant W. C., 150
Guards, Hanoverian, 44
Guards of Honour, 176

BB

INDEX.

Guards, The, 200, 204, 208, 216, 219
Guernsey, 354
Guildford, 35
Guise, Sir J., 1
Gustavus Adolphus, King of Sweden, 325
Guy, Major-General, 307, 308, 310
Gwalior Campaign, 369

Hadden, Lieutenant J. M., Royal Artillery (Hadden's *Journal*), 82
Haldimand, Sir F., 334
Hale, Colonel Thomas, 376
Hales, Lieutenant P., 41
Halifax, Nova Scotia, 94, 188, 279, 348
Hallewell, Ensign E. G., 185
Halliday, Private E., 247
Halpin, Corporal Thady, 229
Halpin, Sergeant Thady, 236
Hamilton, Bermuda, 187
Hamilton, Colonel Gustavus (*see* Boyne, Viscount), 2, 6, 8, 9, 325, 326
Hamilton, Brigadier, 85
Hamilton, Captain F., 9
Hamilton, Captain J., 9
Hamilton, Lieutenant C., 104
Harcourt, Captain J. S. C., 311
Hardinge, Lord, 360
Hardinge, Lieutenant-General Hon. A. E., 321
Harnage, Major, 337
Harris, Surgeon J., 41
Hartley, Ensign, 28
Harvey, Lieutenant-General Sir J., 188
Harwich, 125, 138, 139
Haulbowline, Cork Harbour, 282, 317
Hawkins, Private J., 217, 218
Haworth, Lieutenant-Colonel F., 376
Hay, Lieutenant J. G., 190, 214, 218
Hay, Major J. G. (*see* Boyd, Hay-), 234
Hay, Private J., 243
Head, Private J., 243
Heath, Major R. K., 348
Helder, 102, 107
Hennessy, Captain P., 186
Hennessy, Private W., 236
Hensman, Surgeon W., 302
Herrerias, 132
Hesse-Cassell, 385
Hesse-Darmstadt, Prince George of, 5
Hetherington, Major, 17
Hewitt, Captain P. G., 241
Heywood, Oliver, Esquire, 376
Highland Division, 362
Hill, General Sir R., 352, 388
Hill, General Lord, 176, 389
Hill, Major E., 180, 237
Hill, Mrs. E., 237
Hill, Private C., 245, 247, 368
Hill, Private R., 313

Hiller, Private W., 259
"Himalaya," H.M.S., 280, 281, 314
Hinton, Private E. C., 217
Historical Records (*see* Cannon), 385
History of Europe, Allison's, 121
Hobday, Private W., 217
Hobson, Admiral, 18, 20
Hodson's Horse, 266
Hogg, Major, 170
Hogg, Lieutenant, 126
Holbyn, Ensign T. H., 241
Holdich, Colonel A., 267, 268
Holland, 8, 100, 107, 340, 350, 355, 397, 403
Hollinsworth, Sergeant-Major H., 159
Hollinsworth, Lieutenant H., 181
Hollinsworth, Captain H., 102, 359, 360, 361
Hollinsworth, Major George, 360
Holmes, Lieutenant F. G., 230, 241, 268
Holmes, Private, 231
Honeywood, Colonel Philip, 36, 37
Hong-Kong, 301, 309, 310, 311
Hoorn, 105, 350
Hope, Lieutenant-General Sir John, 137
Horn, Lieutenant Frederick, 181
Horn, Captain Frederick, 182, 183
Horn, Major Frederick, 184, 186
Horn, Lieutenant-Colonel Frederick, 188, 190, 192, 193
Horn, Colonel Frederick, 195, 198, 200, 201, 202, 203, 204, 208, 215, 216, 217, 218, 230, 235, 236
Horn, General Sir Frederick, 279, 361, 363, 364, 367
Horn, Lieutenant F. G., 241, 268
Horneck, Brigadier, 99
Houghton, Private H., 217
Houstoun, Lieutenant-General Sir W., 163
Howard, Assistant-Surgeon E., 186, 190, 193
Howard, Surgeon E., 226, 241
Howe, Lord, 43
Howe, Lieutenant-Colonel Hon. W., 43, 92, 93
Howe, General Sir W., 409
Hozier, Captain, 274
Huarte, Town of, 147
Hubbardton, Battle of, 83, 84, 336, 410
Hudson, River, 85, 88, 94, 336, 337
Hules, Private P., 236
Humphreys, Ensign, 106
Hundredth Regiment (French), 388
Huske, Major-General, 29
Hussengunge, Action at, 253, 365, 372
Hussey, Lieutenant and Adjutant C. E., 277
Hussey, Lieutenant-Colonel, 323
Hutchinson, General, 111
Hutchinson, General W. N., 177, 180, 181, 184, 185, 188
Hutchinson, Lieutenant W. L., 308
Hyde, Surgeon R. A., 302
Hythe, 368

INDEX. 419

Iäkoutsk Regiment, 210, 212, 221
Ilchester, Earl of, 335
Imambarra, 244, 249
Imperial Guard, 352, 353
Independence, American War of, 409
India, 240
Indians (American), 82, 87, 88, 337, 338
Inkerman, Battle of, 199, 219, 362, 363, 364, 367
Inverdouglas, 33
Inverness, 32
Ionian Islands, 354
Ipswich, 124
Ireland, 2, 7, 11, 12, 23, 94, 360, 362
Ireland Island, Bermuda, 186, 278
Irwin, Ensign, 56
Irwin, Lieutenant, 74
Isle Aux Noix, 81, 82, 83, 335, 336
Isle of Wight, 7, 38, 46, 47, 239, 371

Jackson, Sir R., 182
Jackson, Major, 166, 171
Jackson, Captain E., 148
Jackson, Ensign J. R., 186
Jamaica, 11, 95, 360
James, Lieutenant H., 190, 214
"James Baines," Ship, 240
Japan, 299, 300, 301, 306
"Java," Ship, 186
Jeremie, 96
Johnson, Major A. B., 372
Johnson, Captain W., 33
Johnson, Lieutenant, 204
Johnson, Private S., 229
Johnstone, Ensign S., 241
Johnstown, 334
Jokes, Private G., 231
Jomini, *The Art of War*, 346
Jones, Lieutenant C., 276
Jones, Private, 230
"Joseph Somes," Ship, 190
Joyce, Private, 231
Joyce, Private W., 243
Junot, Marshal, 123

Kaiser Bagh, 244, 249, 367
Kane, General, 6
Kane, Colonel, 17, 18
Katcha, Valley of, 196
Katten Dyke, 138
Kavanagh, Corporal, 231
Kazatch, 233
Keane, Lieutenant-General Sir John, 172, 173
Keating, Private P., 229
Keays, Drummer J., 152
Keiskamma Hook, 314
Kekewich, Ensign L., 193, 217, 218
Kellerman, General, 127, 351
Kelly, Lieutenant, 110

Kelsall, Assistant-Surgeon H., 241
Kempt, Lieutenant-Colonel, 115, 117, 118, 119, 120, 121, 351, 357
Kerr, Lieutenant Lord Mark, 181
Kerr, Captain Lord Mark, 183
Khyber Jungle, 265, 369, 372
Kilkenny, 273, 274, 277
Killarney, 284, 290, 315, 317
Kimberley, Earl of, 373
Kinburn Fort, 233
Kincaid, Captain J., 406, 408
King Charles II., 325
King George I., 326
King George II., 33, 63
King George III. (*see* Wales, Prince of), 40
King James II., 1, 2, 7, 12, 325
King Joseph of Spain, 389
King William III., 2, 3, 5, 8, 41, 326
King William's Town, 314, 315
Kinglake, A. W. (*History of the Invasion of the Crimea*), 201, 204, 205, 209, 210, 213, 220, 223, 226
Kinglake, Captain H. A., 287
King's German Legion, 387
Kingsley, Colonel William, 37
Kingsley, Major-General, 55, 57, 58, 60
Kingsley, Lieutenant-General, 79, 326
Kingsley's, 44, 46, 48, 56, 58, 64, 330, 337
Kingston, C. W., 188
Kingston, Jamaica, 94
Kingstown, 182, 273, 318
Kinsale, 139
Kirch-Denkern, Battle of (*see* Vellinghausen), 48, 69
Kirk, Colonel, 6
Kirkee, 323
Kirkham, Private C., 236
Kloster-Kampen, Battle of, 48, 66
Koolapoor, 171
Krabbendam, Village of, 102, 103, 104, 350, 355, 359
Krause, Colonel, 156
Kululu, 234

"Lady Faversham," Ship, 174
Lafayette, Marquis de, 334
Laffeldt, Battle of (*see* Val), 327, 330
La Gudiña, Battle of, 14
La Haie Sainte, 352
Lake Champlain, 81, 82, 83, 335, 358
Lamb, Sergeant R. (*Memoirs and Journal of Occurrences*), 87, 93
Lambert, Lord, 9
Lancashire Fusiliers, 1, 282, 376
Landal, Marquis of, 46
Langley, Private, 197
Langmaid, Corporal J. S., 217
Lanier, Sir John, 3
Lanz, River, 147, 395, 396, 398

420 INDEX.

Laprimaudaye, Captain, 276
Larnaca, 279
Lathom, Private, 231
Laughland, Private D., 236
Lawrence, Colonel, 56
Lawrence, Major-General, 240
Lawrie, Sergeant A., 217
Leeds, 286
Leet, Lieutenant E., 190
Leeward Islands, 11
Leith, 29
Le Marchant, Major Sir Gaspard, 177, 181
"Lennox," H.M.S., 10
"Leopard," H.M.S., 308
Lesaca, 150, 154
Levermore, Private, 194
Lewis, Lieutenant R. L., 148
Lewis, Ensign J. W. D., 193
Lewis, Private J., 229
Lichfield, 100
Light Division, 152, 352, 388, 389
Ligonier, General, 29
Limassol, 280
Limerick, 183
Limerick, Siege of, 2, 7, 326
Lincoln, Private, 245, 368
Lind, Lieutenant-Colonel, 84, 87, 93, 98, 336
Lisbon, 12, 123, 127, 140, 341, 351
Lismore, Dean of, 274
Little, Lieutenant J., 241, 250
Liverpool, 100, 182, 285
Livingston, Colonel, 334
Lloyd, Captain A., 111
"Lloyds," Ship, 166
Loch Earn, 31
Loch Lomond, 33
London, 331
London, C.W., 188
London Gazette, 63, 362
Loughland, Sergeant D., 219
Louisbourg, 40
Louisbourg, Capture of, 328, 330, 409
Love, Private W., 217
Lowe, Sir Hudson, 168, 169
Lowe, Private J., 236
Lucas, Lord, 8
Lucas, Lieutenant, 87
Lucknow, 243, 249, 250, 251, 252, 260, 289, 365, 367, 371, 372
Lugo, 133, 134
Lutyens, Lieutenant, 150
Lutyens, Brevet-Major, 171
Lutyens, Ensign, 190
Lye, Lieutenant R. Leigh, 186
Lye, Captain R. Leigh, 190, 193, 225
Lynch, Private, 198
Lyndhurst, 350
Lyons, Captain T. C., 240, 256, 257, 260
Lyons, Major T. C., 263, 296

Lys, Colonel G. M., 240, 249
Lytton, Earl of, 375

Macaulay, Lord, 5
Maceira, Bay of, 125
Mackay, General, 3, 6
Mackenzie's Farm, 196
Maclagan, Surgeon, 190
Maclean, Colonel, 81
Macneill, Lieutenant W. H., 193
"Macqueen," Ship, 170
Madison, President U.S., 345
Madras, 171
Madrid, 129
Magrane, Corporal M., 217
Maharajpore, Battle of, 369
Mahon, Lord (*History of England*), 92
Maida, Battle of, 119, 120, 341, 355, 359, 406
Maidstone, 35
Maister, Captain, 106
Maitland, Major, 211
Majendie, Colonel V. D. (*Up among the Pandies*), 247
"Malabar," H.M.S., 320
"Malabar," Ship, 174
Malleson, Colonel (*History of the Indian Mutiny*), 253
Mallow, 139, 162
Malta, 113, 114, 115, 122, 124, 234, 279, 280, 351, 355, 357, 359, 362, 363, 371
Malwan, 171
Manchester, 100, 181, 284, 286, 318, 376
Mann, Private W., 236
Mansfield, General Sir W., 269
Mantaban, Capture of, 369
Marines, 96
Markham, Major D., 97
Markham, Lieutenant-Colonel D., 98, 99
Marlborough, Duke of, 3, 8, 9, 46, 47, 168
Marlborough, Life of, 356
"Marsden," Ship, 315
Marshall, Private G., 259
Maryborough, 183, 319
Massey, Ensign W., 41
Masterson, Private J., 217
Mathiati, 279, 280
Mathison, Colour Sergeant J., 217
Matson, Lieutenant J., 41
Mauritius, 314, 315
Mauvillon, Colonel (*Ferdinand of Brunswick's Wars*), 62, 66
Maxwell's Brigade, 69, 70
Maxwell, Captain, 28
Maxwell, Major, 42, 48, 74
Maxwell, Lieutenant, 106
Maya, Pass of, 390, 406, 408
Maycock, Lieutenant, 190
Mayo, Earl of, 374
McCormack, Private, 225

INDEX. 421

McCurry, Ensign, 106
McDonogh, Lieutenant T. S., 241
McDonough, Private B., 217
McDowall, Captain, 44
McGorman, Private, 230
McGovern, Private T., 217
McKay, Quartermaster, 277
McKenzie, Captain Murdoch, 148
McLean, Major, 182
McLean, Captain Murdoch, 117, 118, 351
McNamee, Captain John, 313
Meangunge, Action at, 253, 365, 372
Meares, Captain W. L. D., 297, 298, 301
Meares, Major W. L. D., 270, 273, 274, 276, 278
Meares, Lieutenant-Colonel W. L. D., 279
Meares, Major-General W. L. D., 90
Mearns, Private J., 229
Mehendie Hussien, 242
Mendichuri Pass, 144, 394
Menou, General, 111
Merriday, Private J., 217
Messina, Harbour and Straits, 122, 124
Messina, Town, 116, 117, 122, 123
Meyrac, Captain, 28
Mhow, 320, 321
Middleton, 140, 141
Miller, Major, 255, 256
Mills, Ensign, 139
Milnes, Ensign, 105
Minden, Battle of, 48, 51, 53, 54, 55, 56, 58, 177, 327, 330, 333, 377, 383
Minorca, 16, 17, 18, 108, 340, 351, 355, 359
Mitchell, Lieutenant W., 241
Mohan, Action at, 252, 365, 372
Moles, Private H., 217
Mompleson, Major-General, 73
Monahan, 278
"Monmouth," H.M.S., 137, 138
Monro's Regiment, 30
Montagu, Captain, 228
Montcalm, General, 328
Montreal, 80, 188, 189, 334, 358, 410
Moore, Lieutenant-General Sir John, 123, 124, 128, 131, 133, 134, 135, 136, 341, 349, 351, 403
Morar Mow, Action at, 254, 365, 372
Mordaunt, Lord, 1
Mordaunt, Sir John, 36, 38, 39
Mordaunt, Lieutenant-General Sir J., 326, 328
Morillo, General, 389, 390
Morshead, Lieutenant, 290
Mosley, Paymaster G., 193
Moss, Colour-Sergeant J., 236
Moultan, 360
Mount Tröodos, 280
Muchlee Goan, Action at, 265, 369, 372
Mulcahy, Private, 230
Mullett, Lance-Corporal S., 259

Mullingar, 3, 164, 318
Mullins, Private M., 217, 218
Munday, Assistant Surgeon J., 241
Münster, Westphalia, 44, 47, 50, 67, 76
Murphy, Private T., 229
Murray, Major John, 139
Murray, Captain John, 148, 152, 159
Murray, Captain R. S., 186
Murray, Ensign H., 186
Murray, Ensign J., 159
Murray, Private J., 217, 218
Musjeidia, Fort of, 261

Naas, 164, 319
Nana Sahib, 261, 264
Nanclares, 388
Nanparah, 260, 261
Napier, Sir Charles, 182
Napier, Sir William (*History of the Peninsular War*), 126, 127, 148, 158, 352, 405
Naples, 114, 115, 116, 340, 351, 357, 359
Naples, King of, 115
Napoleon, Emperor, 129, 160, 166, 167, 168, 169, 349, 353, 356, 357, 360
Nasirabad, 321, 322, 323
Nassau, Regiment of, 156
Natal, 314
Nawabgunge, 251, 252, 253, 260, 365, 372
Neemuch, 321, 323
Nenagh, 282
Nesbitt, Lieutenant H., 41
Nesbitt, Lieutenant J., 41
Netherlands, 30, 352
New Brunswick, 334, 409
New Holland, 171
New South Wales, 171
New York, 334, 339, 410
Newcastle, 282
Newman, Captain, 106
Newman, Captain B., 186, 187
Newry, 278, 333
Ney, Marshal, 352
Nicholson, Private R., 247
Ninth Regiment, 84, 85
Nineteenth Regiment, 11
Ninetieth Regiment, 340
Ninety-first Regiment, 133
Ninety-second Regiment, 109
Ninety-fifth Regiment, 128, 133, 213, 214
Ninety-seventh Regiment, 242
Nive, Battle of, 352, 359
Nivelle, Battle of, 155, 352, 355
Noagles, 132
Norbury, Lieutenant, 56
Norman, Lieutenant, 81
Northbrook, Earl of, 374
Nova Scotia, 32, 409
"Nubia," Ship, 301
Nugent, Lieutenant, 56, 66

INDEX.

Nuggur, 257, 258
Nunn, Lieutenant W. D., 241
Nunn, Captain W. D., 269

Oakley, Ensign R. C., 145, 342
Obins, Lieutenant, 87
Obins, Captain H., 160
O'Brien, Sir T. N., 377
O'Callaghan, Lieutenant-Colonel Hon. W., 115
Ocana, Battle of, 352
O'Connell, Sergeant H., 307
Odessa, 233
Ogilvie, Lieutenant-Colonel J., 169, 170, 171
O'Kelly, Private P., 217
Okhotsk Regiment, 213
O'Neill, Lieutenant J. J. S., 230
O'Neill, Captain J. J. S., 257
O'Neill, Major J. J. S., 279, 280
O'Neill, Lieutenant-Colonel J. J. S., 319, 320, 321
O'Neill, Corporal W., 217
O'Neill, Private, 231
Oomeriah, Fort, 260, 365
Orange, Prince of (*see* William III.), 1, 352
Ord, Captain, 290
Ord, Major, 298, 309, 313, 315
Ormond, Duke of, 9, 11
"Orontes," H.M.S., 279
Orthes, 157
Orthes, Battle of, 158, 159, 343, 344, 352, 356, 358, 359, 393, 403
"Orwell," Ship, 170
Osborne, Captain T., 41
Osborne, Corporal J., 217
Osnabrück, 50
Osnaburg, 60, 72
Ostend, 327
Owen, Captain E. R., 286
O'Toole, Lieutenant-Colonel, 399
Oude, 242, 259, 262, 267, 366
Outram, Major-General Sir James, 247, 248, 249

Pachawn, 183
Paddon, Captain G., 102
Paderborn, 59, 60, 69, 70
Padfield, Ensign F., 189
Padfield, Lieutenant and Adjutant, 190, 193, 217, 218, 230
Paget, Lord, 129
Paget, Major-General, 131, 133, 135
Palencia, 142
Palmer, Lance-Sergeant D., 230
Palmerston, Lord, 361
Pampeluna, 143, 144, 342, 358, 387, 388, 389, 395, 398, 402, 404, 406, 407
Paris, 358
Parkes, Sir H. S., 308, 309

Parker, Captain, 9
Parker, Sergeant J., 217
Parkinson, Lieutenant C. E., 193, 207, 218, 237
Parkinson, Captain C. E., 240, 250
Parr, Captain J., 40, 42, 43, 44, 56, 385
Parr, Lieutenant-Colonel J., 409
Parr, Ensign T., 193
Parr, Lieutentant F., 229
Parry, Captain-Lieutenant, 56
Paull, Private, 230
Passages, 150, 154
Paston's Regiment, 13, 14
"Patrician," Ship, 270
Paulet, Major-General Lord W., 297
Payne, Private C., 217
Peace of Amiens, 113
Pearce, Major-General, 14, 16
Peard, Ensign G. S., 190
Peard, Lieutenant G. S., 193, 216, 222
Peel, General, 310
Peninsula, 397, 403
Peninsular Army, 405
Pennefather, Major-General, 199, 201
Pennefather, Lieutenant-General, 296
Perry, Private W., 217
Perryar, Private, 231
Perth, 30, 32
Peterborough, Earl of, 11
Petersfield, 297
Pethebridge, Ensign J., 186, 187
Peyton, Sir R., 1, 2
Phayre, Lieutenant Sir R., 322
Philadelphia, 92, 409
Phillipi, Lieutenant-Colonel T. R., 376
Phillips, Major-General, 86, 87
Picton, Major-General Sir Thomas, 395
Pietermaritzburg, 314
Pilkington, Major-General Sir A., 189
Pitt, Right Hon. William, 40, 47, 50
Plymouth, 99, 136, 192, 193, 270, 271, 273, 284, 318, 366, 371
Poley, Ensign G. F. Weller-, 185
Polymedia, 280
Poonah, 171
Poor, Private E., 217
Poorwah, Action at, 254, 365, 372
Port au Prince, 98
Port Blair, Andaman Islands, 374
Port Louis, 314, 315
Porter, Private W., 243
Portland, 318
Portmore, Lord, 21
Portsmouth, 37, 44, 124, 136, 239, 240, 272, 273, 297, 298, 331, 365
Portugal, 12, 13, 16, 100, 124, 131, 341, 351, 352, 355, 357, 387
Portumna, 183
Potomac, River, 344, 345
Powell, Brigadier, 83

INDEX. 423

Power, Ensign D. O'Neil, 301, 307
Power, Lieutenant Bolton, 66, 74, 106
Power, Captain Manley, 106, 386
Powlett, Captain H., 104, 105, 350, 386
Preston, 100, 318, 386
Pretender, The (*see* Prince Edward Charles), 29, 30, 327
Prince Consort, H.R.H., 239
Prince Edward Charles (*see* Pretender), 327
Prince Regent, H.R.H., 348, 352
Pringle, Captain, R.N., 81
Pringle, Lieutenant, 66
Pritchard, Private G., 217
Prome, Capture of, 369
Prospect Hill, 92, 187, 278
Pyrenees, 145, 150, 151, 155, 342, 352, 387, 403, 406
Pyrenees, Battles on, 355, 358, 359, 402

Quarry Ravine, 203, 204, 205
Quebec, 80, 190, 328, 329, 330, 331, 332, 335, 409
Queen Anne, 8, 41, 326
"Queen of England," Ship, 301
Queen Victoria, 26, 176, 239, 285, 375
Queenstown, 281, 284, 315, 320

Radcliffe, Ensign W. P., 186
Radcliffe, Captain, 193, 200, 208, 213, 214, 215, 219, 222, 224, 227
Radcliffe, Major W. P., 240, 244, 245, 249, 250, 289, 291, 292, 294, 295, 296, 298
Radcliffe, General Sir W. P., 366, 367, 368
Raglan, Lord, 201, 216, 225, 226, 229, 360
Rainbrin, Private T., 217
Rajah Pulwan Sing, 242
Rana Bene Mahdo, 257, 258, 259, 365
Randall, Aquila, 348
Randall, Captain R. G., 322
Randolph, Major W., 322
Rangoon, Capture of, 369
Raper, Lieutenant F., 41
Rassulabad, 253
Ravencroft, Lieutenant, 99
Reading, 34
Reay, Private, 231
Redan, 230, 364, 367
Reggio, 116, 122, 359
Regnier, General, 116, 120, 352
Reideseil, Major-General, 84
Reille, General, 146
Renton, Ensign, 56
Reserve Battalion, 186, 362
Richards, Sergeant C., 307
Ridding, Cyrus (*Fifty Years' Recollections*) 56
Rifle Brigade, 126, 260, 261
· Riton, Private, 197
Robb, Private Andrew, 349

Robinson, Lieutenant-Colonel R., 41
Robinson, Captain, 139
Robinson, Lieutenant, 102
Rochdale, 182, 376
Rochfort, 38, 39, 328, 330
Rochfort, Captain G., 306, 309
Rocky Island, Cork Harbour, 317
Rodgers, Private, 230
Rollinson, Captain, 93
Rolph, Sergeant J., 217
Roncesvalles, Battle of, 146, 151, 159, 342, 358, 387, 390, 391, 405, 406, 408
Rooke, Vice-Admiral Sir George, 9
Rorica, Combat of, 125
Rorkee, 269
Roscommon, 360
Roscrea, 282
Rose, General Sir Hugh (*see* Strathnairn, Lord), 268, 269, 371, 372, 373
Rose, Major Alexander, 150, 151, 152, 153, 154, 391, 403
Rose, Lieutenant A., 41
Ross, Major Robert, 101, 104
Ross, Lieutenant-Colonel Robert, 108, 109, 114, 117, 119
Ross, Colonel Robert, 120, 126, 127, 131, 132, 135, 138, 139, 140, 141, 143
Ross, Major-General Robert, 144, 146, 147, 150, 151, 156, 158, 162, 340, 351, 386, 389, 391, 396, 401, 402, 404, 405, 406, 408, 410
Ross of Bladensburg, 348
Ross, Mrs. Robert, of Bladensburg, 343, 347, 350
Ross, David, of Bladensburg, 350
Ross, Robert S., of Bladensburg, 350
Ross, Captain John F. G., of Bladensburg, 350
Ross, Captain E. T., of Bladensburg, 350
Rosstrevor, Co. Down, 162, 340, 349
Rotheram, Lieutenant M. T., 193, 197
Rotton, Lieutenant, 150
Rowan, Lieutenant-General W., 190
Rowe, Private P., 229
"Royal Oak," H.M.S., 344
"Royal William," H.M.S., 331
Royals, The, 95
Rule, Colour-Sergeant A., 217, 235
Russell, Lieutenant W. H., 118
Russell, Captain W. H., 159
Russell, Major W. H., 161
Russell, Private J., 229
Russell, Private, 230
Russians, 105, 106, 116, 362

Sackville, Lord George (*see* Germain), 30, 31, 32, 55, 385
Salamanca, Town of, 128
Saldaña, 129
Salford, 181, 376

Salico, 280
Salisbury, Marquis of, 375
Salter, Brigadier, 174
San Estevan, 148, 149
Sandbag Battery, 200, 203, 208, 209, 215, 219, 367
Sandhurst, 371
Sankey, General, 14
"Santipore," Ship, 190
Saratoga, Battle of (*see* Bemus Heights and Stillwater), 89, 90, 337, 339, 343
Saratoga, Convention of, 91
Sarre, Village of, 155
Sarsfield, General, 3
Satara, 323
Sauroren, Battle of, 147, 342, 387, 396, 399, 402
Saxe, Marshal, 27
Scariff, 282
Scheldt, 102, 137, 138
Schomberg, Duke of, 2
Schore, Village of, 138
Schuylerville, Village of, 89
Scots Brigade, 5
Scots Fusilier Guards, 214
Scutari, 234
Scylla Castle, 121, 122, 359
Seatapore, 260, 365
Seaton, Field-Marshal Lord (*see* Colborne), 107, 292, 350, 354, 355, 385, 386
Sebastopol, 196, 198, 204, 224, 228, 231, 233, 238, 362, 364, 369
Second Battalion, The, 289
Second Division, 198, 199, 201, 204, 213, 215, 389
Second Regiment, 387
Seven Years' War, 48, 75, 327, 333
Seventh Division, 388, 389
Seventh Fusiliers, 141, 149, 340, 387, 389, 390, 391, 393
Seventh Regiment, Cacadores, 387, 399
Seventh Léger, 206
Seventeenth Regiment, 273
Seventy-first Highlanders, 388
Seventy-eighth Highlanders, 164
Seventy-ninth Highlanders, 247
"Severn," H.M.S., 347
Sharpe, Lieutenant J. B., 183
Sharpe, Captain J. B., 186, 190, 192, 193, 213
Sharpe, Bt.-Major, J. B., 217
Sharpe, Private E., 231
Shelburne, Earl of, 92, 410
Sherlock, Private P., 236, 257
Sherwin, Captain G., 41
Shimiduz Seiji, 306
Shôgun, 300, 307
Shortt, Assistant-Surgeon F. J., 241
Sicilians, Company of, 122, 124
Sicily, 115, 121, 123, 340, 351, 355, 357, 359

Sikh Cavalry, 252, 253, 256, 265, 266
Simmonds, Private, 230
"Simoom," H.M.S., 273
Simree, Fort of, 254, 256
Siniavin, Admiral, 123
Sittingbourne, 35
Sixth Division, 401, 402
Sixth Regiment, 149
Sixtieth Regiment, Second Battalion, 335, 387
Sixty-second Regiment, 85, 86, 87
Sixty-third Regiment, 102
Sixty-sixth Regiment, 166
Sixty-seventh Regiment, 41, 328
Skeensborough, 83, 84
Skeffington, Hon. H. M., 350
Skerret, Major-General, 141
Slater, Private J., 217
Sligo, 164, 318
Smith, Admiral Sir Sydney, 117, 123
Smith, Major-General Sir Harry, 192
Smith, Colonel Hugh, 226
Smith, Major, 183
Smith, Captain A., 159
Smith, Lieutenant and Adjutant, 186, 187
Smith, Lieutenant G., 41
Smith, Lieutenant, 145, 342
Smith, Sergeant J., 217
Smith, Corporal, 231
Smithers, Private W., 259
Smollett, Tobias (*History of England*), 57
Smyrna, 234
Smyth, Major-General G. S., 315
Smyth, Lieutenant-Colonel George, 101, 103, 104, 109, 110, 113, 386
Smyth, Colonel James, 285, 301, 308
Smyth, Lieutenant and Adjutant, 99
Sobraon, Battle of, 360
Soest, 47, 49, 68, 69
Somerset, General Lord Fitzroy, 176
Soubise, Marshal, 69
Soult, Marshal, 135, 145, 146, 156, 160, 176, 342, 387, 389, 396, 398, 402, 406
South Beveland, 138, 359
South, Lieutenant and Adjutant S., 104
South, Major S., 164
South, Lieutenant-Colonel S., 164, 166, 167
South, Paymaster C., 185
South, Captain C., 190, 191
Southampton, 190
Spain, 8, 9, 12, 18, 100, 351, 359, 389
Spencer, Brigadier, 233
Spencer, General, 123
Spencer, Lord Robert, 168
Spencer, Major, 97
Sphinx, 112
Spithead, 46, 124, 238, 240, 331
Stair, Earl of, 24
Stanhope, Lord, 27
Stanley, Lieutenant, 87

INDEX. 425

Stanwix, Colonel, 12, 15
Stanwix, Regiment of, 14
Starman, Private J., 243
St. Aurien, Captain J. D., 159
St. Boës, Village of, 157, 158, 343, 359
St. Clair, Captain, 9
St. Domingo, 94, 95, 98, 99
St. Euphemia, Bay of, 116, 117
St. George's, Bermuda, 187, 278
St. Helena, 166, 356, 360
St. Helens, 9, 39, 46, 47
St. John's, New Brunswick, 334
"St. Lawerence," Ship, 298
St. Malo, 46, 47
St. Pèe, Village, 358
St. Ruth, General, 4, 5, 6
St. Sebastian, 150, 152, 153, 154, 388, 389, 403
Stebbins, Private G., 217
Steevens, Lieutenant Charles, 102, 106
Steevens, Captain Charles, 114, 117, 126, 132, 135
Steevens, Major Charles, 138
Steevens, Lieutenant-Colonel Charles, 150, 153, 157, 162, 164, 165
Steevens, Lieutenant-Colonel Charles (*Reminiscences of My Military Life*), 10
Steevens, Lieutenant G., 185
Steevens, Captain G., 193
Steevens, Major G., 235
Steevens, Lieutenant-Colonel G., 238
Steevens, Lieutenant-Colonel N., 164
Stevenson, Private H., 259
Stewart, General Sir Donald, 321
Stewart, Captain, 56
Stewart, Lieutenant, 99
Stillwater, Battle of (*see* Bemus Heights and Saratoga), 89, 337, 410
Stirling, 30, 31
Stockport, 182
Stone, W. L. (*Campaign of General Burgoyne*), 85, 86
Story, Captain, 99
Strathnairn, Field-Marshal Lord (*see* Rose, Sir Hugh), 268, 269, 273, 274, 276, 364, 366, 370, 371, 372, 373
Stuart, Major-General Sir John, 116, 120, 121, 163, 340, 341
Sullivan, Private T., 259
Sultanpore, Battle of, 242, 365, 367, 371
Sye, River, 252
"Symmetry," Ship, 117

Tafalla, 389
Tagus, 123, 126
Taku Forts, 308
Talmash, General, 3, 6
"Tamar," H.M.S., 278, 279, 280, 315
Taylor, Private J., 152
Tchernaya, 196

Telford, Captain R., 159
Templemore, 163, 277, 282
Tennant, Captain, 56, 63
Tenth Regiment, 242, 360
Tenth Regiment (Portuguese), 148
Tevan, Surgeon S., 185
Texel, 102
Thackeray, W. M. (*Virginians*), 58
Third Division, 388, 389, 395
Thirteenth Hussars, 286
Thirteenth Regiment, 17, 22, 95, 96
Thirtieth Regiment, 22, 295
Thirty-second Regiment, 244
Thirty-fourth Regiment, 19, 22
Thirty-fifth Regiment, 11, 119, 122
Thirty-sixth Regiment, 11
Thirty-eighth Regiment, 244, 247
Thirty-ninth Regiment, 12, 14, 15, 19, 22
"Thomas Arburthnot," Ship, 190
Thomas, Lieutenant-Colonel H., 171, 178, 179
Thomas, Colonel H., 182, 184
Thomas, Major-General H., 264, 357, 358, 359
Thompson, Ensign, 145, 342
Thompson, Lieutenant T., 56, 383, 385
Thompson, R. E., Esquire, of Kenfeld, 383
Thompson, Private, 231
Thorn, Major-General, 192
Thorne, Corporal G., 217
Thorne, Sergeant G., 259
Thorpe, Ensign, 99
Tiburon, 95, 96
Tickner, Drummer, 225
Ticonderoga, 44, 82, 83, 336
Tilling, Sergeant G., 259
Times, The, 226, 355
Tinlin, Lieutenant, 97
Tipperary, 163, 277, 282
Toledo, Regiment of, 391
Tomson, Ensign G., 186
Tomson, Lieutenant G., 190
"Tonnant," H.M.S., 348
Torbay, 1
Torquay, 355
Torrens, Captain, 106
Torrens, Brigadier, 209
Toulouse, Battle of, 160, 161, 352, 356, 358
Tournay, 27, 28
Tovey, Captain George, 144, 145, 146, 159, 160
Tovey, Major George, 171
Tovey, Lieutenant-Colonel George, 181, 392, 406, 407, 408, 409
Tower of London, 176, 362
Towley, Private, 194
Townshend, Major-General, 70
Tuam, 319
Tudela, 143, 389
Turkey, 193, 363
Turks, 197, 198
Turner, Corporal J., 236

426　INDEX.

Tralee, 315, 317, 368
Trapaud, Lieutenant, 30
Trapaud, Captain, 33
Trinity College, Dublin, 340
Trowbridge, 272
Twelfth Regiment, 49, 55, 57, 327
Twentieth or East Devonshire Regiment, 375
Twenty-first Regiment, 84, 85, 87
Twenty-second Regiment, 98
Twenty-third Fusiliers, 55, 98, 141, 149, 251, 387, 389, 390, 393
Twenty-third Regiment (Portuguese), 387
Twenty-fifth Regiment, 19, 22, 55, 60, 65, 340
Twenty-sixth Light Dragoons, 110
Twenty-sixth Regiment, 19, 22
Twenty-seventh Regiment, 148, 353, 387, 402
Twenty-eighth Regiment, 133
Twenty-ninth Regiment, 22
Tyrconnell, 325

Ulster, 325
Unao, District of, 253
United Service Journal, 180, 342, 344, 345, 406
United States, 335, 344
Utrecht, Treaty of, 16

Val, Battle of (see Laffeldt), 327, 330
Val Carlos, 390
Valetta, 114
Van Agnew, 360
Varna, 194
Vaughan, Lieutenant H. B., 199, 204, 205, 206, 215, 218, 237, 241
Vaughan, Captain H. B., 266, 267, 276
Veaitch, Captain C., 41
Vellinghausen, Battle of (see Kirch-Denkern), 48, 69
"Vengeance," H.M.S., 188
Vereker, Lieutenant Hon. A. E. P., 241
Vereker, Captain Hon. A. E. P., 302
Vernon, Ensign C. A., 294
"Vesuvius," H.M.S., 182
Vickers, Lieutenant, 28
Vigo, 326
Villa Franca, 132
Villa Viciosa, 126, 127
Villacova, 142
Villalba, 144, 147, 398, 403, 404
Vimiera, Battle of, 125, 126, 341, 355, 359
Virginians, The, 329
Viscaret, 389, 390
Vittoria, Battle of, 142, 342, 343, 355, 358, 359 388, 389, 390, 393, 399, 404
Vivian, General Sir Hussey, 176
"Vulcan," H.M.S., 301

Wade, Colonel, 392
Wade, Field-Marshal, 27, 327

Wager, Admiral Sir C., 19, 20
Wahab, Lieutenant-Colonel G. D., 323
Walcheren, Expedition to, 137, 341, 355
Walcheren Fever, 138
Waldegrave, Major-General, 46, 55, 57, 58, 65
Waldegrave, Lieutenant-General, 73
Wales, Prince of (see King George III), 40
Wales, Their R.H. the Prince and Princess of, 284, 285
Walker, Commodore, 11
Walker, Major, 122
Walker, Lieutenant H. W., 111
Walker, Lieutenant, 145, 342
Wallace, Captain W., 106, 115
Wallace, Lieutenant-Colonel W., 145, 342, 393, 403
Wallis, Private H., 217
Walpole, Horace (*Letters*), 38, 58, 329
Walsh, Private J., 266
Wangenheim, General, 51, 52, 54
War of the Austrian Succession, 24
Warburg, Battle of, 48, 61, 63
Ward, Captain, 9
Warleigh, Devonshire, 366
Warren, Ensign A. R., 190
Warren, Captain A. R., 237, 240
Warren, Lieutenant-Colonel Sir A. R., 248
Warrington, 34
Washington, City, 344, 345, 346
Washington, Private, 231
Waterford, 162, 317
Waterloo, Battle of, 352, 397
Watson, Colonel, 21
Watson, Private, 231
Wauchope, Lieutenant-Colonel A., 143, 149, 150, 151, 400, 403
Waudby, Ensign F., 276
Webber, Private T., 247
Webb's Regiment, 329
Webster, Lieutenant C. H., 309
Webster, Captain C. H., 314
Webster, Lieutenant-Colonel C. H., 321, 322, 323
Weedon, 181, 284
Weightman, Captain, 9
Weighton, Captain, 9
Wellesley, Sir Arthur (see Wellington), 125
Wellington, Field-Marshal the Duke of, 176, 177, 180, 237, 274, 342, 343, 344, 352, 355, 358, 362, 407, 409
Wellington, Lord (see Wellesley), 141, 143, 148, 152, 154, 155, 160, 161, 353, 389, 396, 399, 402
Wellington, Town of, 290
Wemys, Lieutenant, 87
Weser, River, 50, 51, 52, 71
Westbourne, 297
Westcott, Major, 390, 395
Westerham, Kent, 327

INDEX.

West Indies, 11, 12, 376
Wheat, Lieutenant, 93
Wheeler, Drummer H., 216
Whelan, Private M., 217
Whitehead, Lieutenant-Colonel G., 9
Whitelocke, 96
Whitmore, Private, 231
Whybrow, Colour-Sergeant J., 217, 237
Wigan, 40
Wilhelmsthal, Combat at, 73
Williamson, Major-General, 95, 96
Williamstadt, 78
Wilkinson, Lieutenant T., 41
Wilson, Private J., 255
Winchester, 36, 190, 350, 366
Winchester, Captain, 93
Winchester, Mr. C. A., 306
Winder, General, 344
"Windermere," Ship, 123, 166
Winstanley, Private, 247
Witney, Private W., 229
Wood, Captain W. T. W., 190, 215, 217, 372
Wood, Private J., 217
Wood, Private, 230
Wood, Private, 231
Woodward, Surgeon-Major, 302
Wolfe, Major-General James, 31, 32, 33, 34, 35, 36, 38, 39, 40, 42, 44, 45, 58, 114, 327, 349, 350, 375, 377, 409

Wolfe, Lieutenant-General E., 327
Wolseley, Assistant-Surgeon R., 219, 220, 221
Woolmer, Hants, 297
Wosley, Private, 197
Wright, Assistant-Surgeon T., 193
Wright, R. (*Life of Wolfe*), 45
Wright, Private Samuel, 152
Wrixon, Ensign, 150
Würtemburg, Duke of, 5
Wuzurgung, Village of, 265
Wyatt, Private, 197
Wynyard, Lieutenant and Adjutant, 99

Yedo, 300, 303, 308
Yokohama, 300, 301, 302, 304, 306, 307, 308, 309
York, Duke of, 104
Yorke, Lieutenant W., 41
Youghal, 277, 282
Young, Lieutenant-Colonel T. P., 376
Young, Private, 197
Young, Sergeant J., 216

Zadora, River, 142, 388
Zamora, 142
Zieremberg, Surprise of, 48, 63
Zubiri, 395, 396
Zügoh, 280
Zuype Sluys, 104, 386

THE EXAMINER PRINTING WORKS, MANCHESTER.

www.ingramcontent.com/pod-product-compliance
Lightning Source LLC
Chambersburg PA
CBHW052053300426
44117CB00013B/2109